SECOND EDITION

TERRORISM AND WMDs
AWARENESS AND RESPONSE

SECOND EDITION

TERRORISM AND WMDs
AWARENESS AND RESPONSE

JOHN PICHTEL

CRC Press
Taylor & Francis Group
Boca Raton London New York

CRC Press is an imprint of the
Taylor & Francis Group, an **informa** business

CRC Press
Taylor & Francis Group
6000 Broken Sound Parkway NW, Suite 300
Boca Raton, FL 33487-2742

First issued in paperback 2021

© 2016 by Taylor & Francis Group, LLC
CRC Press is an imprint of Taylor & Francis Group, an Informa business

No claim to original U.S. Government works

Version Date: 20160511

ISBN 13: 978-1-03-209783-1 (pbk)
ISBN 13: 978-1-4987-3898-9 (hbk)

Library of Congress Cataloging-in-Publication Data

Names: Pichtel, John, 1957- author.
Title: Terrorism and WMDs: awareness and response / John Pichtel.
Description: Second edition. | Boca Raton, FL : CRC Press, 2016.
Identifiers: LCCN 2016020853 | ISBN 9781498738989
Subjects: LCSH: Terrorism. | Weapons of mass destruction--Health aspects. |
Terrorism--Prevention.
Classification: LCC HV6431 .P528 2016 | DDC 363.325/3--dc23
LC record available at https://lccn.loc.gov/2016020853

Visit the Taylor & Francis Web site at
http://www.taylorandfrancis.com

and the CRC Press Web site at
http://www.crcpress.com

*To all of our nation's emergency responders.
May your courage and dedication serve
as an inspiration to future generations.*

CONTENTS

PREFACE

Chance favors the prepared mind.

Pasteur

Terrorism as a tactic of violence and intimidation has been used by individuals and groups against noncombatant targets for millennia; likewise, weapons of mass destruction have been in use throughout recorded times. However, with greater technical sophistication, man has, in recent decades, been capable of constructing weapons with more devastating effects, both physical and psychological, than ever previously witnessed.

Few references in awareness of chemical, biological, radiological, nuclear, and explosive (CBRNE) weapons provide a satisfactory review of the underlying chemical and biological processes occurring during a release incident; likewise, a discussion of public health impacts during the incident and beyond is often incomplete. This book is intended to serve as an introductory manual for awareness of CBRNE weapons with emphasis on basic chemistry and biology, including microbiology, and human health. Adequate knowledge of the basic sciences is an essential component of responding to a CBRNE release, and a certain degree of proficiency is required to appreciate the reactions of chemicals and organisms at the incident site and within victims, and to formulate an appropriate response to the incident.

Chapter 1 ("Terrorism and Weapons of Mass Destruction") provides an overview of the historical and ideological context of modern terrorism and CBRNE weapons. Subsequent chapters delineate specific weapons, that is, CBRNE (Chapter 2, "Chemical Agents"; Chapter 3, "Toxic Industrial Chemicals"; Chapter 4, "Biological Agents"; Chapter 5, "Nuclear and Radiological Hazards"; Chapter 6, "Explosives Hazards"; Chapter 7, "Delivery Systems for Weapons of Mass Destruction"; and Chapter 8, "Directed-Energy Weapons"). Discussion is provided on the history of the use of each weapon type; the design, structure, properties, and behaviors of these weapons; impacts of CBRNE weapons on human health; and safety precautions for both the emergency responders and the public. The remaining chapters (Chapter 9, "National Incident Management System and the Incident Command System"; and Chapter 10, "Personal Protective Equipment for Emergency Response, Decontamination, and Remediation") address specific responder issues, specifically, the Incident Command System, personal protective equipment (PPE), and decontamination.

This work is not intended to be a complete guide for response to weapons of mass destruction. Such an effort is beyond the scope of a single book; in fact, printed works can only serve as the starting point to understanding CBRNE weapons and how to respond to intentional and accidental releases. Training in the field, using real-world scenarios, PPE, and detection equipment are required to attain maximum proficiency for any response.

ACKNOWLEDGMENTS

The author wishes to thank Robert Sims and Jill Jurgensen at CRC Press who have been indispensable in preparing this work for publication. Many thanks to Adel Rosario for her meticulous work in editing the manuscript. I am grateful to Young Nam of the Ball State University Teleplex for the production of outstanding-quality drawings.

Thanks to my loved ones who provided support throughout the course of this project: Theresa, Leah, and Yozef Pichtel, and my esteemed colleague Joseph Timko.

Sincere gratitude is expressed to Werner Erhard, a modern-day genius who assisted me in opening countless avenues for producing results.

Finally, special thanks to my students—your energy and curiosity always serve to motivate, challenge, and inspire me.

AUTHOR

John Pichtel is a professor of Natural Resources and Environmental Management at Ball State University in Muncie, Indiana, where he has been on the faculty since 1987. He earned his PhD in Environmental Science at Ohio State University, MS degree in Soil Chemistry/ Agronomy at Ohio State, and BS degree in Natural Resources Management at Rutgers University. His primary research and professional activities have been in management of hazardous materials, remediation of contaminated sites, and environmental chemistry. Dr. Pichtel teaches courses in emergency response to hazmat incidents, management of solid and hazardous wastes, environmental site assessment, and site remediation.

Dr. Pichtel is a Certified Hazardous Materials Manager. He holds memberships in the Institute of Hazardous Materials Managers, The International Association of Arson Investigators, and the Indiana Academy of Science. He was selected as a Fulbright Scholar in 1999 and again in 2005. Dr. Pichtel has received extensive training from the U.S. Department of Homeland Security in response to chemical, biological, radiological, and explosive hazards. He has written two books addressing waste management and cleanup of contaminated sites, and has authored or coauthored approximately 50 research articles. He has served as a consultant in hazardous waste management projects and has conducted environmental assessments and remediation research in the United States, the United Kingdom, Ireland, Finland, and Poland.

1

Terrorism and Weapons of Mass Destruction

In vast laboratories in the Ministry of Peace, and in experimental stations, teams of experts are indefatigably at work searching for new and deadlier gases; or for soluble poisons capable of being produced in such quantities as to destroy the vegetation of whole continents; or for breeds of disease germs immunised against all possible antibodies.

George Orwell, 1961

INTRODUCTION

A terrorist attack may be loosely defined as a premeditated incident involving hazardous materials that has the potential to cause extensive damage to property and produce substantial numbers of casualties (Figure 1.1). Such attacks can range from the detonation of a home-made bomb in a crowded market to the hijacking of commercial jetliners and smashing them into skyscrapers.

In the United States, several definitions of terrorism exist at the federal level. For example, U.S. Code (22 USC 2656[d][2]) defines terrorism as

> premeditated politically motivated violence perpetrated against noncombatant targets by subnational groups of clandestine agents usually intended to influence an audience.

The U.S. Department of Defense defines terrorism as

> The calculated use of unlawful violence or threat of unlawful violence to inculcate fear; intended to coerce or to intimidate governments or societies in the pursuit of goals that are generally political, religious, or ideological.

DTIC, 2010

Figure 1.1 Aftermath of the Oklahoma City terrorist bombing, April 1995. (Courtesy of FEMA, http://www.photolibrary.fema.gov/photolibrary/photo_details.do?id=1275.)

And the U.S. Department of Justice (DOJ) definition reads

the unlawful use of force and violence against persons or property to intimidate or coerce a government, the civilian population, or any segment thereof, in furtherance of political or social objectives.

FBI, 2016

All of these definitions share several common components:

- Terrorism involves a criminal act.
- Terrorism attempts to intimidate governments and/or civilians.
- Terrorism refers to the use of violent acts by individuals or groups motivated by ideology.
- Terrorism attempts to further political, religious, or other agendas.

ORIGINS OF TERRORISM

Terrorism has been used over millennia as a tool to achieve political, religious, and ideological goals. During this time, terrorism has evolved in terms of goals and application.

Terror in Ancient Times

The earliest recorded organization that engaged in what could be defined as terrorism was the Sicarii, a radical Jewish splinter group living in Judea during the Roman Empire of the first century C.E. The group was given its name, which is translated as *dagger-men*, by the Roman occupiers.

Resistance was fierce on the part of the Jewish populace to Roman occupation of Judea. The group's primary motive was a strict belief that it could not be faithful to the precepts of Judaism while being Roman subjects. The Sicarii conducted an underground campaign of assassination of Roman occupying forces plus any Jews that had collaborated with the Romans. For example, numerous Jewish high priests were considered to be colluding with the Romans, and it was thus permissible, in the opinion of the Sicarii, to remove these illegitimate rulers by means of violence. The Sicarii began its campaign of terror in the late 50s and became prominent in the 60s, when it used murder, kidnapping, and terror to support its cause (Peterson and Hamblin, 2004).

According to Flavius Josephus, one of the early Sicarii adherents, the Sicarii would hide daggers under its cloaks, mingle with crowds at festivals, murder its victims, and then disappear into the crowd during the subsequent panic. The Sicarii operated primarily in urban Jerusalem, including within the Temple. However, it also committed attacks in villages, which it raided for the spoils, and set afire to create fear among Jews who collaborated with the Roman occupiers. The Sicarii is also known to have kidnapped important individuals as hostage for the release of its own members who were held prisoner (Horsley, 1979). The Sicarii is considered a terrorist group because of its fanaticism, the type of violence it used, and the use of violence against its own people (Fernando, 2010).

The Sicarii revolt went on to become an open confrontation with the Romans. When the great Jewish rebellion against Rome was underway in C.E. 66, the Sicarii quickly joined, capturing Herod's fortress at Masada from the small Roman garrison. The Sicarii ransacked the armory at Masada and marched on Jerusalem, where it joined with other groups to drive the Roman troops from the city. The group's followers were finally besieged by the Romans and committed mass suicide at the fortress of Masada. The revolt culminated in the destruction of the Jewish Temple and the expulsion of the Jews from Judea.

The Hashshashin, from which the English word *assassin* is thought to originate, was a breakaway faction of Shia Islam. Also known as the Nizari Ismalis, this group was a secretive sect active in Iran and Syria from the eleventh to the thirteenth century. Its leader, Hassam-I Sabbah, founded the group in the mountains of northern Iran. The Hashshashin was devoted to building a new utopia, and formulated a strategy of gaining control of strategically important fortresses and establishing fortified settlements in present-day Iran, Iraq, Syria, and Lebanon. The group was unable to mount a conventional military army; therefore, it developed a form of *asymmetric warfare* that used political assassination as a system of survival and defense against its enemies (Tomes, 2004). Its dramatically executed assassinations of political leaders from the Abbasid and Seljuk tribes from modern-day Iran instilled great fear into the local citizenry and political figures.

The Hashshashin would send a lone assassin to kill a key enemy leader. Once his work was complete, the killer waited next to his victim, to be killed or captured. Such a tactic created fear and awe in its enemies. This group trained highly capable sleeper commandos who were skilled in languages, science, and trade, known as *Fedayeen*, who infiltrated enemy positions and remained undercover (Daftary, 1999). If Nizari civilians were facing assault from enemy mercenaries or armies, the Fedayeen was activated.

Fedayeen also used its skills for political goals without necessarily killing; for example, a victim might find a Hashshashin dagger lying on his pillow upon awakening. This

3

was a clear hint to the targeted individual that whatever action had brought him into conflict with the Hashshashins would have to be stopped if he expected to survive (Daftary, 1999; Lewis, 1967).

The Hashshashins brought two new concepts to terrorism: (1) divine duty and (2) a terrorist act that led to one's death would be rewarded by a special place in heaven. Terrorism against the enemy was therefore considered a religious act.

The Hashshashin was eventually eradicated by the invading Mongols in the thirteenth century. It is believed that the Ismaili-Hashashin's imam, Alaud-Din, ordered hundreds of assassins to kill Mongke Khan, the great khan (i.e., Mongol leader), in his palace (Weatherford, 2005). In retaliation, a decree was handed over to the Mongol commander Kitbuqa who assaulted several Hashshashin fortresses. By 1275, the Hashshashin was crushed and its political power was lost.

It is worth noting that even though both the Sicarii and the Hashshashin carried out their operations in antiquity, they are still of relevance today—first as forerunners of modern terrorists in terms of motivation, organization, targeting, and goals; second, although both ultimately failed, the fact that they are remembered hundreds of years later demonstrates the deep psychological impact they caused.

Medieval and Renaissance Periods

The modern concept of terrorism arose during the French revolution of 1789–1799. Early in the revolution, governments in Paris often imposed their new requirements and pronouncements on the populace by means of violence. It was here the term *terrorism* was first coined; as recorded by the Académie Française in 1798, it was defined as a *system or rule of terror*. This rule of terror included the systematic use of intimidation and violence to repress rivals and keep the population in check. Maximilien Robespierre and the Jacobin Party believed that the use of terrorism was a virtue and the proper tool for a government to achieve its objectives and ultimately keep itself in power.

Nineteenth Century

A century later, a group of Russian anarchists called The People's Will (Narodnaya volya) attempted to overturn the autocratic regime of the Tsars. In 1880, the group tried unsuccessfully to assassinate Russian Tsar Alexander II. It eventually assassinated him in 1881 (Radzinsky, 2005). The anarchists of the late nineteenth century introduced the concept of individual terrorism, that is, the use of terror against an individual to topple a government. Anarchists were active in Europe and the United States during the late nineteenth and the early twentieth centuries. From 1890 to 1908, anarchists were responsible for killing Empress Elizabeth of Austria-Hungary, King Elberto of Italy, and King Carlos I of Portugal. Two of the most notorious acts of terror by anarchists include the assassination of Archduke Ferdinand (1914), which precipitated World War I, and the assassination of U.S. President McKinley (1901). Early in the twentieth century, anarchists detonated explosives in front of the New York Stock Exchange on Wall Street to protest capitalist policies of the United States (Figure 1.2).

Figure 1.2 Bombing of the New York Stock Exchange, 1920. (Courtesy of Wikipedia, "Wallstreetbmb." Public Domain, http://en.wikipedia.org/wiki/Image:Wallstreetbmb.jpg.)

Twentieth Century

Russian Vladimir Lenin lifted the principles of Robespierre to expand the concept of government-sponsored terrorism. Now, terror, used in a highly systematic fashion, was applied to an entire nation in the hopes of building a new society. The Lenin program of government-sponsored terrorism was greatly expanded by his successor, Josef Stalin.

At about the same time, resistance of the Irish against English rule (1919–1921) introduced terrorism as a means to achieve national independence. Such terrorism involved the use of bombings and assassinations of governmental representatives (government officials, judges, soldiers, police officers) of the occupying power. The goal of such a terror campaign was to make occupation by another nation too costly.

The structure and functions of terror organizations had advanced significantly by this time. The Irish Republican Army (IRA), under the command of Michael Collins, orchestrated a sustained terror program designed to endure until all goals were achieved (Figure 1.3). It also perfected the concept of *compartmentalized terrorism* through the assignment of cell operations (Garrison, 2007). The IRA established smaller terror groups (cells) to be assigned a specific operational objective; furthermore, cells did not have contact with other cells—each cell was independent. This design protected the larger terrorist movement from dissolution if one cell was discovered.

After World War II, terrorism made its appearance in several of the less-developed nations of the world, with the goal of removing colonial powers. The targets of terror attacks changed from government officers of the colonial rulers to civilians working and living in the colony. In Kenya and Algeria, terror involved the killing of sympathizers of

Figure 1.3 The Seán Hogan flying column during the War of Independence. (Courtesy of Wikimedia Commons, Public Domain, http://commons.wikimedia.org/wiki/File:Hogan%27s_Flying_Column .gif#/media/File:Hogan%27s_Flying_Column.gif.)

the British and British families. Women and children were now considered acceptable targets for terror attacks (Garrison, 2007).

Modern Terrorism

By the late 1960s, terrorism appeared on the international stage. In 1966, Cuba hosted the Tri-Continental Conference sponsored by the Soviet Union. This conference ushered in the internationalization of terrorism. As a result of this conference, Cuba was designated as a training camp for terrorist organizations from Europe and a number of less-developed nations. Also at this time, various terrorist groups began to cooperate with each other for the first time. Terrorism became a worldwide movement rather than a series of isolated events with individual goals. Financial and political support for terrorist groups began to flourish.

The 1960s saw the development of state-sponsored terrorism, in which governments exported terrorists and their weapons and tactics to other parts of the world to accomplish their own political ends. Iran supported the Hezbollah; Libya supported Abu Nidal; and Iraq, Cuba, Sudan, and Algeria provided training camps and economic and political support to other groups.

Since the late 1960s, a significant proportion of terrorism worldwide has emerged from the Israeli–Arab/Palestinian conflicts. After the Six-Day War of 1967 and the Yom Kippur War of 1973, the option of conventional warfare by Arab nations against Israel was abandoned. Terrorism arose as the new tool to be used against Israel and its allies (including the United States). The Palestine Liberation Organization (PLO), founded in 1964, began a terror campaign from Jordan and later Lebanon.

In the 1970s and 1980s, several groups in Europe emerged and engaged in a range of terrorist activities. In Turkey, both communist and fascist terrorist groups arose; Germany was embroiled with the Red Army Faction (later the Baader-Meinhof Gang). In Italy, the Red Brigade became a notorious terror organization. Many such groups sought to overthrow the current government and install a new ideology.

The year 1968 saw the advent of airline terrorism. The Popular Front for the Liberation of Palestine hijacked an El Al airliner en route from Tel Aviv to Rome. This event marked the first time that airline passengers were used as hostages for demands made publicly against a government (Israel). The 1970s went on to be considered the decade of air terrorism. More than 20 events of air terrorism and bombings of airplanes occurred during that decade. Sometimes the goal of airline hijackings was to bring attention to the Palestinian cause; in other cases, to force Israel to release captured comrades (Figure 1.4). By 1988, the PLO developed bombs that would detonate when a plane reached a certain altitude.

Religion-based terrorism became a major security issue during the latter years of the twentieth century. The return of the Ayatollah Khomeini to Iran in 1979 brought to the forefront a religious justification for terrorism. The expansion of Islam in the Middle East and worldwide and the protection of Islam against Jews, Christians, and the West was considered justification for the use of terror (Garrison, 2007).

Modern religious terrorism was supported by the suicide bomber. In 1983, the U.S. Embassy in Beirut was attacked; also, in 1983, the U.S. Marine barracks in Beirut were bombed, as was the U.S. Embassy in Kuwait. However, other forms of terror were routinely applied during this period, including kidnappings.

The 1990s brought another change to terrorism: the indiscriminate killing and mass casualties of civilians. The World Trade Center (WTC) was bombed in 1993 by Islamic extremists in order to cause death, significant financial losses, and ultimately panic to the U.S. population. An additional goal was the destruction of the WTC itself, a key symbol of U.S. financial might. Citizens were considered to be fair targets in this form

Figure 1.4 In September 1970, four airliners bound for New York City and one for London were hijacked by members of the Popular Front for the Liberation of Palestine (PFLP). Three aircraft were forced to land at Dawson's Field, a remote desert airstrip in Jordan. The hijackers demanded the release of prisoners being held in Israel. In this photo, the airliners are on the ground during a September 6 PFLP press conference. (Courtesy of Wikipedia, Image taken in Jordan in 1970, https://en.wikipedia.org/wiki/Dawson's_Field_hijackings#/media/File:Dawsonfieldcamels.jpg.)

of terror, the rationale being that because the U.S. populace pays taxes and supports their government, they, too, are implicitly an ally of Israel and therefore an enemy of the Islamic cause.

September 11, 2001 revealed the latest incarnation of terrorist practice. Islamic terrorists affiliated with al-Qaeda and, more specifically, following the doctrine of Osama bin Laden, perpetrated the now infamous 9/11 attacks to destroy symbols of American power. American Airlines Flight 11 and United Airlines Flight 175 were smashed into the World Trade Center (WTC), a symbol of American capitalism and economic influence. American Airlines Flight 77 was flown into the Pentagon, headquarters of the U.S. Department of Defense. United Airlines Flight 93 was believed to have targeted either the White House or U.S. Capitol—symbols of American political authority.

Other major terrorist attacks have occurred over the past decade or more, including a Bali nightclub car bomb attack (2000); bombing of the Indian Parliament in New Delhi (2001); London subway and bus bombings (2005); Madrid train bombings (2005), and the 2008 attacks in Mumbai (hotels, train station, and Jewish outreach center). However, there are many, many more occurring on a regular basis in many parts of the globe.

Over the course of 2000 years, terrorism appears to have come full circle—from the Sicarii of the first century to religiously motivated terror of the 1990s and beyond, both embracing suicidal martyrdom.

Recent Chemical, Biological, Radiological, Nuclear, and Explosive Terrorist Incidents

The timeline discussed in the following paragraphs provides an overview of selected terrorist activities, occurring primarily in the United States, involving chemical, biological, radiological, nuclear, and explosive (CBRNE) agents over the past three decades. As you review these, note the range of weapons used, the tactics employed, and the ideologies of the terrorist individuals and groups.

- *1972.* Members of a U.S. fascist group, Order of the Rising Sun, dedicated to the rise of a new master race, were found in possession of 30–40 kg of typhoid bacteria cultures with which they planned to contaminate water supplies in Chicago, St. Louis, and other large Midwestern cities.
- *1984.* Members of an Oregon cult headed by Bhagwan Shree Rajneesh cultivated *Salmonella* bacteria and used it to contaminate restaurant salad bars in an attempt to influence the outcome of a local election. A total of 751 people became ill and 45 were hospitalized; however, there were no fatalities.
- *March 1995.* Four members of the Minnesota Patriots Council, a right-wing militia organization advocating the violent overthrow of the U.S. government, were convicted of conspiracy charges for planning to use ricin, a lethal biological toxin. The four men allegedly conspired to assassinate federal agents who had served papers on one of them for tax violations.
- *March 1995.* In five coordinated attacks, members of the Aum Shinrikyo cult released sarin gas on several lines of the Tokyo Metro, killing 12 people, severely

8

injuring 50, and causing temporary vision problems for nearly a thousand others. The attack was directed against trains passing through Kasumigaseki and Nagatachō, home to the Japanese government.

- *April 1995.* A Ryder truck containing about 5000 lb of ammonium nitrate and nitromethane detonated in front of the nine-story Alfred P. Murrah Federal Building, a U.S. government office complex in downtown Oklahoma City, Oklahoma. The attack claimed 168 lives and left more than 800 injured. Within days after the bombing, Timothy McVeigh and Terry Nichols were arrested for their roles in the bombing. McVeigh and Nichols were sympathizers of an antigovernment militia movement. McVeigh was executed by lethal injection and Nichols was sentenced to life in prison.

- *May 1995.* A member of the neo-Nazi organization Aryan Nations was arrested in Ohio on charges of mail and wire fraud. He allegedly misrepresented himself when ordering three vials of freeze-dried *Yersinia pestis*, the bacteria that causes plague, from a Maryland biological laboratory.

- *December 1995.* An Arkansas resident was charged with possession of ricin in violation of the Biological Weapons Anti-terrorism Act of 1989. Canadian customs officials had intercepted the man carrying a stack of currency with a white powder interspersed between the bills. Suspecting cocaine, customs scientists analyzed the material and discovered that it was ricin. The man was arrested, and the next day the man hanged himself in his jail cell.

- *November 1995.* A Chechen separatist organization left a 30-lb package of radioactive cesium and explosives in Ismailovsky Park, Moscow. The organization informed Russian Independent Television that this was one of four such packages smuggled into Russia. The location of the first package was disclosed before it detonated.

- *June 1996.* German authorities arrested a Slovak engineer on suspicion of smuggling 6.1 lb of uranium into Germany. The material was seized from a safety deposit box in the southern German city of Ulm. Only a few pounds of enriched uranium are needed to make a nuclear weapon.

- *April 1997.* Russian police arrested a group that tried to sell 11 lb of uranium stolen from a production plant in Kazakhstan.

- *September 2001.* Terrorists affiliated with al-Qaeda hijacked four commercial passenger jet airliners. The hijackers intentionally crashed two of the airliners into the WTC in New York City, and crashed a third airliner into the Pentagon. The fourth plane crashed into a field in rural Pennsylvania. Approximately 3000 people died immediately from the attacks. The overwhelming majority of casualties were civilians.

- *May 2002.* Luke Helder injures six people by placing pipe bombs in mailboxes in the Midwest. His motivation was to protest against government control over the daily lives of Americans.

- *August 2004.* Shahawar Matin Siraj and James Elshafay are arrested for planning to bomb the 34th Street–Herald Square subway station in New York City during the 2004 Republican National Convention.

- *November 2006.* The Real IRA detonates a series of firebombs in a hardware store, a sports store, and a toy shop, all in Belfast, Northern Ireland. The hardware retailer and sports store were completely destroyed. There were no fatalities.
- *March 2008.* A man on a bicycle is wanted for bombing a military recruiting office in New York City's Times Square. This crime is still under investigation by the Federal Bureau of Investigation (FBI).
- *October 2009.* A 19-year-old Jordanian planning to commit *violent jihad* was arrested after FBI agents foiled his attempt to bomb the 60-story Fountain Plaza office tower in Dallas, Texas. Hosam Maher Husein Smadi tried to set off a bomb attached to a vehicle at the base of the tower.
- *December 2009.* Northwest Airlines Flight 253, from Amsterdam to Detroit, was the target of a failed al-Qaeda bombing attempt on Christmas Day, 2009. Passenger Umar Farouk Abdulmutallab tried to detonate plastic explosives sewn to his underwear. The 23-year-old Abdulmutallab failed to detonate the explosives properly and was overtaken by fellow passengers. There were 290 people on board the flight.
- *April 2013.* Two improvised explosive devices (IEDs) constructed using pressure cookers were detonated at the Boston Marathon on April 15. Three were killed and an estimated 264 were injured, many severely (Figure 1.5). The suspects were identified as Chechen brothers Dzhokhar and Tamerlan Tsarnaev.
- *May 2013.* Three letters were sent from Shreveport, Louisiana, addressed to President Barack Obama, Mayor Mike Bloomberg of New York City, and to a colleague of Bloomberg. Upon the standard screening process of incoming mail within the offices of Obama and Bloomberg, it was discovered that the letters contained ricin (NBC, 2014). The letter sent to Bloomberg's colleague in Washington was opened, but no one was injured.

Figure 1.5 Emergency responders at the scene of the Boston Marathon attack. (Courtesy of Aaron Tang, Licensed under CC BY 2.0 via Wikimedia Commons, http://commons.wikimedia.org/wiki /File:Boston_Marathon_explosions_(8652971845).jpg#/media/File:Boston_Marathon_explosions _(8652971845).jpg.)

TERRORIST CLASSIFICATIONS

Several terrorist types have been documented as capable of using weapons of mass destruction (WMDs). They vary in terms of ideology, weapons used, tactics, targets, and access to technology and funding.

✷ The *Lone Wolf, Lone Operator,* or *Leaderless Resistance* Model of Terrorism✷

Recent examples include Eric Robert Rudolf (Figure 1.6), the convicted bomber of family planning clinics, and Ted Kaczynski (the *Unabomber*). In some cases, the lone-wolf terrorist shares an ideological identification with a particular extremist group, although that individual may not necessarily communicate directly with them. For example, Eric Rudolph identified with the Christian Identity movement. Lone-wolf terrorists may or may not be closely affiliated operationally with, or sponsored and funded by, a particular terrorist group.

The lone-wolf terrorist type is considered the most difficult to detect. This individual can strike a target without a predictable motive or pattern, copying a recent event to draw publicity, or simply acting on a whim (NJSP, n.d.). Individual terrorists have had limited success, as they tend to lack the funding, organization, and technical sophistication of larger groups.

Local Terrorist Groups and Nonaligned Groups

These form a significant threat of domestic terrorism, as they may possess the funding, organization, and ability to build or purchase CBRNE weapons. Local terrorist groups also have an advantage over foreign terrorist organizations in that members fit into the local community and may go unnoticed until they strike. An example of such a group is the Bhagwan Shree Rajneesh cult, which had been established in eastern Oregon. In the 1980s, members of the group released *Salmonella* into restaurant salad bars in an attempt to influence a local election by making neighbors ill (and thereby be unable to vote).

Figure 1.6 Eric Robert Rudolf was active in the 1990s and finally apprehended in 2003. (Courtesy of FBI, http://www.fbi.gov/publications/top_ten_60th/images/famouscases_14.jpg.)

11

Figure 1.7 **(See color insert.)** Remains of Pan Am flight 103 that exploded over Lockerbie, Scotland, 1988. (Courtesy of US Embassy, http://www.america.gov/st/peacesec-english/2009/August/20090820120057esnamfuak0.8462335.html&distid=ucs.)

Internationally Sponsored Groups

These groups may have access to sophisticated technologies, facilities, and technical support not available to nonaligned groups. On December 21, 1988, Pan Am Flight 103 was destroyed by a bomb smuggled on board (Figure 1.7). The remains of the jetliner rained down around the town of Lockerbie in southern Scotland.

The U.S. FBI determined that Abdel Basset Ali al-Megrahi, a Libyan intelligence officer, was involved in the bombing, with the support of the government of Libya. State sponsors risk severe repercussions should their involvement be discovered.

Doomsday Cults

These groups are obsessed with the advent of a global apocalypse. Such cults may prophesy catastrophe and destruction, and some may even attempt to bring such disasters to fruition. The group's leader may believe that, during the ensuing chaos, s/he will step in and take control. Doomsday cults pose a major threat arising from the fanaticism of their members, who are willing to act by any means to accomplish their goals. An example of such a cult is the Aum Shinrikyo, the group responsible for the sarin attacks in Tokyo in 1995 (Figure 1.8).

POTENTIAL TERRORIST TARGETS

What are the terrorists' considerations in selecting targets? A high degree of surprise in the attack, resulting in public panic and general paralysis, is desirable. Also, terrorists seek to create extreme drama and awe resulting from the attack. It is valuable,

Figure 1.8 Wanted poster for several members of the Aum Shinrikyo cult. Three members of the group are still wanted in connection with the 1995 sarin attacks. (Courtesy of Alamy.com, http://www.alamy.com/stock-photo-a-police-wanted-poster-for-members-of-japanese-cult-aum-shinrikyo-41919244.html.)

from the terrorist's perspective, to have media nearby to publicize the attack. This allows for the effects to persist in the public consciousness. Although typically of lesser importance, the magnitude of the attack may inflate the terrorists' sense of control and power. Many terrorist organizations desire the ability to repeat the attacks, thus causing long-term insecurity among the target population (Center for Defense Information, n.d.).

Terrorists seek to produce their effects by attacking a range of targets, including:

- Government buildings, military bases, ships, and weapons
- Government officials and diplomats
- Soldiers, police, and security officers
- Banks and the electronic transmission of currency
- Public monuments
- Transportation infrastructure including mass transit, airplanes, trains, bridges, tunnels
- Business headquarters, factories, and personnel
- Civilian crowds, events, and resorts
- Electric power plants (including nuclear power plants), dams, and power grids
- Water supplies and pipelines
- Communication stations and towers
- Computers and computer networks

Other targets may include:

- Controversial or high-profile private sector businesses
- Research laboratories
- Any location where large groups congregate
- Local response assets (fire stations, Emergency Medical Services stations, police stations)

WMDs

A WMD may be defined as one that can kill or injure large numbers of people and/or cause serious damage to manmade structures, natural structures, or the environment in general.

Among U.S. Federal regulations, 18 USC 2332a(c) defines *weapon of mass destruction* as follows:

Any *destructive device* including

- Explosives, incendiary, or poison gas
- Bomb, grenade, missile having an explosive or incendiary charge, mine, or device similar to any of the devices described above
- Any weapon that is designed to cause death or serious bodily injury through release, dissemination, or impact of toxic or poisonous chemicals, or their precursors
- Any weapon involving a disease organism
- Any weapon that is designed to release radiation or radioactivity at a level dangerous to human life

From the given definition, the term *WMD* covers several weapon types, including chemicals, biological agents, radiological materials, nuclear devices, and explosives (these weapons are collectively abbreviated throughout this book as *CBRNE*). Some potential WMDs are listed in Table 1.1.

Table 1.1 Selected Examples of Potential Weapons of Mass Destruction

Chemical	Biological	Nuclear/Radiological	Explosive
Tabun	Anthrax	Uranium or plutonium device	Pipe bomb
Sarin	Plague	RDD (*dirty bomb*)	Letter bomb
VX	Tularemia		Vehicle bomb
Hydrogen cyanide	Salmonella		Ammonium nitrate–fuel
Chlorine	Ricin		oil
Phosgene	Smallpox		C-4
Ammonia	Botulinum toxin		Military explosives
Sulfur mustard	Ebola virus		Picric acid (picrates)

Note: RDD, radiological dispersal device.

Chemical Weapons

Chemical weapons include compounds designed specifically for military use (e.g., sarin, a potent nerve gas). Additionally, commercially available toxic industrial chemicals (*TICs*) have been weaponized by terrorists. Obviously, the latter category is more popular with terrorists due to ease of acquisition; however, all forms are extremely hazardous (Figure 1.9).

The processes and equipment required to manufacture chemical weapons vary widely; some procedures are highly complex, requiring exotic ingredients and specialized equipment, temperature control, vacuum or high pressure, and continuous monitoring. Published literature and standard principles of chemistry and chemical engineering enable terrorists to learn how to produce chemical weapons. Although some agents such as mustard gas are relatively easy to manufacture, others are synthesized only by complicated processes involving toxic, corrosive, reactive, and explosive reagents.

More than 100 countries have the capability to manufacture chemical weapons such as phosgene, hydrogen cyanide, and sulfur mustard (U.S. DOD, 1998). Fewer countries are able to fabricate nerve agents such as sarin, soman, tabun, and VX. Commercial equipment for production of chemical warfare agents is generally available. For example, industrial facilities that manufacture organophosphorus pesticides or flame retardant chemicals could be modified to develop nerve agents.

An operational capability to use chemical weapons involves design and development of an effective unit of delivery (e.g., canister, missile payload), proper loading prior to use, and incorporation into an appropriate delivery system (U.S. DOD, 1998). Chemical weapons are described in detail in Chapter 2, and TICs in Chapter 3.

Biological Weapons

Biological weapons include microorganisms such as bacteria, viruses, and fungi, which inflict disease among humans, animals, and agricultural crops. Biological weapons also include

Figure 1.9 First responders assessing a clandestine laboratory used for production of sulfur mustards. (Courtesy of U.S. Dugway Proving Ground. With permission.)

toxins, sometimes poisonous in extremely small quantities, which are produced by certain bacteria, fungi, and plants. Biological attacks can cause widespread illness and death of human populations, or result in destruction of crops or livestock, panic in local communities, and possibly devastation of regional or national markets for particular agricultural products.

Biological agents are considered relatively easy and inexpensive to produce compared with many chemical warfare agents or nuclear weapons. Techniques for cultivating micro-organisms are widely available on the Internet and in published literature. Reagents and equipment needed for large-scale production of biological warfare agents, for example, nutrient broth and fermenters, are available commercially.

The method in which a biological weapon is released depends on several factors, including (1) the properties of the agent itself, (2) preparation of the agent, (3) its durability in the environment, and (4) the route of infection. Some agents can be dispersed as an aero-sol, which can be inhaled or can infect an opening on the skin, such as wounds. Attackers can also contaminate water supplies with biological agents. In other cases, microbes or their toxins can be added to raw foods.

Biological agents are living organisms that reproduce; therefore, a small amount can multiply into a significant threat. When disseminated, the organisms are generally slow acting; microbial pathogens require incubation periods of days to weeks from the time of infection to the appearance of symptoms. This delay may be considered an advantage to terrorists, as their victims may experience the onset of illness hours or days after the release of the agent at the crime scene. From the terrorist's perspective, biological agents must maintain their viability during storage, delivery, and dissemination. When weapon-ized for missile or bomb delivery, agents may become attenuated (weakened) by envi-ronmental stressors such as heat, exposure to oxygen, and desiccation (drying). Many biological agents are easily disseminated using commercially available household and agricultural sprayers (Figure 1.10).

Biological weapons are discussed in detail in Chapter 4.

Radiological Weapons

A *dirty bomb*, also known as a radiological dispersal device (RDD), is a simple combination of a conventional explosive, such as dynamite or C-4, with radioactive material (Figure 1.11). The purpose of a dirty bomb is to disseminate radiation in the target location. The effects of a dirty bomb are vastly different from those of a nuclear weapon. Most RDDs will not release sufficient radiation to kill or even cause severe illness—the conventional explosive itself would be more harmful to victims than the radioactive material. However, depending on the scenario, an RDD explosion could create fear and panic, contaminate property, and require potentially costly cleanup.

The extent of contamination by an RDD depends on numerous factors, including (1) the size of the explosive, (2) the amount and type of radioactive material used, (3) the means of dispersal, and (4) weather conditions. Those closest to the RDD would be the most likely to sustain injuries because of the explosion and become contaminated with radioac-tive debris. Prompt detection of the type of radioactive material that had been used in the weapon will greatly assist authorities in advising the community on protective measures such as sheltering in place or evacuating the immediate area. Radiation can be readily

Figure 1.10 Some countries and terrorist groups have attempted to use conventional crop spraying planes to disseminate agricultural toxins. (Courtesy of ARS, USDA, http://www.ars.usda.gov/is/graphics/photos/oct97/k7803–2.htm.)

detected with equipment already on hand by many emergency responders. Subsequent decontamination of the affected area may involve considerable time and expense.

Immediate health effects from exposure to low radiation levels from an RDD would probably be minimal. The effects of radiation exposure are determined by (1) the amount of radiation absorbed by the body; (2) type of radiation (gamma, beta, or alpha); (3) distance from the radioactive material to the individual; (4) means of exposure, that is, outside the body, absorbed by the skin, inhaled, or ingested; and (5) length of time exposed (U.S. NRC, 2007). RDDs are discussed in Chapter 5.

Nuclear Weapons

A nuclear detonation occurs as a result of the extremely rapid release of energy from a nuclear reaction involving plutonium or highly enriched uranium (Figure 1.12). The dominant reaction in a nuclear detonation may be nuclear fission, nuclear fusion, or a combination of the two.

The energy released from a nuclear weapon can be divided into four general categories: (1) shock wave (the majority of total energy released); (2) thermal radiation; (3) ionizing radiation; and (4) residual radiation (e.g., fallout). Against human beings, the shock wave and thermal effects are immediate. Nuclear radiation effects can be both immediate and delayed.

The basic concepts of nuclear weapons technology are widely known. Nuclear bomb–related physics is available in unclassified publications. Despite the wide availability of the basic design concepts, however, a country (or terrorist organization) with nuclear ambitions must also possess the technical expertise to develop such a weapon. Experienced nuclear weapon engineers and designers could be hired from various nations to initiate and manage a fledgling nuclear weapons program.

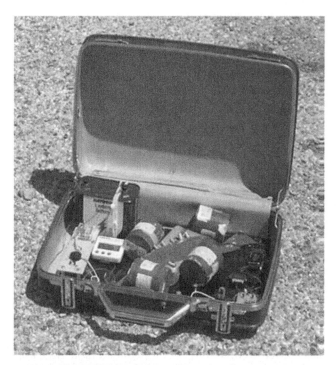

Figure 1.11 Radiological dispersal devices are relatively simple to construct. Lethality from dispersed radiation tends to be relatively minor. Effects from the blast itself may prove more hazardous. (Courtesy of U.S. Department of Homeland Security, Weapons of Mass Destruction Radiological/ Nuclear Awareness, Office for Domestic Preparedness, http://www.nv.doe.gov/nationalsecurity /homelandsecurity/responder.aspx.)

Figure 1.12   An aboveground atmospheric nuclear test conducted at the Nevada Test Site, May 25, 1953. Code-named Grable, the weapon was fired from a 280-mm gun and had an estimated yield of 15 kilotons. (Courtesy of State of Nevada Division of Environmental Protection, https://ndep.nv .gov/boff/ugta0601.htm.)

To construct a nuclear weapon a large, specialized, and costly scientific industrial infra-structure is required. The most difficult and costly part of developing nuclear weapons is obtaining the plutonium or the highly enriched uranium precursors. Procurement of nuclear materials is a significant obstacle to a weapons program; therefore, loss or theft of weapons-grade material from nuclear-capable countries is a serious concern. First-generation nuclear weapons developed by aspiring countries would likely be designed for delivery by short-range ballistic missiles (e.g., a SCUD missile) or tactical aircraft (U.S. DOD, 1998).

Nuclear weapons are described in detail in Chapter 5.

Explosive Weapons

An explosive weapon contains fuel that is energetically unstable and produces a near-instantaneous expansion of the material, accompanied by the generation of heat and a massive increase in atmospheric pressure. Terrorists have used stolen or obsolete military munitions as weapons; much more common, however, are the so-called IEDs (homemade bombs) (Figure 1.13).

Explosives are classified as either low or high explosives according to the rate of decomposition of the *charge* (i.e., the explosive material itself). Low explosives burn rap-idly (or *deflagrate*), whereas high explosives undergo actual *detonation*. The term *detonation* describes an explosive phenomenon whereby decomposition of the charge is propagated by a potent shockwave. The shockwave front traverses the charge at high speed, typically thousands of meters per second. It is the shockwave that shatters concrete and deforms steel, and destroys living tissue. Explosions also injure by flash burns from extremely high

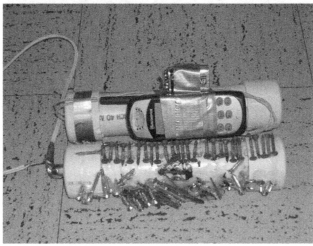

Figure 1.13 Two examples of improvised explosive devices (IEDs).

temperatures. Finally, explosions release significant amounts of fragmentation, typically from the bomb housing, which penetrates materials and living organisms. Some IEDs are intentionally equipped with shrapnel, that is, small articles such as nails or ball bearings, which disperse at high speeds and pose additional hazards to victims.

Explosive weapons are discussed in Chapter 6.

TREND OF CBRNE TERRORISM

In recent decades, the incidence of several forms of CBRNE terrorism has increased at an alarming rate. Is this phenomenon the result of establishing a clearly articulated definition of *terrorism*, or are more events simply occurring? Technically, the answer is *yes* to both; however, we must acknowledge that the numbers and severity of attacks have clearly increased. Some of the more practical reasons for the increase in CBRNE terrorism are discussed in the following subsections.

Information Regarding Manufacture of CBRNE Agents Is Readily Available

Designs for improvised weapons are widespread on the Internet. Likewise, information for culturing and disseminating microbial cultures is easily accessed. Libraries and bookstores provide the recipes required for many chemical agents. In addition, individuals with like interests can gather in appropriate venues (e.g., private clubs and gun shows) to share information on weapons design and construction.

CBRNE Agents Are Relatively Easy to Acquire

A number of chemical and biological agents and explosives can be formulated from readily available components by individuals with only a superficial knowledge of the relevant science. Sponsors and supporters of a cause may provide the necessary materials; precursors may be purchased legally from commercial sources; black market purchases are common; moreover, materials are sometimes obtained by theft. For example, Timothy McVeigh, convicted in the Oklahoma City bombings, had stolen explosive materials from a supply warehouse. Radiological materials are found in many facilities such as research laboratories, hospitals, and industry. Most American homes have small amounts of radioactive material within smoke detectors. Toxic chemicals, and the materials required to manufacture chemical warfare agents, are available in school laboratories, are used in industry, and are located in research facilities. Biological pathogens can be obtained from hospital laboratories and university research facilities.

CBRNE Incidents May Be Difficult to Recognize

CBRNE agents are ideal terrorist weapons because identification is often a formidable task, even with remarkable advances in detection technology. In the case of chemical attacks, it may be difficult to determine the specific chemical agent that was used. Biological agents typically have incubation periods of days or weeks before symptoms appear, thus making it an arduous task to identify the actual source of the release (Figure 1.14). Initial symptoms of a biological release may resemble a common cold or flu, further complicating recognition of an intentional attack. A radiological release would likely not result in obvious radiation casualties; in the event of significant radiation exposure, victims may fall ill days to months afterward. Even if an explosive device was used to disseminate radiological or chemical agents, there may be no immediate indication of any hazard beyond those of the explosives.

CBRNE Agents Are Readily Disseminated

CBRNE agents can be dispersed throughout large areas by air currents. HVAC (heating, ventilation, air conditioning) systems in buildings may carry CBRNE agents far from the source of release. Once disseminated, CBRNE agents can remain in air as vapors or aerosols, or settle on surfaces. The hazard can therefore remain for long periods if not addressed.

Figure 1.14 Biological agents often have lengthy incubation periods before symptoms appear, thus making it difficult to identify the source of the release. (Courtesy of BLS.gov, http://www.bls.gov/ooh /life-physical-and-social-science/biological-technicians.htm.)

CBRNE agents can furthermore be lethal in very small amounts. The degree and persistence of hazard requires that affected facilities be carefully monitored and decontaminated before being returned to service. Such efforts are cumbersome and time-consuming, and are a resource-intensive activity. On October 15, 2001, several suites of the Hart Senate Office Building in Washington, DC, became contaminated by the release of anthrax powder from an envelope mailed to Senate Majority Leader Tom Daschle. The building was closed and then decontaminated using chlorine dioxide gas. Office equipment and files were decontaminated separately using ethylene oxide. The building reopened in January 2002.

Tremendous Psychological Impact

One of the major goals of terrorists is to terrorize a population. The psychological impact of a CBRNE attack will often extend far beyond the actual incident. The scenario of possible exposure to a chemical or biological agent or to radiation will cause panic among potential target populations.

Existing Resources Can Be Overwhelmed

In the event of a significant terrorist event, local emergency response personnel (police, medical, fire, etc.) cannot handle all aspects of scene control, search and rescue, evidence collection, and other immediate needs, at least initially (consider the catastrophic attacks of September 11, 2001) (Figure 1.15). Responders and equipment must be brought in from surrounding counties, states, and the federal government. Some hospitals have the capability to decontaminate a small number of hazardous materials-affected patients arriving in their emergency departments; however, the sheer number of casualties and the

Figure 1.15   (See color insert.) Aftermath of the World Trade Center attacks of 2001. (Courtesy of Centers for Disease Control and Prevention, http://www.cdc.gov/niosh/blog/images/resp-prot.JPG.)

extent of the area involved in a terrorist attack could quickly overwhelm the capabilities of any response agency or medical facility. This reality was demonstrated during the sarin attacks in the Tokyo subway (1995), when literally thousands of citizens self-admitted to local hospitals. It is essential that emergency responders be fully trained, equipped, and integrated in the handling of mass casualty incidents.

LIMITATIONS TO TERRORISTS IN USE OF CBRNE MATERIALS

From a terrorist's perspective, there are a number of practical limitations and disadvantages to using CBRNE agents (Ohio Department of Health, n.d.).

Development and Use Require Skill

Development of effective CBRNE agents may require numerous difficult procedures. One report (NJSP, n.d.) listed 16 steps required to plan and execute a biological terrorist attack that would kill millions, each step of which would pose difficulty for the terrorist group. Problems cited included lack of technical knowledge, difficulty in obtaining equipment and materials, safety, risk of detection, and difficulty in preservation and dissemination. The information, equipment, and skills needed to accomplish these processes are available, but extensive coordination is required.

Effective Agent Dissemination Is Difficult

Chemical agents must be used in relatively large quantities, especially if released in an open area. Many pounds or gallons of chemical agent may be needed to cause a devastating effect. This requirement creates problems with manufacturing, storage and handling, and increases the risk of detection.

Delayed Effects May Diminish the Overall Impact

From the definition given earlier in this chapter, terrorist attacks are carried out to make political or social statements. The delayed effects of some agents, such as biological or radiological weapons, can detract from the intended impact. Determining whether an outbreak of disease or illness is the result of natural causes or terrorism is time-consuming. The uncertainty as to the cause, and the time delay in seeing any effect, can diminish the potency of the political statement or the credibility of the claim (NJSP, n.d.). This delay may, however, be outweighed by the terror that is created.

Counterproductive to Terrorists' Support

The use of CBRNE agents may be counterproductive to a group's cause. A certain balance exists between the magnitude of the terrorist act and the support that it generates. The use of especially gruesome weapons may isolate a terrorist organization from its potential support. Thus far, however, this has not deterred those who have already attempted to use chemical or biological agents.

Potentially Hazardous to the Terrorist

Production of CBRNE weapons is inherently hazardous to the terrorist. Production of chemical or biological agents, or use of radioactive material, pose significant risks to the terrorist. Radiation is difficult to shield, biological agents may infect the user, and chemical agents may kill or injure the producer.

FALLACIES ASSOCIATED WITH TERRORIST ATTACKS

There are many common misperceptions about terrorism and use of CBRNE agents. Some that we can debunk right now are discussed in the following subsections.

There Was Just One Major Terrorist Event, That Being on September 11, 2001

As should be obvious from this chapter, there is a wide range of active terrorist types that have carried out a diverse array of attacks against civilian and other targets. The reader is encouraged to regularly review news from quality, reputable sources (e.g., *New York Times*, *The Washington Post*, *BBC*, *The Guardian*) for updates on terrorist activities worldwide.

It Cannot Happen Here

A terrorist attack can occur anywhere; they already have in many U.S. states and in foreign nations. In the early 1990s, if planners and elected leaders had been asked to list the 10 U.S. cities most likely to suffer a major terrorist attack, who would have included Oklahoma City?

There Is Nothing That Can Be Done to Prevent Terror-Related Incidents

There is much that can be done in the name of prevention. Government intelligence networks can only perform so much, however; all citizens are encouraged to be vigilant and to report suspicious or potentially dangerous situations to local authorities.

There Is Nothing That Can Be Done to Respond to Hazardous Incidents

There is plenty that can be accomplished by both professionals and citizenry. Responding agencies can prepare their local emergency departments to treat contaminated and injured victims before an incident ever occurs. Once these skills are mastered, a hospital can build on this capability to treat victims of a mass casualty incident. Dealing with CBRNE agents as a part of the terrorist attack will certainly make that job more difficult, but not impossible. The key is to train, prepare plans, and then regularly practice and revise the plans as necessary.

For the typical citizen, their duty is to become educated, specifically regarding the range of potential hazardous materials incidents that may occur in their area. This includes industrial accidents (e.g., a release from a factory or a rail car carrying hazardous chemicals). In addition, citizens must learn where to obtain accurate and up-to-date information about an incident and how to respond. They must also obtain and stockpile some simple materials at home to assist in their response. The Federal Emergency Management Agency web site (U.S. FEMA, n.d. [a]) provides many useful tips about citizen response to a release of hazardous materials. Lastly, citizens are encouraged to join their county's

Figure 1.16 Community Emergency Response Teams provide training to citizens in handling a range of hazardous incidents. (Courtesy of FEMA, Community Emergency Response Teams, http://www.fema.gov/community-emergency-response-teams.)

emergency response team (CERT) (U.S. FEMA, n.d. [b]) (Figure 1.16). Such organizations provide training in response to various hazards, and welcome the participation of individuals from a wide range of backgrounds and capabilities.

QUESTIONS

1. Conduct an Internet search and locate a chronology of terrorism-related incidents, whether in the United States, Europe, or worldwide. Do you find any prevailing motivations among organizations that carry out terrorist activities? What are the most commonly used weapons?
2. Using the web site(s) for question 1, can you determine the first well-documented use of bacteriological agents as weapons? Describe the event and its long-term implications. Do the same for chemical agents as weapons.
3. List and discuss the motivations of terrorist groups. Which ones are the most common? Which are most difficult to counter?
4. On the Internet, locate the Southern Poverty Law Center's *Hate Map* at http://www .splcenter.org/get-informed/hate-map. What types of groups are represented on the map? Which groups are active in your state?
5. List and discuss the *advantages* to terrorists in using CBRNE weapons. What are the disadvantages?
6. What is the rationale to a terrorist organization in destroying a government monument, even if no human casualties are intended?
7. All disasters, whether terrorist-related or natural, are *local* incidents first. Explain.

REFERENCES

Center for Defense Information. n.d. Targets of terrorists. http://www.cdi.org/terrorism/more targets.html (accessed October 22, 2010).

Daftary, F. 1999. *The Isma'ilis: Their History and Doctrines*. Cambridge, UK: Cambridge University Press.

DTIC. 2010. U.S. Department of the Army, U.S. Marine Corps, U.S. Department of the Air Force, U.S. Department of the Navy, Joint Chiefs of Staff. Antiterrorism. Joint Publication 3-07.2. November 24, 2010. http://www.dtic.mil/doctrine/docnet/courses/operations/icdjo/resources/JP3 _07X2.pdf (accessed March 12, 2016).

The Federal Bureau of Investigation. 2016. Definition of terrorism in the U.S. Code. https://www.fbi .gov/about-us/investigate/terrorism/terrorism-definition (accessed March 12, 2016).

Fernando, L. 2010. The menace of terrorism and its early origins. http://www.asiantribune.com /?q=node/12854 (accessed October 22, 2010).

Garrison, A.H. 2007. *How the World Changed: A History of the Development of Terrorism*. Dover, DE: Delaware Criminal Justice Council.

Horsley, R. 1979. The Sicarii: Ancient Jewish "terrorists." *The Journal of Religion* 59(4): 435–458.

Lewis, B. 1967. *The Assassins: A Radical Sect in Islam*. London: Weidenfeld and Nicholson.

NBC News. 2014. Woman Who Mailed Ricin Letters to Obama Sentenced to 18 Years. July 16, 2014. http://www.nbcnews.com/news/us-news/woman-who-mailed-ricin-letters-obama-sentenced -18-years-n157531.

New Jersey State Police Homeland Security Branch. n.d. New Jersey HazMat Emergency Response Course. 06085. Special Operations Section, Technical Services Bureau, Hazardous Materials Response Unit. 3rd Edition. Trenton, NJ.

Ohio Department of Health. n.d. Emergency preparedness. http://www.odh.ohio.gov/slides /dpslides/wmd/module6/awr_st~1/tsld011.htm (accessed October 22, 2010).

Orwell, G. 1961. *1984*. Signet Classics Random House, New York: Penguin.

Peterson, D.C., and W.J. Hamblin. 2004. Who were the Sicarii? *Meridian Magazine*. http://www .meridianmagazine.com/ideas/040607Sicarii.html.

Radzinsky, E. 2005. *Alexander II: The Last Great Tsar*. New York: Freepress.

Tomes, R. 2004. Relearning counterinsurgency warfare. Parameters (U.S. Army War College). http:// findarticles.com/p/articles/mi_m0IBR/is_1_34/ai_115566394/ (accessed October 22, 2010).

U.S. Department of Defense. 1998. *The Militarily Critical Technologies List Part II: Weapons of Mass Destruction Technologies*. February 1998. Washington, D.C.: Office of the Under Secretary of Defense for Acquisition and Technology.

U.S. Federal Emergency Management Agency. n.d. (a). Are you ready? An in-depth guide to citizen preparedness. http://www.fema.gov/pdf/areyouready/areyouready_full.pdf (accessed October 22, 2010).

U.S. Federal Emergency Management Agency. n.d. (b). Citizens emergency response team. http:// www.citizencorps.gov/pdf/brochure/CERT.pdf.

U.S. Nuclear Regulatory Commission. 2007. Fact sheet on dirty bombs. http://www.nrc.gov/reading -rm/doc-collections/fact-sheets/dirty-bombs.html (accessed October 22, 2010).

Weatherford, J. 2005. *Genghis Khan and the Making of the Modern World*. New York: Crown Publishing Group.

2

Chemical Agents

Armis bella non venenis geri
(War is fought with weapons, not with poisons)

Declaration of Roman Jurists

Chemical weapons are a kind of poor man's atomic bomb.

Iranian President Ali Akbar Hashemi, 1988

INTRODUCTION

Chemical hazards may be divided into two broad categories, that is, those from *dedicated* chemical weapons agents and those from toxic industrial chemicals. Both have the capacity to inflict injury and kill biota, and both occur in massive quantities worldwide. The two categories differ in many ways; for example, toxic industrial chemicals tend to be commercially available, whereas chemical weapons are kept under heavy guard and are considered *hardened targets*.

Dedicated chemical weapons agents comprise a diverse group of highly toxic substances. Major categories include:

- Nerve agents (e.g., sarin, soman, cyclosarin, tabun, VX)
- Vesicating or blistering agents (e.g., mustards, lewisite)
- Choking agents (chlorine, phosgene, diphosgene)
- Blood agents (hydrogen cyanide)
- Riot control agents (e.g., pepper gas, cyanide, CS)
- Vomiting agents (e.g., adamsite)

Toxic industrial chemicals comprise thousands of substances in everyday use for the manufacture of commercial products, for example:

- Chlorine (used in polymer and pesticide manufacture)
- Cyanide (electroplating, mining)

- Phosgene (polymer manufacture)
- Carbon tetrachloride (industrial solvent)
- Sulfuric acid (metals processing)

Due to the possibility of chemical agent use in future military conflicts and/or terrorist attacks, response agencies (police, fire, emergency medical services) as well as military personnel must possess accurate knowledge of these agents, their effects, and the appropriate methods for treating casualties.

In this chapter, we will discuss the properties and effects of dedicated chemical weapons. Toxic industrial chemicals will be presented in Chapter 3.

HISTORY OF CHEMICAL WEAPONS

Nations have waged war via chemical means for millennia. Archeological evidence from civilizations in Egypt, Babylon, India, China, and elsewhere has revealed the application of chemical warfare in ancient and classical times. With each new armed confrontation between warring parties, weapons have evolved to become more innovative and lethal than were previously.

Ancient China

Chemical warfare appears to have been highly developed by the ancient Chinese. Some historians have proposed that the development of chemical weapons originated from the fumigation of Chinese dwellings to eliminate fleas, which was practiced as far back as the seventh century B.C.E.

Early Chinese writings contain hundreds of recipes for the production of poisonous or irritating smokes for use in war along with accounts of their success. The use of arsenic trioxide smoke is mentioned in early Chinese manuscripts. Accounts from the Mohist sect in China (fourth century B.C.E.) describe the use of ox-hide bellows to pump smoke from burning balls of mustard and other toxic plants into tunnels under construction by a besieging army. One of the first known riot control agents involved the use of finely divided lime dispersed into the air to suppress a peasant revolt in C.E. 178. The use of irritating *five-league fog*, formed from a slow-burning black powder to which varied ingredients, including wolf excrement, was added to produce an irritating smoke, is recorded. Much later, the use of poisonous gas by the Mongol army in 1241 is noted at the Battle of Legnica (in Silesia, southern Europe).

Weapons delivery systems were also described in artillery manuals of the ancient Chinese military. During the Jurchen siege of Xiangyang from 1206 to 1207, defenders of the Song dynasty prepared baked mud balls filled with noxious substances to be launched by catapults (Figure 2.1; Meng, 2005). The rationale for this design was twofold: the first was to release a spray of poisoned shrapnel on impact so as to inflict widespread damage, and the second was to deny the attacking Jurchens the opportunity to reuse the weapons by throwing them back over the city walls.

Figure 2.1 Illustration from thirteenth century China showing soft case grenades thrown from battlements to explode and release noxious fumes. (Reproduced with kind permission from Leong Kit Meng.)

Ancient Egypt, Greece, and Rome

The first pharaoh, Menes, cultivated, studied, and collected poisons from plants, animals, and minerals in 3000 B.C.E. Egyptians also studied the lethal effects of hydrocyanic acid (Osius, 1957). During the First Sacred War in 590 B.C.E., Athens and Sicyon plotted to lay siege to the city of Kirrha in retaliation for the harassment of pilgrims to the Oracle of Apollo at Delphi. Solon, the sage of Athens, had the main water supply to Kirrha poisoned with hellebore roots, causing diarrhea that led to the defeat of the besieged city (Hilmas et al., 2008). In 423 B.C.E., during the Peloponnesian War between Athens and Sparta, Spartan forces besieging an Athenian walled fort ignited a mixture of wood, tar, and sulfur and directed the smoke through a hollowed-out beam into the fort. The intent was for the noxious smoke to incapacitate the Athenians, thus rendering them susceptible to the Spartan assault that followed (the Spartans eventually took the fort). Also during that war, sulfur-containing substances were ignited and the gases were carried by the wind onto the besieged Spartan city of Sphacteria by Demosthenes. During the assault on Ambracia in Epirus in 187 B.C.E., the Roman army used choking smoke and caustic ash as a siege weapon. The inhabitants of the town, however, surprised Roman soldiers who were tunneling under their city wall by using their own blend of choking smoke:

> Filling a huge jar with feathers, they ignited it and attached a perforated bronze cover. After carrying the jar into the mine and turning its mouth toward the enemy, they inserted a bellows in the bottom, and by pumping the bellows vigorously they caused a tremendous amount of disagreeable smoke, such as feathers would naturally create, to pour forth, so that none of the Romans could endure it. As a result the Romans, despairing of success, made a truce and raised the siege.

> Cassius Dio
> *Roman History, Book XIX*

31

The Roman general, Sertorius, when fighting the Characitanes, had to overcome what were considered impregnable defensive positions within a series of well-protected caves. Sertorius noted that the prevailing winds blew from the North and that the openings of most of the caves faced the North. He ordered his soldiers to pile huge mounds of soil in front of the caves. As the breezes came in, he had his soldiers turn the soil over and his cavalry ride over it, raising a cloud of irritating dust that blew into the caves, blinding and choking the Characitanes. After 2 days of continued exposure to this dust, they surrendered—

> adding, by their defeat, not so much to the power of Sertorius, as to his renown, in proving that he was able to conquer places by art, which were impregnable by the force of arms.

> Plutarch
> *The Life of Sertorius*

The Romans are also known to have practiced chemical warfare against enemy's crops. One famous, although still-debated, event followed the defeat of Carthage in the Third Punic War (146 B.C.E.), where all farm fields in and around Carthage were sown with salt to prevent resettlement.

The use of irritating or caustic compounds is documented in numerous ancient military writings. Sand was heated to the point of being red-hot and hurled at the enemy (it often penetrated chinks in armor). Quicklime (calcium oxide) was found to be an effective lachrymatory (tear generating) material and skin irritant, and is described by Quintus Curtius in the first century C.E. (Partington, 1960). Later, during the thirteenth century, pots filled with lime and caustic potash were hung from the rigging of ships to be thrown into the eyes of the enemy. The Greek weapon *Kovía* (*dust*) included quicklime and incense that had been distilled from resinous wood (Partington, 1960). Some of the ancients associated *Kovía* with sulfides of arsenic.

Probably the most common use of chemicals in war during ancient times was via flame weapons. A primitive flamethrower was used as early as the fifth century B.C.E. By the fourth century B.C.E., a number of recipes existed for producing incendiary compositions, such as that provided by Aineias in his *On the Defense of Fortified Positions*, where a mixture of pitch, sulfur, granulated frankincense, and pine sawdust in packages were set aflame (Langford, 2004). One benefit of the mixture, according to Aineias, is the difficulty of extinguishing it. The sulfur would also produce toxic fumes. According to historical documents, a major interest in the use of additives in flaming mixtures was related to their value in producing a hotter flame; for example, salt had been added because it was thought to produce a hotter flame, rather than for the production of an irritating smoke.

The most famous incendiary composition of the ancients was the so-called *Greek fire* of the Byzantine Empire. This secret weapon of the Eastern Roman Emperors is said to have been invented by a Syrian engineer in 673 C.E. This mysterious material had the amazing property of burning on contact with water. The *liquid fire* was hurled onto enemy ships from spray devices and burst into flames on contact. As the mixture was reputed to be inextinguishable and burned even on water, it caused panic and dread among enemies. Using Greek fire against enemy ships, the Byzantines were able to rout the Arab fleet at the battle of Kyzikos in 678 C.E.

The Renaissance

During the Renaissance, developments in chemical warfare continued, even with Leonardo da Vinci as a proponent of the technology. In the fifteenth century, da Vinci proposed a powder of sulfide of arsenic and verdigris:

> throw poison in the form of powder upon galleys. Chalk, fine sulfide of arsenic, and powdered verdegris may be thrown among enemy ships by means of small mangonels, and all those who, as they breathe, inhale the powder into their lungs will become asphyxiated.

It is unknown whether this powder was actually used in warfare. Da Vinci was also one of the early designers of chemically protective clothing. His notes include a description of a protective mask that shields the eyes, nose, and mouth of the user from dust and smoke. This mask was found to be a more effective protection against his toxic powders than a damp cloth, which had originally been proposed (CBWinfo.com, 2005a).

Warring armies enhanced their capabilities by filling incendiary shells, termed *carcasses* or *stinkpots*, with noxious substances and firing them at enemy lines. Contents included sulfur, tallow, rosin, turpentine, saltpeter, and antimony. The primary function of these projectiles was to start fires; however, it was observed that hurling carcasses could at least distract the enemy as a result of the fumes. A variety of fills were developed to maximize the effects of the smoke. Gunners of the Imperial Artillery were reputed to have extensively used toxic fills during the Thirty Years' War. The experience with noxious smokes would lead to further experimentation in the ensuing years. During his siege of the city of Groningen in 1672, the Bishop of Munster, Christoph Bernhard van Galen, gained the nickname *Bommen Berend* (or *Bombing Berend*) because of his extensive use of artillery. He used various explosive and incendiary devices packed with belladonna, intended to produce toxic fumes. These weapons did not alter the course of the battle, however, in part because wind direction was not considered.

In 1854, a British chemist named Lyon Playfair proposed an arsine cyanide artillery shell for use against enemy ships as means to break the stalemate during the siege of Sevastopol. The proposal had the support of Admiral Cochrane of the Royal Navy, but the British Ordinance Department rejected his proposal as "as bad a mode of warfare as poisoning the wells of the enemy" (U.S. Department of the Army, 1997). Playfair's response is provided below, and was used to justify chemical warfare for decades to come (U.S. Department of the Army, 1997):

> There was no sense in this objection. It is considered a legitimate mode of warfare to fill shells with molten metal which scatters among the enemy, and produces the most frightful modes of death. Why a poisonous vapor which would kill men without suffering is to be considered illegitimate warfare is incomprehensible. War is destruction, and the more destructive it can be made with the least suffering the sooner will be ended that barbarous method of protecting national rights. No doubt in time chemistry will be used to lessen the suffering of combatants, and even of criminals condemned to death.

During the U.S. Civil War, a New York schoolteacher proposed the use of chlorine gas as an offensive weapon against Confederate forces, delivered by filling artillery shells with 2 to 3 quarts of liquid chlorine, which could release giant clouds of toxic chlorine gas. Apparently, his plan was never seriously considered.

In 1874, the Brussels Convention on the Law and Customs of War was adopted. The Convention prohibited the use of poison or poisoned weapons and the use of arms or material to *cause unnecessary suffering*. In 1899, an international peace conference held in The Hague led to the signing of an agreement that prohibited the use of projectiles filled with asphyxiating or poison gas. The proposal was passed, with a single dissenting vote from the United States. The Americans argued that "the inventiveness of Americans should not be restricted in the development of new weapons."

World War I

World War I became known as *the chemists' war*, for the deadly gases it introduced to combat (Jacobs, 2013). It is commonly believed that the German army was the first nation to use poison gas during World War I; however, gas was initially deployed by the French. In August 1914, the first month of the war, the French fired 26-mm tear gas grenades containing xylyl bromide against the Germans. The grenades were considered to be of little military worth; regardless, however, the French continued to consider the use of *lachrymating* (i.e., causing the eyes to tear) agents against the Germans (Smart, 1997). Newspapers reported that France had developed a liquid explosive, turpinite, which released toxic fumes. After a French bombardment had asphyxiated soldiers, Germany blamed the deaths on turpinite. The German troops later uncovered a French document describing chloroacetone cartridges and grenades, and instructions regarding their use. This evidence convinced the German High Command that Germany was justified in using poison gas (FirstWorldWar.com, 2007).

The research and use of poison gas by both the Allies and Axis Powers was eventually considered necessary during the war to overcome the stalemate that had occurred during trench warfare. During the battle for Neuve Chapelle in October 1914, the German army fired 105-mm shells containing powdered *o*-dianisidine chlorosulfonate, a lachrymating chemical, at the French, resulting in excessive eye tearing and violent fits of sneezing.

On January 31, 1915, tear gas was used by the Germans for the first time on the Eastern Front; 18,000 15-cm artillery shells containing liquid xylyl bromide tear gas (termed *T-Stoff* by the Germans) were fired on Russian positions on the Rawka River, west of Warsaw, during the Battle of Bolimov. Instead of vaporizing, however, the chemical froze, thus rendering it ineffective.

Fritz Haber of the Kaiser Wilhelm Institute of Physics is credited with the idea of releasing toxic gas late in 1914. Due to shortages of artillery shells, Haber reasoned that a chemical gas cloud could overcome the enemy's trenches and earthworks (Figure 2.2). Furthermore, gas released from storage cylinders would cover a much broader area than would gas dispersed from artillery shells. Haber suggested chlorine as a weapon because it was abundant in German industries (Smart, 1997).

Chlorine gas was released on battlefields near Ypres, Belgium, on April 22, 1915. Immediately upon inhalation, it brought on choking attacks and severe damage to victims' respiratory tracts, skin, and mucous membranes. The Germans' use of chlorine triggered immediate widespread condemnation, and Germany was criticized for abrogating The Hague Conventions of 1899. Germany justified its actions by stating that The Hague Conventions addressed only *projectiles* that diffused asphyxiating or hazardous gases, and

Figure 2.2 Trench warfare, World War I. (Courtesy of Wikipedia, https://en.wikipedia.org/wiki/Trench_warfare#/media/File:Cheshire_Regiment_trench_Somme_1916.jpg.)

did not address gases released by cylinders (Figure 2.3). The Germans added that France broke the poison gas conventions first.

On September 25, 1915, 400 chlorine gas emplacements were established (140 tons arrayed in 5100 cylinders) among the British frontline around Loos-en-Gohelle, France. The gas was released by opening a valve on each cylinder (Figure 2.4). The attack was dependent on a favorable wind, which did not occur—the wind shifted and much of the chlorine gas either persisted between the opposing sides or drifted back on the British.

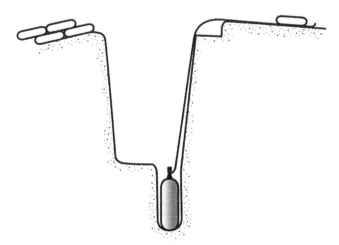

Figure 2.3 Typical German chemical cylinder setup ready for discharge. Thousands of cylinders were opened simultaneously, creating the gas cloud. (Courtesy of Army War College, *German Methods of Offense*, Volume 1, in: *Gas Warfare*, War Department, Washington, D.C., p. 14, 1918. With permission.)

Figure 2.4 Chlorine being released from canisters, World War I. (Courtesy of U.S. Army Medical Department Center and School, http://www.bordeninstitute.army.mil/published_volumes/chemBio /Ch2.pdf.)

Owing to British injuries, experiments were conducted to deliver gas payloads via artillery shells. These efforts provided the additional benefits of expanding target range as well as the variety of gases released (FirstWorldWar.com, 2007).

Citizens and military personnel expressed outrage and alarm over the use of poison gas in the war; however, its use was firmly established by this point. The commander of British II Corps, Lt. Gen. Ferguson, said of the use of gas (Bryen, 2015):

> It is a cowardly form of warfare which does not commend itself to me or other English soldiers. We cannot win this war unless we kill or incapacitate more of our enemies than they do of us, and if this can only be done by our copying the enemy in his choice of weapons, we must not refuse to do so.

The British Army went on to use poison gas with enthusiasm and mounted more gas attacks than any other adversary.

At this point in the war, delivery methods for chemical agents were either by cylinder emplacements or artillery shells. Delivery by cylinders was common initially because they were refillable and, in the case of Germany, large-scale gas shell production capabilities were lacking. Once artillery shells were developed that could be filled with chemical agents, properly sealed, and follow a steady flight path, the Germans stopped using cylinder-based attacks and relied solely on artillery shells.

Chlorine was not terribly efficient as a weapon; it produced a distinct greenish cloud and an obvious odor, making it easy to detect. Enemy soldiers in the trenches might have sufficient warning of its arrival, and thus time to don protective gear. Chlorine was water-soluble, so the simple act of soaking a cotton cloth with water or a solution of bicarbonate of soda (urine was also recommended) and covering the face was sufficient to protect many soldiers. A more discrete weapon was therefore needed on the battlefield.

The practical difficulties of chlorine use in battle were overcome with the introduction of phosgene. This chlorinated compound was first synthesized by the chemist John Davy a century earlier, who directed sunlight on a mixture of carbon monoxide and chlorine. Phosgene became important in the chemical industry during the nineteenth century in dye manufacturing.

Phosgene, a potent killing agent, was first used in World War I by France. Phosgene was colorless and had an odor of cut hay or fresh corn; thus, it was difficult to detect, making it a highly effective weapon. One drawback to its use was that the symptoms of exposure took 1–2 days to appear; therefore, those exposed were still capable of fighting. However, the receiving side feared that apparently fit troops might be incapacitated by effects of the gas by the next day. Later in the war, the Germans added chlorine to phosgene to increase its overall toxicity and to purge the denser phosgene from its containers. The Allies termed this combination *White Star*, based on the marking placed on artillery shells containing the mixture.

On December 19, 1915, 88 tons of the combined phosgene/chlorine gas was released from cylinders by Germany against British troops at Nieltje near Ypres, Belgium. The effect of the German attack was lessened because the British had previously developed a *gas helmet*, which was basically a flannel hood with a celluloid eyepiece impregnated with phenate hexamine solution that neutralized the phosgene. Despite the use of this so-called *P helmet*, the attack resulted in more than 1000 casualties, including 69 deaths. In January 1916, shortly after the first phosgene attack, modified protective helmets—in which hexamethylenetetramine was impregnated into the hoods to allow enhanced protection against phosgene—were issued to soldiers.

In June 1916, the British used the White Star phosgene mixture during attacks in the Somme. Almost 10,000 cylinders were used within 1 week (CBWinfo.com, 2007).

Approximately 36,600 tons of phosgene were manufactured during the war, making it second only to chlorine (93,800 tons) in terms of quantity produced. Phosgene killed far more soldiers and civilians than either chlorine or mustard gas, and was responsible for about 80% of all deaths caused by chemical weapons during World War I (Lohs, 1963).

Germany introduced sulfur mustards (commonly known as mustard gas) against the Russians at Riga in September 1917. It was used by the Germans against Canadian soldiers in 1917 and later against the French. At that time, mustard gas was termed *Yperite*, which is derived from its use near the Belgian city of Ypres. Delivered in artillery shells, mustard gas was dispersed as an aerosol mixed with other chemicals, giving it a characteristic yellow-brown color and distinctive odor. The gas caused severe blisters both internally and externally, usually hours after being exposed (Figure 2.5). The British eventually developed a mustard gas weapon, first using it in September 1918 during the breaking of the Hindenburg Line.

Personal protection against mustard gas was less effective than against either chlorine or phosgene gas. A simple gas mask did not protect against skin absorption.

In only a very small percentage of cases was mustard gas lethal to troops. Its primary military use was as an incapacitating agent. The gas was later used as a so-called *area denial weapon*, that is, it was disseminated over a village or airstrip to prevent access by the enemy.

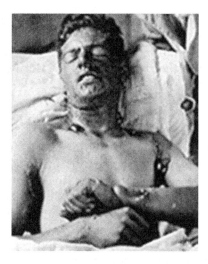

Figure 2.5 Canadian soldier suffering from mustard gas burns sustained during World War I. (Courtesy of Wikipedia, http://en.wikipedia.org/wiki/File:Mustard_gas_burns.jpg.)

Final Days of World War I

By 1918 the use of poison gas had become widespread, particularly on the Western Front. If the war had continued into 1919 both sides had planned on inserting poison gases into 30%–50% of all manufactured shells (Firstworldwar.com, 2007).

Other types of gases produced for the war included bromine and chloropicrin. The French army occasionally made use of a nerve gas obtained from prussic acid. However, the most widely used gases continued to be chlorine, phosgene, and mustard gas (FirstWorldwar.com, 2007). Of all chemical warfare agents used, chlorine, phosgene, diphosgene, chloropicrin, hydrogen cyanide, cyanogen chloride, and mustard were produced and used in largest quantities. As the war continued, many other toxins were tested for utility as chemical warfare agents (Cowell, 1939; Gibson, 1937):

- Bromine
- Chlorine
- Chloropicrin
- Cyanogen bromide
- Cyanogen chloride
- Dibromomethyl ether
- Dichloromethyl ether
- Diphosgene
- Ethanesulfonyl chloride
- Ethyl cyanoformate
- Ethyldibromoarsine
- Ethyldichloroarsine
- Hydrogen cyanide (AC)
- Hydrogen sulphide

- Methanesulfonyl chloride
- Methyl cyanoformate
- Methyldichloroarsine
- Monochloromethyl chloroformate
- Phenylcarbamine dichloride (phosgene anilide)
- Phosgene
- Sulfur mustards
- Trichloromethylsulfuryl chloride
- Trichloronitromethane (PS, chloropicrin)

During World War I, approximately 190,000 tons of toxic chemicals including chlorine, phosgene, and mustard gas were deployed against both soldiers and civilians, resulting in more than 100,000 deaths and more than 1 million casualties. The German army was the heaviest user of gas during the war. Historians estimate that German use reached 68,000 tons; the French used 36,000 tons; and the British 25,000.

By 1918, combatants had become much better prepared to respond to gas attacks. Filter respirators (using charcoal or antidote chemicals) were available and proved effective; however, use of such gear in trenches was cumbersome.

Fritz Haber (Figure 2.6), a German chemist and zealous proponent of chemical weaponry, likened chemical warfare to *an intellectual challenge*, telling industrialist Carl Duisberg that "gas weapons and gas defense turn warfare into a chess match" (Coffey, 2014).

Figure 2.6 Fritz Haber is considered by many to be the *Father of Chemical Warfare*. (Courtesy of the Nobel Prize, http://nobelprize.org/nobel_prizes/chemistry/laureates/1918/index.html.)

Regardless, however, poison gas did not prove itself as the weapon to turn the tide of the war. With the Armistice, the horrors of chemical warfare prompted the banning of chemical weapons in war. This commitment resulted in the signing, by 16 nations, of the 1925 Geneva Protocol for the Prohibition of the Use of Asphyxiating, Poisonous or Other Gases, and Bacteriological Methods of Warfare. The United States did not sign the Protocol until 1975. The Geneva Protocol does not, incidentally, prohibit the development, production, or possession of chemical weapons, only its use on the battlefield. Many nations signing the Geneva Protocol included the caveat that they had the right to retaliate with chemical weapons should they be attacked in such a way.

Interwar Years

After World War I, a number of isolated incidents were documented in which mustard gas was used against both military personnel and civilian populations. During this period, the United States and many European nations attempted to establish new colonial possessions; in other cases, they were faced with holding on to increasingly restless colonies. During the interwar period, chemical agents were sometimes used to repress populations and quash rebellions.

In 1920, the Arab and Kurdish populations of Mesopotamia revolted against British occupation. With time and with rising British casualties, the British resorted to increasingly repressive measures. Colonial Secretary Winston Churchill argued for the use of mustard gas on the Mesopotamian resistors. Churchill believed that chemical weapons could be inexpensively used against the Mesopotamian tribes (Gilbert, 1976):

> I do not understand this squeamishness about the use of gas. I am strongly in favour of using poison gas against uncivilised tribes.

Opposition to the use of gas and technical difficulties may have prevented it from being used in the Mesopotamian uprising.

From 1921 to 1927 during the Rif War in Spanish-occupied Morocco, Spanish forces allegedly dropped mustard gas bombs from airplanes to help defeat the forces of Abd el-Krim. In 1935, Italy, ignoring the Geneva Protocol (which it signed 7 years earlier), is believed to have used mustard gas against Abyssinia (now Ethiopia). Aerial spraying was developed as a new means of gas delivery, described by Ethiopian Emperor Haile Selassie, while making an appeal to the League of Nations (Brett, 1936):

> Special sprayers were installed on board aircraft so they could vaporize over vast areas of territory a fine, death-dealing rain. Groups of 9, 15, or 18 aircraft followed one another so that the fog issuing from them formed a continuous sheet. It was thus that, as from the end of January 1936, soldiers, women, children, cattle, rivers, lakes, and pastures were drenched continually with this deadly rain. In order more surely to poison the waters and pastures, the Italian command made its aircraft pass over and over again. These fearful tactics succeeded. Men and animals succumbed. The deadly rain that fell from the aircraft made all those whom it touched fly shrieking with pain. All those who drank poisoned water or ate infected food also succumbed in dreadful suffering. In tens of thousands the victims of Italian mustard gas fell.

A total of 15,000 chemical casualties were reported, mostly from mustard gas.

World War II

Chemical agents were not used by either the Allies or Axis Powers during World War II. Hitler is known to have been a victim of a sulfur mustard attack during World War I and was therefore opposed to its use by Germany. In addition, Germany decided not to use the newly discovered nerve agents, fearing a devastating Allied retaliation with those same highly toxic agents.

Civilians and prisoners of both the Germans and Japanese were victims of chemical weapons during the war. Mustard gas was intentionally used in so-called *medical experiments* on prisoners, presumably to obtain data on its effects and possible treatment. The Germans conducted experiments at both the Sachsenhausen and Natzweiler concentration camps to investigate mustard gas injuries. The Japanese subjected Chinese prisoners and civilians to experiments with sulfur mustards as well. The Allies also carried out experiments with mustard gas, but on volunteers. The Allied experiments were not conducted to the point of death of the experimental subjects, as had occurred in the German and Japanese experiments. The Allied experiments were also better designed and led to improvements in protective gear and treatment methods (CBWinfo.com, 2005a).

In 1938, chemical warfare was revolutionized by Germany's accidental discovery of the nerve agents sarin and tabun by Gerhard Schrader, a chemist of IG Farben. Another nerve agent, soman, was discovered by Nobel laureate Richard Kuhn at the Kaiser Wilhelm Institute in Heidelberg in 1944. The Nazis developed and manufactured large quantities of several such agents, which are discussed later in this chapter.

Postwar

After World War II, several countries were accused of or documented using chemical weapons. Between 1963 and 1967, the United Arab Republic (Egypt) intervened in the Yemeni Civil War, aiding the armies fighting royalist forces. Egypt was accused of using sulfur mustard during the conflict. Other chemicals such as phosgene were also reported to have been used.

Iraq began conducting research in chemical weapons development and deployment in the 1970s. Iraq used mustard gas during its war with Iran (1982–1988), with the first confirmed use in August 1983 near Haj Umran. Over the following months, both the physical and psychological effects of mustard on the Iranians were obvious; several thousand fatalities due to mustard were claimed; however, the exact numbers are under debate. In an attempt to establish whether chemical warfare agents had been used during the war, three United Nations (UN) missions (in 1984, 1986, and 1987) conducted field inspections, clinical examination of casualties, and laboratory analyses of chemical ammunition. The missions concluded that (Khateri et al., 2003):

- Aerial bombs containing chemical weapons were used in some areas of Iran.
- Sulfur mustard was the primary chemical agent used.
- There was some use of the nerve agent tabun.

In March 1986, UN Secretary General Javier Perez de Cuellar formally accused Iraq of using chemical weapons against Iran. This accusation resulted in an interruption in shipping of precursor materials for those chemical agents. Iraq was repeatedly charged with using chemical weapons, one notorious example occurring in Halabja in 1988 (see Box 2.1).

In the 1960s, The Committee on Disarmament in Geneva opened discussion on the question of chemical and biological disarmament. In 1971, the Convention on the Prohibition of the Development, Production and Stockpiling of Bacteriological

BOX 2.1   CHEMICAL WEAPONS USAGE IN IRAQ

From March 16 to 17, 1988, Iraqi warplanes and helicopters dropped a mixture of chemical weapons agents on the Kurdish city of Halabja, Iraq (population 60,000). The attack involved multiple chemical agents, including mustard gas and the nerve agents sarin, tabun, and VX. Some sources have also claimed that hydrogen cyanide was released (Figure 2.7).

This chemical attack, ordered by Iraqi President Saddam Hussein, caused the deaths of more than 5000 victims, most of whom were women and children. An estimated 7000–10,000 received permanent injuries to the skin, eyes, and membranes of the nose, throat, and lungs. Many victims attempted to escape along the roadways leading out of Halabja; however, Iraqi pilots, expecting evacuation from the city, sprayed roads with chemical weapons.

The incident, which Human Rights Watch defined as an act of genocide, is the largest chemical weapons attack directed against a civilian populated area in history. It has been estimated that as many as 30,000 Kurds were killed from Saddam Hussein's chemical weapons attacks in the late 1980s.

Figure 2.7   Victims of Iraqi chemical weapons, early 1980s. (Courtesy of Wikipedia, http://en.wikipedia.org/wiki/File:Chemical_weapon2.jpg.)

(Biological) and Toxin Weapons (The Biological Weapons Convention [BWC]) was completed. The BWC was opened for ratification in 1972 and entered into force in 1975. This treaty, however, contained no means of verifying a nation's compliance with its provisions.

The Chemical Weapons Convention

The countries participating in BWC negotiations further committed themselves to negotiate a treaty to ban the use and production of chemical weapons. In 1980, an ad hoc working group on chemical weapons was established at the Committee on Disarmament. This group received a formal mandate to negotiate the text of a Convention banning chemical weapons. The treaty was designed to include a verification protocol to ensure the compliance by nations with the treaty's provisions.

Negotiations on a chemical weapons treaty continued from 1980 to 1992. The text of the treaty was adopted by the Conference on Disarmament in Geneva on September 3, 1992, and became known as the Convention on the Prohibition of Development, Production, Stockpiling, and Use of Chemical Weapons and on Their Destruction (Chemical Weapons Convention [CWC]). The CWC was the first disarmament agreement negotiated with the ultimate goal of the elimination of an entire category of weapons of mass destruction under international control.

A unique feature of the CWC is its incorporation of the *challenge inspection*, whereby any nation in doubt about another nation's compliance can request the Director General to send out an inspection team. Under the CWC's challenge inspection procedure, nations have committed themselves to the principle of *anytime, anywhere* inspections with no right of refusal.

The CWC entered into force on April 29, 1997. By this time, 87 countries had ratified the CWC and became original *States Parties* to the Convention. With entry into force, the Organisation for the Prohibition of Chemical Weapons (OPCW) was formally established. The OPCW is the implementing body of the CWC and is given the mandate to achieve the purpose of the Convention, to ensure implementation of its provisions, and to provide a forum for cooperation among States Parties (OPCW, 2015) (see Box 2.2).

Recent Events Involving Chemical Weapons

In 1995, Aum Shinrikyo, a religious sect based in Japan, released sarin in the Tokyo Metro system, killing 11. The attack was directed against trains passing through Kasumigaseki and Nagatacho, home to the Japanese government. Approximately 6000 persons were exposed. A total of 3227 went to the hospital (see Box 2.3).

In 2005, Scotland Yard claimed to have thwarted an al-Qaeda sarin gas attack on the British Parliament. The plot to release nerve gas on the House of Commons was devised the previous year and uncovered through decoded e-mails on computers seized from terror suspects in Britain and Pakistan. Police and the secret service identified a six-person al-Qaeda cell that carried out extensive research and videotaped reconnaissance missions in preparation for the attack (Leppard and Winnett, 2005).

BOX 2.2   DESTRUCTION OF SYRIA'S STOCKPILE
OF CHEMICAL WEAPONS

In the 1970s, Egypt and the Soviet Union equipped Syria with chemicals, equipment, and training in order to initiate a chemical weapons program. Production of chemical weapons began in the mid-1980s. It was estimated that approximately 1100 tons of agent, including sarin, had been stockpiled (Berkowitz and Lindeman, 2013). In 2013, UN weapons inspectors found *clear and convincing evidence* that sarin was delivered by surface-to-surface rockets *on a relatively large scale* in the suburbs of the Syrian capital Damascus (Levs and Yan, 2013).

By 2013, Syria joined the Chemical Weapons Convention and agreed to the destruction of its weapons, to be supervised by the OPCW. Due to the hazards associated with many methods of destroying chemical weapons, it was decided that the safest and most effective route was chemical hydrolysis. Hydrolysis involves decomposing a compound by mixing with hot water and a caustic agent such as sodium hydroxide (lye) or bleach. The resultant products are significantly less toxic and can either be safely incinerated, treated further at an industrial waste facility, or decomposed by microorganisms (Jeavans, 2014). The hydrolysis process was carried out aboard a United States ship, the MV *Cape Ray*, over international waters in the Mediterranean Sea. By August 2014, it was declared that Syria's stockpile of chemical weapons was completely destroyed.

BOX 2.3   SARIN ATTACKS IN JAPAN

In the Tokyo attacks, liquid sarin contained in plastic bags wrapped in newspapers, each containing 1 liter, were delivered by five teams. (Note: a single drop of sarin the size of the head of a pin can kill an adult.) The packages were placed on five different subway trains in the Tokyo Metro system.

Carrying their packets of sarin and umbrellas with sharpened tips, the terrorists boarded their appointed trains; at prearranged stations, each dropped his package and punctured it several times with the sharpened tip of his umbrella. As the liquid volatilized, the vaporous agent spread throughout the car. On the day of the disaster, 641 victims were seen at St. Luke's International Hospital. Among those, five victims arrived with cardiopulmonary or respiratory arrest with significant miosis and extremely low serum cholinesterase values; two died and three recovered completely. In addition to these five critical patients, 106 more, including four pregnant women, were hospitalized with symptoms of mild to moderate exposure. Other victims had only mild symptoms and were released after 6 hours of observation. This incident underscores the potential dangers should chemical weapons fall into the hands of terrorist groups.

In mid-2015, the Islamic State of Iraq and the Levant (ISIL) had used sulfur mustard against civilians in Syria's northern Aleppo province. The mustard gas was delivered by mortar shells to residential areas of the town of Marea (Al-Jazeera, 2015).

With the exception of the Aum Shinrikyo attacks in 1994–1995 and ISIL in 2015, terrorists have not been successful in releasing chemical weapons. Although the manufacture of several chemical weapons involves relatively minor technical expertise, their limited use may be explained by fear of a particularly severe response by a nation and alienation of supporters, and simply that terrorists believe they can achieve their aims with conventional explosives. Regardless, however, the sarin attacks in Japan and sulfur mustard in Syria demonstrate that a small-scale release that causes relatively few deaths can create a significant and disruptive response in the population (Parliamentary Office of Science and Technology, 2001).

CHEMICAL WEAPONS TYPES

Nerve Agents

Nerve agents (also known as *nerve gases*, although these chemicals are liquid at room temperature) comprise a class of phosphorus-containing organic chemicals that inhibit the acetylcholinesterase enzyme in mammals and which are used both as insecticides and weapons (Table 2.1).

These extremely toxic agents are classified as G-series or V-series. The G-agents (named for the German scientists who discovered them) tend to volatilize and dissipate relatively quickly; therefore, G-agents are considered to be nonpersistent chemical weapons. In contrast, all V-agents are persistent, that is, they do not readily degrade biologically or chemically, nor do they readily volatilize (Figure 2.8).

Nerve agents were first developed in secrecy by the German military before and during World War II. The G-series of nerve agents was accidentally discovered in 1936 by a research team led by Dr. Gerhard Schrader. Schrader had been in charge of a laboratory to develop new insecticides for IG Farben pharmaceutical company. During his research, Schrader experimented with several innovative compounds, eventually leading to the development of tabun (see "Tabun" section). Tabun was discovered to be extremely potent

Table 2.1 Primary Categories of Nerve Agents

Series	Agents
G-series	Tabun (GA)
	Sarin (GB)
	Soman (GD)
	Cyclosarin (GF)
V-series	VE
	VG
	VM
	VX

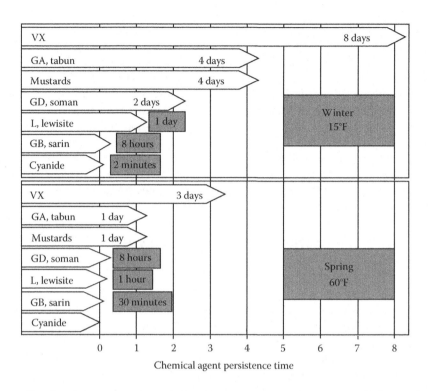

Figure 2.8 Graphical representation of the persistence of various types of chemical weapons agents during two times of year. (Courtesy of Swedish Defence Research Agency. With permission.)

against insects: concentrations as low as 5 parts per million (ppm) killed all leaf lice in initial experiments. Shortly afterward, Schrader personally observed the effects of nerve agents when he accidentally touched a droplet of spilled tabun. Within minutes, he began to experience *miosis* (constriction of the pupils of the eyes), dizziness, and severe shortness of breath. It took him weeks to recover fully.

In 1935, the Nazi government passed a decree that required all inventions of possible military significance to be reported to the Ministry of War, so in May 1937 Schrader provided a sample of tabun to the Army Weapons Office in Berlin and gave a demonstration, after which all of Schrader's nerve agent research became classified. A facility for large-scale manufacture of tabun began production in 1942. About 12,500 tons were manufactured before the plant was overrun by advancing Soviet forces. Large volumes of the agent were dumped into the sea.

Much of our basic knowledge about the clinical effects of nerve agents is the result of research performed in the decades after World War II. Poisoning by a nerve agent leads to miosis, profuse salivation, convulsions, involuntary urination and defecation, and eventual death by asphyxiation due to loss of control over respiratory muscles. Nerve agents can be absorbed through the skin; therefore, those individuals likely to be exposed to such agents must wear a Level A suit in addition to a supplied air respirator (e.g., self-contained breathing apparatus, or in-line respirator). Personal protective equipment (PPE) and respirators are described in Chapter 10.

Tabun

Tabun (military abbreviation: GA) is an extremely toxic nerve agent that is a clear to brown, tasteless liquid with a faint fruity odor. Tabun is a member of a class of phosphorus-containing organic chemicals (organophosphates) and is classified as a weapon of mass destruction by the UN; its production is strictly monitored, and stockpiling is prohibited by the CWC of 1993. Tabun, along with GB (sarin), GD (soman), and GF (cyclosarin) comprise the so-called *G-series* nerve agents.

The chemical formula of tabun is *n,n*-dimethylphosphoramidocyanidate, and its structure is shown in Figure 2.9.

Tabun is volatile and evaporates readily at ambient temperatures; it is, however, less volatile than sarin or soman. Tabun is much easier to produce than the other G-series weapons, and the procedures are rather widely understood; because of these factors, countries that are developing nerve agent capability but which lack advanced industrial technology often start by producing GA. During the Iran–Iraq War, Iraq used large quantities of chemical weapons against Iran's ground forces. Although the most commonly used agents were mustard gas and sarin, tabun and cyclosarin were also used (Norris and Fowler, 1997).

As is the case with all the nerve agents discussed in this chapter, tabun functions by short-circuiting the mammalian nervous system, specifically by binding to and blocking the enzyme acetylcholinesterase. During a normal nerve impulse, the release of acetylcholine over a nerve synapse stimulates muscle contraction. The acetylcholine is then broken down to nonreactive compounds (i.e., acetic acid and choline) by the enzyme. Tabun and the other nerve agents block the action of the enzyme, thus causing the synapses to fire continuously, resulting in contractions of all the muscles in the body. Sustained contraction of the diaphragm muscle causes death by asphyxiation.

Symptoms of tabun exposure are similar to those caused by all nerve agents. Most of our knowledge about lethal dosages is derived from laboratory studies on monkeys. The number and severity of symptoms that appear vary according to the amount of agent absorbed and rate of entry into the body. Very small skin dosages sometimes cause local sweating and tremors accompanied by constricted pupils with few other effects (Gulfweb .org, n.d.). Tabun breaks down slowly in living tissue. After repeated exposures, tabun accumulates in the body. The effects of exposure appear much more slowly when tabun is absorbed through the skin rather than when inhaled.

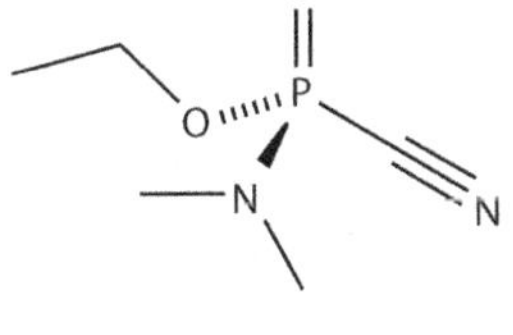

Figure 2.9 Structure of tabun.

Although a lethal dose may be absorbed quickly, death may be delayed for 1–2 h. Inhaled lethal dosages kill in 1–10 min, and liquid deposited on the eye kills almost as rapidly. Most victims who experience mild to moderate exposure to tabun can recover completely, however, if treated soon after exposure.

Sarin

Sarin is a colorless, odorless liquid at room temperature. The compound has a structure and mechanism of action similar to that of tabun and some commonly used insecticides. The chemical structure of sarin is shown in Figure 2.10.

Sarin, along with the other G-series and V-series agents, is classified as a weapon of mass destruction by the UN; stockpiling is prohibited by the CWC of 1993. Sarin was discovered by Gerhard Schrader and his associates in 1938; it was code-named T-144 and Trilon-46. It is the most toxic of the so-called G-agents created by German scientists and more than 10 times as potent as tabun.

At room temperature, the low vapor pressure of sarin (2.9 mm Hg at 25°C) makes it relatively ineffective as a weapon to be inhaled. It is made more persistent by the addition of certain petroleum products.

Sarin gained notoriety as a result of the terrorist attack on the Tokyo subway, perpetrated by members of the Aum Shinrikyo cult on March 20, 1995 (see Box 2.3). In five coordinated attacks, the perpetrators released sarin gas on several lines of the Tokyo Metro, killing 11, severely injuring scores, and causing temporary vision problems for nearly a thousand others.

VX

The V-series of nerve agents (where *V* stands for *venomous*) is another class of phosphorus-containing organic chemicals that inhibit the acetyl cholinesterase enzyme in mammals, essentially inhibiting nerve function and/or causing paralysis and ultimately death. The structure and mode of action of the V-agents are similar to those of the organophosphate insecticides; like the G-series agents, several of the V-agents were derived from early insecticide formulations.

The V-series of nerve agents includes VE, VG, VM, and VX. All the V-agents are persistent, that is, they do not readily degrade via biological or chemical means, nor do they readily volatilize (see Figure 2.8). These agents are therefore considered more hazardous than the G-series agents such as GB (sarin) and GA (tabun), which dissipate quickly and incur only short-term effects.

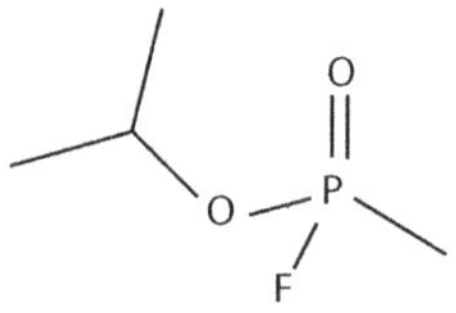

Figure 2.10 Structure of sarin.

VX is the most studied of the V-series nerve agents. The chemical name for VX is *o*-ethyl-*S*-[2(diisopropylamino)ethyl]methylphosphonothiolate, and its molecular formula is $C_{11}H_{26}NO_2PS$. Its chemical structure is shown in Figure 2.11.

The V-series nerve agents were originally studied by Dr. Ranajit Ghosh, a chemist at the British firm Imperial Chemical Industries (Croddy and Wirtz, 2005). Dr. Ghosh determined that the V-agents were extremely effective insecticides; however, they were considered too toxic for conventional use. In 1952, the British military took a strong interest in the new formulation and studied it in Porton Down, U.K. Several newly formulated and chemically similar compounds became the V class of nerve agents. VX was not considered the U.K.'s optimal chemical agent, however; sarin was the weapon of choice.

In 1956, the United Kingdom unilaterally renounced the use of both chemical and biological weapons, and in 1958 the British government traded their research on VX technology with the United States in exchange for information on nuclear weapons. By 1961, the United States went into large-scale production and weaponizing of VX, placing it in rockets, howitzer shells, and landmines (Robinson, 1971).

VX is classified as a weapon of mass destruction by the UN; its stockpiling is prohibited by the CWC. The only countries known to possess VX are the United States, France, and Russia.

VX is also the most potent of all nerve agents; the V-series agents are estimated to be about 10 times more toxic than sarin by entry through the skin and somewhat more toxic by inhalation. The lethal dose to 50% of the exposed population (LD_{50}) for VX is 10 mg min/m^3 compared with 100 mg min/m^3 for sarin and 400 mg min/m^3 for tabun (Table 2.1) (Sidell, 1997). As little as 200 µg is sufficient to kill an average person, depending on mode of entry into the body.

After the release of VX into the air, victims are exposed through inhalation, skin absorption, or eye contact. Clothing can release VX for about 30 min after contact with the vapor, which can result in exposure of other persons (U.S. CDC, 2006a). The extent of VX poisoning depends on the dosage received, mode of exposure (i.e., inhalation versus ingestion), and duration of exposure. When aerosolized to the vapor form, VX becomes most deadly, acting almost immediately on the victim.

VX is odorless and tasteless. It occurs in a viscous liquid state (Table 2.2), similar to that of motor oil, and can be dispersed as a liquid or via atomization as a mist. VX is the least volatile of the nerve agents; it has been engineered to be virtually impossible to remove from the surface it contacts. By virtue of its slow evaporation rate, this weapon can remain absorbed to surfaces (including skin and clothing) for long periods; in the event of a release (e.g., during warfare or a terrorist event), this persistence allows V-agents to remain a surface contact hazard. VX can thus serve as a long-term as well as a short-term threat (U.S. CDC, 2006a).

During mild weather conditions VX will remain for days on surfaces, and under very cold conditions it can persist for months (see Figure 2.8). Its longevity is advantageous in a military context, in that attacks on enemy targets will render an area hazardous to anyone

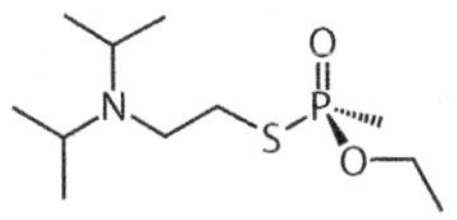

Figure 2.11 Structure of VX.

Table 2.2 Selected Chemical, Physical, Environmental, and Biological Effects of Selected Nerve Agents

Properties	Tabun (GA)	Sarin (GB)	Soman (GD)	VX
Boiling point	230°C	158°C	198°C	298°C
Vapor pressure	0.037 mm Hg at 20°C	2.1 mm Hg at 20°C	0.40 mm Hg at 25°C	0.0007 mm Hg at 20°C
Density				
Vapor (compared to air)	5.6	4.86	6.3	9.2
Liquid	1.08 g/ml at 25°C	110 g/mlat 20°C	1.02 g/ml at 25°C	1.008 g/ml at 20°C
Volatility	490 mg/m^3 at 25°C	22,000 mg/m^3 at 25°C	3.900 mg/m^3 at 25°C	10.5 mg/m^3 at 25°C
Appearance	Colorless to brown liquid	Colorless liquid	Colorless liquid	Colorless to straw-colored liquid
Warning properties	Fruity odor	No odor	Fruity; oil of camphor	Odorless
Solubility				
In water	9.8 g/100 g at 25°C	Miscible	2.1 g/100 g at 20°C	Miscible < 9. 4°C
In other solvents	Soluble in most organic solvents	Soluble in all solvents	Soluble in some solvents	Soluble in all solvents
Detectability				
Vapor	M8A1, M256A1, CAM, ICAD	M8A1, M256A1, CAM, ICAD	M8A1, M2561, CAM, ICAD	M8A1, M2561, CAM, ICAD
Liquid	M8, M9 paper	M8, M9 paper	M8, M9 paper	M8, M9 paper
Persistence				
In soil	Half-life 1–1.5 d	2–24 h at 5–25°C	Relatively persistent	2–6 d
On material	Unknown	Unknown	Unknown	Persistent
Decontamination of	M258A1, diluted	M258A1, diluted	M258A1, diluted	M258A1, diluted
Skin	hypochlorite, soap and water, M291 kit	hypochlorite, soap and water, M291 kit	hypochlorite, soap and water, M291 kit	hypochlorite, soap and water, M291 kit
Toxicity data				
Vapor	LCt$_{50}$: 400 mg min/m^3	LCt$_{50}$: 100 mg min/m^3	LCt$_{50}$: 50 mg min/m^3	LCt$_{50}$: 10 mg min/m^3
Liquid	LD$_{50}$(skin): 1.0 g/70-kg man	LD$_{50}$(skin): 1.7 g/70-kg man	LD$_{50}$(skin): 350 mg/70-kg man	LD$_{50}$(skin): 10 mg/70-kg man

Source: Agency for Toxic Substances and Disease Registry, Medical Management Guidelines for Nerve Agents: Tabun (GA); Sarin (GB); Soman (GD); and VX, 2008. http://www.atsdr.cdc.gov/mhmi /mmg166.html; U.S. Department of Defense, *Potential Military Chemical/Biological Agents and Compounds*, Headquarters, Departments of the Army, Navy, and Air Force, Washington, D.C., 1990. Field Manual 3–9, Air Force Regulation 355–7, NAVFAC P–467. With permission.

attempting to occupy it. VX is a so-called *area denial weapon* because of its physical properties as well as its health effects. Area denial weapons are used to prevent an adversary from occupying or moving across an area. Most area denial weapons pose long-term risks to anyone entering the affected location, including civilians.

Since VX vapor is heavier than air, it will sink to low-lying areas and create a greater exposure hazard there. VX does not readily mix with water; however, populations can be exposed by drinking contaminated water or via foodborne contamination.

VX breaks down slowly in the body; therefore, repeated exposures to VX or other nerve agents impart a cumulative effect. Symptoms appear within seconds after exposure to the vapor and from minutes to hours after exposure to the liquid. The effects are often fatal. It is possible that any VX liquid on the skin, unless washed off immediately, will be lethal (U.S. CDC, 2006a). Full body protection, including the use of securely fitting respirator masks, is essential to avoid exposure in the event of a VX release.

In the event of VX exposure, primary consideration should be given to removal of the liquid agent from the skin before removal of the individual to an uncontaminated area. After removal from the contaminated location, the victim must be decontaminated by washing the affected areas with dilute household bleach and flushing with extensive clean water. After decontamination, clothing is removed and skin contamination washed away. If possible, decontamination should be completed before the victim is provided with extensive medical treatment (GulfWeb.org, n.d.).

Death can be avoided if the appropriate antidote is injected immediately after exposure. The most commonly used antidotes are atropine and pralidoxime, which are issued for military personnel in the form of an autoinjector (Figure 2.12). The administration of chemical agent resistance pills is also effective. Atropine is a toxin itself, but it counteracts the effect of the VX by binding with and blocking certain acetylcholine receptors, so that buildup of acetylcholine VX-induced can no longer affect the nerve synapses. This prevents involuntary muscle contractions. The injection of pralidoxime regenerates

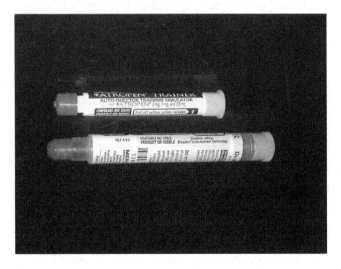

Figure 2.12 Atropine autoinjectors.

acetylcholinesterase, which was bound to the nerve agent. Atropine is typically injected into the arm or thigh but for attacks of VX vapor the atropine must be delivered immediately into the heart.

Destruction of VX Stockpiles

Before the CWC of 1997, chemical agent disposal practices included the U.S. Army's CHASE (Cut Holes And Sink 'Em) program, initiated in 1964, in which old ships were loaded with chemical weapons stockpiles and then sunk. CHASE 8 was conducted on June 15, 1967, in which the S.S. *Cpl. Eric G. Gibson* was filled with 7380 VX rockets and scuttled in 7200 ft of water off the coast of Atlantic City, New Jersey (DailyPress.com, 2005). The long-term environmental impacts of exposing VX to seawater and marine life are unknown.

Since 1990, workers and robots at plants in six states and at Johnston Atoll in the South Pacific have systematically destroyed millions of pounds of liquid VX, as well as sarin and mustard agent in a variety of containers and weapons. The remaining American VX stockpile will be eliminated in two facilities in Kentucky and Colorado (Gustafson, 2013). The VX is hydrolyzed to less toxic by-products using concentrated caustic solution and rendered nontoxic. In other locations such as at Johnston Atoll, VX stockpiles were destroyed by high-temperature incineration.

After the Gulf War of 1990, the UN Special Commission conducted inspections in Iraq to ensure its compliance with requirements to halt production and use of weapons of mass destruction. During this period, Iraq admitted that it had conducted research on VX but denied using the agent for offensive purposes owing to problems with its production (GlobalSecurity.org, 2008a). Subsequent investigation after the 2003 U.S.-led invasion indicated that Iraq had weaponized VX in 1988 and had dropped VX-filled bombs on Iran in the 1980–1988 Iran–Iraq War. Iraq again deployed VX in a 1988 chemical attack on Iraqi Kurds in the town of Halabja (see Figure 2.7), which reportedly killed 5000 people and created serious health problems for thousands more.

Choking Agents

The so-called choking agents have been used in warfare to kill, although historically they have been effective as incapacitating agents by causing irritation and severe coughing. Members of the choking agent weapons category include:

- Chlorine (Cl)
- Phosgene (CG)
- Diphosgene (DP)
- Chloropicrin (PS)

The typical mechanism of agent toxicity is a reaction with linings of the lungs, causing perforations where water leaks into the air sacs. The result is delayed pulmonary *edema* (fluid buildup in the lungs). Severe adverse effects may not become apparent until many hours after exposure. If pulmonary edema occurs within about 4 h of exposure, the victim will likely die despite all medical efforts. Medical management includes admission to the hospital with bed rest, administration of supplemental oxygen, and *intubation* (i.e., insertion of a tube into an orifice of the body).

Chlorine

Chlorine gas can be pressurized and cooled to convert it to liquid form to facilitate shipping and storage. When liquid chlorine is released, it converts quickly to a gas that remains close to the ground (vapor density = 2.5; air = 1.0) and spreads rapidly.

The degree of poisoning caused by chlorine depends on the location of exposure, the quantity a victim is exposed to, and the duration of exposure. Chlorine gas is highly corrosive when it contacts moist tissues such as the eyes, skin, and upper respiratory tract; acids are produced that inflame and damage tissues. Chlorine is highly water-soluble; on contact with H_2O, it forms hypochlorous acid (HClO) and hydrochloric acid (HCl); the unstable HClO readily decomposes, forming free radicals. As a consequence of these reactions, water greatly enhances the oxidizing and corrosive effects of chlorine.

Chlorine gas acts as a pulmonary irritant that causes acute damage to the upper and lower respiratory tracts. Low concentrations irritate the nasal passages and constrict the chest. In larger quantities, chlorine causes death by asphyxiation. A common sign of acute chlorine exposure is suffocation. The lowest lethal concentration reported is 430 ppm for 30 min (Noltkamper and O'Malley, 2008). Exposure to 15 ppm causes throat irritation, exposures to 50 ppm are dangerous, and exposures to 1000 ppm can be fatal, even if exposure is brief. More details about chlorine appear in Chapter 3 (Toxic Industrial Chemicals).

Phosgene

Phosgene, also called collognite or *D-Stoff* by the Germans, was first used in the dye industry before being used as a chemical weapon.

Phosgene is a colorless gas under standard pressure. Its boiling point is 8.2°C (47°F); thus, it is highly volatile and therefore a nonpersistent agent. Its vapor density is 3.4 (air = 1.0); therefore, it may remain for long periods in low-lying areas. At low concentrations, phosgene has a smell resembling newly-mown hay or fresh corn. This highly reactive compound has the formula CCl_2O (its structure is shown in Figure 2.13).

Approximately 2 million tons of phosgene are produced annually, primarily in the manufacture of polymers, including polyurethane and polycarbonates. At the industrial scale, phosgene is produced by passing purified carbon monoxide and chlorine gas through a carbon catalyst bed (Schneider and Diller, 2002):

$$CO + Cl_2 \rightarrow COCl_2 \tag{2.1}$$

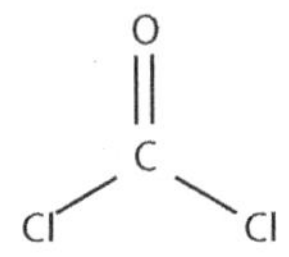

Figure 2.13 Structure of phosgene.

53

As a result of safety concerns, phosgene is typically produced and used within the same facility. It is listed in Schedule 3 of the CWC, that is, all facilities manufacturing more than 30 tons per year must be declared to the OPCW (2015).

During World War I, the Germans escalated their chemical weapons use beyond chlorine gas to include phosgene. By May 1916, the Germans started using diphosgene on the battlefield (DTIRP, 2008). Soon after the first German phosgene attack, the British began manufacturing stockpiles of phosgene gas at Porton Down. The gas was pumped into British artillery shells for the Second Battle of the Somme in June 1916. It is estimated that more than 80% of chemical agent fatalities in World War I were caused by exposure to phosgene (DTIRP, 2008).

Phosgene gas will incapacitate an adult within seconds if exposed to a concentration of 10 ppm. Fatalities are possible if the victim is exposed to concentrations of 20 ppm for 1 or 2 min. The key characteristic effect of phosgene poisoning is massive pulmonary edema. Phosgene attacks the lung capillaries followed by the membranes of the lung sacs, causing them to flood with fluids. Immediately after exposure, the victim experiences coughing, choking, tightness in the chest, nausea, vomiting, headache, and/or lachrymation (tearing). A period may follow during which chest discomfort disappears and the patient appears symptom-free. This interval commonly lasts 2–24 h and is followed by symptoms of pulmonary edema, beginning with cough, *dyspnea*, rapid shallow breathing, and cyanosis. Nausea and vomiting may also occur. As the edema progresses, discomfort and dyspnea increase and frothy sputum develops. The patient may develop shock-like symptoms, with low blood pressure and rapid heartbeat (NATO, 1996). In most fatal cases, pulmonary edema reaches a maximum in 12 h followed by death in 24–48 h. The effect has been termed *dry land drowning*. If the victim survives, the respiratory system will repair within 48 h and, in the absence of infection, there may be little residual damage.

In addition to acute effects, phosgene is dangerous because it does not detoxify naturally, has a cumulative effect on its victims, and may persist in sheltered areas and buildings.

Diphosgene

Diphosgene is a colorless liquid that emits an odor similar to newly-mown hay or fresh corn. Diphosgene has the formula $ClCO_2CCl_3$ and its structure is shown in Figure 2.14. Diphosgene is not listed as a Scheduled Chemical in the CWC.

The compound was originally developed for use in chemical warfare, shortly after the first use of phosgene. It was placed in German artillery shells during World War I, with the first known use on the battlefield in May 1916. Diphosgene was developed because the vapors could destroy the filters in gas masks in use at the time (Kurita, 2004). Diphosgene

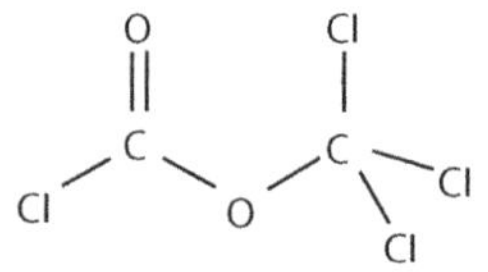

Figure 2.14 Structure of diphosgene.

has a strong lachrymating (tearing) effect; therefore, it has less surprise value than phosgene when used on troops (Globalsecurity.org, 2008b).

Diphosgene is used for the synthesis of several organic compounds, and has replaced phosgene in some industrial reactions. It is widely used in the pharmaceutical, pesticide, perfume, dye, and adhesive industries.

Diphosgene is considered more convenient and safer than phosgene during production, transportation, storage, and use, in part because it is a liquid at ambient temperatures whereas phosgene is a gas. Since it occurs as a liquid at room temperature, it is more persistent than chlorine or phosgene. The boiling point of diphosgene is 128°C (262°F). At temperatures of approximately 300°C (572°F), it will decompose to phosgene.

The hazards of diphosgene exposure are similar to those of phosgene. Symptoms can be delayed by 3 h or more; however, immediate symptoms may appear after exposure to high concentrations. The body converts diphosgene into phosgene, producing the same results as if the victim were exposed to phosgene gas (Globalsecurity.org, 2008b).

Chloropicrin

Chloropicrin is an oily, colorless, or pale yellow liquid that is an irritant to skin and other body surfaces. Chloropicrin has the formula CCl_3NO_2 and the structure is shown in Figure 2.15. This agent is not listed as a Scheduled Chemical in the CWC.

Chloropicrin was initially synthesized in 1848 by John Stenhouse, a Scottish chemist. It was first used as a chemical weapon by Russia during World War I and was eventually delivered in artillery shells and cylinders by both sides. During the war, chloropicrin was often released in combination with other agents because chloropicrin often broke through gas mask filters, making soldiers vulnerable to other gases. After World War I the impor tance of chloropicrin as a weapon declined. Due to its strong odor and having only one-fourth the toxicity of phosgene, chloropicrin did not receive the same attention as other, more potent chemical weapons agents (DTIRP, 2008).

The freezing point of chloropicrin is –69.2°C (–93°F) and its boiling point is 112°C (234°F), where it partially decomposes to phosgene and nitrosyl chloride. Chloropicrin is a relatively stable liquid that is prepared by reaction of picric acid with calcium hypochlorite or by chlorinating nitromethane (WHO, 2004). In the chemical industry, chloropicrin is widely used for organic synthesis as well as in fumigants, fungicides, and insecticides. Chloropicrin is used to sterilize soil and seed and for the extermination of rats. Chloropicrin is more toxic than chlorine but less so than phosgene (Table 2.2). Chloropicrin vapor is highly poisonous if inhaled—at very low concentrations (approximately 1 ppm), exposed individuals experience pain in the eyes; at 4 ppm victims are incapacitated, and at 20 ppm the victim experiences bronchial or pulmonary lesions (ACGIH, 1992).

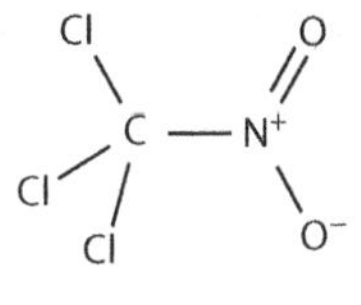

Figure 2.15 Structure of chloropicrin.

Exposure to high concentrations results in irritation of the nose and throat and eventually coughing, difficulty in breathing, sore throat, dizziness, bluish skin, vomiting, and in some cases pulmonary edema. Injury to the lungs can be fatal. Skin contact can result in chemical burns. Chloropicrin also has an intense odor that can serve as a useful warning property. In the open environment, the chloropicrin molecule undergoes *photolysis* (i.e., decomposition caused by light), thereby rendering it less hazardous with time.

Blister Agents

Sulfur Mustards

Sulfur mustards are a class of *cytotoxic vesicant* chemical warfare agents that form large, painful, liquid-filled blisters on exposed skin. At room temperature, most sulfur mustards are colorless, odorless, and viscous liquids. Some are yellow-brown in color and have an odor resembling mustard, garlic, or horseradish (hence the name of this weapon). Sulfur mustard vapor is heavier than air (vapor density = 5.5; air = 1), so it will settle in low-lying areas.

Sulfur mustard is a thioether—that is, a molecule having a generic structure R–S–R'. Specifically, sulfur mustard is a β-chlorothioether with the formula $C_4H_8Cl_2S$. Its structure is shown in Figure 2.16. Although the compound is commonly termed *mustard gas*, it is a viscous liquid at normal temperatures. The pure compound has a melting point of 14°C (57°F) and decomposes before boiling at 218°C (423°F). Mustard agents, including sulfur mustard, are regulated under the CWC. Since its creation, several mixtures of sulfur mustard have been used in various conflicts. Some formulations are listed in Table 2.3.

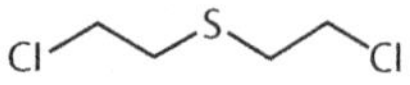

Figure 2.16 Structure of sulfur mustard.

Table 2.3 Selected Sulfur Mustard Formulations

Name	Composition
H	Undistilled sulfur mustard. Contains 20–30% impurities, which result in problems with storage. Also, as it decomposes its vapor pressure increases, with the potential for damaging its container with subsequent leakage.
HD	Distilled sulfur mustard (bis-(2-chloroethyl) sulfide); approximately 96% pure. The term *mustard gas* usually refers to this form of sulfur mustard.
HT	A mixture of 60% sulfur mustard (HD) and 40% T ([bis[2-(2- chloroethylthio)ethyl] ether]), a related vesicant with lower freezing point, lower volatility, and similar vesicant characteristics.
HL	Mixture of distilled mustard (HD) and lewisite (L).

Source: National Institute for Occupational Safety and Health, The Emergency Response Safety and Health Database: Mustard–lewisite mixture (HL), 2009. http://www.cdc.gov/niosh/ershdb /EmergencyResponseCard_29750007.html; U.S. Army, *Chemical Reference Handbook*, FM 3-8, Washington, D.C., January 1967. With permission.

Sulfur mustard has been in existence for almost two centuries; it is believed to have been first synthesized by Depretz in 1822, by Richie in 1854, and again in 1859 by Guthrie, who reported in the *Quarterly Journal of the Chemical Society* that blisters formed if the liquid was allowed to contact the skin. These early synthesis reactions resulted in the discovery of related vesicant compounds. By 1886, synthesis reactions allowed for the production of high yields of relatively pure sulfur mustard (CBWinfo.com, 2005b).

Sulfur mustard was not given much further consideration until World War I, when chlorine gas attacks by the German army instigated a chemical arms race by both sides. Mustard gas was first used on the battlefield on July 12, 1917, when the German army fired shells at British troops in the trenches near Ypres, Belgium. The gas was later used against French forces. The term *Yperite* for mustard gas originated from its use near Ypres. Yperite was such a potent weapon that only small amounts had to be added to high explosive shells to be effective. Once in the soil, mustard gas remained active for weeks (U.S. CDC, 2006b).

The effects of sulfur mustard attacks on the Allies were devastating; in the first week of German use of the agent, the British suffered more than 2900 casualties. Before the use of mustard gas, medical units had treated about 350 gas casualties per week. In the first 3 weeks of German use of mustard gas, the British reported 14,296 gas casualties (CBWinfo.com, 2005b). Sulfur mustard soon became a prominent battlefield weapon. It became the primary chemical agent used by the Germans, as they discovered both its physical as well as its psychological effects.

PPE was very crude and in short supply during the Great War. Some troops were equipped with oilcloth uniforms that could provide limited protection. Many troops had to settle for simple protection such as a mixture of zinc stearate and vegetable oil that was rubbed over the body. This lotion would have to be removed as soon as possible after an attack, as it would absorb mustard gas and eventually allow it to reach the skin (CBWinfo.com, 2005b).

Sulfur mustard is believed to have caused the vast majority of the chemical injuries in World War I (see Figure 2.5); the remaining chemical injuries were caused by chlorine and phosgene. Few of the sulfur mustard casualties were, however, fatal. For example, of the 36,765 single-agent U.S. chemical casualties, the injuries of 27,711 (75%) were caused solely by mustard. Of the casualties who reached a medical treatment facility, 599 (2.2%) died (Sidell et al., 1997). Most of those who eventually died had been hospitalized for days or weeks. Survivors of mustard attacks required prolonged periods of hospitalization— the average length of stay was 42 days. The effects of both lengthy hospital stays and the many casualties caused by mustard combined to substantially reduce an army's effectiveness.

If sulfur mustard contacts PPE, the vesicant property can be neutralized by oxidation or chlorination; household bleach (sodium hypochlorite) is effective. For liquid mustard that contacts skin, the LD_{50} is approximately 100 mg/kg (Sidell et al., 1997). Symptoms of sulfur mustard exposure are not apparent immediately after exposure; however, within 4–24 h deep, itching or burning blisters develop wherever the mustard has contacted the skin; exposed eyes become sore and the eyelids swollen, and may possibly lead to conjunctivitis and blindness.

Sulfur mustard can have the following effects on specific parts of the body (U.S. CDC, 2006b):

- *Skin:* redness and itching of the skin may occur 2–48 h after exposure and change eventually to yellow blistering.
- *Eyes:* irritation, pain, swelling, and tearing may occur within 3–12 h of a mild to moderate exposure. A severe exposure may cause symptoms within 1–2 h and may include light sensitivity, severe pain, or blindness (lasting up to 10 days).
  Cases are documented where the patient has suffered miosis, or pinpointing of pupils (U.S. AMRIID, 1999).
- *Respiratory tract:* runny nose, sneezing, hoarseness, bloody nose, sinus pain, shortness of breath, and cough within 12–24 h of a mild exposure and within 2–4 h of a severe exposure. At very high concentrations there is bleeding and blistering within the respiratory system, damaging the mucous membranes and causing pulmonary edema.
- *Digestive tract:* abdominal pain, diarrhea, fever, nausea, and vomiting.

In addition to its vesicant properties, sulfur mustard is also carcinogenic and mutagenic. Several mechanisms are suggested for the damage caused by mustard agents; one involves the bonding of the sulfur mustard molecule to the bases in DNA. The bonding may result in breakages of DNA strands followed by the formation of new bridges between the strands. Such bridges prevent DNA from functioning normally during cell division and may lead to cell death. Damage to DNA may also cause mutations and disturb natural DNA repair mechanisms. Such damage to DNA may be responsible for the increased frequency of cancer observed after exposure to sulfur mustard (Ivarsson et al., 1992; OPCW, n.d.).

Another possible mechanism involves the interaction between the mustard agent and the glutathione molecule. One of the functions of glutathione is to remove free radicals formed during cell respiration. If too much glutathione is tied up by mustard, then free radicals can no longer be regulated. Free radicals are highly toxic; therefore, this effect may lead to disturbances within the cells. Mustard agent can also bind to different proteins in the cell. However, it is not known how much this contributes to the injuries observed (OPCW, n.d.).

Although no antidote exists for sulfur mustard, exposure is usually not fatal (U.S. CDC, 2006b). There is no treatment or antidote that can ameliorate injury from mustard agent. Instead, efforts are made to treat the symptoms. The most important measure is to rapidly and thoroughly decontaminate the patient and thereby prevent further exposure. Clothing must be removed, and the skin decontaminated with a suitable solution and washed with soap and water. If the hair is contaminated it must be shaved off. Eyes are rinsed with water or a physiological salt solution for at least 5 min (OPCW, n.d.). It is essential to control infections using antibiotics. Pain can be eased by administration of local anesthetics. After skin injuries have healed, it may be necessary to apply plastic surgery. Lung injuries are treated with bronchodilatory treatment. Medicine to relieve coughing and also cortisone preparations may be used. Eye injuries are treated locally with painkillers and with antibiotics if required (OPCW, n.d.).

Disposal of Mustard Gas

After World War II, most of the mustard gas located in Germany was disposed by dumping into the Baltic Sea. For decades afterward, fishermen discovered hundreds of chemical weapons containers outside Bornholm, most of which contained mustard. When sulfur mustard comes into contact with seawater it forms a viscous gel that maintains its lethality for years.

In 1972, the U.S. Congress banned the disposal of chemical weapons into the ocean. However, by this point 64 million lb of nerve and mustard agents had already been dumped into waters off the U.S. coast by the Army (Table 2.4). According to a 1998 report by the U.S. Army Chemical Materials Agency, the Army established at least 26 chemical weapons dump sites offshore from at least 11 states on the West and East Coasts. In addition, because of poor recordkeeping, the approximate location of only half these sites is currently known.

Table 2.4 Locations of Historical Dumping Areas for Sulfur Mustard in U.S. Coastal Waters

Location of Loading	Destination	Date	Munition	Quantity (tons)
Attu and Adak, AK	12 mi off Chichagoff	1947	Bulk agent	Unknown
Charleston, SC	Site *Baker*	August–October 1946	Bombs, projectiles, mines, bulk	More than 7
Colts Neck Naval Pier, Earle, NJ	39°39′ N, 70°57′ W	June 15, 1967	Rockets, Bulk	3890
Colts Neck Naval Pier, Earle, NJ	39°33′ N, 71°02′ W	August 7, 1968	Contaminated water	2975
Edgewood Arsenal, Maryland	38°30′ N, 72°10′ W	June 18, 1962	Projectiles, Bulk	3
Edgewood Arsenal, MD	38°30′ N, 71°06′ W	August 6–7, 1964	Bulk, Projectiles	65
Naval Mine Depot, Yorktown, VA	Site *Baker*	March 21–25, 1945	Projectiles	13
New Orleans Port of Entry, Braithwaite, LA	Gulf of Mexico	March 1–7, 1946	Projectiles	207
NWS Concord, CA	37°40′ N, 125°0′ W	April 8–19, 1958	Bulk	9030
Theodore Naval Magazine, Mobile, AL	Gulf of Mexico	July 13, 1946	Bombs (German)	7

Source: Brankowitz, W.R., *Chemical Weapons Movement, History compilation,* Office of the Program Manager for chemical munitions (demilitarization and binary), ADA193348, Aberdeen Proving Ground, MD, 1987. With permission; Agency for Toxic Substances and Disease Registry, Toxicology profile for sulfur mustard, Chapter 6, Potential for human exposure, 2016. http://www.atsdr.cdc.gov/toxprofiles/tp49-c6.pdf.

A significant portion of the U.S. stockpile of mustard agent was stored at the Edgewood Area of Aberdeen Proving Ground (Maryland). A disposal plant constructed on-site neutralized the last of this stockpile by 2005. The largest mustard agent stockpile, more than 6000 tons, was stored at the Deseret Chemical Depot in Utah. Destruction of this stockpile began in 2006 and was completed by 2011.

Lewisite

Lewisite is a member of the arsine chemical family. As a pure liquid lewisite is colorless and odorless; however, impure lewisite is amber to black with a characteristic odor similar to geraniums (Sidell et al., 1997). Lewisite has the formula β-chlorovinyldichloroarsine, and the structure is shown in Figure 2.17.

Lewisite is named after the U.S. chemist Winford Lewis (1878–1943), who in 1918 discovered a graduate thesis describing its synthesis and went on to formulate a battlefield weapon. The methods in the original thesis called for the reaction of arsenic trichloride with acetylene in the presence of mercuric chloride in HCl. German scientists are believed to have studied this compound earlier (Buscher and Conway, 1944; Prentiss, 1937).

After World War I, the U.S. military became interested in lewisite; however, field trials during World War II demonstrated that casualty effects were not consistent under high humidity due to its high rate of hydrolysis. In addition, its distinct odor and ability to cause lachrymation induced troops to don protective gear and avoid contaminated areas. The United States produced about 20,000 tons of lewisite. It was replaced by sulfur mustard and ultimately declared obsolete by the 1950s. Stockpiles of lewisite were neutralized by oxidation with chlorine and disposed into the Gulf of Mexico (National Research Council, 2001).

There has been no verified use of lewisite on the battlefield although Japan may have used it against China between 1937 and 1944 (Beebe, 1960). China and Japan are known to still be jointly cleaning up Japan's buried World War II stock of lewisite in northeastern China. Several Chinese citizens have died in recent decades from accidental exposure to lewisite (Koijima, 2001; NTI Center for Nonproliferation Studies, 2007). Lewisite is listed in Schedule 1 of the CWC.

As a chemical weapon and a blister agent, lewisite is much more volatile than mustard; however, it is persistent in colder climates. Lewisite remains fluid at lower temperatures, which renders it effective for dispersal in winter, high altitudes, and in other cold situations. Lewisite hydrolyzes rapidly; therefore, maintaining active concentrations of vapor in moist, humid weather may prove difficult (U.S. Army, 2005; U.S. DOD, 1990).

Lewisite hydrolyzes in water to form hydrochloric acid, and in contact with alkaline solutions can form trisodium arsenate. Lewisite readily penetrates ordinary clothing and even rubber materials. The effects of lewisite are similar to those of the sulfur mustards,

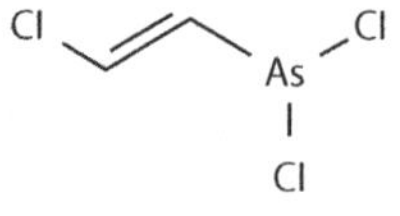

Figure 2.17 Structure of lewisite.

that is, the vapor and liquid damage the skin, eyes, and airways; however, lewisite differs from mustard because pain or irritation occur within seconds of exposure rather than hours (Sidell, 1997). It causes immediate itching with a rash and swelling. Blisters develop after 12 h, and discomfort lasts for 2–3 days. Pain caused by a lewisite lesion is much less severe than that caused by mustard lesions, and it tends to diminish after blisters form (Buscher and Conway, 1944).

A victim is less likely to experience severe eye injury from lewisite vapor than from mustard vapor because the immediate irritation and pain caused by lewisite will produce *blepharospasm* (an involuntary closure of the eyes and lids), thus preventing further exposure. A droplet of lewisite (0.001 ml) can cause perforation and loss of an eye (Mann et al., 1946). Inhalation of lewisite results in a burning pain to the chest, sneezing, coughing, vomiting, and pulmonary edema. Inhalation causes exposed individuals to seek immediate protection, thus limiting further exposure. Ingestion results in severe pain, nausea, vomiting, and tissue damage. Other generalized symptoms include restlessness, weakness, below-normal core temperature, and low blood pressure (Sidell, 1997). With high rates of absorption, systemic poisoning may occur leading to liver necrosis, pulmonary edema, and possibly death.

As with other arsenical chemical weapons, lewisite inhibits many enzymes in the body, in particular those with thiol groups such as pyruvic oxidase, alcohol dehydrogenase, and succinic dehydrogenase. The exact mechanism by which lewisite damages cells has not been completely determined. Inactivation of carbohydrate metabolism, primarily because of inhibition of the pyruvate dehydrogenase enzyme, is considered a key factor (Trammel, 1992).

British antilewisite (BAL, dimercaprol), is highly effective for treatment of the effects of lewisite if used soon after exposure (Sidell, 1997). BAL binds to the arsenic component of lewisite more strongly than do tissue enzymes, thereby displacing lewisite from the cellular receptor sites (Goldman and Dacre, 1989; Trammel, 1992). The reaction is shown below.

$$\text{(2.2)}$$

Medical personnel are directed to follow the same principles for managing lewisite skin, eye, and airway lesions as they would follow for managing mustard lesions. BAL will prevent or substantially decrease the severity of skin and eye lesions if applied topically within minutes after the exposure and decontamination (Sidell, 1997).

QUESTIONS

1. If the Geneva Conventions had never been established and you were a military general, would you allow the use of chemical weapons? If yes, under what circumstances?

2. Check the Internet and determine the current status of chemical weapons stockpiles in your state or a nearby state. How much is currently in storage? How are these stockpiles being destroyed? Is there concern by the public or elected

representatives regarding destruction methods and/or transportation of weapons or their wastes?

3. What is the most common method of chemical weapon destruction in the United States? What are the products of this destruction technology? Are there any hazards with use of this technology? Be specific.
4. By what routes can chemical agents enter the body? Which route is most effective for VX? For sarin?
5. Define the following terms: LD_{50}; edema; miosis; lachrymation; emesis, cytotoxic; vesicant.
6. The G-series nerve agents are based on the chemical properties of what common chemical(s)? Discuss the mode of action of the nerve agents in general.
7. Does the dose rate of a nerve agent affect the body's response? Explain. What is the effect of daily exposure to small doses of a nerve agent over several days?
8. Explain *persistence* of a chemical weapons agent, in terms of its reactions with air, microorganisms, sunlight, and so on. Which chemical agents are persistent? Is there a practical advantage to an army or terrorist organization using a persistent weapon? Explain.
9. Define and explain an *area denial weapon*. How could it be used in modern warfare? By a terrorist group?
10. Response to chlorine or phosgene exposure involves rapid administration of an antitoxin such as atropine. True or false? Explain.

REFERENCES

Agency for Toxic Substances and Disease Registry. 2008. Medical Management Guidelines for Nerve Agents: Tabun (GA); Sarin (GB); Soman (GD); and VX. http://www.atsdr.cdc.gov/mhmi/mmg166.html.

Agency for Toxic Substances and Disease Registry. 2016. Toxicology profile for sulfur mustard. Chapter 6. Potential for human exposure. http://www.atsdr.cdc.gov/toxprofiles/tp49-c6.pdf (accessed February 22, 2016).

Aineias the Tactician. (FL. 357 B.C.) *On the Defense of Fortified Positions*. As cited in Atchity, K.J., and R. McKenna. 1996. *The Classical Greek Reader*. UK: Oxford University Press.

Aljazeera. 2015. ISIL suspected of using mustard gas in Syria's Aleppo. http://www.aljazeera.com/news/2015/08/isil-chemical-weapons-syria-aleppo-mustard-gas-150824051212809.html.

American Conference of Governmental Industrial Hygienists. 1992. *Documentation of Threshold Limit Values and Biological Exposure Indices*. 6th Edition. Cincinnati, OH: ACGIH.

Army War College. 1918. *German Methods of Offense*. Volume 1. In: *Gas Warfare*. Washington, D.C.: War Department, p. 14.

Beebe, G.W. 1960. Lung cancer in World War I veterans: Possible relation to mustard-gas injury and 1918 influenza epidemic. *Journal National Cancer Institute* 25(6): 1231–1252.

Berkowitz, B., and T. Lindeman. 2014. What chemical weapons does Syria have? *Washington Post*. 15 Sept. 2013. Web. 1 Nov. 2014. http://apps.washingtonpost.com/g/page/world/what-chemical-weapons-does-syria-have/454/.

Brankowitz, W.R. 1987. *Chemical Weapons Movement. History Compilation*. Aberdeen Proving Ground, MD: Office of the Program Manager for chemical munitions (demilitarization and binary), ADA193348.

Brett, H.H. 1936. Chemicals and aircraft. *Chemical Warfare Bulletin* 22(4): 151–152.

Bryen, S.D. 2015. *Technology Security and National Power: Winners and Losers*. Piscataway, NJ: Transaction Publishers.

Buscher, H., and N. Conway. 1944. *Green and Yellow Cross. Kettering Laboratory of Applied Physiology*. Cincinnati, OH: University of Cincinnati.

Cassius Dio. *Roman History. Book XIX*. As cited in Cary, E. 1970. *Dio's Roman History*. Portsmouth, NH: Heinemann Press.

CBWinfo.com. 2005a. A brief history of chemical, biological, and radiological weapons. http://www.cbwinfo.com/History/ancto19th.shtml (accessed October 23, 2010).

CBWinfo.com. 2005b. Blister agent: Sulfur mustard (H, HD, HS). http://www.cbwinfo.com/Chemical/Blister/HD.shtml (accessed October 23, 2010).

Coffey, P. 2014. *American Arsenal: A Century of Weapon Technology and Strategy*. OUP, USA.

Cowell, E.M. 1939. Chemical warfare and the doctor. *The British Medical Journal* 2: 736–738.

Croddy, E., and J.J. Wirtz. 2005. *Weapons of Mass Destruction: An Encyclopedia of Worldwide Policy, Technology, and History*, Vol. 1. ABC-CLIO, Santa Barbara, CA.

DailyPress.com. 2005. A generation of indiscriminate dumping. http://www.dailypress.com/media/acrobat/2005-10/20226301.pdf (accessed October 23, 2010).

Defense Treaty Inspection Readiness Program. 2008. Choking agents. http://dtirp.dtra.mil/CBW_References/Agents/AgentsCW.aspx.

FirstWorldWar.com. 2007. Weapons of war: Poison gas. http://www.firstworldwar.com/weaponry/gas.htm (accessed October 23, 2010).

Gibson, A. 1937. Chemical warfare as developed during the world war—Probable future development. *Bulletin of the New York Academy of Medicine*. 13 (7): 397–421. http://www.ncbi.nlm.nih.gov/pmc/articles/PMC1966130/pdf/bullnyacadmed00849-0025.pdf (accessed October 27, 2010).

Gilbert, M. 1976. *Winston S. Churchill*. Volume 4, Part 1. London: Heinemann Pub.

GlobalSecurity.org. 2008a. Iraq Survey Group Final Report. http://www.globalsecurity.org/wmd/library/report/2004/isg-final-report/isg-final-report vol1_rsi-06.htm (accessed October 23, 2010).

GlobalSecurity.org. 2008b. Choking agents. http://www.globalsecurity.org/wmd/intro/cw-choking.htm (accessed October 23, 2010).

Goldman, M., and J.C. Dacre. 1989. Lewisite: Its chemistry, toxicology, and biological effects. *Reviews Environmental Contamination and Toxicology* 110: 75–115.

GulfWeb.org. n.d. Material safety data sheet—Lethal nerve agent tabun (GA). http://www.gulfweb.org/bigdoc/report/appga.html (accessed October 23, 2010).

Gustafson, D. 2013. The long, costly process of destroying chemical weapons. Al-Jazeera America. October 7, 2013. http://america.aljazeera.com/watch/shows/america-tonight/america-tonight-blog/2013/10/7/-the-long-costlyprocessofdestroyingchemicalweapons.html.

Hilmas, C.J., J.K. Smart, and B.A. Hill. 2008. History of chemical warfare. Chapter 2. In *Medical Aspects of Chemical Warfare. Textbooks of Military Medicine*, ed. S.D. Tuorinsky. Washington, D.C.: Department of the Army.

Ivarsson, U., H. Nilsson, J. Santesson, J.-O. Andersson, and K. Bald. (Eds.). 1992. *Briefing Book #16; Chemical Weapons: Threat, Effects, and Protection*. Umea, Sweden: Defence Research Establishment, Forsvarets Forskningsanstalt (FOA).

Jacobs, S. 2013. Chemical warfare, from Rome to Syria. A time line. *National Geographic*. August 22, 2013. http://news.nationalgeographic.com/news/2013/08/130822-syria-chemical-biological-weapons-sarin-war-history-science/ (accessed February 22, 2016).

Jeavans, C. 2014. Destroying Syria's chemical weapons. BBC.com. 2 July 2014. 2 Nov. 2014. http://www.bbc.com/news/world-middle-east-25810934.

Khateri, S., M. Ghanei, S. Keshavarz, M. Soroush, and D. Haines. 2003. Incidence of lung, eye, and skin lesions as late complications in 34,000 Iranians with wartime exposure to mustard agent. *Journal of Occupational and Environmental Medicine* 45(11): 1136–1143.

Koijima, S. 2001. *The Destruction of ACW in China*. Tokyo, Japan: Office for ACW, Cabinet Office.

Kurita, K. 2004. Trichloromethyl chloroformate. In *Encyclopedia of Reagents for Organic Synthesis*, ed. L. Paquette. New York: John Wiley and Sons.

Langford, R.E. 2004. *Introduction to Weapons of Mass Destruction: Radiological, Chemical, and Biological*. Hoboken, NJ: John Wiley and Sons.

Leppard, D., and R. Winnett. 2005. Police foil gas attack on Commons. *The Sunday Times*. http://www.timesonline.co.uk/tol/news/uk/article557472.ece (accessed October 23, 2010).

Levs, J., and H. Yan. 2013. 'War crime': U.N. finds sarin used in Syria chemical weapons attack. CNN.com. September 16, 2013. http://www.cnn.com/2013/09/16/politics/syria-civil-war/.

Lohs, K. 1963. *Synthetic Poisons*, 2nd ed. p. 51. East Berlin: Deutscher Militarverlag.

Mann, I., A. Pirie, and B.D. Pullinger. 1946. A study of Lewisite lesions of the eyes of rabbits. *American Journal of Ophthamology* 29: 1215–1227.

Meng, L.K. 2005. Chinese siege warfare. *The Pao*. August 30, 2005. http://www.grandhistorian.com/chinesesiegewarfare/siegeweapons-earlygrenades.html (accessed October 23, 2010).

National Institute for Occupational Safety and Health. 2009. The emergency response safety and health database: Mustard–lewisite mixture (HL). http://www.cdc.gov/niosh/ershdb/EmergencyResponseCard_29750007.html (accessed October 23, 2010).

National Research Council. 2001. *Disposal of Neutralent Wastes. Review and Evaluation of the Army Non-stockpile Chemical Materiel Disposal Program*. Washington, D.C.: National Academy Press.

NATO. 1996. Lung damaging agents (choking agents). Chapter 4. In *NATO Handbook of the Medical Aspects of NBC Defensive Operations AMedP-6(B)*.

Noltkamper, D., and G.F. O'Malley. 2008. CBRNE—Lung-damaging agents, chlorine. *emedicine*. http://emedicine.medscape.com/article/832336-overview (accessed October 23, 2010).

Norris, J., and W. Fowler. 1997. *NBC: Nuclear, Biological and Chemical Warfare on the Modern Battlefield*. London: Herndon Pub.

NTI Center for Nonproliferation Studies. 2007. Abandoned chemical weapons (ACW) in China. http://www.nti.org/db/china/acwpos.htm (accessed October 23, 2010).

Organisation for the Prohibition of Chemical Weapons. 2015. Convention on the prohibition of the development, production, stockpiling and use of chemical weapons and on their destruction. http://www.opcw.org/ (accessed July 28, 2015).

Organisation for the Prohibition of Chemical Weapons. n.d. Mustard agents. http://www.opcw.org/about-chemical-weapons/types-of-chemical-agent/mustard-agents/#c187 (accessed October 23, 2010).

Osius, T.G. 1957. The historic art of poisoning. *University of Michigan Medical Bulletin* 23(3): 111–116.

Parliamentary Office of Science and Technology. 2001. *Chemical Weapons. Postnote*. London. http://www.parliament.uk/documents/post/pn167.pdf (accessed October 23, 2010).

Partington, J.R. 1960. *A History of Greek Fire and Gunpowder*. New York: Barnes and Noble, Inc.

Plutarch. *The Life of Sertorius*. As cited in *The Parallel Lives by Plutarch* and published in Volume VIII of the Loeb Classical Library edition, 1919. Cambridge, MA: Harvard University Press.

Prentiss, A.M. 1937. *Chemicals in War: A Treatise on Chemical War*. New York: McGraw-Hill.

Robinson, J.P. 1971. The rise of CB weapons. Volume 1. In *The Problem of Chemical and Biological Warfare*. New York: Humanities Press.

Schneider, W., and W. Diller. 2002. Phosgene. In *Ullmann's Encyclopedia of Industrial Chemistry*. Weinheim: Wiley-VCH.

Sidell, F.R. 1997. Nerve agents. In *Medical Aspects of Chemical and Biological Warfare*, ed. F.R. Sidell, E.T. Takafuji, and D.R. Franz. Washington, D.C.: Borden Institute Walter Reed Army Medical Center.

Sidell, F.R., J.S. Urbanetti, W.J. Smith, and C.G. Hurst. 1997. Vessicants. In *Medical Aspects of Chemical and Biological Warfare*, ed. F.R. Sidell, E.T. Takafuji, and D.R. Franz. Washington, D.C.: Borden Institute Walter Reed Army Medical Center.

Smart, J.K. 1997. History of chemical and biological warfare: An American perspective. In *Medical Aspects of Chemical and Biological Warfare*, ed. F.R. Sidell, E.T. Takafuji, and D.R. Franz. Washington, D.C.: Borden Institute Walter Reed Army Medical Center.

Trammel, G.L. 1992. Toxicodynamics of organoarsenic chemical warfare agents. In *Chemical Warfare Agents*, ed. S.M. Somani, 255–270. San Diego, CA: Academic Press.

U.S. Army. 1967. *Chemical Reference Handbook*. FM 3–8. Washington, D.C. (January 1967).

U.S. Army, Marine Corps, Navy, Air Force. 2005. *Potential Military Chemical/Biological Agents and Compounds*. Fort Leonard Wood, MO: U.S. Army Chemical School.

U.S. Army Medical Research Institute of Chemical Defense. 1999. Vesicants. In *Medical Management of Chemical Casualties Handbook*. 3rd Edition. Aberdeen Proving Ground, MD: Chemical Casualty Care Division, USAMRICD.

U.S. Centers for Disease Control and Prevention. 2006a. Facts about VX. http://www.bt.cdc.gov /agent/vx/basics/facts.asp (accessed October 23, 2010).

U.S. Centers for Disease Control and Prevention. 2006b. Facts about sulfur mustard. http://www.bt .cdc.gov/agent/sulfurmustard/basics/facts.asp (accessed October 23, 2010).

U.S. Department of the Army. 1997. *Textbook of Military Medicine. Medical Aspects of Chemical and Biological Warfare*. https://www.hsdl.org/?view&did=1018. Office of the Surgeon General Department of the Army, Bethesda, MD.

U.S. Department of Defense. 1990. *Potential Military Chemical/Biological Agents and Compounds*. Headquarters, Departments of the Army, Navy, and Air Force. Field Manual 3–9, Air Force Regulation 355–7, NAVFAC P–467, Washington, D.C.

World Health Organization. 2004. *Public Health Response to Biological and Chemical Weapons*. Geneva: WHO guidance.

3

Toxic Industrial Chemicals

Lady Astor: "Winston, if you were my husband, I'd poison your tea."
Winston Churchill: "Lady Astor, if I were your husband, I'd drink it."

MylesPaul.com, 2016

INTRODUCTION

Discussion of so-called *chemical terrorism* often addresses highly toxic chemical warfare agents such as sarin or phosgene; however, there is the very real possibility that a terrorist may choose instead to use common toxic industrial chemicals (TICs) in an attack. Such chemicals are in routine use at thousands of facilities nationwide; additionally, many such sites are considered *soft* targets, that is, security is substantially less than would occur at a military base. TICs could, therefore, be comandeered from an industrial or commercial facility with less risk to the perpetrator. Chemical plants, pipelines, storage facilities, railroads, and trucks are all possible sources from which TICs could be acquired or intentionally released.

Some common TICs that pose significant threats to human health and the environment and are routinely transported on U.S. roads and railways are as follows:

- Alcohols
- Anhydrous ammonia
- Butane
- Carbon tetrachloride
- Caustic potash
- Chlorine
- Diesel fuel
- Flammable liquids (various)
- Hydrogen cyanide
- Phosgene
- Sulfuric acid
- Vinyl chloride

Sources of TICs include chemical manufacturing plants, research laboratories, food processing and storage facilities, and chemical transportation facilities. Some specific sources of TICs are as follows:

- Chemical manufacturing plants
- Food processing and storage facilities
- Facilities with large anhydrous ammonia tanks (e.g., agricultural chemical products storage and sale)
- Chemical transportation facilities
- Gasoline and jet fuel storage tanks
- Airports, and barge terminals with compressed gases in tanks, pipelines, and pumping stations
- Pesticide manufacturing and supply distributors
- Educational, medical, and research laboratories

In the United States, TICs are regulated primarily by laws and regulations administered by the U.S. Department of Transportation (DOT), the Environmental Protection Agency (EPA), the Occupational Safety and Health Administration (OSHA), and the Nuclear Regulatory Commission (NRC). These agencies also refer to TICs collectively as *hazardous materials*.

RECENT HISTORY OF TICs AS A WEAPON

Terrorist acts against chemical facilities can be classified into two categories: direct attacks on facilities, and efforts to use business contacts and facilities to gain access to hazardous chemicals (Schierow, 2006). In the case of a direct attack, conventional weapons (e.g., firearms) or WMDs may be used. In the latter category, a terrorist may attempt to gain access to a facility by physically entering and stealing supplies, or by using legitimate or fraudulent credentials (e.g., company stationary, order forms, computers, telephones) to order and receive chemicals.

Attempts by terrorists to use chemicals as weapons have increased over the past two decades. Loosely affiliated terrorist groups have demonstrated a growing interest in chemical weapons and other weapons of mass destruction; however, explosives continue to be the most frequently used of the WMDs.

In February 1999, an unidentified man, coughing and wheezing, entered an Atlanta commuter train. After passing three rows of passengers, he turned back and exited the same door as it was closing. During the 3-min ride to the next station, those passengers he passed experienced a burning sensation on their faces and in air passages, shortness of breath, and coughing and vomiting. Victims were met by police and hazmat responders and underwent decontamination. They were sent to a local hospital along with responders who were overcome by the unknown chemical. Before entering the hospital, victims were again decontaminated by emergency medical personnel. One victim remained under mechanical ventilation for 3 days; the others were examined and released. The substance in this attack remains unidentified. The filters removed from the commuter rail cars were examined and found to contain trace amounts of toluene, an industrial solvent. However, cleaning fluids used daily in the cars also contain this chemical.

Over the past two decades, terrorists have used explosives to release chemicals from manufacturing and storage facilities. Most attempts have occurred overseas in war zones such as Croatia, including attacks on a facility manufacturing fertilizer, carbon black, and light fraction petroleum products; other plants producing pesticides; and a pharmaceutical factory using ammonia, chlorine, and other hazardous chemicals (Schierow, 2006). All these facilities were located close to population centers. In the United States, two instances were recorded during the late 1990s when criminals attempted to cause releases of chemicals from facilities. One involved a large propane storage facility, the other a gas refinery (U.S. DOJ, 2000).

Terrorists have also gained access to U.S. chemical facilities in order to acquire toxic chemicals. For example, one of the 1993 World Trade Center bombers, Nidal Ayyad, became a naturalized U.S. citizen and worked as a chemical engineer at Allied Signal, from which he used company stationery to order chemical ingredients to construct his device. According to a prosecutor in the case against the bombers, "some suppliers balked when the order came from outside official channels, when the delivery address was a storage park, or when [a coconspirator] tried to pay for the chemicals in cash"; however, others did not (Parachini, 2000). Moreover, testimony at the trial revealed that Ayyad and his coconspirators had successfully stolen cyanide from a chemical facility and were training to introduce it into the ventilation systems of office buildings (Parachini, 2000). More recently, chemical trade publications were discovered in al-Qaeda hideouts (Bond, 2002).

Over the past decade in Iraq, chlorine, intended for water disinfection, has been used as a terrorist weapon against both military forces and civilians. For example, in 2007 Iraqi police and civilians near Ramadi were attacked by a suicide vehicle-borne improvised explosive device which included a chlorine tank. Along with the suicide bomber, 16 people were killed by the attack. In the same year, insurgents blew up a tanker filled with chlorine in southern Baghdad, killing at least two and wounding more than 30 (see Box 3.1) (*New York Times*, 2007). In 2014, at least 300 people were killed in a chlorine gas attack in the region of Saqlawiyah, north of Fallujah, according to a senior figure in the Iraqi government. Ali al-Badri, a member of Parliament in the Islamic Dawa party said at a press conference that "the terrorist organization ISIS (Islamic State in Iraq and Syria) used chlorine gas for

---

BOX 3.1   CHLORINE AS A WEAPON OF MASS DESTRUCTION

In Baghdad in 2007, a pickup truck carrying chlorine gas cylinders was detonated, killing at least five people and sending more than 55 to hospitals gasping for breath. Two days earlier, a bomb planted on a chlorine tanker left more than 150 villagers stricken north of Baghdad. Scores were placed under medical care (MSNBC.com, 2007).

Also in March 2007, bombers detonated three chlorine-filled trucks in Anbar province. According to military sources, the attacks killed two police officers and sickened about 350 Iraqis and six coalition force members. The bombs went off within 3 h in three different locations: a checkpoint north of Ramadi; Amiriya, about 10 miles south of Falluja; and the Albu Issa region just south of Falluja. About 250 Iraqis were sickened by chlorine in Albu Issa and 100 in Amiriya. The Amiriya bomber fled before the explosion; the other two were suicides (CNN.com, 2007).

the first time in the region of Saqlawiyah after trapping more than 400 troops, resulting in the deaths of many" (Mamoun, 2014).

Two years after President Bashar al-Assad agreed to dismantle Syria's chemical weapons stockpile (see Box 2.3), evidence has revealed that his government is repudiating international law by dropping improvised chlorine bombs on areas held by insurgents (Barnard and Senguptamay, 2015). Chlorine is being released by helicopters in so-called barrel bombs containing canisters that explode on impact, distributing clouds of gas over civilian populations. As of this writing, the Organisation for the Prohibition of Chemical Weapons states that it lacks authorization to say who (i.e., government or the insurgents) are using these weapons.

HAZARDOUS MATERIALS

DOT, OSHA, EPA, and NRC have each developed their own definition of a hazardous material (Table 3.1). Generally speaking, a hazardous material is any substance (biological, chemical, physical) that poses a hazard to humans, other biota, or the environment, either by itself or through interaction with other substances. Hazardous materials occur as explosives, flammable and combustible substances, corrosives, poisons, and radioactive materials. Releases occur via transportation accidents and because of fires, explosions, or other incidents in stationary facilities.

We will use the DOT system of hazardous material classification in this chapter. Table 3.2 identifies the 10 DOT hazard classes along with the DOT definition, examples of materials that fit those classes, and relevant reference in Volume 49 of the Code of Federal Regulations (CFRs).

Table 3.1 Definitions of a Hazardous Material According to Four U.S. Federal Regulatory Agencies

Agency	Definition
DOT	Any item that, when transported, is a risk to public safety or the environment, and is regulated as such under the Hazardous Materials Regulations (49 CFR 100-180) and other federal regulations (e.g., International Maritime Dangerous Goods Code; Dangerous Goods Regulations of the International Air Transport Association; Technical Instructions of the International Civil Aviation Organization; or the U.S. Air Force Joint Manual, Preparing Hazardous Materials for Military Air Shipments).
OSHA	Any substance or chemical that is a health or physical hazard, including carcinogens, toxic agents, irritants, corrosives, sensitizers; agents that damage the lungs, skin, eyes, or mucous membranes; chemicals that are combustible, explosive, flammable, oxidizers, pyrophorics, unstable-reactive or water-reactive; and chemicals that in the course of normal handling may generate dusts, vapors, or smoke that may have any of the previously mentioned characteristics. Full definitions of OSHA hazardous materials appear in Volume 29 CFR 1910.1200.
EPA	Incorporates the OSHA definition and includes any chemical that can cause harm to people, plants, or animals when released into the environment. Volume 40 CFR 355 lists over 350 hazardous substances.
NRC	Regulates chemicals that are *special nuclear source* or by-product materials or radioactive substances (10 CFR 20).

Table 3.2   DOT Hazard Classes

Class or Division No.	Name of Class or Division	49 CFR Reference
1.1 to 1.6	Explosives	§173.50
2.1 to 2.3	Compressed gases	§173.115
3	Flammable and combustible liquids (i.e., alcohols, solvents, lubricants, paints)	§173.120
4.1 to 4.3	Solids that are flammable, spontaneously combustible, or dangerous when wet (i.e., lithium alkyds, naphthalene, phosphorus, calcium hydride, sodium)	§173.124
5.1 and 5.2	Oxidizers and organic peroxides (i.e., bromates, chlorates, permanganates, hydrogen peroxide (>8%), benzoyl peroxide)	§173.127 and §173.128
6.1	Poisonous/toxic (i.e., some pesticides, barium compounds, phenol, chloroform, and some biotoxins)	§173.132
6.2	Infectious substances (i.e., cultures and stocks, patient specimens, biological products, regulated medical waste, and toxins derived from animal, plant, or bacteria that contains or might contain an infectious substance)	§173.134
7	Radioactive	§173.403
8	Corrosives (acids or bases that are corrosive to the skin and other materials having pH <2.0 or >12.5)	§173.136
9	Miscellaneous hazardous materials (i.e., asbestos, dry ice, PCBs)	§173.140
Forbidden	Forbidden materials	§173.21

DOT HAZARDOUS MATERIALS CLASSES

The U.S. DOT has established 10 classes for management of hazardous materials. Requirements exist for each class regarding packaging, labeling, storage, transportation, and so on, in order to minimize hazards to public health and the environment. Each of the 10 hazard classes will be introduced, paraphrasing the standard regulatory language, in the following sections.

Class 1—Explosives (49 CFR 173.50)

An explosive is defined as any substance that is designed to function by explosion, that is, an extremely rapid release of gas and heat. Explosives in Class 1 are further divided into six divisions.

- Division 1.1—Explosives that have a mass explosion hazard. A mass explosion is one that affects the entire load instantaneously. These materials tend to be extremely sensitive to shock, heat, friction, and so on.
- Division 1.2—Explosives that have a projection hazard (i.e., will cause extensive scattering of debris) but not a mass explosion hazard.

71

- Division 1.3—Explosives that have a fire hazard and either a minor blast hazard or minor projection hazard or both.
- Division 1.4—Explosives that present a minor explosion hazard. The explosive effects are largely confined to the package and no projection of fragments of appreciable size or range is expected.
- Division 1.5—Very insensitive explosives that have a mass explosion hazard but are so insensitive that there is little probability of initiation under normal conditions of transport.
- Division 1.6—Extremely insensitive articles that do not have a mass explosion hazard and that contain only extremely insensitive detonating substances and demonstrate a negligible probability of accidental initiation or propagation.

Explosives will be discussed in some detail in Chapter 6. Examples of explosives include the following:

- Ammonium nitrate–fuel oil mixture
- Black powder
- Dynamite
- Lead azide
- Nitrocellulose
- Nitroglycerin
- Picrate salts
- Cyclotrimethylene trinitramine (RDX)
- Trinitrotoluene

Class 2—Compressed Gases (49 CFR 173.115)

- Division 2.1—Flammable gas. A material that exists as a gas at 20°C or below and 101.3 kPa pressure (i.e., ambient temperature and pressure).
- Division 2.2—Nonflammable/nonpoisonous compressed gas. A material that exerts, within its packaging, an absolute pressure of 280 kPa (40.6 lb/in^2) or greater at 20°C and does not meet the definition of Division 2.1 or 2.3. This includes compressed gas, liquefied gas, pressurized cryogenic gas, compressed gas in solution, asphyxiant gas, and oxidizing gas.
- Division 2.3—Gas poisonous by inhalation. A material that is a gas at 20°C or below and 101.3 kPa pressure, and
  - Is known to be so toxic to humans as to pose a hazard during transportation
  - In the absence of data on human toxicity, is presumed to be toxic to humans because when tested on laboratory animals it has an LC_{50} value of ≤5000 ml/m^3

LC_{50} is defined as the concentration of a chemical that will cause death to 50% of a sample population of test organisms under specified conditions (Box 3.2). Some examples of compressed gases are provided in Table 3.3.

BOX 3.2 SELECTED TERMINOLOGY ASSOCIATED WITH CHEMICAL HAZARDS

LD_{50} (lethal dose 50%) is the dosage, administered by any route except inhalation, which is necessary to kill 50% of exposed animals in laboratory tests within a specified time. It is typically expressed in mg/kg body weight.

LC_{50} is the concentration of an inhaled substance, expressed in mg/cm^3 of air, which is necessary to kill 50% of test animals exposed within a specified time. This term is sometimes referred to as "LC_{50} INHALE."

Immediately dangerous to life and health (IDLH) is the atmospheric concentration that poses an immediate threat to life, causes irreversible or delayed adverse health effects, or interferes with a person's ability to escape from a dangerous atmosphere.

The *threshold limit value (TLV)* of a chemical substance is a level at which a worker can be exposed daily for a working lifetime without adverse health effects. The TLV, defined as a concentration in air, is an estimate based on the known toxicity to humans or animals of the substance and the reliability of the latest analytical methods. It is a recommendation by the American Conference of Governmental Industrial Hygienists.

The *permissible exposure limit (PEL)* is a legal limit, established by OSHA, for exposure of an employee to a chemical substance. The established limit is usually expressed in ppm or sometimes in milligrams per cubic meter (mg/m^3). A PEL is usually given as a time-weighted average (i.e., the amount that can be inhaled over an 8-h workday). Unlike TLV, PEL is an enforceable limit.

Table 3.3 Selected Compressed Gases Regulated as DOT Class 2

Division 2.1 Flammable	Division 2.2	Division 2.3 Poisonous
Aerosols	Aerosols	Ammonia, anhydrous
LPG (propane)	Carbon dioxide	Hydrogen sulfide
Acetylene	Most refrigerant gases (R124, R133, etc.)	Carbon monoxide
Butane	CO_2 fire extinguishers	Compressed coal gas
Some refrigerant gases (R152a, R1132a, etc.)	Helium	Cyanogen
Ethylene	Nitrogen	Chlorine
Hydrocarbon gases	Nitrous oxide	Phosgene
Hydrogen	Oxygen	Hydrogen sulfide
Methane	Xenon	

Class 3—Flammable and Combustible Liquids (49 CFR 173.120)

Flammable liquids are defined as follows:

- A liquid having a flash point of ≤60.5°C (141°F)
- Any material in a liquid phase with a flash point ≤37.8°C (100°F) that is intentionally heated and transported

A *combustible liquid* is one that does not meet the definition of any other hazard class and has a flash point of >60.5°C (141°F) and ≤93°C (200°F).

The concept of flash point will be discussed later in this chapter.

Examples of flammable/combustible liquids are shown in Table 3.4.

Class 4—Flammable Solids (49 CFR 173.124)

- Division 4.1—Flammable solids are defined as follows:
  - Wetted explosives that are Class 1 explosives when dry, which are sufficiently wetted to suppress explosive properties.
  - Self-reactive materials that are thermally unstable and can undergo strong exothermic decomposition even in the absence of oxygen. They also include readily combustible solids that can cause fire through friction, such as matches.

- Division 4.2—Spontaneously combustible materials include the following:
  - Pyrophoric materials—liquids or solids that can, without an external ignition source, ignite within 5 min after coming into contact with air.

Table 3.4 Examples of Combustible and Flammable Liquids, DOT Class 3

Flammable	Combustible
Acetone	Cyclohexanol
Alcohols (various)	Fuel oil nos. 1–6
Acetaldehyde	Kerosene
Benzene	Mineral oil
Carbon disulfide	Shale oil
Diesel fuel	
Methyl ethyl ketone (MEK)	
Gasoline	
Hexane	
Paint thinner	
Some light petroleum oils	
Some paints	
Toluene	
Xylene	

- Self-heating materials—substances that, when in contact with air and without an energy supply, are prone to self-heating. A material of this type that exhibits spontaneous ignition, or if the temperature exceeds 200°C (393°F) during a 24-h test period, is classified as Division 4.2.

- Division 4.3—Dangerous-when-wet materials are those that, when in contact with water, may become spontaneously flammable or give off flammable or toxic gas at a rate of >1 L/kg of material/h.

Some examples of Class 4 materials appear in Table 3.5.

Class 5—Oxidizers and Organic Peroxides (49 CFRs 173.127 and 173.128)

- Division 5.1—Oxidizers are materials that cause or enhance the combustion of other materials, generally by yielding oxygen.
- Division 5.2—Organic peroxides are any organic compounds containing oxygen in an O–O structure and which may be considered derivatives of hydrogen peroxide, where one or more of the hydrogen atoms have been replaced by organic radicals.

Examples of oxidizers and organic peroxides appear in Table 3.6.

Table 3.5 Examples of Flammable Solids, DOT Class 4

Flammable Solids	Spontaneously Combustible	Dangerous When Wet
Matches	Activated carbon	Alkaline earth metal alloys
Nitrocellulose membrane filters	Barium	Aluminum powder
Silicon powder	Phosphorus	Calcium hydride
Wetted explosives	Potassium sulfide, anhydrous	Calcium
Sulfur	Sodium sulfide, anhydrous	Calcium carbide
Titanium powder, wetted		Magnesium
Naphthalene		Lithium
		Sodium
		Sodium borohydride

Table 3.6 Common Oxidizers and Peroxides, DOT Class 5

Oxidizer	Organic Peroxide
Methyl ethyl ketone (MEK)	
Chlorates	Acetone peroxide
Chlorites	Benzoyl peroxide
Nitrates	Cumene hydroperoxide
Perchlorates	Methyl ethyl ketone peroxide
Persulfates	
Permanganates	
Sodium superoxide	
Pool chemicals (e.g., sodium hypochlorite)	

Class 6, Division 6.1—Poisonous/Toxic Materials (49 CFR 173.132)

Poisonous or toxic materials are substances (other than a gas) known to be so toxic to humans as to pose a health hazard during transportation, or which, in the absence of adequate human toxicity data, are presumed to be toxic to humans because of the following properties from testing on laboratory animals:

- Oral toxicity: a material with an LD_{50} of ≤300 mg/kg
- Dermal toxicity: a material with an LD_{50} of ≤1000 mg/kg
- Inhalation toxicity: a dust or mist with an LC_{50} for acute toxicity on inhalation of ≤4.0 mg/L

Toxins that are extracted from a living source such as plants, animals, or bacteria are termed *biotoxins* and could be considered toxic if the LD_{50} meets the criteria stated earlier. Examples of Division 6.1 poisonous/toxic materials are listed in Table 3.7.

Class 6, Division 6.2—Infectious Substances (49 CFR 173.134)

The following categories constitute Division 6.2 materials.

- *Infectious substances* (Division 6.2)—A material known or suspected to contain a pathogen. A pathogen is a microorganism (including bacteria, viruses, rickettsiae, parasites, fungi) or other agents, such as a proteinaceous infectious particle (prion), that can cause disease in humans or animals.
- *Category A*—An infectious substance in a form capable of causing permanent disability or life-threatening or fatal disease in otherwise healthy humans or animals.
- *Category B*—An infectious substance not in a form generally capable of causing permanent disability or life-threatening or fatal disease in otherwise healthy humans or animals.
- *Culture*—An infectious substance containing a pathogen that is intentionally propagated. The label *culture* does not include a human or animal patient specimen.

Table 3.7 Examples of Poisonous Materials, DOT Class 6

Chemical Toxins	Biological Toxins
Acrylamide	Aflatoxins
Aniline	Enterotoxins
Arsenic	Mycotoxins
Barium compounds	Shigatoxin
Chloroform	Phalloidin
Cresols	Tetrodotoxin
Cyanides	Ricin
Mercury compounds	T-2 toxin
Pesticides	Aflatoxins
Phenol	Enterotoxins
Sodium azide	Mycotoxins

Cultures may be categorized as Category A or B depending on the microorganism concerned.

- *Regulated medical waste*—Waste derived from the medical treatment of humans or animals or from biological research. Typically, regulated medical waste is classified as Category B.
- *Patient specimens*—Materials collected directly from humans or animals and transported for research, diagnosis, investigational activities, or disease treatment or prevention. Patient specimens include excreta, secreta, blood and its components, tissue and tissue swabs, body parts, and specimens in transport media (e.g., culture media and blood culture bottles).
- *Biological products*—Derivations of living organisms that are manufactured for use in the prevention, diagnosis, treatment, or cure of diseases in humans or animals and are certified by the United States Department of Agriculture, Food and Drug Administration, or other national authority. Examples of biological products include certain viruses, therapeutic serums, toxins, antitoxins, vaccines, blood, and blood products.

Class 7—Radioactive Materials

Radioactive material is defined as any material having a specific activity greater than 0.002 µCi/g. The *specific activity* of a radionuclide relates to the number of radioactive disintegrations per unit mass. One curie (Ci) of activity, for example, represents 37 billion atoms decaying every second (37 billion dps).

Class 8—Corrosive Materials (49 CFR 173.136)

Corrosive materials are liquids or solids that cause destruction of human skin at the site of contact within a specified length of time, or a liquid that has a severe corrosion rate on steel or aluminum based on criteria in §173.137(c)(2). A liquid is considered to have a severe corrosion rate if it corrodes steel or aluminum faster than 6.25 mm (0.246 in) per year at a temperature of 55°C (131°F). Corrosive materials may be acid or alkaline, organic, or inorganic. Table 3.8 provides some examples of corrosives.

Table 3.8 Examples of Corrosives, DOT Class 8

Acid	Base
Acetic acid	Soda lime
Sulfuric acid	Sodium hydroxide (lye)
Nitric acid	Ammonium hydroxide
Hydrochloric acid	Potassium hydroxide
Perchloric acid (<50%)	
Hydrofluoric acid	
Hypochlorite solutions	
Chromic acid	
Maleic anhydride	

Class 9—Miscellaneous Hazardous Materials (49 CFR 173.140)

Miscellaneous hazardous materials are those that present a hazard during transportation but do not meet the definitions of hazard classes 1–8. Class 9 materials have an anesthetic, noxious, or similar property that could cause extreme annoyance or discomfort to a flight crewmember so as to impair the correct performance of their duties. Examples of Class 9 materials include the following:

- Air bag inflators
- Asbestos
- Dry ice
- Polychlorinated biphenyls (PCBs)
- Polymeric beads
- Resource Conservation and Recovery Act (RCRA) hazardous wastes that do not meet the definition of Classes 1–8
- Wheelchairs/electric vehicles

SELECTED TICs AND RELEVANT PROPERTIES

This section provides some detailed information regarding a select group of TICs, all of which are in common use and are transported daily via highway, rail, air, and sea. Several of these materials have been misused, including as weapons of terrorism. Understanding the properties and behavior of these TICs is useful in appreciating the hazards involved with their use, and ultimately how to protect populations in the event of a release.

Anhydrous Ammonia

Ammonia (NH_3) exists at ambient temperatures as a colorless gas with a characteristic irritating odor. In the United States, the most common use of ammonia is by agriculture as a fertilizer, by virtue of its high nitrogen content. Anhydrous ammonia is also commonly used as a refrigerant in large refrigeration installations, and as an ingredient in explosives manufacture. The entire nitrogen content of all manufactured nitrogen-containing organic compounds is derived from ammonia (Appl, 2006). Anhydrous ammonia has been used for illicit purposes as well, for example, in the manufacture of methamphetamine (see Box 3.3).

The U.S. DOT classifies ammonia as a Class 2.2 hazardous material (nonflammable gas). Anhydrous ammonia is not listed as a Scheduled Chemical in the Chemical Weapons Convention (CWC). Some of its important physical properties are noted in Table 3.11.

Ammonia is produced directly from the heating of hydrogen and atmospheric nitrogen over a metallic catalyst. At elevated temperatures and pressures, these gases combine in the so-called Haber process

$$N_2(g) + 3H_2(g) \rightarrow 2NH_{3(g)} \tag{3.1}$$

Ammonia is liquefied by applying pressure to the confined gas. This relatively pure, water-free form is termed *anhydrous* ammonia (Greek, *without water*). Ammonia has a vapor

BOX 3.3   AMMONIA AND METHAMPHETAMINE PRODUCTION

Anhydrous ammonia is a key ingredient in the illegal production of methamphetamine (*meth*), a powerful central nervous system stimulant (Figure 3.1). The ammonia is often stolen from farms and agricultural chemical dealerships.

Thieves cause anhydrous ammonia releases when ammonia is transferred into makeshift containers, when nurse tank valves are left open, or when hoses or fittings are loosely attached to nurse tanks, causing leaks. In 2000, approximately 1000 lb of anhydrous ammonia were released when someone intentionally opened a valve during the night at a fertilizer dealer in Missouri. Three hundred residents had to be evacuated from their homes, and two people reported respiratory problems (US EPA, 2000). Several additives are being developed to limit anhydrous ammonia thefts and releases. For example, researchers are studying an additive that is mixed with ammonia, rendering it useless for meth production. Glotell™ (Royster Clark, Inc.; Norfolk, VA), a new, commercially available additive, is being used as a marking agent, leak detector, and theft deterrent (U.S. CDC, 2005).

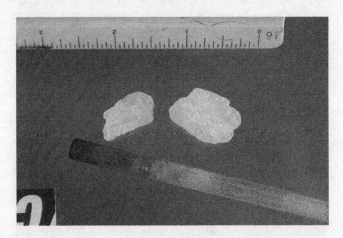

Figure 3.1   Methamphetamine crystals and pipe. (Courtesy of U.S. Drug Enforcement Administration, http://www.justice.gov/dea/photos/meth/ice_methamphetamine%20_pipe .jpg.)

density of 0.59 (Table 3.9); thus, it is lighter than air and readily disperses when released from its container.

Ammonia is shipped to some agricultural locations via pipeline and stored in pressurized tanks (Figure 3.2). For other commercial uses, anhydrous ammonia is transported in steel cylinders, insulated and uninsulated tank cars, barges, and tankers.

Farmers dispense anhydrous ammonia directly to soil or irrigation water. Typically, the ammonia is discharged to the soil from a nurse tank mounted behind the tillage tool through a distribution pod (Figures 3.3 and 3.4).

Table 3.9 Selected Physical Properties of Ammonia

Property	Value
Boiling point	−28°F (−33°C)
Freezing point	−108°F (−78°C)
Density	0.048 lb/ft³ (0.771 g/L)
Vapor density (air = 1)	0.596
Autoignition temperature	1204°F (651°C)
Lower explosive limit	16%
Upper explosive limit	25%
TLV	25 ppm
Solubility	Highly soluble

Source: Agency for Toxic Substances and Disease Registry, *Toxicological Profile for Ammonia*, U.S. Department of Health and Human Services, Public Health Service, Atlanta, GA, 2004; Occupational Safety and Health Administration, Properties of ammonia, 2004. http://www.osha.gov/SLTC/etools/ammonia_refrigeration/ammonia/index.html.

Figure 3.2 Anhydrous ammonia storage tank at an agricultural facility.

Effects of Ammonia on Humans

In the event of a release of ammonia, for example, during a transportation incident, extremely large quantities of ammonia gas may concentrate in the area of release. Ammonia is first visible as a fog caused by condensation of atmospheric moisture. This is a useful feature as it may permit detection of a release. In such situations, it is essential to minimize exposure.

Figure 3.3 Anhydrous ammonia tank used in agriculture.

Figure 3.4 Application of anhydrous ammonia to soil. (Courtesy of USDA-NRCS.)

Ammonia has a high affinity for water and will readily dissolve to form ammonium hydroxide, NH_4OH, a strong and corrosive base. It follows, then, that ammonia vapors will seek out locations on the body where moisture occurs. Exposure to low concentrations of anhydrous ammonia will irritate the eyes, nose, mucous membranes, and lung tissue. The ammonium hydroxide destroys living tissue within minutes. Effects range from mild irritation to tissue loss, depending on concentration and length of exposure. The eyes are a primary concern with regard to ammonia—eyes are continually being rinsed by a natural saline solution and will therefore attract anhydrous ammonia. Damage may include cataracts, glaucoma, and possibly permanent vision loss and disfigurement. When inhaled, ammonia also causes extreme irritation of the bronchial tissues; continued inhalation causes respiratory and pulmonary edema and disease. The respiratory system may essentially become paralyzed because of the pain. A concentration of more than 5000 ppm

81

Table 3.10 Ammonia Exposure Effects on the Human Body

Exposure (ppm)	Effect on the Body	Permissible Exposure
5–10	Odor detectable by human nose	n/a
50	No chronic effects from prolonged or repeated exposure	
134	Irritation of nose and throat	8 h maximum exposure
150–200	General discomfort; eye tearing; irritation and discomfort of exposed skin; irritation of mucous membranes	
700	Coughing, severe eye irritation, may lead to loss of sight	1 h maximum exposure
1700	Serious lung damage, death unless treated	No exposure permissible
2000	Skin blisters and burns within seconds; lung edema, asphyxia, death within minutes	No exposure permissible
	Barely tolerable for more than a few moments; serious blistering of the skin; lung edema, asphyxia, death within minutes following exposure	
5000	Suffocation within minutes	No exposure permissible

Source: Adapted from Nowatzki, J., Anhydrous ammonia: Managing the risks, AE-1149 (Revised), 2008. http://www.ag.ndsu.edu/pubs/ageng/safety/ae1149–1.htm; Fertilizer Institute, Health effects of ammonia, n.d. http://www.tfi.org/publications/HealthAmmoniaFINAL.pdf; Agency for Toxic Substances and Disease Registry, *Toxicological Profile for Ammonia*, U.S. Department of Health and Human Services, Public Health Service, Atlanta, GA, 2004.

will disable a person so that escape is impossible. Elevated blood ammonia concentrations can cause death by suffocation (Meyer, 2004).

The armpits and groin also accumulate substantial moisture and become highly irritated; however, owing to natural perspiration, moisture can be present on any part of the body. Table 3.10 provides symptoms and effects of ammonia explosive.

As water is capable of absorbing large volumes of ammonia, water should be applied directly to skin in cases of dermal exposure to remove any ammonia that has dissolved in surface body fluids.

Flammability Hazards

Anhydrous ammonia is not considered to be a flammability hazard. Its temperature of ignition is 1204°F, which makes it difficult to ignite. The *flammable range* of ammonia is relatively narrow, from 16% to 25% by volume, thus further reducing the likelihood of ammonia fires.

Although listed as a nonflammable gas by DOT, ammonia will burn when confined. In the presence of oxygen, ammonia burns with a yellow flame to form nitrogen and water:

$$4NH_3(g) + 3O_2(g) \rightarrow 2N_2(g) + 6H_2O(g) \tag{3.2}$$

Flammability ranges are discussed later in this chapter.

Occupational Safety and Emergency Response

OSHA has established a 15-min exposure limit for gaseous ammonia of 35 ppm by volume in air and an 8-h exposure limit of 25 ppm (ATSDR, 2004).

Response to ammonia releases will likely occur where it is used commercially, or during transportation accidents (see Box 3.4). The greatest commercial consumption of ammonia is associated with fertilizer manufacture and its application to fields as a fertilizer. However, ammonia releases have also occurred at refrigeration facilities.

Several challenges confront professionals responding to anhydrous ammonia emergencies, including skin and respiratory damage, fires, and thermal effects. Ammonia is colorless; as a result, there may be no visual indication of the location of the gas. Remote detectors, for example, colorimetric Draeger® tubes, may be used (Figure 3.5). Other

---

BOX 3.4   INCIDENTS INVOLVING AMMONIA

In Shreveport, Louisiana, one firefighter was killed and one badly burned in a 1984 fire involving anhydrous ammonia. Ammonia was leaking inside a cold-storage building. The firefighters donned Level A chemical protective clothing and went inside to stop the leak. However, the ammonia reached an ignition source and ignited.

On June 21, 2009, an ammonia leak at a poultry processing plant near Lumber Bridge, North Carolina, killed one worker and injured four others. The leak occurred while workers were conducting maintenance work on machinery at the plant.

On January 18, 2002, a Canadian Pacific freight train derailed outside Minot, North Dakota. Five cars were carrying anhydrous ammonia. Leaking ammonia killed one person and sent dozens to area hospitals. Some local residents were evacuated, whereas others were instructed to shelter in place (Witte, 2002).

In Verdigris, Oklahoma, a tank car was being filled with anhydrous ammonia while a weakened point on the car ruptured, resulting in a boiling liquid expanding vapor explosion (BLEVE). Although no fire occurred, a vapor cloud traveled downwind, defoliating trees and turning other vegetation brown. A worker filling the tank car was killed.

In Delaware County, Pennsylvania, ammonia was being removed from an abandoned cold-storage facility when a leak occurred. Firefighters were exposed to ammonia and experienced irritation and burning of the face and other exposed skin surfaces. Several were transported to local hospitals for treatment after undergoing decontamination at the scene.

In Ortanna, Pennsylvania, two workers were killed while conducting routine maintenance on liquid ammonia lines in a cold storage building used for fruit storage. Both men were splashed with liquid ammonia after a leak occurred. Several firefighters were injured by the vapors while trying to rescue the workers.

A meat packing plant explosion in Booneville, Arkansas, triggered an ammonia leak forcing 180 people from their homes. Firefighters were unable to fight the blaze because of the dangers posed by the ammonia gas and decided to let it burn out. The fire involved 88,000 lb of anhydrous ammonia, which was used in refrigeration systems (*Dallas Morning News*, 2008).

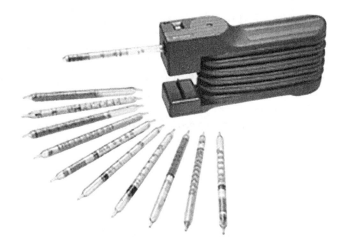

Figure 3.5 Draeger® devices can be equipped with tubes specifically designed for the detection of ammonia as well as for many other chemicals. (Courtesy of Draeger.)

indicators may include rapid browning of local vegetation. If vegetation appears brown during spring or summer months, this may indicate ammonia release. Extensive insect and/or animal kills may also indicate a significant ammonia release (Figure 3.6).

To provide adequate respiratory protection from ammonia, a self-contained breathing apparatus (SCBA) is essential. A respirator equipped with anhydrous ammonia cartridges approved by the National Institute for Occupational Safety and Health is designed only for exposures that do not exceed 300 ppm. Such filters are not capable of protecting a responder from high-level exposures. Since ammonia has a very high affinity for water, including moisture on the skin, it is crucial that no skin be exposed during a response. Responders

Figure 3.6 Ammonia vapor cloud from a pipeline rupture. (Courtesy of NTSB.gov.)

to incidents involving anhydrous ammonia require Level A personal protective equipment (PPE). Respirators and PPE will be discussed in Chapter 10.

Responders can take advantage of the affinity of ammonia to water and use water sprays or mists to remove ammonia vapors from the air and also to decontaminate exposed victims. After decontamination is complete, runoff from the affected site must be captured and treated. Recall that anhydrous ammonia reacts with water to form ammonium hydroxide, a strong base. A simple dilute acid such as acetic acid (vinegar) will neutralize the ammonium hydroxide.

Anhydrous ammonia is stored under pressure and is a very cold liquid. When released from its container its temperature is –28°F (–33.3°C); therefore, it can quickly cause serious thermal burns. No protective clothing is available to protect responders from the severe cold of liquid ammonia.

Regulations

The DOT regulates the transportation of anhydrous liquefied ammonia as a poisonous gas. Its containers are labeled POISON GAS, and transport vehicles are placarded POISON GAS.

Chlorine

Chlorine (Cl) is a chemically reactive halogen appearing in Group VII in the Periodic Table of the Elements. As a consequence of its reactivity, chlorine does not occur in nature in the free state as Cl_2 gas; it occurs instead as chloride ion (Cl^-) in combination with metals such as sodium, potassium, and magnesium. Chlorine shares certain properties with fluorine, bromine, and iodine.

Chlorine gas is greenish-yellow, noncombustible, and highly corrosive at room temperature. It is easily recognized by its pungent, irritating odor, essentially that of household bleach. This obvious odor can provide some warning of exposure. Chlorine is almost three times heavier than air (Table 3.11) and highly poisonous. Due to its density of its density and tendency to settle, chlorine gas is hazardous in low-lying areas and confined spaces. Its IDLH value is 10 ppm (see Box 3.2). Chlorine is not listed as a Scheduled Chemical in the CWC.

Chlorine is one of the most commonly manufactured chemicals in the United States. It is best recognized by consumers as a household cleaning agent and as a disinfectant in the treatment of drinking water and swimming pools. By virtue of its versatile chemical

Table 3.11 Selected Physical Properties of Chlorine

Property	Value
Boiling point	–34.4°C (–29.9°F)
Freezing point	–101.5°C (–150.7°F)
Density	3.2 g/L (0°C, 100 kPa)
Vapor density (air = 1)	2.5
TLV	0.5 ppm

reactivity, however, chlorine has many industrial and commercial uses. It is required in the manufacture of chlorinated solvents and in numerous other synthesis reactions. Chlorine-containing compounds are used in industry as pesticides and dyes; others are used to produce plastics, synthetic rubber, refrigerants, fire extinguishers, automotive antifreeze and antiknock compounds, and other commercially important substances. Chlorine is highly valued in the paper and pulp and textile industries for bleaching cellulose. Chlorine also has extensive application is the manufacture of flame-proofing materials, lubricants, adhesives, and in hydraulic fluids.

Chlorine is manufactured by passing an electric current through either molten sodium chloride or aqueous solutions of sodium chloride. The gas is pressurized and stored for commercial use in 100-lb and 150-lb (45.4 and 68 kg) and 1-ton (908 kg) steel cylinders under a pressure of 84 lb/in^2 at 70°F (21°C). Chlorine may be transported by truck or in rail tank cars.

Safety Issues

Chlorine is very reactive in a chemical sense; however, toxicity is considered its principal hazard. In the workplace, OSHA mandates only 1 ppm as the maximum PEL (see Box 3.2) for chlorine. Common routes of chlorine exposure include inhalation, absorption through the skin, absorption through the eyes, and ingestion. Inhalation is the most common means of chlorine entry into the body. Signs and symptoms of chlorine inhalation include (OSHA, n.d. [a]):

- Rapid, labored breathing
- Bluish skin color
- Wheezing and congestion
- Strong cough
- Nausea and dizziness
- Burning, irritated throat
- Swelling or narrowing of the airways
- Possible lung collapse

Even minor exposures to chlorine can cause immediate burning of the eyes, nose, throat, and skin. Continued exposure can lead to tolerance to these irritant effects and victims may no longer be aware of the presence of chlorine. Chlorine is attracted to the moisture of the eyes and is therefore absorbed through the eyes, resulting in burning and discomfort, excessive tearing, irregular blinking, involuntary closing of the eyelids, and redness. Higher concentrations may cause severe eye burns, pain, and blurred vision. Inhalation may cause inflammation of the nose and throat and congestion of lung tissue; prolonged inhalation may be fatal. As chlorine is heavier than air, it displaces ambient air as it migrates. This effect can lead to suffocation in poorly ventilated, enclosed, or low-lying areas. If ingested, chlorine will cause injury to tissue of the gastrointestinal tract.

Chlorine has a strong affinity for water and is therefore readily absorbed through the skin. Burns ranging from mild to severe will result, depending on chlorine concentration and length of contact. The victim may experience pain, inflammation, and blisters. Symptoms of exposure to liquid chlorine are similar to those of frostbite (U.S. CDC, 2006). Individuals exposed to chlorine should be removed from the area, and a physician should be contacted immediately. Chlorine is a nonflammable gas, but it does support combustion. In an atmosphere of chlorine, several metals and nonmetals burn with incandescence (Meyer, 2004):

$$Cu(s) + Cl_2(g) \rightarrow CuCl_2(s) \tag{3.3}$$

$$2Sb(s) + 3Cl_2(g) \rightarrow 2SbCl_{3(s)} \tag{3.4}$$

Chlorine also supports the combustion of many organic compounds (Box 3.5).

Regulatory Requirements

DOT classifies chlorine as a Class 2.3 hazardous material. Steel cylinders and other containers of chlorine are labeled POISON GAS; likewise, vehicles used to transport any quantity of chlorine are placarded POISON GAS (Figure 3.7).

Rail tank cars and tank trucks that transport chlorine are lined with 4 in of insulation. Thus, if fire impinges on these vessels, the heat does not immediately threaten to rupture the container. This provides time for firefighters to cool the tanks with water to prevent a BLEVE-type incident. BLEVEs are discussed later in this chapter.

Liquid chlorine is significantly more concentrated than the gas. When released, the liquid readily evaporates, producing a massive volume of gas. When chlorine-filled cylinders or rail tank cars are involved in transportation accidents, it is important for responders to locate points from which the chlorine is escaping. Liquid chlorine may leak from valves, fittings, or other openings. Even when leaks cannot be stopped, attempts must be made to prevent liquid

---

BOX 3.5   INCIDENTS INVOLVING CHLORINE

On January 10, 2005, nine men died after a 42-car Norfolk Southern freight train slammed into a parked train in Graniteville, South Carolina. Fourteen cars on the moving train derailed, including three chlorine tank cars, one of which leaked a cloud of the green gas. Eight of the deaths resulted from inhalation of chlorine gas from the leaking tank car. At least 234 people went to area hospitals, most with respiratory injury from inhaling chlorine. Authorities ordered all 5400 people within 1 mi of the incident to evacuate because the leaking chlorine formed a choking, toxic plume.

On June 28, 2004 at 5:03 A.M., in Macdona, Texas, a Union Pacific train collided with a Burlington Northern train resulting in a derailment of 35 railcars. A 90-ton chlorine railcar was breached releasing 60 tons (120,000 lb) of chlorine. Two residents in a house nearby died from chlorine inhalation, and about 40 were hospitalized.

On April 11, 1996, two railcars released chlorine gas west of the town of Alberton, Montana, after a derailment. One person died and at least 350 people were injured from chlorine inhalation, some permanently. Victims included residents of Alberton plus others who drove through the toxic cloud while traveling on Interstate 90. The Interstate was closed for 19 days forcing traffic to take a 200-mi detour. Trees in the area were killed or severely damaged by the chlorine cloud.

Figure 3.7 (See color insert.) Chlorine rail tanker. (Courtesy of ATSDR Report on Chemical Terrorism, http://www.mapcruzin.com/scruztri/docs/cep1118992.htm.)

chlorine from further escaping. This may be achieved by rolling the container so that the opening is located upward, thus keeping the liquid chlorine confined (Meyer, 2004).

White Phosphorus

Elemental phosphorus has several *allotropic* forms, two of which are commercially important—white phosphorus (WP) and red phosphorus. We will discuss WP because of its unique chemical properties and its importance as a weapon.

WP is a colorless to yellow translucent waxlike substance with a pungent, garlic-like odor. Its density is about twice that of water and it has the chemical formula P_4. WP is a *pyrophoric* material—that is, it is spontaneously flammable. When exposed to air, WP ignites immediately and is oxidized to tetraphosphorus hexoxide or tetraphosphorus decoxide (Meyer, 2004):

$$P_{4(s)} + 3O_{2(g)} \rightarrow P_4O_{6(s)} \tag{3.5}$$

$$P_{4(s)} + 5O_{2(g)} \rightarrow P_4O_{10(s)} \tag{3.6}$$

Such intense heat is produced by these reactions that the phosphorus bursts into a yellow flame and generates dense white, choking smoke. Burning phosphorus is highly luminous; this property is valued in tracer bullets used at night by the military. Phosphorus pentoxide (Equation 3.6) is extremely *hygroscopic* and quickly absorbs even minute traces of moisture to form liquid droplets of phosphoric acid:

$$P_4O_{10} + 6H_2O \rightarrow 4H_3PO_4 \tag{3.7}$$

The phosphoric acid also forms polyphosphoric acids such as pyrophosphoric acid, $H_4P_2O_7$.

Safety Issues

WP is volatile at ambient conditions and is highly poisonous. It can cause injuries and death by burning deep into tissue, by being inhaled as a smoke, and by ingestion. Extensive exposure by any of these routes is fatal. The lethal dose is only about 0.1 g for the average adult (Lisandro et al., 2009). The PEL for WP is 0.1 mg/m^3. Repeated inhalation causes a malady known as phossy jaw (phosphorus necrosis), that is, the rotting or disintegration of the jawbone (Marx, 2008).

Burns produced from phosphorus are extremely painful and slow to heal (Meyer, 2004). Burning particles of WP can produce extensive, deep second- and third-degree burns. WP continues to burn unless deprived of oxygen or until it is completely consumed. Phosphorus burns carry a greater risk of death than other types of burns because of the absorption of phosphorus into the body through the burned area, resulting in liver, heart, and kidney damage, and in some cases multiple organ failure (ATSDR, 2008).

To extinguish phosphorus fires, commercial fire extinguishers may be used, but wet sand works most effectively. Precautions should be taken by emergency responders to prevent exposure to the oxides of phosphorus as they irritate the eyes, throat, and lungs.

Regulatory Requirements

Under DOT regulations, containers of WP are labeled SPONTANEOUSLY COMBUSTIBLE and POISON. WP is transported in bulk by rail tank cars or tank trucks as either a solid or liquid. To prevent contact with atmospheric oxygen, solid WP is stored under water; as a liquid, it is maintained under a blanket of an inert gas such as nitrogen (N_2). Motor vehicles, rail tank cars, and freight containers carrying bulk quantities of WP are placarded SPONTANEOUSLY COMBUSTIBLE.

Use as a Weapon

WP, also known as Willy Pete, is used in the military for signaling, screening, and incendiary purposes. WP can be used to obscure the enemy's vision via smoke formation. Used at night, WP aids in target location and navigation. WP is usually dispersed by an explosive charge (Figure 3.8).

The CWC does not designate WP as a chemical weapon; furthermore, WP is legal for purposes such as illumination and production of obscuring smoke. WP experienced heavy use during World War II in military formulations for smokescreens, marker shells, incendiaries, hand grenades, smoke markers, colored flares, and tracer bullets (Globalsecurity .org, 2009). WP weapons have been controversial because of their recent use against civilian populations. WP munitions had been used extensively in Korea and Vietnam. It was also heavily used by Russian forces in Chechnya. WP was used by the Argentine Army during the 1989 attack on La Tablada Regiment, in a violation of the Geneva Convention according to the Human Rights Commission of the United Nations (UN, 1998).

In Iraq, Saddam Hussein ordered the use of WP, as well as chemical weapons listed in the CWC, in the Halabja attack during the Iran–Iraq War in 1988 (Ranucci, n.d.). During the 2006 Israel–Lebanon conflict, Israel stated that it had used phosphorus shells "against military

Figure 3.8 (See color insert.) Ignition of white phosphorus. (Courtesy of Wikipedia, https://en.wikipedia.org/wiki/White_phosphorus_munitions; USAF—National Museum of the U.S. Air Force photo 110310-F-XN622-009, Public Domain, https://commons.wikimedia.org/w/index.php ?curid=14856340.)

targets in open ground" in south Lebanon. Israel declared that its use of WP bombs was permitted under international conventions (BBC, 2006); however, Lebanese President Emile Lahoud claimed that phosphorus shells were used against civilians in his country (Haaretz .com, 2006). In 2014, Israeli aerial and ground forces were alleged to have used white phosphorus bombs to pound several residential areas across the besieged Gaza Strip (PressTV, 2014).

FLAMMABLE LIQUIDS

According to DOT regulations (49 CFR 173.120(a)), a *flammable liquid* (Class 3) is defined as a liquid having a flashpoint of ≤141°F (60.5°C), or any material in a liquid phase with a flashpoint >100°F (37.8°C) that is intentionally heated and transported above its flashpoint.

A *combustible liquid* is one that does not meet the definition of any other hazard class specified in the DOT regulations and has a flashpoint above 141°F and below 200°F. The National Fire Protection Association (NFPA) has formulated a separate classification system for flammable and combustible liquids in fixed storage.

Flammability and Explosion Considerations

All Class 3 materials will burn under certain conditions; therefore, appropriate precautions must be taken in their handling and transport. The most important precaution is to control ignition sources. According to DOT, flammable liquids are involved in more than 50% of all hazardous materials incidents. This finding may be obvious because flammable liquids are used as motor fuels for highway vehicles, railroad locomotives, marine vessels, and aircraft. In addition, many flammable liquids are used to heat homes. To effectively handle flammable liquids at an incident, emergency responders must understand certain key physical characteristics of flammable liquids.

Explosive Limits

The *flammability range* (also known as the *explosive range*) is that range of vapor concentrations that will support combustion in the presence of an energy source such as a flame (Figure 3.9). The *lower explosive limit* (LEL) is defined as the lowest percent by volume of a mixture of explosive gases in air that will propagate a flame at 25°C and atmospheric pressure.

The *upper explosive limit* (UEL) is the maximum concentration of a gas above which the substance will not explode when exposed to a source of ignition. For example, gasoline vapors are explosive when present in the range of 1.4%–7.6% by volume in air. At concentrations greater than 7.6% (the UEL), gasoline vapor will not ignite as the air–vapor mixture is considered *rich*. Below the LEL, sufficient air is available but there is too little vapor, so the mixture is too *lean* to burn. It must be noted that at gasoline concentrations above the UEL, ignition and fire may still be possible, and asphyxiation will also occur. In addition, a sudden dilution of the gasoline vapors within the local atmosphere can bring the mixture back within the explosive range.

A number of hydrocarbon-based substances possess very wide flammable ranges. This fact makes them highly dangerous to emergency responders. Acetylene has a very wide range (2% to more than 80%). Alcohols, ethers, and aldehydes also have wide flammable ranges and should be managed with extreme caution. The explosive ranges of several compounds are provided in Table 3.12.

Flashpoint

During a fire involving any liquid, it is the vapor directly above it that actually burns, not the liquid. Flashpoint is defined as the lowest temperature at which a flame will propagate

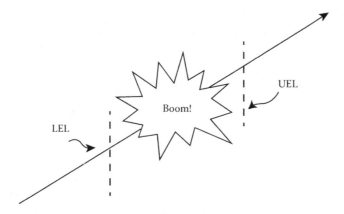

Figure 3.9 The explosive range.

Table 3.12 Flammability Ranges for Selected Hydrocarbon-Based Substances

Substance	LEL (%)	UEL (%)
Acetone	3.0	13.0
Acetylene	2.5	82.0
Benzene	1.2	78.0
Butane	1.8	8.4
Diesel fuel	0.6	7.5
Ethanol	3.0	19.0
Ethylbenzene	1.0	7.1
Ethylene	2.7	36
Gasoline	1.4	7.6
Hexane	1.1	7.5
Hydrogen	4.0	75
Kerosene	0.6	4.9
Methane	4.4	17
Octane	1.0	7.0
Propane	2.1	9.5
Toluene	1.2	7.1
Xylene	1.0	7.0

Source: Agency for Toxic Substances and Disease Registry, Chlorine, Toxic Substances Portal, Atlanta, GA, U.S. Department of Health and Human Services, Public Health Service, 2010. http://www.atsdr.cdc.gov/substances /toxsubstance.asp?toxid=36; Occupational Safety and Health Administration, Hydrogen cyanide, n.d. [b]. http://www.osha.gov/SLTC/health guidelines/hydrogencyanide/recognition.html.

through the vapor of a combustible material. In other words, flashpoint is the minimum temperature at which a liquid produces a sufficient concentration of vapor that forms an ignitable mixture with air. Since it is the vapor that burns, the amount of vapor present is critical in determining whether the liquid will burn.

Even if the ambient temperature is not at the flashpoint of a liquid, the liquid may have been heated, for example, by the radiant heat of the sun; if an ignition source is present, ignition can occur.

Flashpoint should not be confused with fire point. *Fire point* is the temperature at which the vapors will continue to burn after the vapor flash occurs. The fire point temperature is 1° to 3° above the flashpoint (Burke, 2002).

Autoignition Temperature

Ignition temperature (also known as autoignition temperature) is defined as the minimum temperature to which a material must be heated to cause ignition without applying any other energy source. In other words, a material will autoignite simply by being heated to its ignition temperature. For example, kitchen fires have occurred because cooking oils

Table 3.13 Ignition Temperatures of Common Combustibles

Material	Ignition Temperature (°F)
Wood	392
#1 Fuel oil	444
Paper	446
60 Octane gas	536
Acetylene gas	571
Wheat flour	748
Corn	752
Propane gas	871

or grease were overheated and their autoignition temperatures were attained. Corn oil, commonly used for cooking, has an ignition temperature of 460°F; therefore, if corn oil is heated to 460°F or above, it will autoignite. Table 3.13 provides the autoignition temperatures of common combustible materials.

Vapor Pressure

Vapor pressure (also known as volatility) is the tendency of a molecule to leave the surface of a liquid and occur as a vapor. This property is approximately the inverse of molecular weight. Some refined petroleum products, especially gasoline, are relatively low in molecular weight and vaporize readily. Incidentally, such compounds also have relatively low flashpoints. At the other end of the spectrum are heavy, viscous products such as lubricating oils and fuel oils that vaporize minimally.

Vapor Density

Vapor density is defined as the weight of the vapor of a substance compared with the weight of air. Air is assigned a weight of 1.0. If the vapor of a compound has a density greater than 1.0, it is considered to be heavier than air so the vapor will remain close to the ground and collect in low-lying areas. This property is important for emergency responders as they may become asphyxiated working in a trench or confined space. In addition, because many ignition sources, for example, furnaces, are placed on lower floors, an explosive hazard may exist. If the vapor density is less than 1.0, the vapor is considered to be lighter than air and will rise and may travel away from a release.

Solubility

Most flammable substances are petroleum hydrocarbons and are, with few exceptions, insoluble in water. Solubility in most cases is inversely proportional to molecular weight; lighter hydrocarbons are more soluble in water compared with higher molecular weight compounds. Lighter hydrocarbons, that is, butane and hexane and also many aromatics (benzene and xylene), are relatively soluble. Gasoline is the only petroleum product in common use that contains constituents that are sufficiently soluble in water to cause health problems. Aromatic compounds such as benzene and alkyl benzenes are the primary concern.

BLEVEs

A *BLEVE* is a type of explosion that can occur when a container storing a pressurized liquid is heated, causing it to burst.

If the container is ruptured, for example, due to a puncture, the vapor portion may rapidly leak, lowering the pressure inside the container. This sudden drop in pressure inside the container causes violent boiling of the liquid, which rapidly generates large amounts of vapor. The pressure of this vapor can be extremely high and create a strong wave of overpressure (i.e., an explosion) that may completely destroy the container (Figures 3.10 and 3.11).

A BLEVE can occur with a nonflammable substance. However, if a flammable substance is involved, the resulting cloud may ignite after the BLEVE has occurred, forming a fireball and possibly a fuel-air explosion, also termed a vapor cloud explosion.

Health Effects and Routes of Exposure

Health hazards associated with flammable and combustible liquids vary depending on the individual chemical. Hazards may include the following:

- *Inhalation* of flammable liquids can damage mucous membranes, irritate respiratory passages, and cause nausea, headaches, muscle weakness, drowsiness, loss of coordination, disorientation, confusion, unconsciousness, and ultimately death.
- *Eye contact* with flammable liquids can cause burning, irritation, and eye damage.
- *Skin contact* with flammable liquids can remove the oils from the skin resulting in irritated, dry skin, rashes, and dermatitis.

Chronic Exposure

Long-term (i.e., chronic) exposure hazards associated with flammable and combustible substances may include damage to the lungs, heart, liver, kidneys, and central nervous system. For several chemicals, cancer and adverse reproductive effects may result from long-term exposure.

Proper protective clothing is essential when working around flammable materials. Proper respiratory equipment, whether a cartridge air-purifying respirator or an SCBA, may be needed for long-term work. Skin protection must be considered in the PPE ensemble as well.

Figure 3.10 Schematic showing the sequence of steps in a BLEVE. (From International Fire Service Training Association (IFSTA), *Hazardous Materials for First Responders*, 1st edition, Fire Protection Publications, Oklahoma State University, Stillwater, OK, 1988. Reprinted with permission.)

Figure 3.11 BLEVE occurring during a highway accident involving a fuel truck. (Courtesy of the City of Pensacola, http://www.ci.pensacola.fl.us/upload/images/Fire/GAS%20bleve.JPG.)

CORROSIVE MATERIALS

Corrosive materials are solids and liquids classified by the DOT as Hazard Class 8. No subclasses of corrosives are included. Two types of corrosive materials occur in Class 8: acids and bases (alkalis). Although acids and bases are in some ways chemical opposites, they have the common property of causing corrosive effects on biological tissue and certain materials. The most accurate terminology for acids, however, is that they are corrosives, and bases are considered to be caustic. The DOT, however, does not differentiate between the two. The DOT definition of a corrosive (Code of Federal Regulations, 2015) is as follows:

> a liquid or solid that causes visible destruction or irreversible alterations in human skin tissue at the site of contact, or a liquid that has a severe corrosion rate on steel or aluminum. This corrosive rate on steel and aluminum is 0.246 inches per year at a test temperature of 131°F.

Two general categories of acids exist: organic and inorganic (Table 3.14). Inorganic acids, sometimes referred to as mineral acids, do not contain carbon; in contrast, organic

Table 3.14 Examples of Inorganic and Organic Acids

Inorganic	Organic
Hydrochloric, HCl	Acetic, CH_3COOH
Hydrofluoric, HF	Citric, $C_6H_8O_7$
Hydroiodic, HI	Formic, HCOOH
Nitric, HNO_3	Oxalic, $H_2C_2O_4$
Perchloric, $HClO_4$	
Sulfuric, H_2SO_4	

acids contain carbon. Although inorganic acids are corrosive, they do not burn. Inorganic acids may be oxidizers and support combustion.

Most acids are produced by dissolving a gas or a liquid in water. For example, hydrochloric acid is generated by dissolving hydrogen chloride gas in water. Most bases are produced by dissolving a solid, usually a salt, in water.

Measurement of Acidity or Alkalinity

The pH scale measures the degree of acidity or alkalinity of a solution (Figure 3.12). Solutions with a pH value of 7.0 are considered to be chemically neutral; that is, they are neither acidic nor basic. Acids have a pH value of less than 7.0 and bases have pH values from 7.1 to 14.

It is important to note that the intervals between the whole numbers on the pH scale are exponential, not arithmetic. For example, a solution with a pH of 6 is *10 times* more acidic than a solution at pH 7.0. A pH of 5 is 10 times more acidic than a pH of 6, and 100 times (10 × 10) more acidic than pH 7. A solution with a pH of 1 is 1,000,000 times more acidic than a solution having pH 7.0.

In the event of a hazmat incident, a responder may be able to check vehicle DOT or NFPA placards to determine whether a released substance is corrosive. More detailed information, such as the UN number appearing on a DOT placard, will allow the responder to look up the chemical name in a reference source such as the *North American Emergency Response Guide* to obtain more detailed information, for example, the required PPE and evacuation distances. However, in unknown situations (e.g., clandestine laboratories or terrorist incidents), conducting a simple pH measurement can provide a general clue as to whether an acid or base is present.

Several methods are available to determine the pH of a solution. The most reliable methods incorporate commercially available pH meters. Such instruments range in sophistication from handheld (e.g., for field use) laboratory-scale instruments. pH meters are highly accurate, providing immediate digital readouts. Such equipment must be calibrated regularly and can be expensive, however. The simplest and least expensive pH measurement method is via the use of pH paper (litmus paper). The pH paper changes color based on the pH value of the solution. Litmus paper turns blue if the suspect liquid is a base and turns red if the liquid is an acid. The paper, once color is formed, can be compared to a pH color chart provided by the manufacturer. The chart will provide approximate numerical pH values similar to that of the pH scale. Litmus paper is not as accurate as a pH meter; however, the emergency responder can at least obtain a rapid assessment of solution pH in the field.

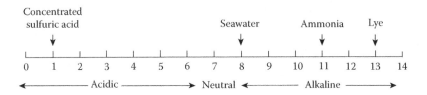

Figure 3.12 The pH scale.

Common Acids and Bases

Sulfuric Acid

Sulfuric acid, also known as *oil of vitriol*, is the most widely used industrial chemical in the United States. Sulfuric acid is used by iron and steel making industries for preparing sheet metal for sale; it is used in electroplating baths at metal plating facilities, in vehicle batteries, and in the manufacture of fertilizers, dyes, pigments, and explosives. Sulfuric acid is also used to manufacture other acids.

Sulfuric acid has a strong affinity for water. Even small amounts of water that come into contact with sulfuric acid can cause it to splatter and boil violently. Sulfuric acid also acts as an oxidizer. The vapors are toxic at 1 ppm in air. Fuming sulfuric acid ($H_2S_2O_7$) is a solution of sulfur trioxide in sulfuric acid. It is violently water-reactive. The fuming form is far more hazardous than standard sulfuric acid; violent explosions have resulted when it has come into contact with water. Fuming sulfuric acid is such a strong dehydrating and oxidizing agent that it can ignite combustible materials.

Risks to emergency response personnel include severe chemical burns if sulfuric acid contacts tissue, and burns to mucous membranes if the vapor is inhaled. There have been reports of severe erosion of tooth enamel from inhalation of sulfuric acid vapor.

Hydrochloric Acid

Hydrochloric acid (HCl) is corrosive, toxic, and extremely irritating when the vapors are inhaled. Technical-grade hydrochloric acid is called *muriatic acid*. It is water-soluble and is used in food processing, steel pickling and metal cleaning processes, and as an alcohol denaturant.

HCl is a strong corrosive and is toxic by ingestion and inhalation. In the event of an HCl release, hydrogen chloride vapor is released into the air. The PEL of hydrogen chloride is 5 ppm, and the IDLH value is 100 ppm.

Sodium Hydroxide

Sodium hydroxide (NaOH) is a strong base with a pH of approximately 13.0. Sodium hydroxide is the most important industrial caustic material; it is used in the manufacture of pulp and paper, textiles, soaps, and detergents, and as a drain cleaner. NaOH is also important in electroplating and as a neutralizer in petroleum refining. Sodium hydroxide is sold as white solid pellets, granules, or flakes. It is water-soluble and readily absorbs water and carbon dioxide from the air.

Other Hazards of Corrosive Materials

In addition to being corrosive, many Class 8 materials impart other hazards. Compounds in this class may be poisons, oxidizers, or flammables. Many acids and alkalis are violently water-reactive; contact with water may cause splattering, generation of toxic vapors, and generation of heat that may ignite nearby combustible materials. If the corrosive material is enclosed in a container, water added to the solution may be converted to steam, thereby increasing the pressure of the container and creating a bursting hazard.

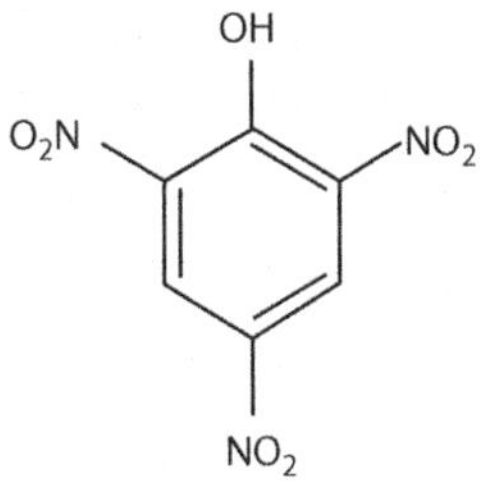

Figure 3.13 Structure of picric acid. Compare with the structure of TNT (Figure 6.12).

Many corrosives are also unstable and reactive. Several are known for exploding, polymerization, and decomposition, with the consequent generation of toxins. A notorious example of an unstable Class 8 substance is picric acid, $C_6H_2(NO_2)_3OH$ (Figure 3.13). When shipped, picric acid is prepared as a mixture containing 12% or more H_2O to maintain stability. However, over long periods in storage the water evaporates, creating unstable picrate salts. The nascent material becomes a high explosive that is extremely sensitive to shock and heat. The slightest movement (even twisting the cap of the container) may cause it to detonate.

Perchloric acid ($HClO_4$) is used in the manufacture of explosives, in electropolishing, as a *catalyst*, and in analytical chemistry. This acid is dangerously corrosive, unstable in its concentrated form, and readily forms explosive mixtures. Perchloric acid is a colorless, fuming, strong oxidizing agent—it will spontaneously ignite when in contact with organic materials. Likewise, when shocked or heated, it may detonate. Contact with water produces excessive heat. It is toxic by ingestion and inhalation (ILO, 2008).

Hydrocyanic acid (HCN) is used in the manufacture of rodenticides and other pesticides, acrylonitrile, acrylates, cyanide salts, and dyes. HCN is a highly toxic corrosive material. It is also a fire and explosion risk, with a wide flammable range (6%–41% in air). HCN is toxic by inhalation, ingestion, and absorption through skin. An HCN concentration of 300 mg/m^3 in air will kill a human within a few minutes (OSHA, n.d. [b]). Toxicity of HCN is caused by the cyanide ion, which impairs cellular respiration. Hydrogen cyanide, packaged under the codename Zyklon B, was used by the Nazi regime during World War II in the gas chambers of numerous concentration camps.

Transport of Corrosives

Corrosives are transported in MC 312/DOT 412 tanker trucks (Figure 3.14). The tanks are designed with a small diameter with heavy reinforcing rings around the circumference. Tank diameter is small because most corrosives are very dense and heavy. No other type of hazardous material is carried in this type of tanker. Lighter corrosives may also be found in MC 307/DOT 407 tankers and may be placarded corrosive, flammable, poison, and oxidizer. Corrosives are also transported in rail tank cars, intermodal containers, and varying sizes of portable containers.

Figure 3.14 MC 312/DOT 412 corrosive tanker truck.

Responder Safety

The main danger of corrosive materials to responders is contact with the body. Many strong acids and bases severely damage skin upon contact. It is estimated that a chemical burn is nine times more damaging to tissue than a thermal burn (Burke, 2002).

There are four basic methods of limiting the chemical action of corrosives on skin in the event of exposure:

- *Physical removal* of the corrosive material (e.g., using cloth wipes) is difficult to accomplish and will likely leave a residue.
- *Neutralization* is a chemical reaction that may be violent and produce heat. This type of reaction on body tissues may cause more damage than it prevents. Neutralization should not be attempted on responders wearing chemically protective clothing, in part because of concerns about generation of excessive heat. The PPE layer is very thin and heat from the neutralization reaction may melt the suit or cause burns to the skin.
- *Dilution* requires very large quantities of water to bring the pH to near neutral.
- *Flushing* is the method of choice for corrosive materials and should be started as soon as possible to minimize the extent of damage. Most corrosives are very water-soluble. Flushing should continue for a minimum of 15 min. Treatment after flushing involves standard first aid for burns.

QUESTIONS

1. Locate, on a map, the fixed facilities in your city, town or county that store and use hazardous chemicals. Where are population centers located in relation to these facilities? Locate the main roads. Can some serve as adequate evacuation routes in the event of a release?

2. Using DOT and local emergency response data, determine the types and quantities of hazardous chemicals being transported through your city, town, or county by road and/or railway. What are some of the primary hazard properties of these chemicals?
3. Check with your county's emergency response agency and ask to view their response plan for release of a hazardous chemical. How are local citizens to respond—should they evacuate or shelter in place? Where are the evacuation routes located?
4. Where can you find detailed information about potential human health and environmental impacts of hazardous chemicals? Cite four or five key sources.

REFERENCES

Agency for Toxic Substances and Disease Registry. 2004. *Toxicological Profile for Ammonia.* Atlanta, GA: U.S. Department of Health and Human Services, Public Health Service.

Agency for Toxic Substances and Disease Registry. 2008. White phosphorus: Health effects. Toxicological profile information sheet. http://www.atsdr.cdc.gov/toxprofiles/tp103-c2.pdf (accessed October 26, 2010).

Agency for Toxic Substances and Disease Registry. 2010. Chlorine. Toxic substances portal. U.S. Department of Health and Human Services, Public Health Service, Atlanta, GA. http://www.atsdr.cdc.gov/substances/toxsubstance.asp?toxid=36 (accessed October 26, 2010).

Appl, M. 2006. Ammonia. In *Ullmann's Encyclopedia of Industrial Chemistry*, 2006. Weinheim: Wiley-VCH. 10.1002/14356007.a02_143.pub2. December 15, 2006.

Barnard, A., and S. Senguptamay. 2015. Syria is using chemical weapons again, rescue workers say. *New York Times.* May 6, 2015. http://www.nytimes.com/2015/05/07/world/middleeast/syria-chemical-weapons.html?_r=2#story-continues-4.

BBC. 2006. Israel admits phosphorus bombing. October 22, 2006. http://news.bbc.co.uk/2/hi/middle_east/6075408.stm (accessed October 26, 2010).

Bond, C. 2002. Statement on S. 2579. *Congressional Record*, Daily edition, June 5, 2002, p. S5043.

Burke, R. 2002. *Hazardous Materials Chemistry for Emergency Responders.* 2nd Edition. Boca Raton, FL: CRC Press.

City of Pensacola, FL. n.d. Fire suppression and safety. http://www.ci.pensacola.fl.us/live/pages.asp?pageID=7598 (accessed October 26, 2010).

CNN.com. 2007. Iraq gas attack makes hundreds ill. http://www.cnn.com/2007/WORLD/meast/03/17/iraq.main/index.html (accessed October 26, 2010).

Code of Federal Regulations. 2015. Class 8 (corrosive) materials. Vol. 49. http://www.gpo.gov/fdsys/pkg/CFR-2011-title49-vol2/pdf/CFR-2011-title49-vol2-sec177-839.pdf.

Dallas Morning News. 2008. Explosion rocks meat plant, October 7, 2008. http://www.dallasnews.com/sharedcontent/dws/news/texassouthwest/stories/DN-arexplosion_24tex.ART.State.Edition1.45f50a1.html (accessed October 26, 2010).

Fertilizer Institute. n.d. Health effects of ammonia. http://www.tfi.org/publications/HealthAmmonia FINAL.pdf (accessed October 26, 2010).

Globalsecurity.org. 2009. White phosphorus (WP). http://www.globalsecurity.org/military/systems/munitions/wp.htm (accessed October 26, 2010).

Haaretz.com. 2006. Israel admits using phosphorus bombs during war in Lebanon. http://www.haaretz.com/news/israel-admits-using-phosphorus-bombsduring-war-in-lebanon-1.203078 (accessed October 26, 2010).

International Fire Service Training Association (IFSTA). 1988. *Hazardous Materials for First Responders.* 1st Edition. Fire Protection Publications, Oklahoma State University, Stillwater, OK.

International Labour Organization. 2008. Perchloric acid. http://www.ilo.org/public/english/protection/safework/cis/products/icsc/dtasht/_icsc10/icsc1006.htm (accessed October 26, 2010).

Lisandro, I., M.V. Williams, G.M. Williams, and J.E. Diaz-Alcala. 2009. CBRNE—Incendiary agents. White phosphorus. eMedicine. http://www.emedicine.com/emerg/topic918.htm (accessed October 26, 2010).

Mamoun, A. 2014. Urgent: ISIS kills 300 Iraqi soldiers by chlorine gas attack in Saqlawiyah. Iraqi News. http://www.iraqinews.com/iraq-war/urgent-isis-kills-300-iraqi-soldiers-chlorine-gas-attack-saqlawiyah/.

Marx, R. 2008. Uncovering the cause of "Phossy Jaw" circa 1858 to 1906: Oral and maxillofacial surgery closed case files—Case closed. *Journal of Oral and Maxillofacial Surgery* 66(11): 2356–2363.

Meyer, E. 2004. *Chemistry of Hazardous Materials*. 4th Edition. Englewood Cliffs, NJ: Prentice-Hall.

MSNBC.com. 2007. Chlorine gas attacks hint at new enemy strategy. http://www.msnbc.msn.com/id/17254507/ (accessed October 26, 2010).

MylesPaul.com. 2016. http://www.mylespaul.com/forums/backstage/136296-one-liners-2.html (accessed February 2, 2016).

New York Times. 2007. Iraq insurgents employ chlorine in bomb attacks. February 22, 2007. 156(53863): A1–A8.

Nowatzki, J. 2008. Anhydrous ammonia: Managing the risks. AE-1149 (Revised), August 2008. http://www.ag.ndsu.edu/pubs/ageng/safety/ae1149–1.htm (accessed October 26, 2010).

Occupational Safety and Health Administration. 2004. Properties of ammonia. http://www.osha.gov/SLTC/etools/ammonia_refrigeration/ammonia/index.html (accessed October 26, 2010).

Occupational Safety and Health Administration. n.d. [a]. Occupational safety and health guideline for chlorine. http://www.osha.gov/SLTC/healthguidelines/chlorine/recognition.html (accessed October 26, 2010).

Occupational Safety and Health Administration. n.d. [b]. Hydrogen cyanide. http://www.osha.gov/SLTC/healthguidelines/hydrogencyanide/recognition.html (accessed October 26, 2010).

Parachini, J.V. 2000. The World Trade Center bombers (1993). In *Toxic Terror: Assessing Terrorist Use of Chemical and Biological Weapons*, ed. B.T. Jonathan. Cambridge, MA: MIT Press. Citing the summation statement of Henry J. DePippo, Prosecutor, United States of America v. Mohammad A. Salameh et al., S593CR.180 (KTD), Feb. 16, 1994, pp. 8435–8439.

PressTV. 2014. Israel drops white phosphorus bombs on Gazans. http://www.globalresearch.ca/israel-drops-white-phosphorus-bombs-on-gazans/5393390.

Ranucci, S. n.d. Fallujah, the hidden massacre. http://www.youtube.com/verify_age?next_url=http%3A//www.youtube.com/watch%3Fv%3DUwrsNRoyblE.

Schierow, L.-J. 2006. *Chemical Facility Security. Resources, Science, and Industry Division*. RL31530. Congressional Research Service, Washington, DC.

United Nations. 1998. E/CN.4/2001/NGO/98. January 12, 2001.

U.S. Centers for Disease Control and Prevention. 2005. Anhydrous ammonia thefts and releases associated with illicit methamphetamine production—16 states, January, 2000–June, 2004. April 15, 2005/54(14): 359–361. http://www.cdc.gov/mmwr/preview/mmwrhtml/mm5414a4.htm#box#box (accessed October 26, 2010).

U.S. Centers for Disease Control and Prevention. 2006. Facts about chlorine. http://www.bt.cdc.gov/agent/chlorine/basics/facts.asp (accessed October 26, 2010).

U.S. Department of Justice. 2000. Assessment of the increased risk of terrorist or other criminal activity associated with posting off-site consequence analysis information on the Internet, April 18, pp. 23–24.

U.S. Environmental Protection Agency. 2000. Anhydrous Ammonia Theft. Office of Solid Waste and Emergceny Response, Washington, DC. EPA-F-00-005. March 2000.

Witte, B. 2002. Train derailment kills one, sends ammonia cloud over Minot. *The Minot Daily News*. January 18, 2002.

4

Biological Agents

You will be well advised to infect the Indians with sheets upon which smallpox patients have been lying, or by any other means which may serve to exterminate this accursed race.

Jeffery Amherst, 1717–1797

For the life of me, I cannot understand why the terrorists have not attacked our food supply, because it is so easy to do.

Tommy Thompson, 2004

INTRODUCTION

Biological warfare has been known, and applied to great effect, for millennia. In recent years, however, with enhanced knowledge of microbiology, culturing techniques, and means of dissemination, the threat has become acute. Bioweapons have been used by terrorists, and several nations are known to be manufacturing tactical biological weapons. Therefore, awareness of this potential threat by first responders, medical care providers, public health agencies, elected officials, and ultimately the general public, including how to identify such weapons and to respond appropriately, is essential.

CATEGORIES OF BIOTERRORISM AGENTS

Given the events of the past two decades, it is essential that the U.S. public health system and primary healthcare providers be prepared to address a wide range of biological agents, including pathogens that rarely occur in the United States. Even before the bioterror attacks of 2001 in which anthrax spores were deliberately released in the U.S. postal system, public health officials expressed concerned regarding the potential for such an event. In 1999, the U.S. Centers for Disease Control and Prevention (CDC), one of the key units of the Department of Health and Human Services, devised a classification scheme for major biological agents that terrorists could use to harm civilians (please see the lists of categories of CDC biological agents and examples of CDC category A, B, and C agents).

Categories of CDC biological agents (U.S. CDC, n.d.):

- Category A diseases/agents
  - High-priority agents include organisms that pose a risk to national security because they
    - Can be easily disseminated or transmitted from person to person
    - Result in high mortality rates and have the potential for major public health impact
    - Might cause public panic and social disruption
    - Require special action for public health preparedness
- Category B diseases/agents
  - Second highest-priority agents include those that
    - Are moderately easy to disseminate
    - Result in moderate morbidity rates and low mortality rates
    - Require specific enhancements of CDC's diagnostic capacity and enhanced disease surveillance
- Category C diseases/agents
  - Third highest-priority agents include emerging pathogens that could be engineered for
    - Mass dissemination in the future because of availability
    - Ease of production and dissemination
    - Potential for high morbidity and mortality rates and major health impact

Examples of CDC category A, B, and C agents (U.S. CDC, n.d.):

- Category A
  - Anthrax (*Bacillus anthracis*)
  - Botulism (*Clostridium botulinum* toxin)
  - Plague (*Yersinia pestis*)
  - Smallpox (variola major)
  - Tularemia (*Francisella tularensis*)
  - Viral hemorrhagic fevers (filoviruses [e.g., Ebola, Marburg] and arenaviruses [e.g., Lassa, Machupo])
- Category B
  - Brucellosis (*Brucella* species)
  - Epsilon toxin of *Clostridium perfringens*
  - Food safety threats (e.g., *Salmonella* species, *Escherichia coli* O157:H7, *Shigella*)
  - Glanders (*Burkholderia mallei*)
  - Melioidosis (*Burkholderia pseudomallei*)
  - Psittacosis (*Chlamydia psittaci*)
  - Q fever (*Coxiella burnetii*)

- Ricin toxin from *Ricinus communis* (castor beans)
- Staphylococcal enterotoxin B
- Typhus fever (*Rickettsia prowazekii*)
- Viral encephalitis (alphaviruses [e.g., Venezuelan equine encephalitis, eastern equine encephalitis, western equine encephalitis])
- Water safety threats (e.g., *Vibrio cholerae, Cryptosporidium parvum*)
  - Category C
    - Emerging infectious diseases such as Nipah virus and hantavirus

The CDC bioterror lists include those biological agents that pose the greatest threats to national security because of their ease of transmission, high rate of death or serious illness, potential for causing public panic, and special public health measures an epidemic would require. Since the creation of the CDC lists, public health officials and researchers have been planning and preparing intensively for a possible bioterror attack. After the 2001 anthrax attacks, federal funding for these efforts increased dramatically (NIH, 2007).

HISTORY OF BIOLOGICAL WEAPONS

The use of *biological weapons* has been detected as far back as the proto-Neolithic (late Stone Age, approximately 10,000 B.C.E.) hunter–gatherer societies in Southern Africa. Hunters used poisoned arrows, tipping stone points with venom obtained from scorpions or snakes. Extracts from poisonous plants were also used. The arrow was fired into the target, and the hunter tracked the animal until the poison caused its death.

Documented usage of biological weapons on the battlefield is abundant. In ancient times, many varieties of biological warfare were used, often with startling success, for example, Scythian archers used arrows dipped in decomposing corpses (and also blood and manure) as far back as 400 B.C.E. The Assyrians poisoned enemy wells with rye ergot, which contains a psychoactive agent. The fungus that causes ergot produces ergotamine, a hallucinogen that causes delusions, paranoia, seizures, and cardiovascular problems that can lead to death. Those affected seemed to go insane, which intensified the terror aspect and demoralized fellow soldiers.

In the sixth century B.C.E., Solon of Athens used the purgative herb hellebore (skunk cabbage) to poison drinking water supplies during the siege of Krissa. The effects rendered the entrenched enemy unable to conduct battle. The use of decomposing bodies as the carrier of biological agents also proved effective against enemy water supplies. Ancient Persian, Greek, and Roman literature cites examples of the use of dead animals to contaminate wells and other water sources. Barbarossa used this same tactic much later at the battle of Tortona in 1155.

Hannibal, the brilliant general of Carthage, hurled clay pots filled with venomous snakes on to the ships of Pergamus during the battle of Eurymedon in 190 B.C.E. When the pots broke on the decks, the Pergamene were forced to fight against both snakes and Hannibal's forces (Hannibal's troops were eventually victorious). Roman armies catapulted hives of bees and hornets at their enemies. Some historians claim that such military usage was responsible for a shortage of hives and honey during the latter years of the Roman Empire.

One of the best-documented historic incidents of biological warfare occurred in 1346 during the siege of Kaffa (now Feodossia, Ukraine), a port city located on the Crimean Peninsula of the Black Sea. The attacking Tatar forces of Kipchak khan Janibeg, backed by Venetian forces, catapulted plague-infected corpses into the city. The ensuing epidemic within the already weakened city forced the defenders to surrender. Some infected citizens who fled Kaffa by ship may have started the Black Death pandemic, which spread throughout Europe. This same stratagem of hurling infected corpses was repeated in 1710 by the Russians besieging Swedish forces at Reval in Estonia.

The Spanish deliberately contaminated wine with the blood of leprosy patients for use against the French near Naples in 1495. Another innovative attempt at biological warfare occurred in 1650 by Kazimierz Siemienowicz, a Polish artillery general, who placed saliva from rabid dogs into hollow projectiles for firing against his enemies.

On the North American continent, smallpox served as a highly effective biological weapon—the disease proved devastating to the Native American population. Pizarro is said to have presented South American natives with variola-contaminated clothing in the fifteenth century (variola is the causative organism of smallpox). During Pontiac's Rebellion in 1763, Colonel Henry Bouquet, a British officer, suggested giving the Indians at Fort Pitt, Pennsylvania, blankets infected with smallpox. In the French and Indian War of 1754–1767, British forces under Jeffrey Amherst gave blankets that had been used by smallpox victims to the Native Americans in efforts to spread the disease.

During the U.S. Civil War in 1861, Union troops advancing south into Maryland and other border states were warned not to eat or drink anything provided by unknown civilians for fear of being poisoned. Many cases were documented where soldiers thought they had been poisoned after eating or drinking in occupied areas. Confederates retreating in Mississippi in 1863 left dead animals in wells and ponds to deny water sources to the Union troops (Smart, 1997).

World War I

The use of biological weapons during World War I was not nearly as widespread as that of chemical warfare (see Chapter 2). However, it is believed that by 1915 the Germans infected the Allies' horses and cattle with various microbes on both the western and eastern fronts. Also in 1915, the Germans allegedly inoculated pathogenic bacteria into horses and cattle leaving U.S. ports for shipment to the Allies in Europe (Figure 4.1) (Smart, 1996, 1997; Stockholm, 1971). Erich von Steinmetz, a captain in the German navy, entered the United States with cultures of glanders to inoculate horses intended for the western front. His efforts were not successful, however. Dr. Anton Dilger, a German-American physician, developed a microbiology facility in Maryland, where he produced large quantities of anthrax and glanders bacteria, using starter cultures provided by the German government. German agents inoculated horses in Baltimore that were awaiting shipment to the Allied forces in Europe; they inoculated 3000 horses, mules, and cattle. Several hundred military personnel were reported to have received secondary infections.

Other bioattacks included a reported attempt to spread plague in St. Petersburg, Russia, in 1915 (Smart, 1996, 1997; Stockholm, 1971). In 1916, German agents attempted to

Figure 4.1 Horses being prepared for transport to Europe during World War I. (Courtesy of Queen's University Archives, Kingston, Ontario, Canada.)

infect horses with glanders, and cattle with anthrax in Bucharest. In 1917, Germany was accused of poisoning wells in the Somme area with human corpses, and dropping fruit, chocolate, and children's toys infected with pathogenic bacteria into Romanian cities. The authenticity of many of these reports was, however, called into question and was strongly denied by German officials.

The only bioagent studied by the United States during World War I was ricin toxin, which was intended for retaliatory purposes. Ricin, which is extracted from the castor bean, was studied for dissemination via attachment to shrapnel in an artillery shell, or via generation of a ricin dust cloud. Both methods were tested in the laboratory; however, neither was optimized for use during the war (Hunt, 1918).

The Interwar Years

In 1928, Shiro Ishii (Figure 4.2), a Japanese military officer, toured foreign research laboratories and came to the conclusion that several of the world powers were secretly researching biological warfare (his conclusion was at least accurate for the Soviet Union). In 1929, the Soviets were reported to have established a biological warfare facility north of the Caspian Sea (Robertson and Robertson, 1995; Smart, 1997; Stockholm, 1971; Williams and Wallace, 1989). In 1933, Germany began military training in offensive biological warfare and was reported to have secretly tested *Serratia marcescens*, considered a biological simulant, in the Paris Metro ventilation shafts and near several French forts (Smart, 1997). Soon afterward, the Germans conducted experiments on livestock infections with foot and mouth disease (FMD). The German Military Bacteriological Institute in Berlin began developing anthrax as a biological weapon, while the Agricultural Hochschule in Bonn examined spraying of crops with bacteria (Robertson and Robertson, 1995; Smart, 1996).

107

Figure 4.2 General Shiro Ishii of the Japanese military, ca. 1933. (Courtesy of Wikipedia, http://en.wikipedia.org/wiki/File:Shiro-ishii.jpg.)

By 1936, France had established a large-scale biological warfare research program that investigated microbial viability while in storage and during detonation of explosives. Canada also initiated biological warfare research, studying anthrax, botulinum toxin, plague, and psittacosis. By 1940, Britain instituted a biological warfare laboratory at Porton Down.

In 1933, Japan—under the direction of General Ishii—set up an offensive biological warfare laboratory near Harbin in occupied Manchuria. The laboratory complex, code-named Unit 731, was used for research on the effects of biological agents on numerous organisms and also prisoners of war (Figure 4.3). About 1000 human autopsies were carried out at Unit 731, mostly on victims exposed to anthrax. Many more prisoners and Chinese nationals may have died in this facility, however. Unit 731 developed and tested a biological bomb within 3 years. Additional biological warfare facilities were established in 1939.

Some key U.S. military officials considered it highly unlikely that biological agents would ever be suited for warfare, particularly because of concerns about the safety of those individuals loading the weapons, and also because of the technical difficulties inherent in cell culturing and preservation. As a result, U.S. weapons research during the interwar years did not place significant emphasis on biological warfare agents.

Figure 4.3   Japanese Unit 731 complex in Manchuria. (Courtesy of Wikipedia, http://en.wikipedia
.org/wiki/File:Harbin _maj_enh_731_1.JPG. Copyright 2002 Markus Kallander.)

World War II

By 1940, Japan had developed and tested several different biological devices in the field;
more than 1600 bombs were constructed. Some are known to have been filled with a
mixture of shrapnel and anthrax spores. By 1945, Ishii's program had stockpiled 400 kg
of anthrax to be carried in specially designed fragmentation bombs (Smart, 1997). The
Japanese had apparently used cholera, dysentery, typhoid, plague, anthrax, and paratyphoid on Chinese troops. Hundreds of Chinese citizens are known to have died from
plague epidemics. By the start of World War II, Japanese laboratories devoted significant
attention to the use of vectors such as the common flea to carry biological agents (Smart,
1996; U.S. Army, 1945; Williams and Wallace, 1989).

In 1943, the U.S. military began research into the use of biological agents for offensive purposes. This work was conducted at Camp Detrick, the Chemical Corps Biological
Warfare Center (now Fort Detrick). During the war, anthrax became the highest-priority
agent for development for the U.S. military arsenal (Smart, 1997).

Post–World War II

During the 1950s, the biological warfare programs of many nations were geared toward
standardizing selected biological agents and weaponizing them. Highest priority was
placed on antipersonnel agents. In the United States, Major General Bullene, Chief Chemical
Officer, continued to give utmost priority to the development of anthrax (Smart, 1997).

Biological agents were produced at several sites in the United States until 1969,
when President Nixon halted all offensive biological weapon research and production by Executive Order. Between 1971 and 1972, all stockpiles of biological agents from
the U.S. program were destroyed. The agents eliminated included *Bacillus anthracis*,

Francisella tularensis, *Coxiella burnetii*, Venezuelan equine encephalitis virus, *Brucella suis*, Staphylococcal enterotoxin B, and botulinum toxin. The United States created a medical defensive program in 1953 that continues today at the U.S. Army Medical Research Institute for Infectious Diseases (USAMRIID) at Fort Detrick, Maryland.

In 1972, the United States, United Kingdom, and Union of Soviet Socialist Republics (USSR) signed the "Convention on the Prohibition of the Development, Production and Stockpiling of Bacteriological (Biological) and Toxin Weapons and on Their Destruction," also known as the Biological Weapons Convention (BWC). This treaty prohibits the stockpiling of biological agents for offensive military purposes and also forbids research into offensive deployment of biological agents. More than 140 countries have since ratified this convention. Despite this promising international agreement, however, biological warfare research continued in many countries. In addition, several cases of suspected or actual use of biological weapons have been reported. For example, during the Vietnam conflict, Laos and Kampuchea (formerly Cambodia) were attacked by planes delivering aerosols of varying color (later dubbed *yellow rain*). Some exposed villagers and livestock became ill, and a small percentage died. Some of these clouds were thought to be composed of trichothecene toxins (e.g., T2 mycotoxin).

In April 1979, public attention became focused on an incident that occurred in Sverdlovsk (now Yekaterinburg) in the former Soviet Union. Spores of *B. anthracis* were accidentally released from the Soviet Military's Compound 19, a microbiology laboratory. Workers at a ceramic plant across the street fell ill during next few days, and almost all died within a week. Some residents living downwind from the facility also became ill and died within days of the event. All cases occurred within a narrow zone extending 4 km downwind in a southerly direction from the facility (Figure 4.4). The Soviet Ministry of Health claimed that the deaths were the result of consumption of contaminated meat; however, controversy as to the actual cause continued for years. The death toll from the incident totaled at least 105, but the exact number is unknown as all hospital records and other evidence were destroyed by the Komitet Gosudarstvennoy Bezopasnosti (KGB), according to former Biopreparat deputy director Ken Alibek (Alibek and Handelman, 1999). Livestock downwind from the site also succumbed to the disease.

In 1992, the new Russian President Boris Yeltsin acknowledged that the Sverdlovsk incident was in fact related to military-related biological programs underway at Compound 19. A detailed review of the Sverdlovsk incident was published shortly afterward (Meselson et al., 1994). Among the findings was that the accident was caused by failure to replace a filter in an exhaust system at the facility, thus allowing anthrax spores to escape.

After the accident and the closing of the Sverdlovsk facility, and in order to continue biological weapons production, a new biological warfare R&D facility was created in Stepnogorsk in Kazakhstan. An even more virulent strain of anthrax was produced at the new location, one that was three times as lethal as that produced in Sverdlovsk. The Stepnogorsk operation is recorded to have had a production capacity estimated at 300 tons of anthrax spores in 220 days (Miller and Broad, 2001). Efforts to clean up the Soviet biological warfare installations continues today, as does the effort to determine if any technical expertise or the products of their operations fell into the hands of terrorist organizations (CNS, 2014; NSA, 2001).

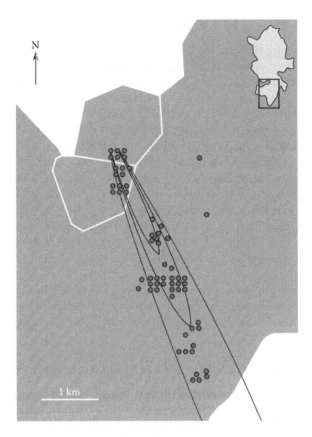

Figure 4.4 Sverdlovsk, USSR, showing direction of a *Bacillus anthracis* spore plume, 1979. (From M.J. Meselson et al., *The Sverdlovsk anthrax outbreak of 1979*. American Association for the Advancement of Science. With permission.)

In August 1991, in the aftermath of the Gulf War, Iraq's biological weapons program was inspected by the United Nations (UN). Representatives of the Iraqi government declared to the UN Special Commission that research had been ongoing into the offensive use of *B. anthracis*, botulinum toxins, and *Clostridium perfringens*. By 1995, it was determined that Iraq's offensive program conducted research and development activities on anthrax, botulinum toxin, *C. perfringens*, aflatoxins, wheat cover smut, and ricin. Field trials were conducted with *B. subtilis* (an organism that simulates the behavior of anthrax), botulinum, and aflatoxin. Biological agents were tested in numerous delivery systems including rockets, aerial bombs, and spray tanks. In December 1990, the Iraqi military loaded 100 bombs with botulinum toxin, 50 with anthrax, and 16 with aflatoxin. In addition, 13 al-Hussein (SCUD) warheads were filled with botulinum toxin, 10 with anthrax, and 2 with aflatoxin. These weapons were deployed in 1991 to four locations (USAMRIID, 2005).

Current Threat

Biological threats relating to both warfare and terrorism continue today. There is increasing concern regarding possible terrorist use of biological agents to threaten both military installations and civilian populations. In addition, there is apprehension that a number of countries, some known to be hostile to the United States, may be developing biological agents for offensive purposes. It was reported in January 1998 that Iraq had sent scientists involved in bioweapons research to Libya to help that country develop a biological warfare complex disguised as a medical facility in the Tripoli area. In a report issued in 1997, Secretary of Defense William Cohen identified Libya, Iraq, Iran, and Syria as countries *aggressively seeking* chemical, biological, and nuclear weapons (USAMRIID, 2005).

Recent reports from Russia have revealed an intensive ongoing biological warfare program that includes active research into genetic engineering, binary biological formulations, and industrial capacity to produce bioagents. Furthermore, there is concern that the smallpox virus, known to be stored in only two laboratories at the CDC in Atlanta and the Institute for Viral Precautions in Moscow, may actually occur in other nations as well (Box 4.1).

In August 1984, the Bhagwan Shree Rajneeshee cult, based in eastern Oregon, served water laced with *Salmonella typhimurium* to two county commissioners. Both became ill and one was hospitalized. Later that year, several cult members contaminated salad bars

---

BOX 4.1 DISCOVERY OF SMALLPOX CULTURES, 2013–2014

By international agreement, only two official World Health Organization (WHO)–designated repositories exist for smallpox: the U.S. CDC in Atlanta, Georgia, and the State Research Centre of Virology and Biotechnology in Novosibirsk, Russia. The WHO oversees the inspection of both smallpox facilities and conducts periodic reviews to certify the repositories for safety and security.

In 2014, the National Institutes of Health (NIH) notified the CDC that employees discovered six vials labeled *variola*, commonly known as smallpox, in a storage room in a Food and Drug Administration (FDA) laboratory located in Bethesda, Maryland. Scientists discovered the vials while preparing for the laboratory's move to another campus. The vials appear to date from the 1950s. Upon discovery, the vials were immediately secured in a CDC-registered agent containment laboratory in Bethesda. The vials were transported safely to the CDC's high-containment facility in Atlanta, Georgia. Testing carried out by the CDC confirmed the presence of variola virus DNA. After completion of testing, the samples were destroyed. There is no evidence that any of the vials labeled variola had been breached, and there has been no identification of exposure risk to laboratory workers or the public.

At about the same time, the NIH stated that in different facilities, it found small amounts of samples containing pathogens that cause botulism, plague, tularemia, and a rare tropical infection called melioidosis. They also discovered a bottle of ricin, found in a box with microbes dating from 1914 and thought to be 85 to 100 years old (Aleccia, 2014; U.S. CDC, 2014a; Neergaard, 2014).

in restaurants of nearby communities with *S. typhimurium*. More than 750 were poisoned and 40 hospitalized. The group was attempting to influence a local election by making people too sick to vote. The deliberate food poisoning event was only discovered a year later when certain members turned informants. There is evidence that the cult had considered using *S. typhi*, the causative agent of typhoid fever; however, that organism was rejected because of the risks of having it traced back to the group.

In 1991, the Minnesota Patriots Council extracted ricin from castor beans obtained through a mail order. They planned to disseminate the agent as an aerosol but were arrested after the FBI infiltrated the group and learned of their plan. Two members of the group, Doug Baker and Charles Wheeler, were the first individuals to be indicted and convicted under the Biological Weapons Anti-Terrorism Act of 1989.

In October 1992, Shoko Asahara, leader of the Aum Shinrikyo cult, with 40 followers, traveled to Zaire reportedly to assist victims of an outbreak of Ebola hemorrhagic fever. According to a report by the U.S. Senate's Permanent Subcommittee on Investigations, however, the cult's true motive was to obtain virus samples to be used for biological attacks. By 1995, it was reported that on at least 10 occasions Aum Shinrikyo attempted to disperse anthrax, botulinum toxin, Q fever, and Ebola against civilian populations and government figures in Japan (see Chapter 7).

In 1995, a group called The Covenant and the Sword smuggled ricin into the United States from Canada. The ricin was baked into cakes that were to be given to the local Internal Revenue Service office at Christmas. The perpetrator hanged himself shortly after his arrest. Also in 1995, a Kansas City oncologist, Deborah Green, attempted to murder her husband by contaminating his food with ricin.

In May 1995, a laboratory technician from Ohio (Larry Wayne Harris) ordered plague bacterium (*Yersinia pestis*) from a Maryland biomedical supply firm using a credit card and a false letterhead. He received three vials of *Y. pestis*. As a result of his suspicious behavior, the supplier contacted federal authorities. An investigation revealed that he was a member of a white supremacist organization. Harris was arrested after he threatened to release anthrax in Las Vegas. The strain in his possession, however, was a harmless veterinary vaccine strain.

In China in 2001, 120 people became ill after food products were laced with rat poison by manufacturers of competing products. In 2002, a similar rat poisoning incident killed at least 38 people and made more than 300 seriously ill (BBC, 2002; CNN, 2002). In 2003, it was discovered that 200 lb of ground beef was contaminated with an insecticide containing nicotine by a disgruntled supermarket employee in Michigan. This episode resulted in 111 people becoming ill, including 40 children (U.S. CDC, 2003).

BACTERIAL DISEASES

Bacteria are one-celled organisms that can survive in a wide variety of environments. The majority of bacteria are either beneficial or do no particular harm to other organisms. Only a minority are *pathogenic*, that is, disease-causing, in animals and humans. As a consequence of the differences in physiology between bacteria and their hosts, it is possible to treat most bacterial diseases by using antibiotics.

Two pathogenic bacterial agents—*B. anthracis* and *Coxiella burnetii*—have the capability of converting to a highly resistant form, that is, a spore, when the environment becomes hostile to the organism's survival (too dry, too cold, extremes of pH, etc.). The spore is capable of remaining viable for extended periods and will subsequently revert to the vegetative, disease-producing form when favorable environmental conditions return. The following section will describe a spore-forming bacterial species with a long history of adverse public health impacts.

Anthrax

Anthrax is an acute infectious disease caused by the bacterium *B. anthracis*. The CDC has classified *B. anthracis* as a Category A bioterrorism agent. Anthrax is thought to be the *fifth plague* of Egypt as chronicled in the book of Exodus. The disease is probably best known for its role in the 2001 bioterrorist attacks in the United States in which lethal anthrax spores were sent via U.S. mail to offices in the U.S. Senate and several news media companies (Box 4.2). Twenty-two people became ill and five died as a result of the attacks. The perpetrator is believed to have been Dr. Bruce Ivins, a biodefense scientist who was working on a vaccine for anthrax at the U.S. Army Biodefense Laboratories at Fort Detrick, Maryland. In 2009, he committed suicide during the FBI investigation of his possible role in the attacks.

There were two waves of letters containing anthrax spores sent from the unknown perpetrator. The anthrax spores caused pulmonary anthrax (lung infection) and cutaneous anthrax among victims. As many as 30,000 people were placed on medication to prevent illness.

BOX 4.2

In October 2001, two letters contaminated with *B. anthracis* spores were processed at the U.S. Postal Service Brentwood Mail Processing and Distribution Center in Washington, D.C. Four postal workers became ill with what was eventually diagnosed as inhalational anthrax, and two died. The facility was closed, and postexposure prophylaxis was recommended for approximately 2500 workers and business visitors.

The subsequent investigation disclosed that both letters contained the same strain of anthrax, which was isolated and sent to the Army's Biodefense Laboratories at Fort Detrick, Maryland. All the letters were postmarked in Trenton, New Jersey.

The anthrax episodes occurred as follows:

- Palm Beach County, Florida—October 3, 2001
- New York City—October 12, 2001
- Washington, D.C.—October 15, 2001
- Trenton, New Jersey—October 17, 2001
- Oxford, Connecticut—November 20, 2001

All affected sites were subjected to simultaneous investigations, including public health (case finding) and medical response (treatment); forensics (crime investigation); environmental (worker safety/cleanup); and tactical (operations and intelligence). Multiple state and local jurisdictions were involved, as well as multiple federal agencies.

Lessons learned from these episodes include the following:

- The value of integrated emergency response to the incidents
- Dramatic expansion of health information about anthrax and its behavior
- Improved risk communications to media and the public

Anthrax is primarily a disease of ruminant animals, most commonly affecting wild and domestic mammals (cattle, sheep, goats, camels, antelope, and other herbivores), but it can also occur in humans when they are exposed to infected animals or their tissue (U.S. CDC, 2008). Naturally occurring anthrax infections occur worldwide, but the disease is most often a risk in countries with inadequate public health programs. Common locations of infections include South and Central America, Southern and Eastern Europe, Asia, Africa, the Caribbean, and the Middle East.

Human exposure to anthrax is usually caused by occupational exposure to infected animals or their products. Anthrax most commonly occurs in rural/agricultural regions; those who work on farms, ranches, or in slaughterhouses and handle animal hides, hair, or wool may be at risk of contracting the disease. Anthrax in wild livestock has occurred in the United States (U.S. CDC, 2008). Cases occur annually, with outbreaks occurring most frequently in the central United States from North Dakota to Texas.

The Agent

The causative agent of anthrax, *B. anthracis,* is a relatively large (approximately 1 by 6 µm) Gram-positive, spore-forming, rod-shaped bacterium. Anthrax was the first bacterium ever to be documented to cause disease, by Robert Koch in 1877. *B. anthracis* lives in soil, and the vegetative form has evolved a survival tactic (i.e., spore formation) that allows it to withstand harsh conditions for decades. The spore, which measures approximately 1 by 0.5 µm, serves as a resilient resting phase that can tolerate extreme heat, cold, and desiccation. When environmental conditions eventually become favorable, the spores germinate into active bacteria.

Although the spore stage will allow the bacteria to survive in unfavorable environments, the potency of anthrax as a killer is the ability of the vegetative form to produce toxins. The resilience of the spore and the production of toxins combine to make *B. anthracis* a formidable bioterrorism agent. *B. anthracis* possesses several virulence factors: a capsule surrounding the vegetative cell, a protective antigen, and two protein exotoxins, termed *lethal factor* and *edema factor.* The capsule prevents the bacterial cell from being engulfed and killed by *phagocytes* (i.e., specialized white blood cells). The protective antigen binds to the cell of the infected organism, creates a pore, and channels the edema factor and lethal factor into the cell. Once inside, the edema factor causes fluid to accumulate at the site of infection. The edema factor can contribute to a fatal buildup of fluid in the cavity surrounding the lungs; it can also inhibit some of the body's immune functions. The lethal factor also works inside the cell, disrupting a key molecular process that regulates cell

115

function. The lethal factor can kill infected cells or prevent them from functioning properly (NIH, 2007).

Clinical Manifestations and Symptoms

Three human forms of anthrax are known, depending on route of exposure: cutaneous, gastrointestinal (GI), and inhalation. Each form produces its own unique symptoms.

Cutaneous Anthrax

Cutaneous anthrax is the most common manifestation of natural *B. anthracis* infection. Individuals with cuts or open sores can succumb to cutaneous anthrax if they come in direct contact with the bacteria or its spores through broken skin, usually on the hands, arms, or face. Handling contaminated animal products is a common source of infection. The spores germinate within hours after infection and the vegetative cells multiply and produce toxins.

The first obvious sign of cutaneous anthrax is typically is a small reddish *macule* that develops within a few days after infection. The macule progresses to a *papular* and eventually a *pustular* stage (a fluid-filled vesicle), and the surrounding tissue becomes swollen. Secondary vesicles may surround the initial infected site. The final stage involves the formation of an ulcer with a blackened necrotic *eschar* surrounded by a zone of edema (Figure 4.5). The term *anthrax* arises from the Greek word meaning *coal*, because of the development of the black lesions in cutaneous victims. The fully developed lesion is painless.

Most victims of the cutaneous form have no fever and often have no systemic symptoms of infection. Natural healing occurs in the majority (80–90%) of untreated cases, but

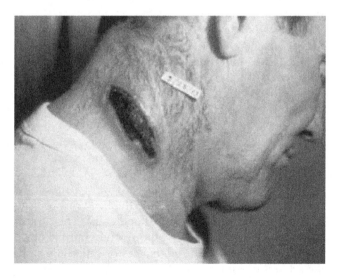

Figure 4.5 Anthrax eschar. (Courtesy of Centers for Disease Control and Prevention, http://www .bt.cdc.gov/agent/anthrax/anthrax-images/cutaneous.asp.)

edema may persist for weeks. In untreated patients who do not naturally heal, cutaneous anthrax can progress to a systemic infection (i.e., septicemia) that can be fatal. Cutaneous anthrax responds favorably to antibiotics; if exposed individuals are administered antibiotics promptly, most will recover within 10 days of onset.

No form of anthrax is considered contagious; however, the fluid in the vesicles of cutaneous anthrax contains viable *B. anthracis*. If fluid from a victim's vesicles comes into contact with the open wound of another individual, the bacteria can be transferred. The use of gloves and other protective clothing will prevent such transfer.

Cutaneous anthrax is rare in the United States—according to the U.S. CDC, only one to two cases are diagnosed per year. Cutaneous anthrax is not likely to be significant in a bioterrorism event, although it may erupt in conjunction with an aerosol anthrax attack. This occurred in 2001, when 11 of the exposed individuals contracted the cutaneous form.

GI Anthrax

Humans can become infected with GI anthrax from eating undercooked meat contaminated with anthrax bacteria or their spores. GI anthrax is most likely to occur in warm, tropical regions of Asia, Africa, and the Middle East. There have been no confirmed cases of GI anthrax in the United States, although a Minnesota farm family experienced symptoms of the disease in 2000 after eating meat from an anthrax-infected steer (NIH, 2007). The infections were discovered early and treated successfully.

GI anthrax is characterized by an acute inflammation of the intestinal tract. Clinical symptoms begin within days after ingesting spores. If the spores germinate in the upper intestinal tract, ulcers may develop in the mouth or esophagus and cause swelling in the lymph nodes of the neck and surrounding tissues. *Septicemia* may follow. Spores that germinate in the lower intestinal tract will create lesions and may be severe enough to cause intestinal hemorrhage. Early symptoms include loss of appetite, nausea, vomiting, and fever. These symptoms are followed by abdominal pain, vomiting of blood, and severe diarrhea. If left untreated, GI anthrax results in death in 25–60% of cases (U.S. CDC, 2008). Antibiotic treatment can cure the GI form of anthrax.

Researchers generally report that the cutaneous form of anthrax is much more common than the GI form (Dixon et al., 1999; Jaax and Fritz, 1997). Other researchers (Sirisanthana and Brown, 2002), however, propose that the apparent predominance of the cutaneous form is, rather, attributable to the difficulty of diagnosis of the GI form.

Although there are no reports of anthrax having ever been used in a foodborne bioterrorism attempt, such an act would likely result in severe illness in those individuals consuming the contaminated food.

Inhalation Anthrax

The inhalation form of the disease, also known as Woolsorters disease, is highly lethal, causing a hemorrhagic inflammation of the mediastinum (generally speaking, the space in the chest between the pleural sacs of the left and right lungs) and often, hemorrhagic *mediastinitis* (Figure 4.6). Fatality rates are very high in untreated cases and may occur in as many as 95% of treated cases if therapy is delayed after the appearance of symptoms.

Spores of *B. anthracis* occurring as airborne particles measure less than 5 µm in diameter and can be deposited directly into the alveoli of the lungs. After spores are inhaled,

117

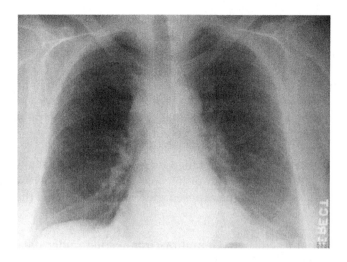

Figure 4.6 Mediastinitis as a result of inhalation anthrax. (From U.S. Centers for Disease Control and Prevention. 2001. Bioterrorism-Related Inhalational Anthrax: The First 10 Cases Reported in the United States. Atlanta, GA. http://wwwnc.cdc.gov/eid/article/7/6/01-0604-f5.)

phagocytes (white blood cells) engulf them. The spores are carried by the phagocytes to the mediastinal nodes where they germinate and release toxins soon afterward. Symptoms usually appear from 1 to 7 days after exposure, but may take as long as 60 days. The time difference is apparently a function of dose received (Fong and Alibek, 2005).

Inhalation anthrax occurs in two stages. The first stage lasts 3–5 days and mimics common flu symptoms; thus, early diagnosis is difficult. The patient exhibits mild, nonspecific upper respiratory symptoms often accompanied by sore throat, mild fever, and *myalgia* (muscle aches). Nausea and vomiting are among other early symptoms. Later symptoms include cough, chest discomfort, shortness of breath, and fatigue. Near the end of the first stage, the patient's condition may appear to improve somewhat. The second stage begins with an abrupt onset of acute respiratory distress, sweating, shock, and *cyanosis* (bluish discoloration of the skin). After 1–3 days fever increases and *dyspnea, hypoxia,* and *hypotension* occur, usually leading to death within 24 h. Once this stage is reached, the disease is almost always fatal (NIH, 2007). The second stage is the direct result of *toxemia* (high concentrations of toxins in the blood) and is not treatable with antibiotics.

Diagnosis and Treatment

Anthrax is not contagious; therefore, communicability is not a concern in managing patients with inhalation anthrax (U.S. CDC, 2008). DNA identification techniques combined with microbial culture of body fluids can provide an accurate diagnosis of the disease. To date, there are several successful rapid diagnostic tests for *B. anthracis.*

Untreated inhalation anthrax has an extremely high fatality rate. In the event of inhalation exposure, the immediate administration of antibiotics is critical. Antibiotics are effective if provided early during the course of the disease; antibiotic treatment is not effective if begun more than 24 h after symptoms appear. Large doses of intravenous and oral antibiotics, such as ciproflaxin (Cipro®), penicillin, doxycycline, tetracycline, and erythromycin, are effective. Antibiotic treatment should ideally begin before the onset of symptoms. It should be noted that some antibiotic-resistant strains of anthrax have been identified. Laboratory studies have shown that *B. anthracis* can develop resistance to ciprofloxacin, doxycycline, and β-lactam antibiotics (Brook et al., 2001; Pomerantsev et al., 1992; Price et al., 2003).

A safe, effective vaccine for inhalation anthrax has been developed from a portion of the toxin from a nonvirulent strain. The vaccine is safe and effective and can be used both prophylactically and therapeutically.

If livestock are located in proximity to an anthrax release and die, their carcasses should be placed in deep burial trenches. Shallow burial is both ineffective and potentially hazardous because other organisms may scavenge carcasses and subsequently disseminate anthrax spores. Incineration of anthrax-infected carcasses may pose practical problems; if incomplete burning occurs, spores may be released downwind in smoke and particulate emissions.

Animals introduced into an environment that had previously been infected should be vaccinated. Animal products from livestock living in anthrax-affected areas should not be consumed or handled by untrained and/or unvaccinated personnel (UTDallas, 2015).

Recent Developments

Anthrax toxins are being studied to learn how to block their production and ultimately their action. Researchers have discovered the three-dimensional molecular structure of the anthrax protective antigen protein that is used to enter host cells; they have subsequently been able to block the attachment of protective antigen in laboratory experiments, thereby inhibiting anthrax toxin activity (NIH, 2007). In other studies, the National Institute of Allergy and Infectious Diseases has synthesized a molecule that interferes with anthrax toxin in cell culture and in rodents. The molecule blocks the pore formed by anthrax protective antigen, which prevents lethal factor and edema factor toxins from entering cells (NIH, 2007). In 2015, The U.S. FDA approved Anthrasil, Anthrax Immune Globulin Intravenous, to treat patients with inhalation anthrax in combination with appropriate antibacterial drugs. Anthrasil is manufactured from the plasma of individuals vaccinated against anthrax. The plasma contains antibodies that neutralize toxins produced by the anthrax bacteria (U.S. FDA, 2015).

Biowarfare and Terrorism

Anthrax spores were weaponized by the U.S. military in the 1950s and 1960s before the U.S. offensive program was terminated. Other countries have been or are currently suspected of weaponizing this agent.

The anthrax bacterium is relatively easy to cultivate. The formation of spores facilitates both storage and weaponization of the organism. Anthrax spores are highly resistant to sunlight, heat, and disinfectants—properties that are advantageous when choosing a bacterial weapon.

119

VIRAL DISEASES

A virus (from the Latin *poison*) consists of small units of DNA or RNA; a virus does not constitute a complete cell. Virus particles (*virions*) are much smaller than bacteria—they cannot be seen using conventional light microscopy. Each viral particle is enclosed within a protective protein coat termed a capsid. The capsid shape varies from simple helical and icosahedral forms to more complex structures.

Viruses act by parasitizing selected host cells; they are unable to grow or reproduce outside those cells. Viruses are classified into animal, plant, and bacterial types, depending on the type of host infected. Viral infections in human and animal hosts typically result in disease and an immune response. In many cases, an invading virus is completely destroyed and removed by the immune system. A key practical difference between viruses and bacteria is that viruses cannot be treated using antibiotics. However, vaccines are effective in preventing some viral infections or in limiting their effects. In some cases, antiviral drugs have been developed to treat life-threatening infections.

Smallpox

The name *smallpox* is derived from the Latin word for *spotted* and refers to the raised bumps that appear on the face and body of an infected victim. Two clinical forms of smallpox exist; variola major is the most severe and most common form of smallpox, characterized by an extensive rash and high fever. Variola minor is less common and a less severe disease, with death rates historically of 1% or less. Variola is a member of the *Orthopoxvirus* genus of poxviruses, which includes many species isolated from mammals.

Humans are the only natural hosts of variola; smallpox is not known to be transmitted by insects or animals. Smallpox is highly contagious, and outbreaks have been recorded for thousands of years. The last case of smallpox in the United States was in 1949. The last known endemic case was recorded in October 1977 in Somalia. After a successful worldwide vaccination program, the disease was declared eradicated from the planet in 1980. After this historic event, routine vaccination against smallpox ended. The United States discontinued vaccinations for civilians in 1972, and by 1985 the military no longer vaccinated its recruits. The smallpox virus still exists, however—both the United States and Russia retain stocks of the virus. It is fairly certain that some clandestine stocks of smallpox virus exist in other nations as well.

Direct and prolonged face-to-face contact (resulting in inhalation of aerosolized virus) is typically required to spread smallpox from one person to another. Smallpox is also spread through direct contact with infected body fluids or contaminated objects such as clothing. Only in rare circumstances is smallpox spread by virus carried in the air in enclosed settings (e.g., inside buildings) (U.S. CDC, 2007a).

Clinical Manifestations/Symptoms

Following entry into the body the virus travels to nearby lymph nodes where it multiplies and causes *viremia* (contamination of the bloodstream with the virus). The virus later spreads to the spleen, liver, and lungs. An incubation period of about 12–14 days follows, during which no symptoms are apparent and the victim may feel well. During this time, infected individuals are not contagious.

The first obvious symptoms of the disease include fever, malaise, head and body aches, and sometimes vomiting (the *prodrome* phase). The fever is usually high, in the range of 101–104°F. At this time, victims become incapacitated. This phase may last for 2–4 days (U.S. CDC, 2007a). After the prodrome phase, the first visible lesions occur in the mouth as red spots on the tongue and on the oral and pharyngeal mucosa. These lesions enlarge and ulcerate quickly, releasing large amounts of virus into the saliva. It is during this phase that the victim is most contagious. As the sores in the mouth disappear, a rash appears on the skin, starting on the face and spreading to the arms and legs and then to the hands and feet (Figure 4.7). Usually, the rash spreads to all parts of the body within 24 h. During this time, the lesions progress from macules to papules, then to pustular vesicles (a small round raised area of inflamed skin filled with pus). As the rash appears, the fever usually falls and the victim may start to feel better. However, fever often will rise again and remain high until scabs form over the bumps (U.S. CDC, 2007a). The scabs begin to fall off, leaving marks on the skin that eventually become pitted scars. Most scabs fall off within 3 weeks after the rash appears. The victim is contagious until all scabs have fallen off. Fatalities are usually caused by systemic toxicity and occur more frequently during the second week of illness.

Treatment

At the time of the last endemic cases in Somalia, supportive care was the only possible treatment. As is the case with all viral diseases, antibiotics have no effect on the progress of the disease.

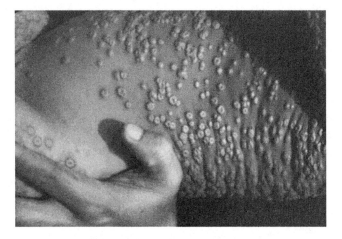

Figure 4.7 Smallpox lesions on skin of trunk. Picture taken in Bangladesh, 1973. Public Health Images Library (PHIL) ID # 284. (Courtesy of CDC/James Hicks, http://www.bt.cdc.gov/agent /smallpox/smallpox-images/smallpox2.htm.)

121

Smallpox vaccine, a live virus preparation derived from vaccinia virus (another member of the *Orthopoxvirus* genus), is highly effective in inducing immunity against the disease before exposure. Dryvax® is the vaccinia-based formulation currently licensed in the United States. Vaccinia preparations do not contain smallpox (variola) virus. The vaccine had previously been prepared using calf lymph tissue; however, a reformulated vaccine, produced using cell culture techniques, was subsequently developed. If administered within 3 days after exposure to smallpox virus, the vaccine may prevent the disease or decrease the severity of disease and the risk of death (U.S. CDC, 2007b).

Smallpox immunity is known to diminish over time. Few in the United States have been vaccinated since 1985; hence, only a small proportion of the population has any residual immunity to the disease. Since the September 11 terrorist attacks, only a few thousand persons have received the vaccine.

In some individuals, smallpox vaccination can result in undesirable reactions. The majority of adverse effects caused by the vaccine are mild complications that are resolved on their own. Serious reactions are rare but can be fatal. Two medications are available to help those with adverse reaction to the smallpox vaccine: vaccinia immune globulin (VIG) and cidofovir. VIG has been extensively used and concluded to be quite effective. Cidofovir is considered effective based on studies in animals. These treatments are investigational and may cause side effects (U.S. CDC, 2007a).

The potential effects of current antiviral drugs on the smallpox virus are unknown.

Biowarfare and Terrorism

Smallpox virus was researched as a weapon by the Soviet Union during their offensive biological program, and the status of former stockpiles is uncertain. Dr. Ken Alibek, a former official of the Soviet bioweapons program, asserts that Russia continues to research and manufacture biological weapons (Alibek and Handelman, 1999). The Soviet government in 1980 is reported to have begun an ambitious program to produce large volumes of smallpox virus and adapt it for payloads in intercontinental ballistic missiles. The program was known to have an industrial capacity capable of producing tons of smallpox virus annually. It is also reported that the Russian research program continues working to produce more virulent and contagious recombinant strains (Henderson et al., 1999). Many scientists in the Soviet bioweapons industry were put out of work when Russia officially discontinued its offensive biological weapons program in the 1990s, and there are concerns that some may be assisting rogue states working to develop their own biological weapons programs.

A single confirmed case of smallpox would constitute an international public health emergency and an international crime. Given the diminished immunity to the disease, there is potential for a global pandemic should smallpox become established. An aerosol release of variola virus would disseminate widely because of the stability of the orthopoxvirus in aerosol form (Harper, 1961), and the probability that the infectious dose is very small (Wehrle et al., 1970).

An occurrence of smallpox would require an immediate and coordinated public health, medical, and law enforcement response to control the outbreak and to protect the public from further spread. Any incidents of smallpox must be reported immediately to

Figure 4.8 Unloading supplies for Strategic National Stockpile. (Courtesy of Strategic National Stockpile SharePoint Site, https://www.orau.gov/sns/.)

public health authorities, local law enforcement, local emergency management officials, and the FBI. Medical personnel must be able to recognize multiple cases of vesicular rash and severe illness as the result of a deliberate attack with smallpox virus. Healthcare and other emergency response personnel must rapidly establish protocols to prevent spread of the disease. Anyone exposed to smallpox should be vaccinated immediately, including those individuals in contact with smallpox patients. Smallpox vaccine is available as a component of the Strategic National Stockpile (SNS) (Figure 4.8) (see Box 4.3). Persons who have had direct contact with a smallpox victim must be held in respiratory isolation for 17 days.

BOX 4.3   THE STRATEGIC NATIONAL STOCKPILE

An act of terrorism or a large-scale natural disaster affecting the U.S. population will require rapid access to large quantities of both medicines and medical supplies. Such quantities have been made readily available via the creation of dedicated stockpiles.

The CDC's SNS is equipped with an extensive inventory of pharmaceuticals and medical supplies to protect the American public in the event of a public health emergency (terrorist attack, flu outbreak, etc.) severe enough to cause local supplies to become depleted. Once federal and local authorities determine that the SNS is needed, medicines will be delivered to any state in the United States within 12 h. Each state has plans to receive and distribute SNS medicine and medical supplies to local communities as quickly as possible (U.S. CDC, 2009).

The SNS contains sufficient medicine to protect citizens in several large cities simultaneously. The medicine is free for all citizens, not only healthcare professionals and emergency responders.

In response to the potential use of biological agents against civilians, the federal government has formulated plans for preparedness, readiness, and national defense. The U.S. CDC has been designated as the lead agency for the national public health response to biological terrorism. The *Smallpox Response Plan and Guidelines* (U.S. CDC, 2007b) incorporates and expands many of the procedures that were successfully used decades ago to control smallpox outbreaks. These protocols for outbreak containment contributed greatly to the eventual global eradication of smallpox. The *Plan* includes criteria for implementation, notification procedures for suspected cases, CDC and state and local responsibilities and activities (including some that should take place before a smallpox emergency), and CDC vaccine and personnel mobilization (U.S. CDC, 2007b).

Ebola Hemorrhagic Fever

Ebola hemorrhagic fever is a disease of humans and other primates caused by ebolaviruses. The virus is a member of the family Filoviridae and the genus *Ebolavirus* with five strains including Ebola (*Zaire ebolavirus*), Sudan virus (*Sudan ebolavirus*), Tai Forest virus (*Tai Forest ebolavirus*), Bundibugyo virus (*Bundibugyo ebolavirus*), and Reston virus (*Reston ebolavirus*) (U.S. CDC, 2014b). Ebola is one of the most virulent viral diseases known, resulting in death in 20–90% of all clinically ill cases (WHO, 2015).

Ebola was first identified in 1976 in two simultaneous outbreaks, one in Nzara, Sudan, and the other in Yambuku, in modern-day Democratic Republic of the Congo, in a village near the Ebola River where the disease takes its name (WHO, 2015). Ebola viruses are currently found in several African countries. Since the 1976 occurrence, outbreaks have occurred sporadically in Africa.

The natural host of Ebola virus remains unknown. However, on the basis of experimental evidence and the nature of similar viruses, researchers believe that the virus is animal-borne and that bats are the most likely reservoir. Four of the five virus strains occur in an animal host native to Africa.

Unlike other outbreaks of similarly fatal diseases such as smallpox and plague, Ebola is not an airborne pathogen; instead, it spreads via infected fluids. The Ebola virus is transferred from one individual to another through contact with an infected victim's bodily fluids, including blood, saliva, vomit, stool, and semen. In addition, one may contract the virus via contact with infected equipment such as used needles or through the consumption of contaminated meat or contact with infected animals (U.S. CDC, 2014b).

Ebola made chilling headlines in 2013 and 2014 when it was revealed that the disease emerged and spread rapidly in a number of West African nations. As of mid-2015 the Ebola outbreak has left more than 11,000 dead in Guinea, Liberia, and Sierra Leone. More than 18 months after the outbreak began, Guinea and Sierra Leone continue to report new cases. In Liberia, the virus reemerged in June 2015, months after the country had been declared Ebola-free.

As a result of its virulence and catastrophic effects on the human body, the organism has figured prominently in discussions of biological warfare, although its practical applications as a biological warfare agent remain speculative.

Clinical Manifestations/Symptoms

The length of time between exposure to the virus and the development of symptoms is usually between 4 and 10 days but can take as long as 3 weeks or more (Goeijenbier et al., 2014; Haas, 2014; U.S. CDC, 2014b; WHO, 2015).

Symptoms begin with the rapid onset of an influenza-like phase characterized by fatigue, weakness, muscle and joint pain, headache, and fever (Gatherer, 2014; Goeijenbier et al., 2014; Magill et al., 2013; WHO, 2015). The fever often exceeds 101°F. The second stage involves vomiting, diarrhea, and sharp abdominal pain. Next, shortness of breath and chest pain may occur, along with swelling, headaches, and disorientation. In about half of the cases, the skin may develop a maculopapular rash, i.e., a flat red area covered with small bumps, 5 to 7 days after symptoms begin (Goeijenbier et al., 2014; Hoenen et al., 2006; Magill et al., 2013).

Infected victims experience decreased blood clotting. In some cases, internal and external bleeding occurs at about 5 to 7 days after the first appearance of symptoms. Bleeding from mucous membranes or from sites of needle punctures has been reported in nearly half of all cases, with resultant vomiting of blood, coughing up blood, or the appearance of blood in stool. Bleeding into the skin may create *petechiae* (i.e., purple spots or rashes). Bleeding into the whites of the eyes may also occur (Fisher-Hoch et al., 1985; Hoenen et al., 2006; King, 2015; Simpson, 1977; WHO, 2014).

Treatment

No specific treatment for the disease is available, although many potential treatments are under investigation. Treatment is primarily supportive. Early supportive care includes either oral rehydration therapy or administering intravenous fluids as well as treating symptoms (management of pain, nausea, fever, and anxiety). Blood products such as packed red blood cells, platelets, or fresh plasma may also be used. Other regulators of coagulation have also been attempted including heparin, and clotting factors to decrease bleeding. These efforts have been found to improve survival (Clark et al., 2012; WHO, 2014).

Vaccine

Many Ebola vaccine candidates had been developed and investigated over the past decade. The WHO announced in mid-2015 that a vaccine has shown great promise in halting the spread of the virus during clinical trials in Guinea (Phillip et al., 2015). The vaccine, VSV-EBOV, contains no live Ebola virus. Instead, it deploys a different virus, one that is alive and replicating, and has been modified to replace one of its genes with a single Ebola virus gene. The result is that the body's immune system has an Ebola-specific response and is better able to fight off an Ebola infection. The vaccine was found to be 100% effective in treated individuals (Phillip et al., 2015). More than 4000 have been vaccinated with VSV-EBOV, and none developed Ebola after 6 to 10 days, the amount of time needed for people to develop immunity.

Biowarfare and Terrorism

As a potential biological weapons agent, the Ebola virus is feared for its high case-fatality rate. Due to its rarity, the disease may not be diagnosed correctly at the onset of an outbreak. Reports suggest that the Ebola virus was researched and weaponized by the former Soviet Union's biological weapons program, Biopreparat. Dr. Ken Alibek, former First Deputy Director of Biopreparat, speculated that the Russians had aerosolized the Ebola virus for dissemination as a weapon (Alibek and Handelman, 1999). In the early 1990s, the Japanese terrorist group Aum Shinrikyo reportedly sent members to Zaire during an outbreak to harvest the virus.

BIOLOGICAL TOXINS

Toxic substances are produced by numerous bacteria, fungi, protozoa, plants, reptiles, amphibians, fish, mollusks, echinoderma (e.g., certain urchins and starfish), and insects. Some can be extracted and purified with relative ease, and some can be manufactured in the laboratory. Biological toxins are nonvolatile, are not dermally active (with the exception of mycotoxins), and tend to be more toxic per weight than many chemical warfare agents (USAMRIID, 2005). The LD_{50} (lethal dose to 50% of the exposed population) values of several biological toxins are shown in Table 4.1.

Some biological toxins have been identified by the intelligence community as biological warfare threats. The most probable routes of toxin entry from a terrorist attack are through the lungs by respirable aerosols and through the GI tract by contaminated food or water.

Table 4.1 LD_{50} Values of Selected Biological Toxins

Toxin	LD_{50}[a]	Toxin	LD_{50}
Abrin	0.7	Diphtheria toxin	0.1
Aerolysin	7.0	Listeriolysin	3–24
Botulinum toxin A	0.0012	Pertussis toxin	15–21
Botulinum toxin B	0.0012	*Pseudomonas aeruginosa* toxin A	3–14
Botulinum toxin C1	0.0011	Ricin	2.7
Botulinum toxin F	0.0025	Shiga toxin	0.5–20
b-Bungarotoxin	14.0	*Shigella dysenteriae* neurotoxin A	0.5–1.3
Cholera toxin	260	*Staphylococcus* enterotoxin B	20–25
Clostridium difficile enterotoxin A	0.5	*Staphylococcus* enterotoxin F	2–10
Clostridium perfringens lecithinase	3	Tetanus toxin	0.001
Clostridium perfringens enterotoxin	80	*Yersinia pestis* murine toxin	10
Clostridium perfringens beta toxin	0.3–0.4		

Source: Gill, D.M., *Microbiol. Rev.*, 46, 1, 86–94, 1982; Sweet, D.V. (Ed.), *Registry of the Toxic Effects of Chemical Substances, Microfiche Edition*, National Institute for Occupational Safety and Health, CAELEM Research Corporation, Silver Spring, MD, 1993; ChemCAS, *Free MSDS Search.* http://www.chemcas.com/.

[a] Oral (μg/kg body weight).

Ricin

Ricin is a highly toxic glycoprotein that occurs naturally in castor beans (*Ricinis communis*). The ricin molecule consists of two polypeptide chains, the A chain and the B chain, linked by a disulfide bond.

Ricin can be produced easily and inexpensively; it is highly toxic, stable in aerosolized form, and has no approved vaccine. Ricin can be disseminated as an aerosol, by injection, or as a contaminant in food or water. The toxin is not communicable from person to person, however.

One of the more notorious incidents involving ricin intoxication in recent years is the case of Georgi Markov, a Bulgarian dissident. Markov was assassinated in 1978 at a London bus stop. Agents of the Soviet KGB are believed to have used a modified umbrella equipped with a compressed gas cylinder to fire a tiny ricin pellet into Markov's leg (Figure 4.9). After the injection, he developed severe gastroenteritis and high fever, and died in a hospital a few days later. His body was autopsied and the ricin pellet was discovered. The initial suspects were the Bulgarian secret police; Markov had defected from Bulgaria and written books that were highly critical of the Bulgarian communist regime. Later, however, some high-profile KGB defectors confirmed the involvement of the Soviet KGB in the assassination.

Clinical Manifestations

Ricin is highly toxic to cells and acts by inhibiting protein synthesis. The B chain binds to cell surface receptors and the toxin–receptor complex is taken into the cell. The A chain has endonuclease activity, and extremely low concentrations will inhibit protein synthesis (USAMRIID, 2005).

The effects of ricin poisoning are a function of route and quantity of exposure. Aerosol exposure results in weakness, fever, and pulmonary edema within 18–24 h, and severe respiratory distress and death within 36–72 h. Death via inhalation appears to be caused by *hypoxemia* resulting from massive pulmonary edema and alveolar flooding (Franz and Jaax, 1996). In rodents, aerosol exposure is characterized by necrotizing airway lesions causing tracheitis, bronchitis, bronchiolitis, and interstitial pneumonia with perivascular and alveolar edema (Mirarchi, 2008). The LD_{50} for aerosol exposure to ricin is 2.7 µg/kg. If ingested in sufficient amounts ricin can cause severe gastroenteritis; GI hemorrhage; and hepatic, splenic, and renal necrosis. The LD_{50} for GI exposure is 30 µg/kg. There

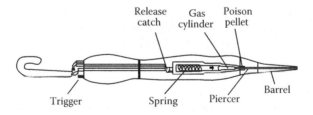

Figure 4.9 Representation of the umbrella-concealed device used to kill Georgi Markov.

127

is disagreement as to the toxic potential from ingestion of multiple castor bean seeds (Mirarchi, 2008). Puncture (parenteral) exposures can cause severe local necrosis of muscle and regional lymph nodes. Injected ricin is rapidly fatal, with an LD_{50} similar to that of aerosol exposure. Dermal exposure of ricin is a minor concern because the amounts absorbed through the skin tend to be quite low. Dermal exposure probably is unable to achieve toxicity.

Treatment

Treatment of ricin poisoning depends on the route of exposure. Treatment is supportive; no antidote is currently available for ricin. In the case of aerosol exposure, treatment should be directed toward acute lung injury and pulmonary edema. It is critical to ensure adequate oxygenation and ventilation for the patient. For GI exposure, the GI tract should be decontaminated (i.e., *lavaged*) with superactivated charcoal. For exposure via puncture, the injection site should be excised, if possible, within the shortest amount of time. Antibiotics may help prevent infection. For dermal exposure, a dilute sodium hypochlorite solution or soap and water will serve to decontaminate the skin. Investigations are underway with potential vaccines and ricin inhibitors as antidotes.

Biowarfare and Terrorism

Ricin can be disseminated as an aerosol, by injection, or as a food and water contaminant. A large quantity of ricin is necessary to produce the effects of a weapon of mass destruction, however. For example, the amount of ricin necessary to cover a 100-km^2 area and cause 50% lethality, assuming an aerosol toxicity of 3 µg/kg and optimum dispersal conditions, is approximately 4 metric tons, whereas only 1 kg of *B. anthracis* will cause the same damage (Kortepeter and Parker, 1999; Mirarchi, 2008). Ricin would, however, be effective as a disabling agent. If used as a food and water contaminant, ricin could easily incapacitate many and overwhelm local healthcare resources.

The U.S. military investigated the potential of ricin as a weapon during World War I. At that time, it was being considered for use either as a toxic dust or as a coating for bullets. The dust cloud method could not be perfected by war's end, and the coated bullet method would have violated The Hague Convention of 1899. During World War II, the U.S. military studied the use of ricin in cluster bombs. Although there were plans for mass production and several field trials with different bomb concepts, it was eventually concluded that ricin was no more economical than using phosgene. Ricin was given the military symbol W and later WA. Interest in ricin continued for a short period after World War II but diminished when the U.S. Army Chemical Corps began a program to weaponize sarin. Ricin was never used in battle (Cookson and Nottingham, 1969; Franz and Jaax, 1996).

Although ricin is easy to produce, it is neither as practical nor likely to cause as many casualties as other agents. Ricin becomes inactivated (i.e., its polypeptide chains become denatured, thus becoming less dangerous) much more readily than anthrax spores, which may remain lethal for decades. It is known that al-Qaeda experimented with ricin, which has been interpreted as an inability by their weapons makers to produce and/or weaponize botulin or anthrax.

AGROTERRORISM

Agricultural terrorism (agroterrorism) is considered by many scientists and policy makers to be a subset of biological terrorism. Agroterrorism is defined by U.S. Federal Emergency Management Agency (2005) as follows:

> the malicious use of plant or animal pathogens to cause devastating disease in the agricultural sector. It may also take the form of hoaxes and threats intended to create public fear of such events.

Acts of agroterrorism may involve contamination of livestock, food crops, and processed foods, and the results can be as catastrophic as other forms of terrorism. The most dangerous mode of agroterrorism is via introduction of pest organisms which may devastate a commercial source of food. Effects from an attack on crops, livestock, or food supplies would be both short- and long-term and include the following:

- Extensive deaths and illness.
- Paralyzes the economy of a nation or region.
- Destroys the livelihood of many citizens.
- The disease may not be detected until it reaches levels that are difficult to control.
- Puts food supply at risk, perhaps for long periods.

Many consider agriculture to be an ideal target for terrorism because of the size of the industry's revenues and its breadth across a nation. The United States is a global leader in food production, and an attack on any segment of the food industry would have disastrous effects on the entire national economy. The magnitude of such damage can be seen from the following data (USDA, 2009):

- The farm sector is the largest contributor to the U.S. trade balance.
- The United States produces nearly 50% of the world's soybeans, more than 40% of its corn, 20% of its cotton, 12% of its wheat, and more than 16% of its meat.
- Approximately 2.2 million farms exist in the United States, totaling more than 920 million acres.

A number of interrelated consequences would contribute to severe financial losses at local to national levels, including (Figure 4.10) (Parker, 2002):

- Direct losses of agricultural commodities to disease
- Decline in sales of agricultural products from diminished consumer confidence
- Costs of diagnosis and surveillance
- Destruction of contaminated crops and animals to contain the disease
- Costs of disposal of animal carcasses

Figure 4.10 Introduction of a pathogen to an agricultural system could result in severe economic consequences. (Courtesy of U.S. Department of Agriculture. 2002. Keeping cattle cool makes sense. http://agresearchmag.ars.usda.gov/2002/jul/cattle.)

- Losses due to export and trade restrictions
- Disruption of commodity markets
- Insurance costs

Threats

Agricultural diseases have evolved to remain viable in soil for months to years in spite of exposure to ultraviolet light, heat, lack of moisture, and other stressful conditions. Thus, they are highly resilient in the natural environment and are expected to persist in storage as well. In addition, the supplies and equipment necessary to carry out an agroterror attack are relatively easy to obtain (Kohnen, 2000). Small quantities may be needed, for example, of a specific livestock pathogen that would be relatively simple to transport to the site of intended use. Infection of a small number of animals may be sufficient to cause a disease outbreak. An epidemic could be caused by placing bird droppings contaminated with Newcastle disease into a feeding trough, or by placing oral scrapings from an FMD-infected animal onto the floor of a cattle barn (U.S. FEMA, 2005).

Animal Diseases

Over many decades, a wide range of diseases were weaponized by the United States, the former Soviet Union, China, Iraq, and other countries. The scientific expertise and technology for developing such weapons on a large scale have been available for more than a century. There are approximately 150 diseases of concern within the livestock disease category alone. Animal pathogens known to have been weaponized or pursued for weaponization potential are shown below.

Animal pathogens pursued for weaponization purposes (U.S. CDC, 2005)

- African swine fever
- Anthrax
- Foot and mouth disease
- Hog cholera/classical swine fever
- Ornithosis/psittacocis
- Rinderpest
- Trypanosomiasis
- Poxvirus
- Ebola virus
- Marburg virus
- Rift Valley virus
- *Bacillus anthracis*
- *Burcella melitensis*
- *Burkholderia mallei*
- *Francisella tularensis*
- *Yersinia pestis*

The most successful agriculture biological warfare program was developed by the former Soviet Union, where a wide range of animal pathogens were studied. The Soviets successfully used ticks to transmit FMD and avian ticks to transmit ornithosis to chickens (Ban, 2006). Disease organisms believed to have been weaponized by the former Soviet Union are shown below.

Disease organisms believed to have been weaponized by the former Soviet Union (U.S. FEMA, 2005)

- African swine fever
- Anthrax
- Avian influenza
- Brown grass mosaic
- Brucellosis
- Contagious bovine pleuropneumonia
- Contagious ecthyma (sheep)
- Foot and mouth disease
- Glanders
- Maize rust
- Newcastle disease
- Potato virus
- Psittacosis
- Rice blast
- Rinderpest
- Rye blast
- Tobacco mosaic
- Venezuelan equine encephalitis
- Vesicular stomatitis

- Wheat and barley mosaic streak
- Wheat stem rust

Plant Pathogens

Plant pathogens typically occur as fungi and, to a lesser extent, as viruses and bacteria. Plant pathogens usually kill or injure a particular crop species; however, in some unusual cases, the disease may produce toxins that can be harmful to humans.

Plant pathogens known to have been weaponized include:

- Rice blast (*Mangaporthe grisea*)
- Wheat stem Rust (*Puccinia graminis* f.sp. *triciti*)
- Wheat smut (*Fusarium graminearum*)

Additional plant pathogens that have the potential for weaponization are shown in Table 4.2.

Rice and wheat are two cereal crops that supply the majority of the world's daily intake of calories. A disease event involving either of these crops, whether by natural outbreak or from terrorist activity, would have significant social, political, and economic consequences.

Rice blast is a destructive disease of rice as well as a number of other agriculturally important cereals including wheat, rye, barley, and pearl millet (Knowledgebank, 2005). The disease is particularly damaging to upland rice crops (Figure 4.11). A fungus, *Magnaporthe grisea*, is responsible for the disease, which is known to occur in 85 countries worldwide. Rice blast is widespread and causes severe economic losses—each year, it is estimated to destroy enough rice to feed more than 50 million people.

During World War II, *M. grisea* spores were prepared as a biological weapon by the United States and the USSR. The U.S. Chemical Warfare Service is known to have researched

Table 4.2 Selected Plant Pathogens That Have Potential for Weaponization

Crop	Pathogen
Wheat	Wheat dwarf (*Geminivirus*)
	Barley yellow dwarf virus (*Pseudomonas fascovaginaei*)
Corn (maize)	Barley yellow dwarf virus (*Pseudomonas fascovaginaei*)
	Brown stripe mildew (*Sclerophthora rayssiae*)
	Sugarcane downy mildew (*Peronosclerospora sacchari*)
	Java downy mildew (*Peronosclerospora maydis*)
Soybean	Soybean dwarf virus (*Luteovirus*)
	Red leaf blotch (*Pyrenochaeta glycines*)

Source: Parker, H.S., Agricultural Bioterrorism: A Federal Strategy to Meet the Threat, McNair Paper 65, National Defense University, March, 2002. http://www.ndu.edu/inss/McNair/mcnair65/McN_65.pdf; Steele, N., Econoterrorism: U.S. Agricultural Productivity, Concentration, and Vulnerability to Biological Weapons, Unclassified Defense Intelligence Assessment for DOD Futures Intelligence Program, January 14, 2000.

Figure 4.11 Typical eye-shaped lesion of rice blast disease on a U.S. rice cultivar inoculated with *Magnaporthe grisea*. (Courtesy of U.S. Department of Agriculture. 2008. Markers for Rice Blast Resistance Discovered. Alfredo Flores. Agricultural Research Service, http://www.ars.usda.gov/is /pr/2008/080912.htm.)

the agent for use against Japan's rice crop during the war (Croddy and Wirtz, 2005). The United States worked with Canadian and British scientists to weaponize rice blast, but it was not ready for use by war's end (Levy, 2000).

Karnal bunt, a fungal disease of wheat, was first discovered in wheat-growing areas of India in 1931. It has subsequently been located in all major wheat-growing areas in India, Pakistan, Iraq, Afghanistan, and South Africa. The disease was introduced to Mexico in 1960, and by 1996 Karnal bunt was found in the United States in Arizona. The disease does not severely impact crop production; however, because of international regulations, an outbreak of Karnal bunt would significantly restrict export of wheat overseas. The U.S. Department of Agriculture conducts an annual national survey to certify the U.S. wheat crop is free from Karnal bunt (USDA, 2006).

Transmission of Plant Pathogens
Fungi, viruses, and bacteria that cause crop diseases can be transmitted by the following methods (U.S. FEMA, 2005):

- *Airborne*—Most fungal diseases are carried by the wind, possibly over great distances. Spores also readily attach to surfaces (packaging, farm equipment, clothing, etc.). It is difficult to eradicate spores from infected areas, and once-productive land may have to be abandoned as *useless* for long periods.
- *Vectors*—Both viruses and bacteria can be spread by insect vectors. Diseases that depend on vectors spread slowly because transmission depends on the movement of the insect hosts.
- *Water-borne*—Bacteria typically spread in moist materials and environments.

Zoonotic Diseases

Zoonotic diseases are those transferred from animals to man or from man to animals. Approximately 150 such diseases are known to exist (University of Minnesota, 2005). Zoonotic diseases are of significant concern to U.S. public and animal health sectors. The recent emergence of avian influenza and West Nile virus demonstrates the vulnerability of industrialized nations to the spread of zoonotic diseases, and the general inability to contain such diseases once they become established in wild animal populations.

Indicators of an Agroterrorism Event

The indicators of an agroterrorism event might not appear for days or weeks. Certain patterns may appear to alert veterinarians, healthcare providers, and other public health professionals of the intentional release of an infectious disease (Moore, 2002):

- Unusual clustering of illness or mortality in a particular region or within a short span of time for large numbers of animals or humans. This may include atypical, unexplained symptoms.
- Symptoms occurring in an area where a particular disease is extremely rare.
- Normally healthy individuals becoming suddenly ill.
- An unusual age distribution for common diseases.
- A disease occurring outside its typical season.

Response to a Disease Event

Response to agroterror events is different from responses to human disease events in a number of ways. The primary intent of response to an agricultural disease event is to contain and destroy the disease by isolating the infected crops or animals. This usually includes destruction of the crops and euthanasia of the animals involved. Emergency responders may be involved in the containment, eradication, and/or quarantine enforcement to limit the spread of agricultural diseases.

Responders must remain alert to the hazards presented by an agricultural disease event. Many such diseases can affect humans as well as animals. A number can be life-threatening, and can be passed along to other persons once contracted or if proper decontamination procedures are not followed. The following steps in response can be applied to agroterrorism events as well as other chemical, biological, radiological, nuclear, and explosive events:

- *Recognize*—Recognize the indicators of an agricultural disease event.
- *Avoid*—Practice avoidance measures to prevent the accidental exposure or spread of the disease.
- *Isolate*—Isolation or quarantine procedures are essential in the control and eradication of a disease.
- *Notify*—Know whom to call at the first possible indications of a disease event so that the identification and response process can begin.

QUESTIONS

1. Would the sealing of windows with duct tape and plastic sheeting help protect you in your home during a bioterrorist attack with anthrax spores? Explain.
2. What regulations or guidance documents exist that would help with investigation and development of safe and effective new products that might be used in countering bioterrorism? Check the FDA.gov web site.
3. What is the most effective route for dispersal of a biological agent to enter a target population?
4. What atmospheric properties might affect migration of an aerosol plume (cloud) of biological agent? Consider barometric pressure, wind, moisture, etc.
5. Explain the difference between an *infectious* disease and a *contagious* disease.
6. Any identification of smallpox outbreak should be considered an international emergency, and most likely a terrorist event. True or false? Explain.
7. Could biological agents be effective in contaminating large water supplies (e.g., reservoirs)? Discuss.
8. List and discuss two possible indicators of a terrorist biological attack.
9. Define or discuss the following terms: edema, eschar, mediastinitis.

REFERENCES

Aleccia, J. 2014. Smallpox vials discovered in lab Storage room, CDC Says. NBC News. http://www.nbcnews.com/health/health-news/smallpox-vials-discovered-lab-storage-room-cdc-says-n150806.

Alibek, K., and S. Handelman. 1999. *Biohazard: The Chilling True Story of the Largest Covert Biological Weapons Program in the World—Told from inside by the Man Who Ran It*. New York: Random House.

Ban, J. 2006. Agricultural biological warfare: An overview. *The Arena* 9: 1–8.

BBC. 2002. Death sentence for China poisoning. September 30, 2002. BBC News. http://news.bbc.co.uk/2/hi/asia-pacific/2287801.stm (accessed October 26, 2010).

Brook, I., T.B. Elliott, H.I. Pryor, T.E. Sautter, B.T. Gnade, J.H. Thakar, and G.B. Knudson. 2001. In vitro resistance of *Bacillus anthracis* Sterne to doxycycline, macrolides and quinolones. *International Journal of Antimicrobial Agents* 18: 559–62.

Center for Nonproliferation Studies. 2014. Former Soviet Biological Weapons Facilities in Kazakhstan: Past, Present, and Future. James Martin Center for Nonproliferation Studies. http://cns.miis.edu/opapers/op1/op1.htmC.

ChemCAS. 2010. Free MSDS Search. http://www.chemcas.com/ (accessed August 18, 2010).

Clark, D.V., P.B. Jahrling, and J.V. Lawler. 2012. Clinical management of filovirus-infected patients. *Viruses* 4(9): 1668–86.

CNN Staff and Wires. 2002. Death sentence over Chinese poisonings. September 30, 2002. CNN News. http://edition.cnn.com/2002/WORLD/asiapcf/east/09/30/china.poison/ (accessed October 26, 2010).

Cookson, J., and J. Nottingham. 1969. A survey of chemical and biological warfare. *Monthly Review Press*. 6.

Croddy, E., and J.J. Wirtz. 2005. *Weapons of Mass Destruction: An Encyclopedia of Worldwide Policy, Technology, and History*. Santa Barbara, CA: ABC-CLIO.

Dixon, T.C., M. Meselson, J. Guillemin, and P.C. Hanna. 1999. Anthrax. *New England Journal of Medicine* 341: 815–826.

Fisher-Hoch, S.P., G.S. Platt, G.H. Neild, T. Southee, A. Baskerville, R.T. Raymond, G. Lloyd, and D.I. Simpson. 1985. Pathophysiology of shock and hemorrhage in a fulminating viral infection (Ebola). *Journal of Infectious Diseases* 152(5): 887–894.

Fong, K., and L. Alibek. 2005. *Bioterrorism and Infectious Agents: A New Dilemma for the 21st Century.* New York: Springer-Verlag.

Franz, D.R., and N.K. Jaax. 1996. Ricin toxin. In *Medical Aspects of Chemical and Biological Warfare*, eds. F.R. Sidell, E.T. Takafuji, and D.R. Franz. Washington, D.C.: Borden Institute Walter Reed Army Medical Center, pp. 631–642.

Gatherer, D. 2014. The 2014 Ebola virus disease outbreak in West Africa. *Journal of General Virology* 95(8): 1619–1624.

Gill, D.M. 1982. Bacterial toxins: A table of lethal amounts. *Microbiological Reviews* 46(1): 86–94.

Goeijenbier, M., J.J. van Kampen, C.B. Reusken, M.P. Koopmans, and E.C. van Gorp. 2014. Ebola virus disease: A review on epidemiology, symptoms, treatment and pathogenesis. *Netherlands Journal of Medicine* 72(9): 442–448.

Haas, C.N. 2014. On the quarantine period for Ebola virus. *PLOS Currents Outbreaks.* http://currents .plos.org/outbreaks/article/on-the-quarantine-period-for-ebola-virus/.

Harper, G.J. 1961. Airborne micro-organisms: Survival test with four viruses. *Journal of Hygiene* 59: 479–486.

Henderson, D.A., T.V. Inglesby, J.G. Bartlett, M.S. Ascher, P.B. Jahrling, J. Hauer, M. Layton, J. McDade, M.T. Osterholm, T. O'Toole, G. Parker, T. Perl, P.K. Russell, and K. Tonat. 1999. Smallpox as a biological weapon. Medical and public health management. *Journal of the American Medical Association* 281: 2127–2137.

Hoenen, T., A. Groseth, D. Falzarano, and H. Feldmann. 2006. Ebola virus: Unravelling pathogenesis to combat a deadly disease. *Trends in Molecular Medicine* 12(5): 206–215.

Hunt, R. 1918. Ricin. American University Experiment Station. Chemical Warfare Monograph 37, Washington, D.C., pp. 107–117.

Jaax, N.K., and D.L. Fritz. 1997. Anthrax. In *Pathology of Infectious Diseases*, eds. D.H. Connor, F.W. Chandler, H.J. Manz, D.A. Schwartz, and E.E. Lack, 397–406. Stamford, CT: Appleton and Lange.

King, J.W. 2015. Ebola virus infection clinical presentation. Medscape. http://emedicine.medscape .com/article/216288-clinical#showall (accessed September 30, 2015).

Knowledgebank. 2005. Rice blast. http://www.knowledgebank.irri.org/riceDoctor_MX/Fact_Sheets /Diseases/Rice_Blast.htm (accessed October 26, 2010).

Kohnen, A. 2000. *Responding to the Threat of Agroterrorism: Specific Recommendations for the U.S. Department of Agriculture.* BCSIA Discussion Paper 2000–29, ESDP Discussion Paper ESDP-2000-04, John F. Kennedy School of Government, Harvard University, Cambridge, MA, October 2000.

Kortepeter, M.G., and G.W. Parker. 1999. Potential biological weapons threats. *U.S. Army Medical Research Institute of Infectious Diseases* 5(4): 523–527.

Levy, B.S. 2000. *War and Public Health.* Washington, D.C.: American Public Health Association.

Magill, A., E.T. Ryan, T. Solomon, and D.R. Hill. 2013. *Hunter's Tropical Medicine and Emerging Infectious Diseases.* New York: Elsevier Health Sciences.

Meselson, M.J., J. Guillemin, and M. Hugh-Jones. 1994. The Sverdlovsk anthrax outbreak of 1979. *Science* 266(5188): 1202–1208.

Miller, S.E., and W. Broad. 2001. *Germs: Biological Weapons and America's Secret War,* New York: Simon and Schuster.

Mirarchi, F.L. CBRNE—Ricin. February 14, 2008. http://emedicine.medscape.com/article/830795 -overview (accessed November 10, 2008).

Moore, D.H. 2002. Zoonotic diseases, bioterrorism and agroterrorism: Prevention by preparedness. *The ASA Newsletter.* http://www.asanltr.com/newsletter/04-4/articles/044a.htm.

National Institutes of Health, National Institute of Allergy and Infectious Diseases. 2007. Anthrax. http://www3.niaid.nih.gov/healthscience/healthtopics/anthrax/overview.htm (accessed October 26, 2010).

National Security Archive. 2001. *Volume V. Anthrax at Sverdlovsk, 1979. U.S. Intelligence on the Deadliest Modern Outbreak*. National Security Archive Electronic Briefing Book No. 61, eds. R.A. Wampler and T.S. Blanton. November 15, 2001.

Neergaard, L. 2014. Forgotten vials of ricin, smallpox and plague uncovered in NIH labs review. PBS News hour. http://www.pbs.org/newshour/rundown/forgotten-vials-ricin-smallpox-plague -uncovered-nih-labs-review/.

Parker, H.S. 2002. *Agricultural Bioterrorism: A Federal Strategy to Meet the Threat*, McNair Paper 65, National Defense University, March 2002. http://www.au.af.mil/au/awc/awcgate/ndu/mcnair65 .pdf.

Phillip, A., S. Larimer, and J. Achenbach. 2015. Ebola vaccine appears to be highly effective, could be 'a game-changer.' *Washington Post*. July 31. http://www.washingtonpost.com /news/to-your-health/wp/2015/07/31/ebola-vaccine-appears-to-be-highly-effective -could-be-a-game-changer/.

Pomerantsev, A.P., N.A. Shishkova, and L.I. Marinin. 1992. Comparison of therapeutic effects of antibiotics of the tetracycline group in the treatment of anthrax caused by a strain inheriting tet-gene of plasmid pBC16. *Antibiotiki i Khimioterapiia* 37: 31–4.

Price, L.B., A. Volger, T. Pearson, J.D. Busch, J.M. Schupp, and P. Keim. 2003. In vitro selection and characterization of *Bacillus anthracis* mutants with high-level resistance to ciprofloxacin. *Antimicrobial Agents and Chemotherapy* 47: 2362–2365.

Robertson, A.G., and L.J. Robertson. 1995. From asps to allegations: Biological warfare in history. *Military Medicine* 160(8): 369–372.

Simpson, D.I.H. 1977. Marburg and Ebola virus infections: A guide for their diagnosis, management, and control. *WHO Offset Publication* 36: 10f.

Sirisanthana, T., and A.E. Brown. 2002. Anthrax of the gastrointestinal tract. Perspectives. http://www .cdc.gov/ncidod/eid/vol8no7/02–0062.htm (accessed October 26, 2010).

Smart, J.K. 1996. *History of Chemical and Biological Warfare Fact Sheets*. Special Study 50. Aberdeen Proving Ground, MD: U.S. Army Chemical and Biological Defense Command.

Smart, J.K. 1997. History of chemical and biological warfare: An American perspective. In *Medical Aspects of Chemical and Biological Warfare*, eds. F.R. Sidell, E.T. Takafuji, and D.R. Franz. Washington, D.C.: Borden Institute Walter Reed Army Medical Center.

Steele, N. 2000. *Econoterrorism: U.S. Agricultural Productivity, Concentration, and Vulnerability to Biological Weapons*. Unclassified Defense Intelligence Assessment for DOD Futures Intelligence Program, January 14, 2000.

Stockholm International Peace Research Institute. 1971. *The Rise of CB Weapons. Vol. 1. In: The Problem of Chemical and Biological Warfare*. New York: Humanities Press.

Sweet, D.V. (Ed.). 1993. *Registry of the Toxic Effects of Chemical Substances, Microfiche Edition*. Silver Spring, MD: CAELEM Research Corporation, National Institute for Occupational Safety and Health.

University of Minnesota. 2005. Health concerns to be aware of when working with wildlife (a.k.a.—Zoonoses). http://www.tc.umn.edu/~devo0028/zoonos.htm (accessed October 26, 2010).

U.S. Army. 1945. *Scientific and Technical Advisory Section, US Army Forces, Pacific. Biological warfare*. Volume 5. In Report on Scientific Intelligence Survey in Japan. HQ, U.S. Army Forces, Pacific, 1945.

U.S. Army Medical Research Institute of Infectious Diseases. 2005. *USAMRIID's Medical Management of Biological Casualties Handbook*. 6th Edition. April 2005. Fort Detrick, Frederick, MD.

U.S. Centers for Disease Control and Prevention. 2003. Nicotine poisoning after ingestion of contaminated ground beef—Michigan, 2003. *Morbidity and Mortality Weekly Report*. 52(18): 413–416.

U.S. Centers for Disease Control and Prevention. 2005. Bioterrorism agents/diseases. Emergency preparedness and response. http://www.bt.cdc.gov/agent/agentlist-category.asp (accessed October 26, 2010).

U.S. Centers for Disease Control and Prevention. 2007a. Smallpox fact sheet—Information for clinicians and public health professionals. Medical management of smallpox (vaccinia) vaccine adverse reactions: Vaccinia immune globulin and cidofovir. http://www.bt.cdc.gov/agent /smallpox/vaccination/mgmtadv-reactions.asp (accessed October 26, 2010).

U.S. Centers for Disease Control and Prevention. 2007b. Smallpox response plan and guidelines. http:// www.bt.cdc.gov/agent/smallpox/response-plan/files/exec-sections-i-vi.doc (accessed October 26, 2010).

U.S. Centers for Disease Control and Prevention. 2008. Anthrax. Atlanta, GA. http://www.cdc.gov /nczved/dfbmd/disease_listing/anthrax_gi.html (accessed October 26, 2010).

U.S. Centers for Disease Control and Prevention. 2009. Strategic national stockpile. http://www .bt.cdc.gov/stockpile/ (accessed October 26, 2010).

U.S. Centers for Disease Control and Prevention. 2014a. CDC Media Statement on Newly Discovered Smallpox Specimens. http://www.cdc.gov/media/releases/2014/s0708-nih.html (accessed October 17, 2014).

U.S. Centers for Disease Control and Prevention. 2014b. Ebola Virus Disease: Signs and Symptoms. http://www.cdc.gov/vhf/ebola/symptoms/index.html (accessed October 15, 2014).

U.S. Centers for Disease Control and Prevention. n.d. Bioterrorism agents/diseases. http://www.bt .cdc.gov/agent/agentlist-category.asp (accessed October 26, 2010).

U.S. Department of Agriculture. 2006. Karmal bunt: A fungal disease of wheat. Plant protection and quarantine. http://www.aphis.usda.gov/research/atlas02/pdf/02-moo1-RGBDot1-largetext .pdf (accessed October 26, 2010).

U.S. Department of Agriculture. 2009. *Census of Agriculture*. Volume 1, Geographic Area Series. Part 51. AC-07-A-51. December 2009. http://www.agcensus.usda.gov/Publications/2007/Full_Report /usv1.pdf (accessed October 26, 2010).

U.S. Federal Emergency Management Agency. 2005. Appendix E: Agriterrorism. Toolkit for managing the emergency consequences of terrorist incidents. http://fema.gov/pdf/onp/toolkit _app_e.pdf (accessed October 26, 2010).

U.S. Food and Drug Administration. 2015. FDA approves treatment for inhalation anthrax. FDA News Release March 25, 2015. http://www.fda.gov/NewsEvents/Newsroom/PressAnnounce ments/ucm439752.htm.

UTDallas. E-Plan—Emergency Response Information System. Biological Agent Information Papers. https://erplan.net/WMD/BioFiles/Links/BiologicalAgents/FactSheets/FS.htm (accessed March 7, 2010).

Wehrle, P.F., J. Posch, K.H. Richter, and D.A. Henderson. 1970. An airborne outbreak of smallpox in a German hospital and its significance with respect to other recent outbreaks in Europe. *Bulletin of the World Health Organization* 43: 669–679.

Williams, P., and D. Wallace. 1989. *Unit 731: Japan's Secret Biological Warfare in World War II*. New York: The Free Press, pp. 13–30.

World Health Organization. 2015. Ebola virus disease. Fact sheet No. 103. Media Centre. http:// www.who.int/mediacentre/factsheets/fs103/en/.

5

Nuclear and Radiological Hazards

These atomic bombs which science burst upon the world that night were strange even to the men who used them.

H.G. Wells, 1914

That is the biggest fool thing we have ever done. The atomic bomb will never go off, and I speak as an expert in explosives.

Admiral William D. Leahy, commenting to President Harry S. Truman, 1945

Malicious acts involving nuclear or other radioactive material are a continuing worldwide threat.

IAEA, 2008

INTRODUCTION

Nuclear weapons are by far the most powerful of all weapons of mass destruction (WMDs). The detonation of a nuclear device by a terrorist group would result in catastrophic physical effects, including blast overpressure, thermal effects, and radiation contamination, and also cause tremendous psychological impacts worldwide.

During the Cold War between the United States and the Soviet Union (late 1940s to early 1990s), the nations of the world lived with the constant threat of nuclear war. With the end of the Cold War came the hope that the nuclear arsenals stockpiled by these and other countries would eventually be dismantled. Unfortunately, however, international terrorist organizations have been attempting to gain access to WMDs, including nuclear weapons, by trying to recruit nuclear weapon scientists. In addition, several nuclear nations still pose a military threat to others.

NUCLEAR WEAPONS

Nuclear weapons are designed and constructed based on two unstable materials, uranium and plutonium.

The uranium-based weapons are not manufactured directly from this metal; the naturally occurring mineral must be enriched before it is usable in a weapon. Enrichment processes are costly and extremely complex; therefore, only large national institutes or industries possess the resources needed to carry out enrichment and weapon fabrication. In other words, a terrorist group is unlikely to engage in such activities without being detected. Plutonium does not exist in nature and is only produced within a nuclear reactor, which is another complex technology limited solely to large-scale enterprises.

As a consequence of these limitations, a terrorist organization can acquire a nuclear weapon only by limited means, including the following:

- Obtaining an intact nuclear weapon from a national stockpile
- Obtaining fissile material from stocks produced in industrial facilities and then converting the fissile material into a nuclear weapon

The most important and effective steps for reducing the threat of nuclear terrorism are therefore to secure, consolidate, reduce, and, where possible, eliminate nuclear weapons and fissile material. Programs to implement such measures are under way in many countries but are far from reaching their goals (NTI, n.d.).

HISTORY OF NUCLEAR AND RADIOLOGICAL WEAPONS

Early in the twentieth century, the science of physics achieved remarkable advances; much was discovered regarding the nature of atoms and their behavior. In the late 1800s at the University of Wurzburg (Germany), Wilhelm Konrad Roentgen conducted experiments involving high voltage currents in vacuum tubes and in 1895 discovered x-rays. In 1898, Pierre and Marie Skladowska Curie discovered a new substance occurring within pitchblende (an ore of uranium) that emitted massive amounts of energy (this energy was later to be termed *radioactivity*). The work of the Curies led to the discovery of polonium in 1896 and radium in 1897. Different types of radioactive emissions were soon identified; in 1899, Henri Becquerel found that some radiation emissions were electrically charged. British chemist and physicist Ernest Rutherford went on to distinguish two types of charged emissions—alpha and beta. He demonstrated that alpha particles were actually helium atoms minus their planetary electrons. In 1900, Paul Villard, a French physicist, identified gamma rays, which were determined to be uncharged waves of electromagnetic radiation.

Experiments by Rutherford in 1911 indicated that the vast majority of an atom's mass is concentrated within the center, or nucleus, and is composed of protons surrounded by a cloud of electrons. In 1932, James Chadwick discovered that the nucleus contained another fundamental particle, later termed the *neutron* because of its lack of electrical charge.

Also in 1932, John Cockcroft and Ernest Walton (English and Irish physicists, respectively) were the first scientists known to have split the atom, and by late 1933 Hungarian physicist Leo Szilard conceived the idea of using a *chain reaction* of neutron collisions with

140

atomic nuclei to release energy. He also realized the potential of using this chain reaction to make bombs. In 1934, Szilard received a patent for the atomic bomb, although he had no intentions of pursuing such a weapon; rather, his intent was to protect the concept of the bomb to prevent its destructive use. He offered his theory to the British government so that it could be made classified and protected under British secrecy laws. The British War Office rejected Szilard's offer; however, a few months later in February 1936, he succeeded in getting the British Admiralty to safeguard the new discovery (Atomicarchive, 2008a).

Nuclear *fission* (splitting) was documented in December 1938, when German chemists Otto Hahn and Fritz Strassmann reported that they had detected the element barium after bombarding uranium with neutrons (Hahn and Strassmann, 1939). On January 25, 1939, a research team at Columbia University conducted the first nuclear fission experiment in the United States (Anderson et al., 1939).

World War II

With the start of World War II, many of Europe's most distinguished physicists fled the continent. Scientists now understood that nuclear fission could be used in a weapon; however, no one had yet determined how this could be accomplished. There was a sense of alarm among scientists of the Allied nations that Nazi Germany might develop its own project to create fission-based weapons. Urgent research began in the United States and Britain with the intention of beating Hitler in the race to construct the bomb. By 1942, the U.S. nuclear program was placed under the supervision of a military team led by General Leslie Groves and became known as the Manhattan Project. Led by the American physicist Robert Oppenheimer (Figure 5.1), the project brought together top scientific minds including many European exiles. The United States and Britain agreed to combine their resources for the project; however, the Soviet Union, the other major Allied power, was not informed of plans for the bomb. In the early years of the war, physicists halted all publishing on the topic of nuclear fission to prevent Nazi Germany (and the Soviets, whom the United States and Britain did not trust) from gaining any advantage in nuclear weapons development.

The U.S. government invested enormous energy and resources into wartime research for the project, which was distributed across more than 30 sites in the United States and Canada. Scientific knowledge was centralized at a secret laboratory named Los Alamos near Santa Fe, New Mexico. On December 2, 1942, Enrico Fermi achieved the world's first controlled and sustained nuclear chain reaction in the first *atomic pile* (i.e., a crude nuclear reactor) at the University of Chicago. At the same time, large reactors were secretly being constructed in eastern Washington State at what is now known as the Hanford Site, to manufacture weapons-grade plutonium.

By early 1943, Oppenheimer determined that two weapons projects should be given highest priority: the so-called Thin Man (a plutonium gun) and Fat Man (a plutonium implosion device). Development of the latter bomb was given top priority. A gun-type uranium bomb was next in line for development.

Germany surrendered on May 8, 1945, thus closing the European Theater of the war. A team of Allied scientists followed Allied troops into Europe to assess the status of the German nuclear program. This effort was also designed to prevent the Soviets, marching in from the east, from discovering any nuclear materials or locating scientists. It was

Figure 5.1 Physicist J. Robert Oppenheimer (right, with General Leslie Groves) led the Manhattan Project, the Allied atomic weapons program. (Courtesy of the Department of Energy, http://www .cfo.doe.gov/me70/manhattan/images/GrovesOppenheimerLarge.jpg.)

eventually discovered that in early 1945, a Nazi scientific team had been directed by physicist Kurt Diebner to develop a primitive nuclear device in Ohrdruf, Thuringia (Furlong, 2005; Karlsch, 2005). However, although Germany had been developing its own atomic bomb program, it was far from becoming operational.

The Manhattan Project was still months away from having a working weapon available. In April 1945, after the death of U.S. President Franklin Roosevelt, Vice President Harry Truman was informed about the secret wartime project. On July 16, 1945, the first nuclear test, code-named *Trinity*, took place in the desert north of Alamogordo, New Mexico. The detonation released the equivalent of 19 kilotons (kt) of trinitrotoluene (TNT), far greater than any weapon ever used before. While observing the massive fireball, Manhattan Project Director Oppenheimer quoted *The Bhagavad Gita*, a Hindu holy book:

> If the radiance of a thousand suns
> were to burst at once into the sky,
> that would be like the splendor of the Mighty One...
> I am become Death,
> the shatterer of Worlds.

Figure 5.2 Aftermath of the atomic bombing of Hiroshima, 1945. (Courtesy of Wikipedia, http://en.wikipedia.org/wiki/File:AtomicEffects-Hiroshima.jpg.)

After considering arguments from scientists and military officers regarding the possible use of atomic weapons against Japan, President Truman ordered dropping them on Japanese cities with the hope that these weapons would stun the Japanese government to the point of their country's capitulation. Initial proposed targets of the first atomic bomb included Tokyo, but this suggestion was dropped. The Target Committee recommended Kyoto, Hiroshima, Yokohama, and a weapons depot at Kokura as possible targets. On August 6, 1945 a uranium-based weapon, *Little Boy*, was dropped on Hiroshima (Figure 5.2). Three days later, a plutonium-based device, *Fat Man*, was dropped onto Nagasaki. The two bombs, specifically the blast wave, heat, and radiation that were generated, killed at least 100,000 Japanese immediately, most of them civilians. Tens of thousands died later of radiation sickness and cancer.

Truman threatened to destroy Japanese cities one by one until Japan accepted unconditional surrender. Japan surrendered on August 15. Truman's threat was actually a bluff, because the United States had no more atomic bombs in its arsenal at the time (Rhodes, 1996).

Postwar

The Soviet Union was not privy to intelligence about the U.S. atomic bomb program; however, a substantial unit of Soviet spies was directly involved with the Manhattan Project and regularly forwarded detailed plans about Allied weapons development to their home country. One of the most notorious moles was Klaus Fuchs, a German émigré physicist who had participated in the early British nuclear program (Figure 5.3). During the war, Fuchs went on to work with the U.K. division at Los Alamos. Fuchs was closely involved with the development of the plutonium weapon and passed on detailed cross sections

Figure 5.3 Klaus Fuchs. (Courtesy of the Department of Energy, http://www.cfo.doe.gov/me70 /manhattan/espionage.htm.)

of the device to his Soviet contacts. The diverted information, in combination with the Soviet's own nuclear program led by physicist Yuli Khariton, provided that country with the necessary resources for developing a tactical nuclear weapon.

Soon after the war, the Soviets became focused on the development of their own atomic weapons. Early on, however, the Soviet program stalled because of insufficient nuclear fuel resources; little data were available regarding potential uranium deposits within the Soviet Union. The United States had already made progress in monopolizing the largest known and highest quality uranium reserves in the Belgian Congo. The Union of Soviet Socialist Republics (USSR) decided to mine uranium deposits in Czechoslovakia, which was under its control. They eventually discovered new domestic deposits as well.

On August 29, 1949, the USSR tested its first fission bomb (dubbed *Joe-1* by the United States) at its test site in Kazakhstan, years ahead of predictions by American scientists. The news of the first Soviet detonation was announced to the world by the United States, which had detected nuclear fallout from reconnaissance aircraft patrolling near the Arctic Circle. The U.S. response to the Soviet test was one of apprehension and alarm. In early 1950, President Truman announced the development of a crash program to develop a nuclear *fusion* device—a *hydrogen bomb* or *thermonuclear bomb*—a far more powerful weapon than the fission devices dropped on Japan during the war. At this point, however, the components and design of a nuclear fusion weapon were unknown. It was agreed, however, that the goal of this weapons project was to construct a device that would harness the same reactions as those that powered the Sun.

A number of scientists, including several who had developed the first atomic bombs for the Manhattan Project, were vehemently opposed to the concept of creating a weapon thousands of times more powerful. Technical issues were raised; for example, it seemed

144

impossible to be able to generate sufficiently high temperatures to support a nuclear fusion reaction. Scientists also presented moral objections: such a powerful weapon could not be used solely on military targets—large civilian populations would inevitably be annihilated. This weapon therefore seemed to serve as a weapon of genocide.

The first fusion device, code-named *Mike*, was tested by the United States during *Operation Ivy* on November 1, 1952, at Eniwetok Atoll of the Marshall Islands (Figure 5.4). The device was very large, standing more than 20 ft tall and weighing more than 60 tons. The detonation yielded 10.4 megatons (Mt) of energy, almost 500 times the power of the bomb dropped onto Nagasaki—obliterating the atoll and leaving an underwater crater 6200 ft wide and 160 ft deep. On January 7, 1953, President Truman announced the development of the hydrogen bomb to the world.

The Soviet Union detonated its first thermonuclear device, designed by physicist Andrei Sakharov, on August 12, 1953. The Soviet weapon was cause of great concern within U.S. government and military agencies because unlike *Mike*, the Soviet device was a deliverable weapon, which the United States did not yet have. Although its yield was not in the megaton range, it was nonetheless a powerful propaganda tool for the Soviets. On February 28, 1954, the United States detonated its first deliverable thermonuclear weapon during the *Castle Bravo* test at Bikini Atoll in the Marshall Islands. The yield of the device was 15 Mt, more than twice its expected energy. This detonation also became the worst radiological disaster in U.S. history. The exceptionally large blast combined with poor weather conditions caused a cloud of radioactive nuclear fallout to contaminate more than 7000 mi², including Marshall Island natives, and the crew of a Japanese fishing boat.

As the Cold War intensified during the 1950s, a program of nuclear testing was undertaken to improve the U.S. nuclear arsenal. The Nevada Test Site, located 90 mi north of Las Vegas in the Nevada desert, became the primary location for all U.S. nuclear testing

Figure 5.4 The *Mike* test in 1952 ushered in the age of fusion weapons. (Courtesy of the Department of Energy, http://www.cfo.doe.gov/me70/manhattan/images/IvyMikeWhiteLarge.jpg.)

145

(Figure 5.5). In the USSR, the Semipalatinsk Test Site in Kazakhstan served as the primary nuclear test site (NTI, 2001). Tests by the United States were divided into two primary categories: weapons-related (verifying the feasibility of a new weapon) and weapons effects (observing how weapons behaved under selected conditions).

Early during U.S. and Soviet nuclear programs, most tests were conducted either above ground (*atmospheric tests*) or under water. Concerns began to be raised about the safety of the tests, which were now known to release nuclear fallout to the atmosphere. Several prominent scientists and leaders called for an outright ban on nuclear testing. In 1958, the United States, USSR, and the United Kingdom (which had recently become a nuclear state) declared a temporary testing moratorium for both political and public health reasons. In 1961, the Soviet Union renounced the moratorium, and both the USSR and the United States began testing their latest devices with greater urgency and frequency.

The Soviets tested the massive Tsar Bomba, the largest-ever nuclear weapon, in October 1961. The device was detonated in a reduced state with a yield of about 50 Mt. The weapon was impractical for actual military use; however, it was hot enough to induce third-degree burns at a distance of 62 mi (100 km) (Adamsky and Smirnov, 1994; *Time Magazine*, 1961).

In 1963, all nuclear and many nonnuclear states signed the Limited Test Ban Treaty, pledging to refrain from testing nuclear weapons in the atmosphere, under water, or in outer space. The treaty permitted underground tests, however. Most tests were devoted to increasing the efficiency and power of detonations or to reducing the size of the weapons so that they could be more easily transported. This latter modification prompted the installation of nuclear warheads into missiles. The first nuclear-tipped rockets such as the MGR-1 Honest John, first deployed by the United States in 1953, were surface-to-surface missiles with relatively short ranges (about 15 mi) with yields about twice that of the

Figure 5.5 Hundreds of nuclear tests, both above- and belowground, were conducted at the Nevada Test Site. (Courtesy of the Nevada Division of Environmental Protection, http://ndep.nv .gov/boff/atomic.jpg.)

Hiroshima-era weapons. The limited range of these weapons meant that they could only be used for tactical purposes (i.e., in small-scale military situations) (Figures 5.6 and 5.7).

For strategic weapons (i.e., those that would serve to threaten an entire country), long-range bombers were the only vehicles initially capable of penetrating deep into enemy territory. In the United States, the Strategic Air Command (SAC), a system of bombers directed

Figure 5.6 Honest John nuclear-tipped rocket. (Courtesy of Redstone Arsenal, http://www.redstone .army.mil/history/archives/missiles/honest_john_02.jpg.)

Figure 5.7 The Davy Crockett was the smallest and lightest nuclear weapon ever deployed by the U.S. military. It was designed for use in Europe against Soviet troop formations. (Courtesy of Wikipedia, http://en.wikipedia.org/wiki/File:DavyCrockettBomb.jpg.)

by General Curtis LeMay, was created in 1946. The SAC kept a number of nuclear-armed planes in the sky at all times, ready to attack Moscow upon command from Washington, D.C. (Figure 5.8). By the 1960s, both the United States and the USSR developed intercontinental ballistic missiles (ICBMs), which could be launched thousands of miles from their target (Figure 5.9). In addition, submarine-launched ballistic missiles had a shorter range but could be launched very close to the target without any radar warning.

By the 1950s and 1960s, other nations became members of the *nuclear club*. In 1952, British Prime Minister Winston Churchill announced that the United Kingdom had an atomic bomb; a successful test took place in October of that year. Early U.K. weapons were freefall bombs, soon followed by missiles, for example, *Blue Steel*, and later by submarine-based ballistic missiles. In the 1950s, a French civil nuclear research program began, which eventually generated plutonium as a by-product but also as a potential nuclear fuel. A successful nuclear test, called *Gerboise bleue* (blue jerboa) took place on February 13, 1960 in the French Sahara. On October 16, 1964, China's first atomic bomb was successfully tested at Lop Nur. A hydrogen bomb became operational less than 3 years later, in June 1967. It is believed that Chinese warheads had been improved and miniaturized using designs obtained by espionage from the United States. The current number of Chinese nuclear weapons is unknown; however, it is thought that up to 2000 warheads may have been produced.

On January 27, 1967, more than 60 nations signed the Outer Space Treaty, banning the use of nuclear weapons in space. Twenty-five years later, in a dramatic move after the end of the Cold War, Russian President Boris Yeltsin announced in 1992 that Russia would stop targeting U.S. cities with nuclear weapons. All former Soviet bloc nations housing nuclear weapons including Ukraine, Belarus, and Kazakhstan, returned their warheads to Russia by 1996.

Nuclear proliferation among lesser powers began with the end of the Cold War (Bracken, 2003). In 1974, India tested its first atomic weapon, named *Smiling Buddha*, which

Figure 5.8 Long-range bomber aircraft, such as the B-52 Stratofortress, allowed for a wide range of strategic nuclear forces to be deployed. (Courtesy of Wikipedia, http://en.wikipedia.org/wiki /File:YB-52sideview.jpg.)

Figure 5.9 Intercontinental ballistic missile, the Minuteman-III. (Courtesy of Wikipedia, http://en.wikipedia.org/wiki/File:YB-52sideview.jpg.)

it described as a *peaceful nuclear explosion*. India tested fission and perhaps fusion devices in 1998. Its neighbor Pakistan successfully tested fission devices also in 1974, raising concerns of a nuclear conflict between the two hostile nations. South Africa had an active program to develop nuclear weapons; however, the program was scrapped in the 1990s. There is no firm evidence of a nuclear test on South African soil, although it later claimed to have constructed several crude devices, which it eventually dismantled. Israel has never officially confirmed or denied the presence of a nuclear program; however, Israel is believed to possess an arsenal of possibly up to several hundred nuclear warheads.

In January 2004, Pakistani nuclear scientist Abdul Qadeer Khan confessed to his participation in illicit trafficking of nuclear materials, technical information, and equipment from Pakistan to Libya, Iran, and the Democratic People's Republic of Korea (North Korea). In 2003, North Korea announced that it had constructed several nuclear devices. The first detonation of a nuclear weapon by North Korea took place in 2006, resulting in the adoption of United Nations (UN) Resolution 1718 (Box 5.1). In mid-2009, North Korea continued nuclear testing, in violation of Resolution 1718.

In Iran on August 9, 2005, Ayatollah Ali Khamenei issued a fatwa forbidding the production, stockpiling, and use of nuclear weapons. The full text of the fatwa was released in an official statement at the meeting of the International Atomic Energy Agency (IAEA)

BOX 5.1   UN RESOLUTION 1718

United Nations Security Council Resolution 1718 was adopted unanimously by the UN Security Council on October 14, 2006. The resolution imposes a number of economic and commercial sanctions on North Korea (the Democratic People's Republic of Korea) in the aftermath of their nuclear test of October 9, 2006.

---

in Vienna (Mathaba.net, 2005). Despite this, however, there is mounting concern in many nations about Iran's refusal to halt its nuclear power program, which many fear is an attempt to obscure weapons development activities.

PROPERTIES OF THE ATOM

The tremendous power of nuclear weapons originates from reactions occurring within atomic nuclei. In nuclear reactions, matter is converted to energy. The amount of energy generated is many orders of magnitude greater than that available from any chemical reaction.

Elements and Atomic Structure

A total of 92 elements are known to occur naturally; hydrogen (H) is the lightest (having 1 proton) and uranium (U) the heaviest, with 92. There are also at least 25 artificially created elements, termed *transuranic* (i.e., *beyond uranium*) elements, used in research and industry. These elements comprise all matter on earth.

The *atom* is the simplest structural unit of any element that can exist, while still retaining the unique chemical and physical characteristics of the element. An atom is composed of a central nucleus containing most of its mass, with *electrons* orbiting in shells around the nucleus. The nucleus consists of two fundamental particles, *protons* and *neutrons* (Figure 5.10). The proton is a particle that possesses a positive charge. The neutron is an uncharged particle with mass similar to that of the proton. Electrons are negatively charged particles of extremely low mass.

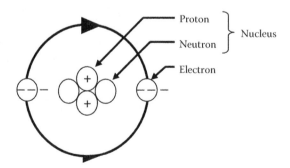

Figure 5.10   Generic structure of an atom.

Table 5.1 Selected Isotopes of Uranium

Isotope	Abundance	Protons	Neutrons	Electrons
Uranium-238	99.3%	92	146	92
Uranium-235	0.7%	92	143	92

Isotopes

Atoms of different elements possess unique numbers of protons in their nuclei. The term *atomic number* describes the number of protons in a nucleus. An element may contain varying numbers of neutrons, however. The total number of protons plus neutrons in a nucleus is termed the *atomic mass*. When atoms have the same number of protons but different numbers of neutrons, they remain the same element, but are termed isotopes (Table 5.1). Some isotopes are known to be quite unstable. This instability is termed *radioactivity*, which is truly the cornerstone of our discussion of nuclear science (and nuclear weapons).

If we refer to the Periodic Table of the Elements, the element with atomic number 92 is uranium (chemical symbol, U). The atomic mass number 235 identifies a uranium isotope having 92 protons and 143 neutrons (235 − 92 = 143) in its nucleus. To identify the individual isotopes of a given element, the following notation is used:

$$^{A}_{Z}X$$

where:
  X = chemical symbol of the element
  Z = atomic number (number of protons)
  A = atomic mass number (protons + neutrons)

An example of the standard notation would be:

$$^{235}_{92}U$$

The atomic number is often deleted, and an isotope will then be represented by its mass number and chemical symbol, for example, ^{235}U.

RADIOACTIVITY

The nuclei of certain naturally occurring isotopes, and of others produced artificially, contain excess energy, that is, they are unstable. To attain stability, those energetic nuclei emit their excess energy in the form of nuclear radiation. Isotopes that emit ionizing radiation from their nuclei to achieve stability are termed *radioactive*. Radioactive isotopes are also referred to as *radioisotopes* or *radionuclides*. Each radioisotope has its own unique radioactive *decay scheme*. A decay scheme identifies the types of ionizing radiation emitted, the range of energies of the radiation emitted, and the half-life of the decaying radioisotope (Figure 5.11).

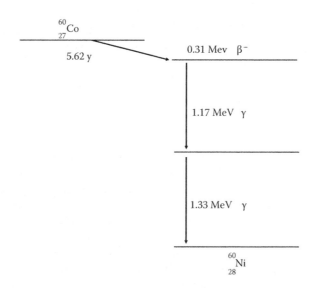

Figure 5.11 Radioactive decay scheme for ⁶⁰Co. Note that, after several stages of decay, cobalt has been converted to nickel.

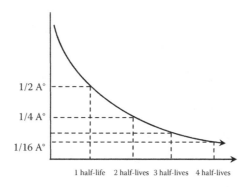

Figure 5.12 Plot of radioactive decay of an isotope.

The *half-life* of a radioisotope is the time required for half of the atoms of a sample to decay to nonradioactive forms. Half-life values range from fractions of a second to thousands of years, depending on the isotope. The concept of half-life is extremely important in discussions of soil, structures, and debris contaminated by radiation, and *radioactive fallout*. Radioactive decay can be plotted in linear or semilogarithmic form (Figure 5.12). These line forms are used to determine, by simple inspection, an isotope's activity at a specific time.

IONIZATION: WHEN RADIATION INTERACTS WITH MATTER

Why is radiation such a significant hazard to the human body and to all biota? It is well established that ionizing radiation significantly increases the risk of certain forms of cancer. There are conflicting reports regarding the potential for radiation to increase the risk of birth defects, however. Let us look at the root cause of the concern to emergency responders, healthcare officials, and the public as regards radiation.

Ionizing radiation results in the deposition of energy in living tissue. Radioactive particles or waves (alpha, beta, gamma radiation, and neutrons, discussed later) all possess significant energy. The transfer of energy to the atoms of a recipient material (in this discussion, human tissue) may occur via several mechanisms (U.S. Army, Navy, Air Force, 1996).

Excitation

This process involves the addition of energy to an atom, thereby elevating it from its stable state (*ground state*) to an excited state. Excitation occurs when relatively small amounts of energy are transferred. Depending on the type of interaction, either the nucleus of the atom or one of its electrons will absorb the excitation energy. The excited nucleus or electron will not retain this higher energy but tends to return to its original energy level either by transferring the excess energy to other atoms or by emitting it as electromagnetic radiation, often in the form of light or of *x-rays*.

Ionization

Ionization will occur if incoming radiation transfers sufficient energy to dislodge one or more electrons from the outer orbitals of the recipient atom. Ionization thus creates an ion pair consisting of a free electron and a *cation*, that is, the positively charged atom (Figure 5.13).

The ionization process is especially significant in DNA, the genetic repository that codes for structure, physiology, and behavior of an organism. It is accepted that random mutation of DNA is a natural process (and is, in fact, the basis for natural selection and evolution); however, when living tissue is bombarded with radioactive particles or waves, the incidence of DNA mutation is considerably increased. DNA chains will therefore have a significantly greater chance of fragmenting and recombining, resulting in the coding of new, undesirable, and possibly detrimental changes in the affected organism (e.g., development of *carcinomas*).

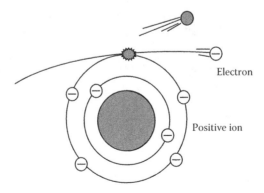

Figure 5.13 Ionization of an atom resulting from bombardment by radiation.

FORMS OF RADIATION

There are four types of ionizing radiation that can be emitted from radioactive elements. All are potentially hazardous to organisms and include the following:

- Alpha particles
- Beta particles
- Gamma/x-rays
- Neutrons

Alpha Radiation

When large, unstable nuclides such as uranium or radium decay, they may emit several forms of radiation. One common form is a particle composed of two protons and two neutrons, essentially the nucleus of a helium atom minus its planetary electrons (Figure 5.14). This form is termed *alpha radiation*. Alpha radiation is relatively heavy, of low energy, and carries a net positive charge.

Alpha travels only a few centimeters in air and has little penetrating power. Most alpha radiation is stopped by 1–2 in of air or a sheet of paper or cloth. Alpha cannot even penetrate the outer layer of dead skin on the body. For this reason, alpha is considered an *internal hazard* only, that is, it must enter the body to cause biological damage. For example, if radon gas (an alpha emitter) is inhaled, the alpha particles can reach cells deep in the lungs and deposit large quantities of energy in a small volume of unprotected tissue. Radon gas is therefore known to increase the risk of lung cancer.

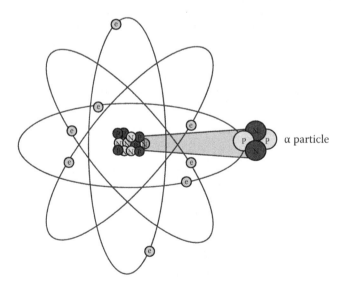

Figure 5.14 Alpha radiation.

Sources of alpha radiation include the following:

- Uranium (nuclear power plant fuel and nuclear weapons)
- Plutonium (nuclear weapons)
- Americium (smoke detectors)
- Thorium (tungsten welding rods, coatings on large lenses of telescopes)

Beta Radiation

Beta radiation is essentially an electron minus an electrical charge, ejected from the nucleus at high energy (Figure 5.15). Given its small size, beta particles have extremely low mass.

Externally, beta radiation is potentially hazardous to the skin and eyes. Beta particles cannot penetrate through all skin layers to damage internal organs, however. Beta radiation becomes an internal hazard if the beta emitter is ingested or inhaled; in such cases, the source of the beta radiation is in proximity to living cells and deposits energy over a small area. The range of beta radiation in air is about 10 ft. Most beta radiation can be shielded by about ¼ in of plastic sheeting, aluminum foil, thick clothing, or safety glasses.

Beta particles are emitted from the following:

- Used nuclear reactor fuel and nuclear weapons fallout (e.g., as strontium-90)
- Some industrial radioactive sources such as cesium
- Tritium in glow-in-the-dark EXIT signs, watch dials, night-sights on firearms
- Radioactive nickel in chemical agent detectors

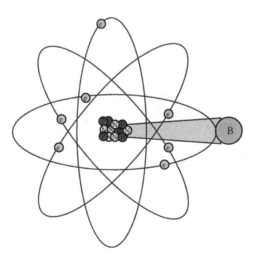

Figure 5.15 Beta radiation.

Gamma Radiation/X-Rays

Gamma rays and x-radiation have no mass and no charge; they are composed of electromagnetic energy, not matter. Gamma radiation is illustrated in Figure 5.16.

As gamma and x-ray radiation have no charge and no mass, they have very high penetrating power. Gamma rays travel great distances in air (thousands of yards to miles) at the speed of light. They are considered a whole body hazard, that is, internal and external. Gamma radiation can be extremely destructive to living tissue via ionization. A single gamma ray may ionize many thousands of atoms along its path of travel. The more electrons it removes (ionizes), the less energy remains. Eventually, the gamma radiation gives up the last of its energy and disappears.

Gamma radiation and x-rays must be shielded by very dense materials such as concrete (6 in or more), lead (1 in or more), water (1 ft or more), soil (1 ft or more), or thick steel (several inches). The thicker the shielding, the greater the success in blocking the radiation.

Sources of gamma radiation include the following:

- Uranium, plutonium, radioactive cobalt, and cesium
- Industrial radiation sources
- Medical sources and cancer treatment machines

Many beta emitters are also known to emit gamma radiation.

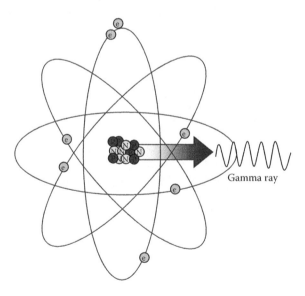

Figure 5.16 Gamma/x-ray radiation.

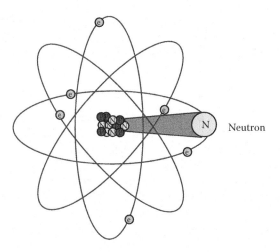

Neutron

Figure 5.17   Neutron radiation.

Neutron Radiation

As mentioned earlier, neutrons are one of the key subatomic particles occurring within an atom's nucleus. A neutron has mass, but no electrical charge. Emission of a neutron particle is illustrated in Figure 5.17.

Ionization of matter occurs as the result of collisions between neutrons and target atoms. The neutrons continue on, smashing into other atoms until they dissipate all their energy. Neutron radiation has a high penetrating ability—they are difficult to shield and stop. The range for neutrons in air is up to several miles. It follows that neutron radiation is a whole body hazard (internal and external)—it easily penetrates body tissues and is quite destructive to cells.

Neutron radiation is best shielded by materials with high hydrogen content such as water or thick plastic (6–10 in or more). In addition, thick concrete (1 ft or more), water (several feet), and soil (several feet) are very effective for neutron shielding.

The sources of neutrons include:

- Nuclear fuels within a nuclear reactor
- The burst of radiation from a detonating nuclear weapon (discussed later)
- Plutonium, californium, and americium

MEASUREMENT OF RADIATION

The measurement of radiation emitted from a source is critical for safety and correct response actions; likewise, the amount of radiation absorbed by victim(s) will give an indication of possible degree of harm. Units of radiation will vary as a function of whether it is being emitted or being absorbed.

Most scientists in the international community measure radiation using the System Internationale (SI), a protocol that evolved from the metric system. In the United States, however, the conventional system of measurement is still widely used.

Measuring Emitted Radiation

The quantity of radiation emitted by a radioactive source is measured using the *curie* (Ci), named for Marie Curie, or the SI unit *Becquerel* (Bq). The Ci or Bq expresses the number of disintegrations of radioactive atoms over a period of time. For example, 1 Bq is equal to 1 disintegration/s. One Curie is equal to 37 billion (37×10^9) disintegrations/s; therefore, 1 Ci is equal to 37 billion (37×10^9) Bq. These units may be used to refer to the amount of radioactive materials released during an incident. For example, during the Chernobyl nuclear accident that took place in the former Soviet Union in 1986, an estimated 81 million Ci of radioactive cesium was released (Atkinson and Rosenthal, 2010).

Measuring Radiation Dose

When a human is exposed to radiation, energy is deposited in the body's tissues. The amount of energy deposited per unit weight of human tissue is termed the *absorbed dose*. Absorbed dose is measured using the conventional *rad* or the SI unit Gray (*Gy*). A value of 1 Gy is equal to 100 rad. The biological risk of exposure to radiation is measured using the conventional unit *rem* or the SI unit *sievert* (Sv). The amount of rems received from exposure to a radioactive source can be correlated with possible harm (Table 5.2).

Table 5.2 Estimated Effects on Human Health as a Function of Radiation Dose

Dose (rem)	Effects
5 to 20	Possible latent effects (cancer), possible chromosomal aberrations
25 to 100	Changes in blood chemistry
>50	Fatigue; temporary sterility in males
100	Hemorrhage; double the normal incidents of genetic defects
100 to 200	Vomiting, diarrhea, reduction in infection resistance, possible bone growth impaired cognitive development in children
200 to 300	Serious radiation sickness, nausea
>300	Permanent sterility in females
300 to 400	Bone marrow and intestine destruction; possible death
400 to 1000	Acute illness and early death (usually within days)
2000	Damage to central nervous system; loss of consciousness; death in minutes to days

Source: U.S. Environmental Protection Agency, Radiation protection, Health effects, 2010. http:// www.epa.gov/rpdweb00/understand/health_effects.html; U.S. Nuclear Regulatory Commission. 2010. Fact sheet on biological effects of radiation. http://www.nrc.gov/reading-rm/doc-col lections/fact-sheets/bio-effects-radiation.html.

NUCLEAR REACTIONS

Fission

The fission process, whether in a commercial nuclear power plant or a nuclear weapon, relies on the inherent instability of certain naturally occurring and artificially produced elements. The nuclei of some heavy isotopes, in particular, uranium-235 (^{235}U) and plutonium-239 (^{239}Pu), can split when they are bombarded by outside neutrons. This splitting is termed nuclear *fission*.

As illustrated in Figure 5.18, a free neutron smashes into the nucleus of a fissionable atom, resulting in splitting of the unstable nucleus. This results in the production of two or more fission products, more free neutrons, and a tremendous amount of energy in the form of heat and light.

When nuclear materials are tightly packed such as in nuclear reactors and nuclear weapons, such a process will cascade, resulting in a virtual avalanche of neutrons being released that go on to split more and more nuclei. Each generation of neutrons released can generate a tremendous number of fissions. This phenomenon is the so-called *nuclear chain reaction*, or self-sustaining reaction. Ultimately, the energy recovered from such a process may be extremely large.

In theory, a single neutron could initiate a chain reaction of nuclear fissions that could result in the splitting of each fissionable atom in a fuel mass. In reality, however, not all the neutrons produce more fission reactions. Many escape from the fissionable mass; others are removed by nonfission reactions. Both of these effects were significant practical problems affecting the development of the first atomic weapons.

In commercial nuclear reactors, the fission chain reaction takes place in a controlled manner. The resulting energy is used to generate electricity in discrete quantities. In contrast, in a nuclear detonation, the chain reaction occurs at an extremely rapid and uncontrolled rate.

Isotopes capable of fission are termed *fissionable isotopes*. The most common fissionable isotope is uranium-238 (^{238}U). Large quantities of U-238 exist in nature; however, U-238 does not readily undergo fission and therefore cannot be used in a commercial nuclear reactor or nuclear weapon. Some isotopes, such as U-235 or Pu-239, undergo fission relatively easily and are termed *fissile isotopes*. As a result of this capability, fissile isotopes are valuable for generating energy in nuclear reactors. This fissile capability is also important to cause a nuclear detonation.

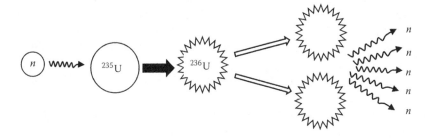

Figure 5.18 Nuclear fission of U-235 showing generation of daughter nuclei and additional neutrons.

Fissile isotopes are extremely rare in nature. Natural uranium consists of 99% U-238 but less than 0.7% U-235 (see Table 5.1). Plutonium-239 does not occur naturally. Highly complex industrial processes are needed to isolate and concentrate sufficient quantities of U-235 and to generate Pu-239; these activities are considered to be beyond the capabilities of terrorist organizations. To initiate a chain reaction, sustain the reaction sufficiently long to build up the explosive energy, and confine the released energy for as long as possible to maximize the weapon's explosive effect, requires that a variety of important requirements be fulfilled (U.S. Army, Navy, Air Force, 1996). Some are discussed below.

Critical Mass

The first requirement for generating a fission detonation is that sufficient material be present and in the proper configuration so that successive generations of neutrons can cause greater numbers of fission reactions. The quantity of fuel capable of sustaining a chain reaction is termed a critical mass. A tremendous number of fissions is required for the release of such immense amounts of energy as occurs in a nuclear detonation. One of three types of chain reactions may occur for a given mass of fissionable fuel (U.S. Army, Navy, Air Force, 1996):

- *Subcritical chain reaction*—a reaction in which the number of neutrons decreases in succeeding generations, thus not sustaining itself
- *Critical chain reaction*—a reaction in which the number of neutrons remains constant in succeeding generations
- *Supercritical chain reaction*—a reaction in which the number of neutrons increases in succeeding generations

To initiate a nuclear detonation, a weapon must be equipped with a quantity of uranium or plutonium that exceeds the mass necessary to support a chain reaction, that is, a *supercritical mass* of fissionable material. Several methods can be used to make a mass of fissionable material supercritical (Rhodes, 1996; U.S. Army, Navy, Air Force, 1996):

- The material is purified to eliminate unwanted elements that might absorb neutrons and attenuate the chain reaction.
- Fissionable material is enriched, that is, the proportion of U-235 compared to U-238 is increased.
- The material is machined into the most efficient shape. A spherical shape provides the greatest volume with the least surface area, thereby reducing the probability of neutron loss.
- Moderators are used to slow fission neutrons, increasing the probability of their producing fissions.
- Neutrons that escape the fissile fuel are returned to the mass using suitable reflector materials. Reflectors can also physically delay the expansion of the exploding material thus allowing more fissions to occur, thereby resulting in increased explosive energy.

When constructing a nuclear weapon, it is essential to keep fuel materials below critical mass; otherwise, the critical or supercritical mass may melt or possibly detonate. Before detonation, therefore, the fuel must be separated into several pieces of fissionable material, all below critical mass. At the time of detonation the mass is made supercritical by changing its shape or configuration.

Fusion

Under extreme heat and pressure, the nuclei of two isotopes of hydrogen (deuterium and tritium) can fuse together to form a single atom of helium. This process is known as nuclear *fusion*. For the fusion process to occur, the two nuclei must be forced together by enough energy so that the strong, attractive, short-range nuclear forces overcome the electrostatic forces of repulsion (U.S. Army, Navy, Air Force, 1996). Nuclear fusion occurs in the Sun and is responsible for producing light, heat, and other energy forms.

The two conditions required for fusion to occur are: (1) extremely high temperatures (to accelerate the nuclei) and (2) high pressure density (to increase the probability of interaction). For the development of a weapon, the only practical means to attain the required temperatures and pressures is by means of a fission detonation. Consequently, fusion weapons must contain a fission component. The energy released in the detonation of a fission–fusion weapon originates from approximately equal contributions of fission and fusion processes (U.S. Army, Navy, Air Force, 1996).

Nuclear fusion has been applied to nuclear weapons, but methods for using fusion to produce energy in commercial reactors (e.g., to generate electricity) have not yet been feasible.

NUCLEAR WEAPON DESIGNS

Nuclear weapons are explosive devices that rapidly release the energy generated from the fission or fusion of atomic nuclei. Nuclear devices are thousands of times more powerful than any known chemical explosive. The explosive power, or *yield*, of a nuclear weapon is typically expressed in terms of the quantity of TNT that would release an equivalent amount of energy, often measured in thousands of tons of TNT (kilotons). For the most powerful weapons, however, yield is measured in millions of tons of TNT (megatons). The first of the fission bombs (July and August, 1945) had yields in the range of 10–20 kt. Substantially greater yields have since been designed for fission weapons.

Fission weapons are designed to rapidly assemble a supercritical mass of fissile material to create an uncontrolled fission chain reaction. The energy of this reaction is released within a fraction of a second, resulting in a powerful detonation. Fission weapons are the only type of nuclear weapon ever used in wartime. The United States used a fission weapon against the Japanese city of Hiroshima and a second against the city of Nagasaki near the end of World War II, in August, 1945. Since then, no nuclear weapon of any type has been used in combat.

There is concern that terrorist organizations could build fission weapons if they could acquire sufficient fissile material (either *highly enriched uranium* [HEU] or plutonium). Terrorists could also obtain fission weapons from nations storing them in their nuclear arsenals (see Box 5.2). The most difficult challenge for a terrorist organization attempting to construct an improvised nuclear device (IND) is obtaining the fissile material.

BOX 5.2   PAKISTAN'S NUCLEAR ARSENAL

Pakistan is located at the epicenter of global jihadism. The country warehouses 100 or more nuclear weapons on bases and in facilities across the country. Pakistan would be an obvious location for a jihadist organization to seek a nuclear weapon or fissile material: its national government has difficulty establishing its authority in many corners of the territory; the country's military and security services are infiltrated by jihadist sympathizers; and many jihadist organizations are already headquartered in the country (Goldberg and Ambinder, 2011).

A report by Harvard University's Belfer Centre for Science and International Affairs, entitled *Securing the Bomb 2010*, said Pakistan's nuclear weapons stockpile "faces a greater threat from Islamic extremists seeking nuclear weapons than any other nuclear stockpile on earth" (Nuclear Threat Initiative, 2016). The Institute for Science and International Security has reported that Pakistan's second nuclear reactor, built to produce plutonium for weapons, shows signs of starting operations, and a third is under construction. "Despite extensive security measures, there is a very real possibility that sympathetic insiders might carry out or assist in a nuclear theft, or that a sophisticated outsider attack (possibly with insider help) could overwhelm the defences," the report said. Experts state that the danger is growing because of the arms race between Pakistan and India (Borger, 2010).

HEU has been processed to increase the proportion of the U-235 isotope to more than 20%, which is required for the construction of a *gun-type* nuclear device. The greater the proportion of U-235 (i.e., the greater the degree of enrichment), the less material is needed for a nuclear detonation. *Weapons-grade* quality refers to uranium enriched to at least 90%; however, material of far lower enrichment levels, found in both fresh and spent nuclear fuel, can be used to create a nuclear device (NTI, n.d.).

HEU Production

The process of generating HEU begins with mining natural uranium, a fairly widespread element in the Earth's crust. Uranium is mined primarily from sandstone ores where the uranium occurs at concentrations of 0.03–0.7% by weight, but it is also found in lower concentrations in shales and granites. Uranium-bearing rocks are extracted from underground mines or open pits. The ore is crushed and placed in an acid bath that leaches the uranium into solution. The dissolved metal is then extracted as uranium oxide, U_3O_8.

The uranium-235 isotope must then be separated from the more abundant U-238 form. The goal is to concentrate U-235 well above its natural value of 0.7%. In a chemical sense, different isotopes of uranium behave identically; therefore, most separation methods rely on physical rather than chemical means of separation, based on the slight difference in mass between the U-235 and U-238 isotopes. The primary approaches to separation involve first converting the natural uranium to uranium hexafluoride gas (UF_6), followed by physical separation of the lighter $^{235}UF_6$ molecules from the slightly heavier $^{238}UF_6$ molecules. The most successful technologies for accomplishing this separation are (NTI, n.d.):

- *Gaseous diffusion*, which takes advantage of the difference in diffusion rates of the lighter and heavier molecules through a cascade of thousands of porous barriers
- *Centrifugation*, which uses thousands of sophisticated, ultrahigh-speed, gas centrifuge instruments to separate the molecules based on their differing masses

Plutonium Production

In a commercial or defense nuclear reactor, the starting nuclear fuel will never be pure U-235 and will contain substantial contamination by the U-238 isotope. This contamination is not necessarily detrimental, however, as usable plutonium can be generated. A nuclear reactor that contains U-238 in its fuel produces Pu-239 in the course of operation as a result of the absorption of some of the fission neutrons by this uranium isotope:

$$^{238}_{92}U + n \rightarrow {}^{239}_{92}U \rightarrow {}^{239}_{93}U + {}_{-1}e^{o} \tag{5.1}$$

$$^{239}_{93}Np \rightarrow {}^{239}_{94}Pu + {}_{-1}e^{o} \tag{5.2}$$

Types of Nuclear Weapons

At the time of detonation, the nuclear fuel is made supercritical by changing its shape or configuration. Two general methods have been developed for rapidly converting a subcritical mass into a supercritical one.

Gun Type

The simplest type of nuclear weapon is the so-called gun type. Two pieces of fissionable material, each below critical mass, are rapidly brought together to form a single, supercritical unit. The gun-type assembly (Figure 5.19) is achieved in a tube in which a high explosive blasts a subcritical piece of fissionable material from one end into a second subcritical piece held at the opposite end. When the two masses collide, they form a supercritical mass that results in a nuclear detonation. Although the gun-type weapon is the simplest of the nuclear weapon types to design and construct, they typically require more fissile material than do other designs such as the implosion design (see *Implosion Weapons*, p. 162).

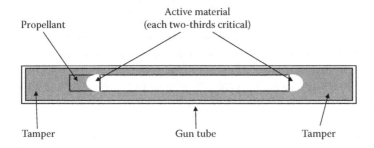

Figure 5.19 Gun-type nuclear weapon assembly.

Figure 5.20 Little Boy gun-type nuclear weapon. (Courtesy of the Department of Energy, http://www.cfo.doe.gov/me70/manhattan/early_bomb_design.htm.)

Depending on the sophistication of the design, at least 25 to 50 kg (55 to 110 lb) of HEU enriched to 90% U-235 is needed to build a gun type nuclear device. The *Little Boy* bomb dropped on Hiroshima during World War II was a gun-type fission weapon containing 64 kg of 80% enriched uranium with an explosive yield of 14 kt (Figure 5.20).

Implosion Weapons

An implosion fission weapon is a significantly more sophisticated device compared with the gun-type design. In the implosion assembly method (Figure 5.21), a subcritical mass of U-235 or Pu-239 is compressed to produce a supercritical mass. Compression is achieved by the detonation of many specially positioned high explosives around a subcritical sphere of fissionable material. When the high explosive is detonated, implosion occurs. The imploding blast wave compresses the sphere of fissionable material, thus making the mass supercritical. Once compressed, the mass will undergo a rapid chain reaction.

The first nuclear weapon ever detonated, at the *Trinity* test near Alamogordo, New Mexico, on July 16, 1945 was an implosion-type weapon. The *Fat Man* bomb used against Nagasaki in World War II was an implosion-type weapon with an explosive yield of about 21 kt (Figure 5.22).

Implosion-type weapons are much more difficult to design and construct compared with gun-type weapons—the explosive components and fusing systems are highly complex. Implosion-type weapons typically require much less fissile material than do gun-type

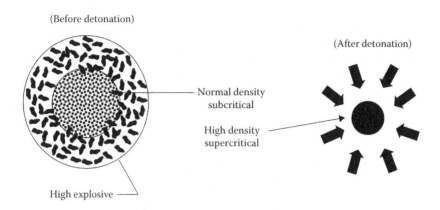

(Before detonation)

(After detonation)

Normal density subcritical

High density supercritical

High explosive

Figure 5.21 Implosion method for nuclear detonation.

Figure 5.22 *Fat Man* nuclear device on transport carriage. (Courtesy of Wikipedia, http://en.wikipedia.org/wiki/File:Fat_Man_Assembled_Tinian_1945.jpg.)

weapons. An implosion weapon requires only about 8 kg (18 lb) of HEU or 4 kg (9 lb) of plutonium. This means that implosion weapons can be relatively small.

Thermonuclear Weapons

Thermonuclear weapons derive their explosive yield from the combined power of nuclear fission and fusion. An initial fission reaction with plutonium fuel generates the extreme temperatures needed to trigger a secondary fusion reaction. The fission component relies on implosion of plutonium fuel. Radiation from the fission detonation heats and compresses a separate core of deuterium and tritium, which undergoes fusion. In thermonuclear weapons, the key fusion reaction is known as the D–T reaction. Using the heat and

165

BOX 5.3   DEUTERIUM AND TRITIUM

Hydrogen (^{1}H) has an atomic mass of 1, because of the presence of one proton and no neutrons in its nucleus. *Deuterium* (^{2}H), also called *heavy hydrogen*, is a stable isotope of hydrogen having one proton and one neutron (atomic mass = 2). *Tritium* (^{3}H) is another radioactive isotope of hydrogen with a nucleus containing one proton and two neutrons (atomic mass = 3).

pressure of fission, deuterium (^{2}H), fuses with tritium (^{3}H) (Box 5.3), to form helium-4 (^{4}He) plus one neutron (η) and energy (Glasstone and Dolan, 1977):

$$2D + 3T \rightarrow 4He + \eta + 17.6 \text{ MeV} \tag{5.3}$$

The fusion reaction generates additional explosive energy, but more importantly, releases more neutrons within the core. These neutrons will bombard more of the fissile plutonium, causing it to undergo fission rather than being dispersed by the detonation. This boosting process significantly reduces the quantity of fissile material that might have been wasted.

Thermonuclear weapons are significantly more difficult to design, build, and maintain than fission weapons (Figure 5.23). Thermonuclear weapons can be extremely powerful, with yields measured in megatons. The largest nuclear weapon ever produced was the *Tsar Bomba* tested by the Soviet Union on October 31, 1961. The USSR claimed that the designed yield of the Tsar Bomba was 100 Mt; however, the yield was reduced to 50 Mt for safety reasons. There was, nevertheless, concern by the weapon's designers that the nuclear reaction might *run away* and cause damage on an even greater scale. U.S. nuclear scientists concluded that the total yield of the weapon was about 57 Mt.

Figure 5.23   Mk-15 thermonuclear device. (Courtesy of Wikipedia, http://en.wikipedia.org/wiki/File:Mk15.jpg.)

INDs

An IND is essentially a *home-made* weapon designed to produce a nuclear detonation. These devices may be fabricated in a completely improvised manner or may be a modification to a weapon already present in a national nuclear stockpile.

The destructive capability of an IND depends on the explosive yield of the weapon and location of the detonation. The possibility exists that an IND could generate a substantial yield, as might be expected for a tactical nuclear weapon; however, the more likely scenario would be a low-yield device of 5 kt or less that could be easily concealed and transported.

In the case of detonation of a low-yield weapon, damage would be much greater than that of the largest high explosive devices deployed in truck bombs. Radiation released from the blast may injure large numbers of people, who may exhibit no symptoms for hours. The spread of radioactive fallout will create panic among the general public. It is possible that substantial radiation exposure would affect first responders working at ground zero.

The potential for terrorist use of INDs will be discussed in some detail later in this chapter.

EFFECTS OF NUCLEAR DETONATIONS

The energy released by a nuclear detonation results in extensive damage to buildings, infrastructure, and humans and other biota. As noted earlier, nuclear detonations can potentially release millions of times more destructive force than the largest conventional explosions (e.g., using TNT or RDX).

Both nuclear weapons and conventional explosives rely on the destructive force of the blast, or shock wave. However, the temperatures attained in a nuclear detonation are markedly higher than are those in a conventional explosion, and a large proportion of the energy is released in the form of heat. Nuclear detonations are also accompanied by radiation, *fallout*, and *electromagnetic pulse* (EMP). Blast, thermal radiation, and *prompt ionizing radiation* occur within seconds or minutes of the detonation. Delayed effects, including radioactive fallout, inflict damage over hours to years. The relative distribution of these effects depends on the yield of the weapon, the location of the detonation, and the characteristics of the blast environment.

Yield

For a low-altitude atmospheric detonation of a 20-kt weapon, it is estimated that the energy is distributed approximately as follows:

- 50% as blast (overpressure and high winds).
- 35% as thermal radiation, composed of a wide range of the electromagnetic spectrum, including infrared, visible, and ultraviolet light, as well as *soft x-rays.*
- 15% as nuclear radiation, including 5% as initial ionizing radiation composed of neutrons and gamma rays emitted within the first minute after detonation, and 10% as residual nuclear radiation. Residual radiation is the hazard in fallout.

Blast

The major proportion (approximately 50%) of energy from a nuclear weapon detonated either on the Earth's surface or within the atmosphere is released in the form of blast and shock waves. At the instant of a nuclear detonation, the heat from the fireball produces a high-pressure wave that moves outward. The front of the blast wave (the *shock front*, *shock wave*, or incident shock wave) is a moving wall of highly compressed air that travels rapidly away from the fireball, sharply increasing air pressure. The pressure can crush structures and create hurricane-force winds at hundreds of miles per hour (Figure 5.24). These winds, in turn, create pressure against objects facing the blast. When this shock wave comes into contact with a solid object, it will either move the object in the direction of the wave propagation or shatter it, depending on the strength of the shock wave and the characteristics of the recipient object. The *overpressure* reaches its maximum value upon the arrival of the shock wave (see Box 5.4). It then decays over a period ranging from a few

Figure 5.24 Effects of a blast wave on a typicalwood frame house. (Courtesy of the Department of Energy, http://www.nv.doe.gov/library/photos/upshot.aspx.)

BOX 5.4   OVERPRESSURE

When a detonation occurs, a shock wave is generated by the rapidly expanding air heated by reaction, whether it be nuclear or chemical. The term overpressure refers to the increase in atmospheric pressure as a result of the detonation. Blast effects are usually measured by amount of overpressure, that is, the pressure in excess of the normal atmospheric value, in pascals (Pa; metric system) or pounds per square inch (lb/in²; English system).

Different influences at the time of the incident (e.g., surface versus air burst, urban area versus open area) make it difficult to accurately predict the magnitude of damage produced by different blast intensities. A general guide is given in Table 5.3.

Shock waves from a nuclear detonation occurring on or below ground can destroy buildings in a manner similar to that of an earthquake (U.S. Army, Navy, Air Force, 1996). Urban, built-up areas are mostly destroyed by overpressures of 5 lb/in², with heavy damage extending out to at least the 3 lb/in² contour. Overpressures of 2 lb/in² will seriously damage frame and composite houses. The blast from a nuclear weapon equivalent in yield to that dropped on Hiroshima (about 13 kt) would flatten all wooden or unreinforced masonry structures within 1 mi (1.6 km) from ground zero. No structure can withstand 10–12 lb/in² overpressure. Industrial facilities might survive 5 lb/in², but most houses will be destroyed (Figure 5.24).

Table 5.3   Physical Effects of Overpressure on Humans and Structures

Overpressure (lb/in²)	Wind Speed (mi/h)	Physical Effects
1	38	Residential structures collapse; serious injuries occur, and fatalities may occur.
2	70	Windows and doors blown down. Humans injured by flying debris.
5	163	Most buildings collapse; injuries are universal, fatalities are widespread.
10	294	Reinforced concrete buildings are severely damaged or destroyed. Most people are killed.
20	502	Heavily built concrete structures are severely damaged or demolished. Fatalities approach 100%.

Source: U.S. Centers for Disease Control and Prevention, Explosions and Refuge Chambers, n.d. Zipf, R.K., Cashdollar, K.L., Effects of blast pressure on structures and the human body. http://www.cdc.gov/niosh/docket/pdfs/NIOSH-125/125-Explosions%20and%20Refuge%20Chambers.pdf; Glasstone, S., Dolan, P., *The Effects of Nuclear Weapons*, 3rd Edition, U.S. Dept. of Defense and U.S. Dept. of Energy, Washington, DC, 1977.

LOCATION OF THE BLAST

The magnitude of a nuclear detonation effect is related to the height of the burst above ground level. For any explosion, there is an optimum burst height that will produce the greatest change in air pressure (overpressure). A detonation on the surface produces the greatest overpressure at very close ranges, but less overpressure over longer ranges than would an air burst.

Some scientists believe that a Hiroshima-sized weapon detonated at ground level in an urban environment would show modified blast effects; a tremendous amount of blast damage would be expected, but damage could be significantly less than what would occur from an equivalent yield weapon detonated high above a city's skyline. The Hiroshima bomb detonation height was set at 2000 ft above the ground surface to maximize blast damage.

tenths of a second to several seconds, depending on the blast strength and the weapon's yield (Figure 5.25) (Atomicarchive, 2008b).

Mach Stem

If the nuclear detonation occurs aboveground, the expanding blast wave will quickly strike the surface of the Earth. This wave is immediately reflected from the surface to form a second shock wave traveling behind the first. This reflected wave travels faster than the first, or incident, shock wave because it is traveling through air already moving at high speed owing to the passage of the incident wave. The reflected blast wave merges with the incident shock wave to form a single wave, known as the *Mach stem*. The overpressure at

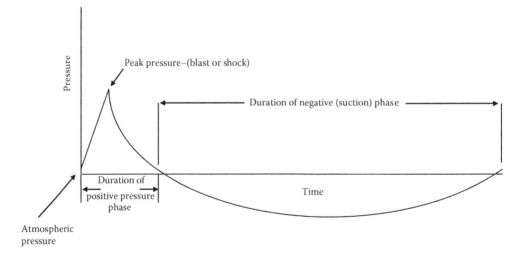

Figure 5.25 Representation of shock front and overpressure following a detonation.

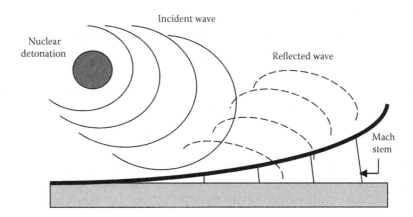

Figure 5.26 Mach effect.

the front of the Mach wave is generally about twice as great as that of the direct blast wave front (Figure 5.26). At first the height of the Mach Stem wave is small, but as the wave front continues to move outward, the height increases steadily. At the same time, however, the overpressure, like that in the incident wave, decreases because of the continuous loss of energy and the increasing area of the advancing front. When the Mach front from a 1-Mt nuclear weapon is 10 mi from ground zero (after approximately 40 s), the overpressure will have decreased to roughly 1 lb/in^2 (Glasstone and Dolan, 1977).

Blast Effects on Humans

Upon contact with human populations, the nuclear shock wave will push the person in the direction of propagation and compress the body as the wave passes, resulting in damage ranging from burst eardrums to destruction and liquefaction of internal organs, depending on the amount of overpressure (Langford, 2004). At overpressures of 1 lb/in^2, people can be knocked down; at 5 lb/in^2 eardrums are ruptured. Pressures of more than 40 lb/in^2 are sufficient to cause death. Serious injury or death can also occur from impact after being propelled through the air.

The blast magnifies thermal radiation burn injuries by tearing away severely burned skin. This creates raw open wounds that may become infected.

An added danger from overpressure involves the collapse of structures. The destruction of buildings in urban areas generates substantial airborne debris. Collapsing structures will crush persons caught inside.

Thermal Effects

Approximately 35% of the energy of a nuclear weapon is released as heat, reaching temperatures at the moment of detonation of 180,000,000°F (100 million °C). In contrast, the temperature due to explosion of a conventional chemical explosive (e.g., TNT or RDX) is a few thousand degrees.

BOX 5.5   HARD X-RAYS AND SOFT X-RAYS

X-rays are commonly defined in terms of the energy they carry, in units of thousands of electron volts (keV). X-rays have energies ranging from less than 1 keV to greater than 100 keV. *Hard x-rays* are the highest energy x-rays, typically those with energies greater than 10 keV; the lower energy x-rays are referred to as *soft x-rays*.

Such temperatures are as hot as those of the sun, and are so extreme that about one-third of the energy is converted into electromagnetic radiation (specifically x-rays). This electromagnetic radiation, consisting mostly of soft x-rays (see Box 5.5), is absorbed by the atmosphere at ground zero, heating it to very high temperatures and forming an extremely hot sphere of air and gaseous weapon residues, the so-called *fireball* (Figure 5.27). The surface temperature of the fireball is about 14,400°F (8000°C). At these temperatures, the nonfissioned components of the weapon are vaporized. The heat obviously incinerates all matter over a large distance. At the point of detonation, humans and structures are vaporized. At greater distances, combustible materials are ignited.

Depending on environmental factors such as building materials and weather conditions at the seat of detonation, the blast heat can also create a firestorm. This storm of flames and air is heated to more than 1000°C and is hot enough to melt glass and many metals. In a Hiroshima-sized detonation, such a firestorm could incinerate everything within about 1.9 km (1.2 mi) from ground zero.

Figure 5.27   (See color insert.) Fireball and mushroom cloud following detonation at the Nevada test site. (Courtesy of the Nevada Division of Environmental Protection, http://ndep.nv.gov/boff /upshot.jpg.)

Prompt Radiation

About 15% of the energy released from a nuclear detonation occurs as various types of radiation. The initial nuclear radiation comprises about one-third of this total. Initial nuclear radiation, also termed prompt radiation, is defined as that produced within about 1 min from detonation. Prompt radiation is quite destructive and is composed mainly of neutrons, gamma rays, x-rays, and alpha and beta particles. Although prompt radiation lasts for only about 1 min, it is lethal to all life forms within a few thousand yards. At these distances, blast and thermal effects are also lethal.

The electromagnetic radiation (chiefly gamma rays) interacts with the molecules in the air (including debris) so that its intensity is eventually reduced. The intensity and effects of such radiation follow the inverse square law (Box 5.6).

The prompt radiation from a Hiroshima-sized detonation would expose people within about 2 km (1.3 mi) of ground zero to a 500-rem dose of radiation, creating a 50% chance of death from radiation sickness, radiation burns, and other health effects within days to weeks (see Table 5.2). The actual radiation exposure a person receives depends on the amount of time exposed, the distance from the radiation source, and the amount of shielding. For instance, in a large modern city such as New York the dense array of structures should significantly reduce the degree of prompt radiation exposure to human populations.

Health Effects

Radiation adversely affects the structure and function of cells. Two general mechanisms of radiation damage are known in biological systems: direct action and indirect action mechanisms. The *direct action mechanism* occurs from the direct attack on a molecule by ionizing radiation and the consequent destruction of the molecule. Thus, radiation damages cells by changing the structure of organic molecules such as DNA, ribonucleic acid (RNA), and enzymes. For example, the molecular structure of a specific enzyme that is essential to substrate metabolism in a cell is altered by radiation. As a consequence, cell metabolism is disrupted and energy can no longer be generated. This disruption causes the cell to die.

The *indirect action mechanism* occurs when water in the cell is irradiated. The water molecule is split and the resulting free radicals subsequently damage the cell. A *free radical* is an atom or molecule that has a single unpaired electron in one orbit (as compared to most electron orbits, which have pairs of electrons). The following reactions show the

---

BOX 5.6   THE INVERSE SQUARE LAW

This law states that the intensity from a radioactive source decreases in relation to the square of the distance. For example, if the radiation at 10 m is 500 R, at twice that distance or 20 m, it is 125 R ($500/2^2$). At 30 m (about 100 ft), radiation intensity is only about 56 R ($500/3^2$), and so on.

processes involved in the breakdown of the water molecule by radiation. H^o symbolizes the hydrogen radical, and OH^o denotes the hydroxyl radical.

Radiation

$\downarrow\downarrow\downarrow$

$H_2O \rightarrow H^o + OH^o$	Free radicals
$H^o + H^o \rightarrow H_2$	Hydrogen gas
$H^o + OH^o \rightarrow H_2O$	Water
$OH^o + OH^o \rightarrow H_2O_2$	Hydrogen peroxide (toxic)
$H^o + O_2 \rightarrow HO_2^o$	Peroxyl radical (toxic)

Free radicals, hydrogen peroxide, and the peroxyl radical are extremely harmful to a living cell. The formation of the highly toxic hydrogen peroxide from recombined free radicals is referred to as the *poison water theory*.

Radiation effects are generally classified as early (or *acute*) and late (or *chronic*). The terms *early* and *late* refer to the length of the latency period after exposure. The *latency period* is the time interval between dose and detection of symptoms. Acute radiation effects are those that are clinically observable within 2 or 3 months after exposure (U.S. FEMA, n.d.). Severity depends on the radiation dose received. Examples of acute radiation effects include skin burns, loss of appetite, nausea, fatigue, and diarrhea. Late effects can occur years after exposure; examples include cancer, leukemia, cataracts, and genetic disturbances. Radiation damage can be repaired if the dose received is not too high and if the dose is received over a long period.

EMP

The radiation from a nuclear detonation creates a powerful electromagnetic pulse (EMP). Radiation ionizes air molecules, imparting an electric charge to them. These ionized air molecules interact with the Earth's magnetic field to create a surge of electromagnetic energy. The EMP effect is similar to the electrical surge caused by lightning, but about 100 times faster and thousands of times stronger. The EMP from some very large nuclear detonations can cause surges of 25,000–50,000 V/m. This surge is strong enough to destroy unprotected electronic equipment, shut down power grids and communications networks, and completely erase the memory on a computer hard drive. The EMP can also cause arcing in electronic equipment.

If a nuclear weapon detonates close to the ground surface, the EMP is generated over a relatively small area. However, an EMP could be conducted by buried electric lines, resulting in loss of electrical power beyond the immediate zone of destruction. Depending on the weapon's yield, EMP effects could potentially lead to loss of electrical communications equipment for emergency responders stationed within miles of ground zero, unless the equipment was electrically shielded in advance.

In the event of a high-altitude nuclear detonation, a tremendous flux of gamma rays from the nuclear device occurs. These gamma rays produce high-energy free electrons, typically at altitudes between 12 and 24 mi above the Earth's surface (Langford, 2004). The high-energy electrons become trapped in the earth's magnetic field, generating an oscillating electric current that creates a rapidly rising electromagnetic field, resulting in a significant EMP. The pulse can cover a radius of hundreds of miles, spanning entire continents, affecting electrical and electronic systems (NTI, n.d.).

The first recorded EMP incident accompanied a U.S. high-altitude nuclear test over the South Pacific, resulting in power system failures as far away as Hawaii. It is highly unlikely that a high-altitude detonation could be achieved by terrorists.

Induced Radiation

Many atoms can be converted into radioactive isotopes by *neutron activation*. In the process, a nonradioactive atom absorbs a *slow neutron* (i.e., one whose kinetic energy is below about 1 keV) and becomes a radioactive isotope having one additional mass unit. The new atom can emit radiation as alpha, beta, or neutron particles, or x-rays or gamma rays. Building materials, water, and soil can undergo neutron activation and thus become radioactive. Most isotopes created by neutron activation have short half-lives and quickly decay. Thus, the intensity of induced radioactivity decreases rapidly.

Fallout

About 10% of the total energy from a nuclear blast occurs in fallout, that is, fine particles of radioactive dust that settle back to earth over a period of minutes to years. This radiation is largely attributable to the radioactivity of the fission products present in weapon debris, plus irradiated soil and moisture thrust into the atmosphere from the detonation. It is estimated that the radioactivity from detonation of a fission-type nuclear weapon results from about 300 different radionuclides representing about 40 elements. As an example, uranium-235 can split via many reactions to form numerous products. Equation 5.4 shows one possible fission reaction, where U-235 is converted to strontium-95, xenon-139, and two neutrons (η), plus energy (Glasstone and Dolan, 1977):

$$^{235}U + \eta \rightarrow {}^{95}Sr + {}^{139}Xe + 2\eta + 180 \text{ MeV} \tag{5.4}$$

During the 1960s, public health officials expressed concern that strontium isotopes from fallout, being chemically similar to calcium, were becoming incorporated into cow's milk and stored in human tissue.

Radioactive materials blasted high into the atmosphere by the force of a nuclear detonation can travel hundreds of miles before falling to earth, depositing radioactive contamination across thousands of square miles. The intensity and duration of contamination from fallout vary with the yield of the nuclear weapon and its proximity to the ground surface at the time of detonation (Figure 5.28).

Ground Blast

Weapons detonated close to ground level generate the greatest quantities of fallout. A significant hazard results from soil particles irradiated by the nuclear detonation that are lifted skyward. The radioactive particles that rise only a short distance (i.e., those in the *stem* of the mushroom cloud) will fall back to Earth within a matter of minutes, landing close to the

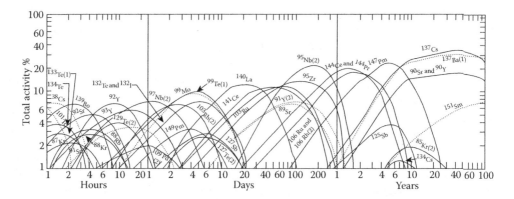

Figure 5.28 Elements occurring in fallout from thermonuclear fission of U-238. (From Crocker, G.R., Turner, T., Calculated Activities, Exposure Rates, and Gamma Spectra for Unfractionated Fission Products, U.S. Naval Radiological Defense Laboratory, San Francisco, CA, 1965. With permission.)

center of the detonation. Such particles are unlikely to cause additional deaths, as they will fall in areas where people have already perished because of blast effects and heat.

Immediately after fallout is deposited near the blast site, radiation intensities will be very high as the short-lived isotopes decay. For 2 days after a Hiroshima-sized explosion at ground level, persons within about 1.5 mi of ground zero could be exposed to a 500-rem radiation dose from fallout carried by low-altitude winds. This level of radiation may result in a 50% fatality rate. Such intense radiation will dissipate relatively quickly, however. The intensity will fall by a factor of 10 after 7 h, a factor of 100 after 49 h and a factor of 1000 after 2 weeks (OTA, 1979). Regardless, however, without extensive decontamination, radiation within the area may not decay to safe levels for 3–5 years. The radioactivity that remains will create difficulties for response and rescue, and also for eventual reconstruction of the affected area.

Air Burst

The fallout from air bursts poses long-term health hazards, but they are relatively minor compared to other consequences of the nuclear blast. The radioactive particles that rise high in the atmosphere are carried significant distances by the wind before returning to Earth; hence, the area and intensity of the fallout is strongly influenced by weather conditions. Much of the material is simply blown downwind in a long plume. A number of attempts have been made to mathematically model the possible path of a fallout plume following a nuclear detonation (Figure 5.28).

The map shown in Figure 5.29 illustrates the plume expected from a 1-Mt surface burst in Detroit if winds were blowing to the northeast. The model assumes that winds were blowing at a uniform speed of 15 mi/h over the region. The plume would be longer and narrower if wind speeds were greater, and broader if the winds were slower. The areas in the plume would become safe (by peacetime standards) in 2–3 years for the outer ellipse, and in about 10 years for the inner ellipse.

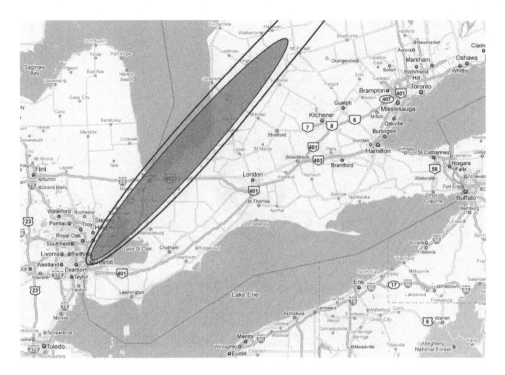

Figure 5.29 Model showing a plume of radioactive fallout over Detroit following a hypothetical detonation. (From U.S. Congress Office of Technology Assessment, Effects of Nuclear War, 1979, http://www.fas.org/ota/reports/7906.pdf. With permission.)

Wind direction will make a substantial difference in radiation intensity on affected populations. Rainfall will also impart a significant influence on the deposition of radiation from weapons, because rain will carry contaminated particles directly to earth. The areas receiving such contaminated rainfall would become *hot spots* having greater radiation intensity than their surroundings (OTA, 1979).

The amount of radiation produced by fallout will decrease with time as the radioactive materials decay. Each isotope decays at a characteristic rate (see Figure 5.11). Some radioactive particles that have been thrust into the stratosphere may not return to earth for years. Only the long-lived particles pose a threat, as they are dispersed around the world over a range of latitudes. Some fallout from United States and Soviet weapons tests in the 1950s and 1960s can still be detected. Some particles in the immediate fallout (notably strontium-90 and cesium-137) remain radioactive for years.

The biological effects of fallout radiation are similar to those from direct radiation. Persons exposed to significant quantities of fallout radiation will become ill and possibly die; those exposed to lesser amounts may experience chronic illness. Areas receiving such fallout must be evacuated or decontaminated; otherwise, survivors would have to be sheltered for months until the most intense radiation is dissipated (Figure 5.30).

Figure 5.30 Soviet test of *Joe 1*, detonated on the ground surface, showing dirty cloud due to soil incorporation. (Courtesy of the Department of Energy, http://www.cfo.doe.gov/me70/manhattan /images/Joe1SovietTest.jpg.)

TIMELINE OF A NUCLEAR DETONATION

A suggested timeline for a blast resulting from a 1-Mt detonation in air is as follows:

- *Time = 0:* Detonation caused by runaway chain reaction. Fireball expands rapidly and rises because of its low density.
- *1 ms after detonation:* Diameter of fireball is about 150 m (450 ft).
- *10 s:* Up to this point, the fireball had increased at the rate of 100 m/s (300 ft/s). It has attained its maximum size (approximately 5700 ft across). The initial rapid expansion of the fireball severely compresses the surrounding atmosphere, producing the powerful blast wave. The shock front is about 3 mi from ground zero. As the fireball expands toward maximum diameter, it cools.
- *50 s:* The fireball is no longer visible. The blast wave has traveled about 12 mi; it is traveling at about 780 mi/h, slightly faster than the speed of sound at sea level.
- *60 s:* The temperature decreases so that the fireball no longer emits significant thermal radiation. The combination of upward movement and the cooling of the fireball induce the formation of the characteristic mushroom cloud. As the fireball cools, the vaporized materials within condense to form a cloud of solid and liquid

particulates. Following an air burst, condensed droplets of water impart a white cloudlike appearance to the fireball. In the case of a surface burst, the cloud will contain large quantities of soil and other debris that are drawn up by the strong updrafts, giving the cloud a dirty gray-brown appearance (Figure 5.30).

The soil and other debris become contaminated with radioisotopes generated by the detonation or activated by neutron radiation and return to earth as fallout.

Varying times. Radioactive fallout lands close to ground zero; debris drawn higher into the atmosphere will travel great distances and may be deposited thousands of miles from ground zero.

EMERGENCY RESPONSE TO A NUCLEAR DETONATION

The detonation of a nuclear device will clearly overwhelm emergency response efforts in any community. Many emergency responders stationed near ground zero may die or be injured by the initial blast. First responders may be contaminated with soil and dust from the detonation before any personnel with the capability of monitoring for radiation arrive on scene.

Victims could overwhelm first responders before a decontamination plan could be established. Many victims may self-admit to local clinics and hospitals before those facilities were aware of the incident and the potential for contamination. Once it is determined that radioactive contamination is present, decisions have to be made rapidly concerning rescue efforts.

The presence of radiological contamination will create extensive physical and psychological stress for responders attempting to recover victims from the debris. As a consequence of brief work shifts (to limit exposure to radiation) and decontamination requirements for the responders, it may be difficult to maintain a sufficient number of trained rescue personnel on-scene immediately following the incident. Emergency responders will be concerned about their own safety as well as that of loved ones who may have been affected by the incident.

In the aftermath of a nuclear detonation, mass decontamination will be needed. Exposure to radiological materials typically indicates no immediate symptoms; thus, it will be difficult to manage large numbers of civilians who have no idea that they have been contaminated. In the case of mass decontamination, there will likely be a shortage of monitoring equipment and trained personnel to determine if victims have been successfully decontaminated.

TERRORISM AND NUCLEAR DEVICES

The possible construction of INDs by terrorist groups is a growing concern. The ability of terrorists to obtain fissile material is a closely related issue, given the fall of the Soviet Union and subsequent black market operations (see Box. 5.7).

BOX 5.7   REPORTED LOSSES, THEFTS, AND SEIZURES
OF NUCLEAR MATERIALS WORLDWIDE

2015

Moldova: Undercover agent buys an ampule of cesium-135; materials contaminated with cesium-137 found in central Chisinau.

2014

1. Moldova: Smugglers allegedly tried to sell 200 g of uranium-235 from Russia to undercover security agents for $1.6 million; 1.5 kg of uranium-235 seized close to the Moldovan border in Ukraine.
2. Militants in Iraq seized low-grade nuclear material from a university in the north of the country.

2013

Mexico: Highly lethal cobalt-60 was stolen in a truck theft and not recovered for 2 days.

2012

1. Egypt: Container of radioactive materials reported stolen from Dabaa nuclear power plant construction site.
2. Lebanon: Inspectors find orphan cesium-137 and strontium-90 sources in scrap-metal trucks at seaports.
3. Bolivia: Police seize 2 tons of uranium.

2011

1. Mexico: Orphan cobalt-60 source found.
2. France: Package with iodine-125 missing in Paris airport.
3. India: 15 cobalt-60 sources stolen from steel plant in Durgapur, two recovered.
4. France: Device with cobalt-57 source stolen in Chalons-en-Champagne.
5. France: Krypton-85 source lost in Mantes-la-Ville.
6. France: Device with cobalt-57 stolen in Gagny.
7. Germany: 2.3 thousand low-enriched uranium and thorium fuel elements missing.
8. France: Cesium-137 source lost in Saint-Grégoire.
9. Russia: Serviceman convicted of theft, attempt to sell cesium-137.
10. Namibia: 700 lb of uranium ore stolen from Areva Mine, four suspects arrested.
11. Abu Dhabi: Radiography equipment with iridium-192 missing.
12. Romania: 162 lb of natural uranium stolen from a storage depot.

13. Egypt: Radioactive material stolen from a university in Alexandria.
14. Russia: Youth sentenced to prison for acquisition and storage of uranium.

2010

1. Georgia: Enriched uranium stolen from Sukhumi Physical-Technical University.
2. France: Americium-241 source missing at Bordeaux University.
3. Russia: Radioactive material found abandoned in Volgograd region.
4. Ukraine: Radioactive scrap metal detected at metallurgical plant in Donetsk.
5. France: Two cadmium-109 sources stolen.
6. France: Cobalt-57 source stolen.
7. Belgium: Radioactive iodine stolen from vehicle in Brussels.
8. Russia: Orphan plutonium-239 sources found in Orsk.
9. Poland: Seven cobalt-60 sources stolen from foundry in Lublin.
10. Canada: Radioactive source missing in Surrey, British Columbia.

2009

1. Pakistan: Radioactive sources stolen from a steel plant.
2. Namibia: 375 lb of natural uranium stolen from Rossing mine.

2008

1. Russia: A device containing strontium stolen in Saratov.
2. Russia: Five men convicted for stealing uranium from the Chepetsk Plant.

2007

3. Russia: Orphan container with plutonium found in Smolensk Oblast.
4. Kazakhstan: Ampules labeled cesium-133 uncovered in water well.
5. Russia: Thieves steal uranium rods in Udmurtia Republic.

2006

Georgia: Radioactive sources recovered.

2005

1. Ukraine: Ukrainian officials recover radioactive materials believed originally stolen in 1995.
2. Russia: A container with 110 lb of radioactive waste found in Samara Oblast.

2004

Russia: Small amount of plutonium-238 found in Alta Kray.

2003

1. Kyrgyzstan: Europium stolen from a factory.
2. Georgia: Radioactive cesium missing from a military base.
3. Kyrgyzstan: Kyrgyzstani police arrest thieves with ytterbium oxide.
4. Russia: Stolen radioisotope thermoelectric generator recovered in Leningrad Oblast.
5. Georgia: Orphaned cesium-137 sources found in Tbilisi.
6. Georgia: Georgian authorities search for a missing radioisotope thermoelectric generator.
7. Russia: Cesium-137 source missing in Vologodskaya Oblast.
8. Russia: Cesium stolen in Yamalo-Nenets autonomous district.

BBC News
Nuclear smuggling deals 'thwarted' in Moldova, 2015

N. Lundeen
Iraq warned U.N. of stolen nuclear materials, agency says, 2014

M. Fisher
This alarming map shows dozens of radioactive materials theft and losses every year, 2013

Table 5.4 Status of World Nuclear Forces

Country	Deployed Strategic	Deployed Nonstrategic	Reserve/ Nondeployed	Military Stockpile	Total Inventory
Russia	1780	0	2720	4500	7500
United States	1900	180	2620	4700	7200
France	290	n.a	10	300	300
China	0	?	250	250	250
United Kingdom	150	n.a.	65	215	215
Israel	0	n.a.	80	80	80
Pakistan	0	n.a.	100–120	100–120	100–20
India	0	n.a.	90–110	90–110	90–110
North Korea	0	n.a.	<10	<10	<10
Total	~4120	~180	~6000	~10,300	~15,700

Source: FAS.org, 2015. http://fas.org/issues/nuclear-weapons/status-world-nuclear-forces/.

Global Nuclear Inventories

Today, nearly three decades since the end of the Cold War, more than 22,000 assembled nuclear weapons exist worldwide (Table 5.4). Nine countries possess these weapons; the five nations with the largest stockpiles are also state parties to the Nuclear Non-proliferation Treaty: Russia, the United States, China, France, and the United Kingdom. The United States and Russia possess the majority (about 95%) of these weapons (Bunn and Zenko, 2007). In addition, U.S. nuclear weapons are located in six other countries: the United Kingdom and five nonnuclear-weapon states (Germany, the Netherlands, Belgium, Italy, and Turkey) (Norris and Kristensen, 2006).

HEU and plutonium-239 have both military and civilian uses. With few exceptions, HEU is no longer used in commercial (civilian) nuclear reactors. However, HEU continues to be widely used in civilian research reactors as well as for medical isotope production and in naval reactors, among other applications. It is estimated that 140 research reactors in more than 40 countries continue to operate with HEU as their fuel (Bunn and Zenko, 2007). Many civilian nuclear facilities, for example fuel fabrication plants, possess sufficient nuclear material on site for construction of a nuclear device. It is estimated that 128 research reactors or associated facilities possess at least 20 kg of HEU (U.S. GAO, 2004).

There are an estimated 61 tons of HEU in civilian use worldwide, and 490 tons of plutonium in stocks worldwide (IPFM, 2013; NTI, 2014). The amount of civilian plutonium increases annually at a rate of about 70 tons (Albright and Kramer, 2005).

Many countries reprocess plutonium from spent reactor fuel and recycle it as plutonium–uranium mixed oxide fuel in civilian reactors. These activities result in the processing and transport of many tons of weapons-usable plutonium annually (Bunn and Zenko, 2007).

Transport of HEU, particularly military-grade material, takes place on a massive scale. Nuclear weapons are dismantled, and HEU is shipped from dismantlement facilities to storage facilities. In some countries, excess HEU is shipped to other locations for blending to low enriched uranium (i.e., that having less than 20% U-235; U.S. GAO, 1999). In contrast, the scale of shipments of civilian HEU is relatively small. However, hundreds of kilograms of HEU are shipped each year for fuel for research reactors and for medical isotope production—primarily within the United States and Russia. These shipments pose risks of theft and use by terrorists (Mendelsohn, 2005).

Transport of military-grade plutonium currently occurs at a much smaller scale than transport of military HEU (Bunn and Zenko, 2007). In the United States and Russia, plutonium from dismantled weapons is stored at the site of dismantling. Final management, including reprocessing and/or disposal of excess plutonium, has not been initiated. Large quantities of weapons-usable separated plutonium are transported every year. Approximately 20 tons of plutonium is reprocessed from spent fuel and about half of that is fabricated into fuel for use in nuclear reactors. Roughly 100 commercial plutonium shipments occur per year, most of which contain more than 100 kg of weapons-usable plutonium per single shipment (Albright, 2007).

Nuclear Smuggling

There is ample evidence documenting that both terrorist groups and states hostile to the United States have sought stolen nuclear weapons or weapons-usable nuclear materials

(Box 5.7); many have furthermore attempted to recruit scientists and engineers with expertise in the construction of nuclear weapons (Bunn et al., 2005). In 2003, a Russian businessman offered $750,000 for stolen weapons-grade plutonium for sale to a foreign client. He went on to make contact with residents of the closed city of Sarov, site of one of Russia's top nuclear weapons research and development centers, to attempt to close the deal (Bunn and Wier, 2003; RIA-Novosti, 2003). There is evidence that groups have carried out reconnaissance at nuclear weapon storage sites and on nuclear weapon transport trains in Russia, whose locations and schedules are state secrets (Associated Press, 2001; Koryashkin, 2001). Finally, there are reports that nuclear materials have simply disappeared from some countries' inventories. In 1998, Russian Army Lieutenant General Lebed was ordered to account for 132 suitcase-size nuclear weapons that the Soviet Union had manufactured during the 1970s and 1980s. He could only locate 48. He explained, "We do not know what the status of the other devices is, we just could not locate them...." The Soviet devices, built by the KGB for sabotage purposes, have an explosive charge of roughly 1 kt of TNT.

Many less-developed countries had nuclear research reactors built in the 1950s under the Eisenhower administration's *Atoms for Peace* program. The thinking of the time was that making reactors available to these countries would make them more receptive to U.S. influence. At this time, the USSR was also actively marketing its research reactors in a similar attempt to draw countries into its sphere of influence (Daly et al., 2005).

In 1958, construction of a research reactor began on the University of Kinshasa campus outside the capital city of the Congo. In 1959, the reactor went critical and was acknowledged as a symbol of progress for the Congo and for Africa in general. The first reactor was retired in 1970, and a newer and larger design began operation in 1972.

In the mid to late 1970s, two of the reactor rods in storage at the Kinshasa facility disappeared (Daly et al., 2005; Kinshasa Digitalcong, 2002). The location of the rods was unknown for over two decades, until 1998. It had been suggested that Congo President Mobutu, overthrown in 1997, took the rods with him as a potentially valuable asset. At the same time, allegations were made of Italian criminal smuggling rings attempting to sell nuclear material from the country. In July 1996, a Portuguese businessman offered to make available a bar of uranium-235 from Zaire worth 7 billion Italian lira. Eventually, two Portuguese citizens involved in the plot admitted to criminal activity. An Italian involved in the plot claimed to be working for the Russian Secret Service. Only one of the two rods was ever recovered. An IAEA official stated that he thought the second rod was probably "lost in the jungle" (Wrong, 1999).

In 2001, U.S. intelligence agencies concluded that the al-Qaeda terrorist network may have made greater strides than previously thought toward obtaining plans or materials to construct a crude nuclear weapon. Osama bin Laden and al-Qaeda have openly attempted to obtain nuclear weapons for use against the United States and its allies. Bin Laden has labeled the acquisition of WMDs a *religious duty*. Al-Qaeda communications reportedly have referred to inflicting a *Hiroshima* on the United States (Risen and Engelberg, 2001). An al-Qaeda spokesman, Sulaiman Abu Ghaith, has asserted that the group "has the right to kill 4 million Americans—2 million of them children," in retaliation for the deaths the group believes the United States and Israel have inflicted on Muslims (Bunn et al., 2005). For more than a decade, al-Qaeda has been attempting to purchase stolen nuclear weapons or nuclear material, and to recruit nuclear expertise (Albright, 2002; Albright et al., 2002).

In 2005, the U.S. intelligence community assessed that al-Qaeda was capable of fabricating at least a *crude* nuclear device if it could obtain the requisite nuclear material, that is, HEU or separated plutonium. Michael Scheuer, member of a Central Intelligence Agency (CIA) team focused on Osama bin Laden, wrote in 2004 to the House and Senate Intelligence Committees that his unit "acquired detailed information about the careful, professional manner in which al-Qaeda was seeking to acquire nuclear weapons." He continued, "there could be no doubt after this date that al-Qaeda was in deadly earnest in seeking nuclear weapons" (Anonymous, 2004). The CIA Counterterrorist Center judged in November 2001 that al-Qaeda "probably had access to nuclear expertise and facilities and that there was a real possibility of the group developing a crude nuclear device."

Osama bin Laden, Mamdouh Mahmud Salim, and others have made efforts to obtain the components of nuclear weapons (CNS, 2001). The best documented case was an attempt in 1993 to purchase HEU in the Sudan, which has been described in some detail in court testimony of Jamal Ahmad al-Fadl, the al-Qaeda operative charged with several key steps in the transaction (McCloud and Osborne, 2001).

In addition to the 1993 attempt, there have been several reports regarding al-Qaeda attempts to purchase nuclear materials or nuclear weapons in the former Soviet Union (Bunn et al., 2005; McCloud and Osborne, 2001). Al-Qaeda and its allies have also actively attempted to recruit individuals with nuclear weapons expertise. For example, Osama bin Laden and his deputy Ayman al-Zawahiri met with two senior Pakistani nuclear weapons experts, both Taliban sympathizers with extreme Islamic views, and pressed them for information regarding the manufacture of nuclear weapons. Pakistani intelligence officials told the *Washington Post* that the two had provided bin Laden with detailed technical information, in violation of Pakistan's secrecy laws (Albright and Hunter, 2003). In 2000, an official of Russia's National Security Council announced that the Taliban regime of Afghanistan attempted to recruit a nuclear expert from a Russian facility (Radio Free Europe, 2000). In 1998, a scientist at one of Russia's nuclear weapons laboratories was arrested for spying for both the Taliban and Iraq (Bunn et al., 2005).

Other terrorist organizations have been documented as having ambitions to obtain or construct a nuclear weapon. Aum Shinrikyo, the Japanese doomsday cult associated with the 1995 Tokyo sarin attacks, recruited nuclear physicists from Moscow. It was also determined that the group tried to mine its own uranium in Australia and to buy Russian nuclear warheads (Willman and Miller, 2001).

TERRORISM AND RDDs

This chapter has thus far presented phenomena associated solely with nuclear detonations, that is, engineered reactions occurring within the nuclei of atoms to release extremely large quantities of energy. In contrast, a *radiological dispersed device* (RDD, *dirty bomb*) occurs as a simple improvised device consisting of explosives such as black powder or dynamite in combination with radioactive material. When the explosives are detonated, the blast disperses radioactive debris into the local area.

The U.S. Department of Defense (DOD) defines an RDD as

any device, including any weapon or equipment, other than a nuclear explosive device, specifically designed to employ radioactive material by disseminating it to cause destruction, damage, or injury by means of the radiation produced by the decay of such material.

P.O. Krehl, 2008

Terrorists could use an RDD to scatter radioactive debris, thereby contaminating a wide area. The threat from an RDD not only includes the blast wave and fragmentation from the explosive, but also radiation exposure from the radioactive material, and fear and panic that would spread among the target population. Depending on the type and strength of radiation involved, RDDs could render a great deal of property unusable for an extended period unless costly remediation practices were undertaken. However, most probable radioactive sources in an RDD would be incapable of releasing sufficient radiation to cause severe illness or death. The explosives contained in the device would likely impart more immediate lethal effect than would the radioactive material.

An RDD is far easier for terrorists to construct, conceal, and detonate as compared with a true nuclear weapon. Unlike the HEU or plutonium required for a nuclear device, the radioactive material for a dirty bomb exists at thousands of locations worldwide. In other words, the probability of a dirty bomb attack is substantially higher than the probability of a terrorist attack with a nuclear weapon. However, the consequences of a dirty bomb attack would be far less than those for a nuclear weapon (Bunn, 2010) (Box 5.8).

Since the September 11, 2001 attacks, concerns of terrorist groups using dirty bombs have increased markedly. Two cases of cesium-containing dirty bombs (neither of which were detonated) have been reported. The first attempt was carried out in November 1995

BOX 5.8   EXPOSURE VERSUS CONTAMINATION

It is important to appreciate the difference between exposure to radiation and contamination with radioactive material. Health effects and countermeasures differ significantly for each.

- *Radiation exposure* (irradiation) occurs when radiation penetrates tissue, for example, when a patient undergoes a diagnostic x-ray. A person can be irradiated without physically contacting radioactive material.
- *Radioactive contamination* involves the placement of radioactive material in random, unintentional locations on the body. Contamination can be external (outside the body), internal, or both. External contamination comprises radioactive material occurring on clothes, skin, or hair. Internal contamination includes radioactive material that has entered the body by inhalation, ingestion, or absorption through skin or wounds.

by a group of Chechen separatists who concealed a cesium-137 source wrapped in explosives at Izmaylovsky Park in Moscow. Chechen rebel leader Shamil Basayev alerted the media and the bomb was removed by security forces.

In December 1998, a second attempt at radiological terror was announced by the Russian-backed Chechen Security Service, who discovered a container filled with radioactive materials attached to an explosive mine. The Security Service safely defused the bomb. The location of the discovery—a suburban area 10 mi east of the Chechen capital of Grozny, where a Chechen rebel group is known to operate an explosives workshop—led nuclear specialists to suspect Chechen rebels' involvement in the incident. Shamil Basayev, the rebel leader who phoned in the dirty bomb threat in Moscow 3 years earlier, had been closely associated with the explosives workshop (NOVA, 2003).

On October 14, 2001, Israel was reported to have arrested a man linked to al-Qaeda who was trying to enter the country from the West Bank city of Ramallah with a radiological bomb hidden in his backpack (Huessy, 2007).

In November 2002, the director of Russia's nuclear regulatory agency, Yuri Vishnyevsky, announced that small amounts—"a few grams here and there"—of weapons-grade and reactor-grade uranium was missing from his country's atomic facilities. Vishnyevsky did not provide details as to when and how the materials disappeared. A few grams of weapons-grade uranium would not be sufficient to construct an effective nuclear device; however, it could constitute adequate material for a dirty bomb. Moreover, small amounts of reactor-grade uranium can be enriched to weapons-grade (NOVA, 2003).

Radionuclides of Concern

Almost any radioactive material can be used to construct an RDD, including fission products, spent fuel from nuclear reactors, and relatively low-level materials such as medical, industrial, and research waste. Millions of radioactive sources have been manufactured and distributed worldwide since the end of World War II, with hundreds of thousands currently in use, storage, and production. Many of these sources are weakly radioactive and pose little radiological risk (IAEA, 2002).

Worldwide, the IAEA has documented more than 20,000 operators of significant radioactive sources; for example, more than 10,000 radiotherapy units for medical care are in use; about 12,000 industrial sources for radiography are supplied annually; and about 300 irradiator facilities containing radioactive sources for industrial applications are in operation (IAEA, n.d.).

The most probable radionuclides for use in an RDD include cesium chloride, cobalt, americium, and iridium (U.S. DHHS, 2010a); however, others may also be used. Multiple agents may be combined in a single explosion. The isotopes of interest for RDDs are shown in Table 5.5.

Cs-137, Co-60, and Ir-192 (Table 5.5) are all strong gamma emitters, which make these isotopes valuable for commercial and medical applications including sterilization of equipment, irradiation of tumors, and evaluation of high-integrity welds. They are also used in industrial gauges. If exposed, these nuclides could pose a whole-body hazard to victims.

Strontium-90 emits beta particles and has important commercial uses, a major one being in radioisotope thermal generators (RTGs). Approximately 1000 RTGs occur in

Table 5.5 Possible Isotopes for Use in RDDs

Nuclide	Primary Radiation Type (Half-Life)	Primary Form	Possible Radiation per Source (Curies)	Application
^{90}Sr	Beta (28.6 years)	Ceramic ($SrTiO_3$)	300,000	Large radioisotopic thermal generator (RTG) (Russian IEhU-1)
^{137}Cs	Beta + Ba (137 months), Gamma (30.17 years)	Salt (CsCl)	200,000	Irradiator
^{60}Co	Beta, gamma (5.27 years)	Metal	300,000	Irradiator
^{238}Pu	Alpha (87.75 years)	Ceramic (PuO_2)	300,000	RTG used for the Cassini Saturn space probe
^{241}Am	Alpha (432.2 years)	Pressed ceramic powder (AmO_2)	20	Single well logging source
^{252}Cf	Alpha (2.64 years)	Ceramic (Cf_2O_4)	20	Several neutron radiography or well-logging sources
^{192}Ir	Beta, gamma (74.02 days)	Metallic	1000	Multiple industrial radiography units
^{226}Ra	Alpha (1600 years)	Salt ($RaSO_4$)	100	Old medical therapy sources

Source: Argonne National Laboratory, *Radiological Dispersal Device (RDD)*, EVS Human Health Fact Sheet, 2005c; U.S. Department of Health and Human Services, Radiological dispersal devices, 2010b. http://www.remm.nlm.gov/rdd.htm.

Russia, with most of them being used as power sources for lighthouses and navigation beacons. All Russian RTGs have long exhausted their designated service periods and are in need of dismantling (Figure 5.31). The urgency of this issue is underscored by three incidents involving vandalism and destruction of these dangerous sources—on the shore of the Baltic Sea, and in the Kola Bay (Alimov, 2003). The poor accountability for Soviet-era RTGs has been widely publicized. RTGs pose a considerable threat because they may contain tens of thousands of curies of Sr-90. Initial radiation levels have declined substantially in older RTGs because of radioactive decay, but levels in newer units could exceed 10,000 Ci. Beta emitters such as Sr-90 are primarily an internal health hazard if ingested or inhaled.

A number of isotopes in Table 5.5, for example, Am-241, Cf-252, Po-210, Pu-238, and Ra-226, are primarily alpha emitters. Alpha particles are easily shielded with minimal layers of protective material, so they do not pose a significant external health hazard. Rather, their health significance relates to ingestion or inhalation. In addition, Am-241 is commonly mixed with beryllium to produce a neutron-emitting source. Similarly, Cf-252 emits neutrons through spontaneous fission. Neutron emitters represent both an external and internal health hazard. Alpha or neutron emitters have been used in soil moisture gauges, medical pacemakers, and well logging gauges used in the petroleum industry.

Figure 5.31 Abandoned RTGs on the Kola Peninsula, Russia. (Courtesy of Finnmark region government, http://www.bellona.no/imagearchive/72029f025e5aa2e80c543023d7f1590b.)

Dispersal of Radioactive Material

One key aspect relating to radiation hazard of RDDs involves the ability of radioactive debris to disperse in the local environment. The ability to disperse is a function of the physical and chemical properties of the material used in the RDD. Solid metallic forms would be difficult to disperse, whereas powder forms could be dispersed readily. Cobalt, iridium, and polonium typically occur in solid metallic forms and are hence not readily dispersible (U.S. EPA, 2009). Several others, however, including americium, californium, and plutonium, tend to occur as oxides that could exist as a powder (Argonne National Laboratory, 2005a,b). Cesium is often prepared as cesium chloride, a powder that is highly soluble in water. Radium and strontium are used in various forms. Strontium fluoride in certain sealed sources is *sintered* such that it is essentially insoluble and nondispersible.

Ultimately, however, the original radioactive material used by a terrorist could be chemically or physically altered to enhance dispersal (Zimmerman, 2006). Finally, detonation of a chemical explosive could also physically and chemically alter radioactive materials to produce oxides as well as nitrates (from the explosives) occurring over a range of particle sizes (Argonne National Laboratory, 2005c).

Accidents with Radioactives

Numerous events have been documented regarding uncontrolled radioactive contamination. Possibly the worst-case example of a radiological accident is that which occurred in Goiânia, Brazil. In September 1987, a radiotherapy clinic, formerly owned by the Instituto Goiano de Radioterapia in Goiânia, moved to a new location and left its radiation cancer therapy unit behind. Metal scavengers entered the abandoned clinic and removed a teletherapy source capsule containing cesium-137. The cesium had an activity of 50.9 T Bq

189

(approximately 1400 Ci) (IAEA, 1988). Cesium-137 has a half-life of 30.1 years, and beta-decays to metastable barium-137. The Ba-137m has a half-life of 2.55 min and emits gamma radiation.

The sealed radioactive source capsule was set within a source wheel manufactured of lead and stainless steel. The source was brought to the home of one of the scavengers in attempts to disassemble and eventually sell it for scrap metal. Later that day, the two men handling the source experienced signs of acute radiation illness; both were vomiting and one had a swollen hand (edema) and diarrhea.

Several days later, one of the men punctured the 1-mm-thick window of the capsule and removed some of the cesium chloride powder. Thinking it might be gunpowder, he attempted to ignite it (there was no reaction). In the evening, noticing that the powder glowed blue in the dark, he brought it home and pieces were distributed to family and friends. People daubed the radioactive powder on their skin, as one might do with glitter at carnival time. The 6-year-old daughter of one of the scavengers handled the source while eating her meal by hand.

Contamination by cesium powder of citizens, homes, and businesses continued for about 2 weeks, resulting in an increasing number of adverse health effects. Early diagnoses were attributed to allergic reaction, food poisoning, or tropical disease. Almost 2 weeks later, hospital staff recognized symptoms of acute radiation syndrome in the victims. By this time, 249 people were contaminated, 151 exhibited both external and internal contamination, of which 20 people were seriously ill and four died (IAEA, 1988).

The panic that followed caused more than 112,000 people—10% of the population—to request radiation surveys to determine whether they had been exposed. At a make-shift facility in the city's Olympic Stadium, 250 persons were found to be contaminated. Twenty-eight had sustained radiation-induced skin injuries (burns), whereas 50 had ingested cesium. For the latter victims, there is concern that the internal deposition may result in an increased risk of cancer over their lifetime (IAEA, 1988).

Once the correct diagnosis of acute radiation sickness was made, the proper precautions were put into action. A local response agency had considered throwing the source into a nearby river; however, they were dissuaded at the last moment. Local citizens were persuaded to vacate the contaminated area, which by this time covered more than 40 city blocks. Of the 85 homes found to be significantly contaminated, 41 were evacuated and seven were demolished. It was also discovered that through routine travels over that short time, people had contaminated houses nearly 100 mi away. It is relevant to note that cesium chloride's high solubility contributed to the extensive contamination of persons, property, and the environment.

Various remedial actions were undertaken in the affected area such as decontamination of property, collection of contaminated clothing, removal of contaminated soil, and placing restrictions on consuming home-grown produce near the area. Cleanup generated 3500 m^3 of radioactive waste at a cost of $20 million.

The impacts of this incident also included psychological effects such as fear and anxiety for a large proportion of the city's inhabitants. Frightened by the possibility of radioactive contamination, neighboring provinces isolated Goiânia and boycotted its products. The price of their manufactured goods dropped 40%. Tourism, a primary industry, collapsed.

Total economic losses were estimated at hundreds of millions of dollars (Argonne National Laboratory, 2005c).

The accident in Goiânia was one of the most serious radiological accidents to have ever occurred. However, it has similarities with a number of other accidents, such as those in Mexico City (1962), Algeria (1978), Morocco (1983), and Ciudad Juarez in Mexico (1983). The Ciudad Juarez event was remarkably similar to the accident in Goiânia (Combs, 2008).

The Goiânia incident to some extent predicts the radiation contamination pattern during an event involving an RDD if it is not immediately realized that the explosion spread radioactive material, and also how hazardous even small amounts of ingested radioactive powder can be (Zimmerman and Loeb, 2004). Such information could be highly useful for responders in the event of an RDD attack.

A Variation on Dirty Bomb: The *Smoky Bomb*

In November 2006, former Russian Security Service officer Alexander Litvinenko died from acute radiation syndrome after his food was poisoned with polonium-210. In contrast to Cs-137, Po-210 is an alpha emitter. As stated in earlier in this chapter, alpha particles are fast-moving helium nuclei ejected during the radioactive decay of certain isotopes, including polonium-210. Alpha radiation cannot travel far and can be easily shielded—for example, by the outer layer of skin, a few sheets of paper or a layer of aluminum foil. Alpha radiation should not injure a person as long as the source stayed outside the body. Mr. Litvinenko was apparently killed by polonium that he ate or drank or inhaled. Mr. Litvinenko's death implies that *smoky bombs*, where alpha emitters are attached as fine particulate matter to airborne dust and other debris from fires or explosions, could be inhaled and/or ingested.

Polonium-210 is used by industry in devices that eliminate static electricity, for example, in certain applications of the photographic and textile industries (Zimmerman, 2006). It is used to control dust in *clean rooms* where computer chips and hard drives are manufactured. The goal for the radiological terrorist may be to have the victim ingest or inhale the alpha-emitting material so that it will cause the most harm. As alpha particles travel such short distances, they deposit all their energy in a relatively small number of cells, killing them or causing them to mutate, thus increasing the long-term risk of cancer. *Smoky bombs* based on alpha emitters might easily be just as dangerous as beta- or gamma-emitting dirty bombs. The terrorist's goal lies in getting very finely divided polonium into the air where people can breathe it. A smoky bomb exploded in a packed theater or in a crowded downtown could possibly kill hundreds.

QUESTIONS

1. Check various web sites and published sources to obtain data on the overpressure from a nuclear detonation. What range of pounds per square inch (lb/in^2) pressure can be generated from a 10-kt detonation? A 1-Mt detonation? Compare this data with that from detonations of conventional chemical explosives in Chapter 6.

2. Define the following terms: isotope, half-life, fissile, critical mass, soft x-rays, EMP.
3. List three natural sources of background radiation. What are the most common naturally occurring radioactive elements? In what materials do they occur?
4. Nuclear weapons are designed and constructed based on which two isotopes? Could other radioisotopes be used, for example, thorium? Discuss.
5. How is uranium processed before it is usable in a weapon? Describe the processes involved.
6. List the hazards to humans and structure from a thermonuclear detonation. The relative distribution of the effects depends on which factors?

REFERENCES

Adamsky, V. and Y. Smirnov. 1994. Moscow's biggest bomb: The 50-megaton test of October 1961. *Cold War International History Project Bulletin* 4(Fall): 19–21.

Albright, D. 2002. *Al Qaeda's Nuclear Program: Through the Window of Seized Documents.* The Nautilus Institute: Special Policy Forum 47 (November 6, 2002).

Albright, D. 2007. Shipments of weapons-usable plutonium in the commercial nuclear industry institute for science and international security, Washington, DC. http://isis-online.org/uploads /isis-reports/documents/plutonium_shipments.pdf (accessed January 3, 2007).

Albright, D. and H. Hunter. 2003. A bomb for the Ummah. *Bulletin of the Atomic Scientists* 59(2): 49–55.

Albright, D., and K. Kramer. 2005. Plutonium watch. Tracking plutonium inventories. In *Global Stocks of Nuclear Explosive Materials.* Washington, DC: Institute for Science and International Security.

Albright, D., K. Buehler, and H. Higgins. 2002. Bin Laden and the bomb. *Bulletin of the Atomic Scientists* 58(1): 2002.

Alimov, R. 2003. Radioisotope thermoelectric generators. Bellona. http://bellona.ru/bellona.org /english_import_area/international/russia/navy/northern_fleet/incidents/31772 (accessed August 3, 2015).

Anderson, H.L., E.T. Booth, J.R. Dunning, E. Fermi, G.N. Glasoe, and F.G. Slack. 1939. The fission of uranium. *Physical Reviews* 55(5): 511–512.

Anonymous. 2004. How not to catch a terrorist: A ten-step program. From the Files of the U.S. Intelligence Community. *Atlantic Monthly* 294(5): 50–52.

Argonne National Laboratory. 2005a. *Americium. Human Health Fact Sheet*, August, 2005.

Argonne National Laboratory. 2005b. *Californium. Human Health Fact Sheet*, August, 2005.

Argonne National Laboratory. 2005c. *Radiological Dispersal Device (RDD).* EVS Human Health Fact Sheet, August, 2005.

Associated Press. 2001. Russia: Terror groups scoped nuke site. October 26, 2001.

Atkinson, A.L. and A. Rosenthal. 2010. Thyroid carcinoma secondary to radiation cloud exposure from the Chernobyl Incident of 1986: A case study. *Case Reports in Oncology* 3(1): 83–87.

Atomicarchive. 2008a. Leo Szilard (1898–1964). http://www.atomicarchive.com/Bios/Szilard.shtml (accessed October 27, 2010).

Atomicarchive. 2008b. Blast effects. http://www.atomicarchive.com/Effects/effects3.shtml (accessed October 27, 2010).

BBC News. 2015. Nuclear smuggling deals 'thwarted' in Moldova. http://www.bbc.com/news /world-europe-34461732.

Borger, J. 2010. Pakistan nuclear weapons at risk of theft by terrorists, US study warns. *The Guardian.* 12 April 2010. http://www.theguardian.com/world/2010/apr/12/pakistan-nuclear-weapons -security-fears.

Bracken, P. 2003. *The Structure of the Second Nuclear Age*. New Haven, CT: Yale University. November 5, 2003. http://web.mit.edu/ssp/seminars/wed_archives_03fall/bracken.htm (accessed October 27, 2010).

Bunn, M. 2010. *Securing the Bomb 2010. Project On Managing The Atom*. Belfer Center for Science and International Affairs. Harvard Kennedy School, Harvard University. April 2010. www.nti.org /securingthebomb (accessed October 27, 2010).

Bunn, M. and A. Wier. 2003. *Plutonium Con Artists Sentenced in Russian Closed City of Sarov*. NIS Export Control Observer, no. 11 (November 2003), pp. 10–11.

Bunn, M. and M. Zenko. 2007. Securing the bomb. Introduction—The threat. Nuclear Threat Initiative. http://www.nti.org/e_research/cnwm/threat/global.asp (accessed October 27, 2010).

Bunn, M., A. Wier, and J. Friedman. 2005. Securing the bomb. The threat: The demand for black market fissile material. Nuclear Threat Initiative. http://www.nti.org/e_research/cnwm/threat /demand.asp#_ftn24 (accessed October 27, 2010).

Center for Nonproliferation Studies. 2001. Draft of indictment, United States of America versus Usama bin Laden. http://cns.miis.edu/reports/pdfs/binladen/060201.pdf.

Combs, S. 2008. El Cobalto. Window on State Government. http://www.webcitation.org/5WJdA3Qgz (accessed October 27, 2010).

Daly, S., J. Parachini, and R. Rosenau. 2005. *Aum Shinrikyo, Al Qaeda, and the Kinshasa Reactor Implications of Three Case Studies for Combating Nuclear Terrorism*. Santa Monica, CA: RAND Corporation.

Fisher, M. 2013. December 6, 2013. This alarming map shows dozens of radioactive materials thefts and losses every year. http://www.washingtonpost.com/blogs/worldviews/wp/2013/12/06 /this-alarming-map-shows-dozens-of-nuclear-materials-thefts-and-losses-every-year/.

Furlong, 2005. BBC. Hitler 'tested small atom bomb'. http://news.bbc.co.uk/2/hi/europe/4348497 .stm (accessed October 27, 2010).

Glasstone, S. and P. Dolan. 1977. *The Effects of Nuclear Weapons*. 3rd Edition. Washington, DC: U.S. Dept. of Defense and U.S. Dept of Energy.

Goldberg, J. and M. Ambinder, 2011. The ally from hell. *Atlantic Monthly*. http://www.theatlantic .com/magazine/archive/2011/12/the-ally-from-hell/308730/.

Hahn, O. and F. Strassmann. 1939. Über den Nachweis und das Verhalten der bei der Bestrahlung des Urans mittels Neutronen entstehenden Erdalkalimetalle. [On the detection and characteristics of the alkaline earth metals formed by irradiation of uranium with neutrons.] *Naturwissenschaften* 27(1): 11–15.

Huessy, P. 2007. *World Trade, Smuggling Nukes, & Homeland Security: The Challenge of Thinking Anew*. U.S. National Center for Critical Incident Analysis, February 15, 2007. http://www.dtic.mil /ndia/2007psa_winter/huessy2.pdf (accessed October 27, 2010).

International Atomic Energy Agency. 1988. *The Radiological Accident in Goiania*. Vienna: Wagramerstrasse.

International Atomic Energy Agency. 2002. Security of radioactive sources. Proceedings of an international conference held in Vienna, Austria, March 10–13, 2003. http://www-pub.iaea.org /MTCD/publications/PDF/Pub1165_web.pdf (accessed October 27, 2010).

International Atomic Energy Agency. 2008. https://www.iaea.org/sites/default/files/publications /reports/2008/anrep2008_full.pdf.

International Atomic Energy Agency. n.d. Features: Radioactive sources. http://www.iaea.org /NewsCenter/Features/RadSources/radsrc_faq.html (accessed October 27, 2010).

International Panel on Fissile Materials. 2013. Increasing Transparency of Nuclear-warhead and Fissile-material Stocks as a Step toward Disarmament. October 22, 2013, pp. 11, 13, http:// fissilematerials.org.

Karlsch, R. 2005. *Hitler's Bomb*. Germany: Deutsche Verlags-Anstal.

Kinshasa Digitalcong. 2002. *DRC: US Reportedly Plans to Buy Uranium to Prevent It from Falling into Terrorist Hands*. October 1, 2002, FBIS document no. AFP20021002000011.

Koryashkin, P. 2001. Russian Nuclear Ammunition Depots Well Protected—Official, ITAR-TASS, October 25, 2001.

Krehl, P.O. 2008. *History of Shock Waves, Explosions and Impact: A Chronological and Biographical Reference*. Berlin: Springer Science and Business Media.

Langford, R.E. 2004. *Introduction to Weapons of Mass Destruction: Radiological, Chemical, and Biological*. New York: Wiley-Interscience.

Lundeen, N. 2014. Iraq warned U.N. of stolen nuclear material, agency says. *Wall Street Journal*. http://www.wsj.com/articles/iraq-warned-u-n-of-stolen-nuclear-material-agency-says-1404992276.

Mathaba.net. 2005. Iran, holder of peaceful nuclear fuel cycle technology. http://mathaba.net/0_index.shtml?x=302258 (accessed October 27, 2010).

McCloud, K. and M. Osborne. 2001. WMD terrorism and Usama Bin Laden. James Martin Center for Nonproliferation Studies. CNS Reports. 11/20/01. http://cns.miis.edu/reports/binladen.htm.

Mendelsohn, C. 2005. Scope and accomplishments of the NNSA nuclear material threat reduction program. In 46th Annual Meeting of the Institute for Nuclear Materials Management. Phoenix, AZ.

Norris, R.S. and H.M. Kristensen. 2006. NRDC nuclear notebook: Global nuclear stockpiles, 1945–2006. *Bulletin of the Atomic Scientists* (July/August): 2006.

NOVA. 2003. Dirty bomb. http://www.pbs.org/wgbh/nova/dirtybomb/chrono.html (accessed October 27, 2010).

Nuclear Threat Initiative. 2001. Kazakhstan: Semipalatinsk test site. http://www.nti.org/db/nisprofs/kazakst/weafacil/semipala.htm (accessed October 27, 2010).

Nuclear Threat Initiative. 2014. Nuclear Confab to Urge 'Minimized' Stocks of Bomb-Usable Plutonium. Global Security Newswire. http://www.nti.org/gsn/article/nuclear-confab-urge-minimum-stocks-bomb-usable-plutonium/.

Nuclear Threat Initiative. 2016. Securing the Bomb. Washington, DC. http://www.nti.org/about/projects/Securing-bomb/ (accessed March 12, 2016).

Nuclear Threat Initiative. n.d. Why highly enriched uranium is a threat. http://www.nti.org/db/heu/index.html (accessed October 27, 2010).

Office of Technology Assessment. 1979. *The Effects of Nuclear War*. Washington, DC: U.S. Congress OTA.

Radio Free Europe/Radio Liberty Daily Report, October 9, 2000. As cited in Bunn., M., A. Wier, and J. Friedman. 2005. The threat: The demand for black market fissile material. Nuclear Threat Initiative. http://www.nti.org/e_research/cnwm/threat/demand.asp#_ftn24.

Rhodes, R. 1996. *Dark Sun: The Making of the Hydrogen Bomb*. New York: Simon and Schuster.

RIA-Novosti. 2003. *Russian Court Sentences Men for Weapons-Grade Plutonium Scam*. October 14, 2003, translated by BBC Monitoring Service.

Risen, J. and S. Engelberg. 2001. Signs of change in terror goals went unheeded. *New York Times*, October 14, 2001.

Time Magazine. 1961. Russia: A bang in Asia. September 8, 1961.

U.S. Centers for Disease Control and Prevention. n.d. Explosions and Refuge Chambers. Zipf, R.K. and K.L. Cashdollar. Effects of blast pressure on structures and the human body. http://www.cdc.gov/niosh/docket/archive/pdfs.NIOSH-125/125-ExplosionsandRefugeChambers.pdf (accessed February 22, 2016).

U.S. Departments of the Army, the Navy, and the Air Force. 1996. *NATO Handbook on the Medical Aspects of NBC Defensive Operations*. AMedP-6(B). FM 8–9. Army Field Manual 8–9. Navy Medical Publication 5059. Air Force Joint Manual 44–151. Washington, DC, February 1, 1996.

U.S. Department of Health and Human Services, 2010a. Public health emergency. http://www.phe.gov/Preparedness/planning/playbooks/rdd/Pages/default.aspx (accessed October 27, 2010).

U.S. Department of Health and Human Services, 2010b. Radiological dispersal devices. http://www.remm.nlm.gov/rdd.htm (accessed October 27, 2010).

U.S. Environmental Protection Agency. 2009. Cobalt. Radiation protection. http://www.epa.gov/radiation/radionuclides/cobalt.html (accessed October 27, 2010).

U.S. Environmental Protection Agency. 2010. Radiation protection. Health effects. http://www.epa
.gov/rpdweb00/understand/health_effects.html (accessed October 27, 2010).

U.S. Federal Emergency Management Agency. n.d. Radiological emergency response. IS-301. http://
training.fema.gov/EMIWeb/IS/is301lst.asp (accessed October 27, 2010).

U.S. Government Accountability Office. 2004. Nuclear nonproliferation: DOE needs to take action to
further reduce the use of weapons-usable uranium in civilian research reactors. GAO-04-807.
Washington, DC http://www.gao.gov/new.items/d04807.pdf as of 10 July 2007 (accessed
October 27, 2010).

U.S. Government Accounting Office. 1999. *Status of Transparency Measures for U.S. Purchase of Russian
Highly Enriched Uranium.* Washington, DC: GAO. p. 7. (GAO is now called the U.S. Government
Accountability Office.)

U.S. Nuclear Regulatory Commission. 2010. Fact sheet on biological effects of radiation. http://www
.nrc.gov/reading-rm/doc-collections/fact-sheets/bio-effectsradiation.html (accessed October 27,
2010).

Wells, H.G. 1914. *The World Set Free.* Seattle, WA: CreateSpace Independent Publishing Platform.

Willman, D. and A.C. Miller. 2001. Nuclear threat is real, experts warn. *Los Angeles Times.* November
11, 2001. http://articles.latimes.com/2001/nov/11/news/mn-2948.

Wrong, M. 1999. More wreck than reactor. *Financial Times.* August 21, 1999, p. 8.

Zimmerman, P.D. 2006. The smoky bomb threat. *New York Times.* December 16, 2006.

Zimmerman, P.D. and C. Loeb. 2004. Dirty bombs: The threat revisited. *Defense Horizons* 38: 1–11.

Figure 1.7 Remains of Pan Am flight 103 that exploded over Lockerbie, Scotland, 1988. (Courtesy of US Embassy, http://www.america.gov/st/peacesec-english/2009/August/20090820120057esnamfuak 0.8462335.html&distid=ucs.)

Figure 1.15 Aftermath of the World Trade Center attacks of 2001. (Courtesy of Centers for Disease Control and Prevention, http://www.cdc.gov/niosh/blog/images/resp-prot.JPG.)

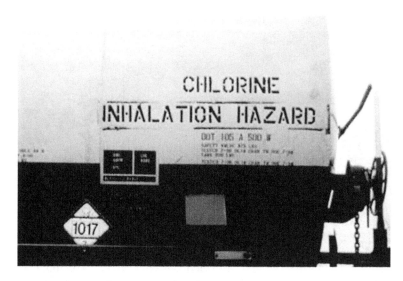

Figure 3.7 Chlorine rail tanker. (Courtesy of ATSDR Report on Chemical Terrorism, http://www
.mapcruzin.com/scruztri/docs/cep1118992.htm.)

Figure 3.8 Ignition of white phosphorus. (Courtesy of Wikipedia, https://en.wikipedia.org/wiki
/White_phosphorus_munitions; USAF—National Museum of the U.S. Air Force photo 110310-F-
XN622-009, Public Domain, https://commons.wikimedia.org/w/index.php?curid=14856340.)

Figure 5.27 Fireball and mushroom cloud following detonation at the Nevada test site. (Courtesy of the Nevada Division of Environmental Protection, http://ndep.nv.gov/boff/upshot.jpg.)

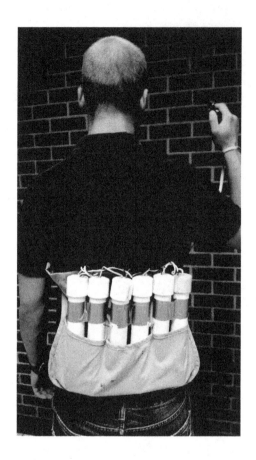

Figure 7.5 Bomb vest.

Figure 8.12 Long-range acoustic device in use by the U.S. Navy. (Courtesy of the National Oceanic and Atmospheric Administration, http://www.vos.noaa.gov/MWL/aug_09/Images/antipiracy tech.jpg.)

Figure 10.9 Example of Level A PPE. (From U.S. Army Dugway Proving Ground. With permission.)

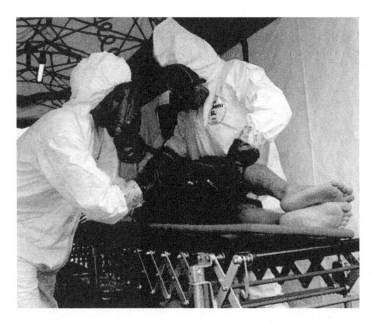

Figure 10.18 Secondary decon of a victim. (Courtesy of Alaska Department of Environmental Conservation, http://www.dec.state.ak.us/SPAR/perp/gallery/MassDeconJune2007/images/Mass Decon_June2007_p009.jpg.)

Figure 10.20 *Star* configuration used in emergency decon.

Figure 10.33 Phytoremediation is a very promising, low-cost technology that can be used for the destruction and/or removal of soil contaminants.

6

Explosives Hazards

Bombs do not choose. They will hit everything.

Nikita Khrushchev

Last night the United States dropped four 2,000-pound bombs on Saddam Hussein. I don't know anything about explosives, but my Heavens, do those things even need to explode?

David Letterman
The Late Show, 2003

INTRODUCTION

In modern societies, the risk of explosive incidents is significant. Beyond military applications, numerous businesses manufacture, transport, and use low and high explosives in daily operations (i.e., mining and demolition). In addition, explosives continue to be the weapon of choice for terrorists worldwide—of all the weapons of mass destruction (WMDs) (chemical, biological, radiological, nuclear, explosive) reportedly used, the most commonly used, by far, are explosive devices.

Emergency responders encounter explosives in a variety of applications. Military and commercial explosives may be adapted for improvised bombs. In addition, many powerful explosives can be home-made from simple ingredients. The hazards of explosive weapons are underscored by their relative ease of manufacture; information on bomb making is available in library books and in bomb training manuals available at many gun shows. In addition, detailed bomb-making instructions are available on the Internet.

DEFINITION OF EXPLOSIVES

An explosive device is any device designed to explode, with concomitant release of a blast wave, gases, light, heat, and sound.

The U.S. Department of Transportation (DOT) defines an explosive as (Code of Federal Regulations):

> Any substance or article, including a device, which is designed to function by explosion (i.e., an extremely rapid release of gas and heat) or which, by chemical reaction within itself, is able to function in a similar manner even if not designed to function by explosion, unless the substance or article is otherwise classed.
>
> 49 CFR 173.50(a)

An *explosion* is defined as the rapid expansion of matter into a greater volume. Conventional high explosives are not the only materials involved in explosions; for example, an industrial boiler can experience a pressure buildup and explode.

There are three general categories of explosions:

1. Nuclear
2. Mechanical
3. Chemical

A nuclear detonation occurs within the nucleus of an atom as a result of either fission or fusion processes (see Chapter 5). Fission occurs when the nucleus of an atom is split, resulting in the release of massive quantities of energy. Nuclear fusion occurs when light nuclei (e.g., hydrogen or deuterium atoms) are fused, forming a heavier element with the generation of substantial energy. Both reactions have been intensively studied and adapted for use in nuclear weapons. Fission devices were dropped on Hiroshima and Nagasaki, Japan, in 1945. Fusion devices have never been used in warfare.

In a mechanical explosion, the internal pressure of a vessel is greater than its ability to withstand the pressure. An example is the bursting of a boiler.

A chemical explosion results from the ignition of an energetic (reactive) substance. A chemical disintegration occurs, along with the production of light, heat, and shock wave. Chemical reactions take place within the electron cloud of an element; this is also where the explosion occurs. This chapter will be devoted solely to chemical explosions.

HISTORY OF EXPLOSIVES DEVELOPMENT

Ancient Times to the Renaissance

Among the first of all energetic (explosive) materials ever developed and tested was black powder. Historians, however, still differ regarding its origins; the Chinese, Hindus, and Arabs have all been credited with its discovery. In 1200 c.e., Arabian Abd Allah recorded the use of saltpeter as a key ingredient of black powder. In 1249, Roger Bacon, an English monk, documented a formula for black powder that included saltpeter, charcoal, and sulfur.

Early in its development, black powder was found to be useful for both military and work purposes. The Chinese and Europeans became aware of the benefits of black powder at about the same time. By 1232, the Chinese developed rockets and a weapon they called *heaven-shaking thunder crash bomb*, an iron bomb attached to a chain that could be lowered from city walls to explode among attacking forces (Langford, 2004; Meng, 2005). The earliest mention of black powder on military supply lists was in 1326.

The explosive mixtures in use to this point were for black powder, not gunpowder. Different proportions of saltpeter, charcoal, and sulfur were required to fire weapons from early cannons. In the middle of the twelfth century, John Arderne, an Englishman, gave the proportions of saltpeter, charcoal, and sulfur as 6:2:1. The Germans used a mixture of 4:1:1 in 1350. Other, mostly useless ingredients such as wine, urine, arsenic, amber, alcohol, and camphor were added to the recipe in attempts to improve stability, reduce absorption of moisture, and prevent crumbling.

In the seventeenth and eighteenth centuries, a number of advancements in explosives manufacture occurred. In 1654, ammonium nitrate was prepared by J.R. Glauber, a German chemist. Picric acid, a highly unstable and powerful explosive, was discovered by Pierre Woulfe, a French chemist, in 1771 by treating silk with nitric acid. Soon afterward, potassium chlorate was prepared by Claude Berthollet, a French chemist. His proposal to use potassium chlorate instead of potassium nitrate in black powder was dropped after a catastrophic explosion during its manufacture in 1788 (U.S. Department of the Army, 1990).

Nineteenth Century

By the nineteenth century, modern energetic materials technology had arrived. New explosives were discovered, replacing the black powder mixtures that had been so popular for centuries for weapons and blasting. New energetic materials influenced the design and performance of weapons; concomitantly, the invention of new weapons prompted the search for more effective and less expensive explosives.

In 1800, Edward Howard, an English chemist, discovered mercury fulminate, a highly sensitive and powerful explosive. In 1807, the use of mercury fulminate as an explosive primer was patented by the Scot Alexander Forsyth. In 1825, Rev. Dr. Clayton in England isolated benzene, creosote, and naphthalene from coal tar. These products were later incorporated into explosives such as trinitrobenzene and nitronaphthalene.

The application of a flame directly to explosive solids (e.g., in mining) was a highly dangerous activity. In 1831, the safety fuse was invented by British engineer William Bickford. The so-called Bickford fuse contained a core of black powder tightly wrapped in jute yarn. The fuse was designed to ensure accurate and consistent burning time. The Bickford safety fuse was later made waterproof by applying a coat of asphalt covered with textile.

Nitrostarch was discovered in 1833 by Henri Braconnot, a French chemist, while dissolving starch in concentrated nitric acid (Labrude and Becq, 2003). In 1845, guncotton (later termed nitrocellulose) was formulated by Christian Schoenbein, a German chemist at the University of Basel, Switzerland, by treating cotton with a nitric acid–sulfuric acid mixture. Schoenbein demonstrated that nitrocellulose was up to four times as powerful as black powder for blasting. During early efforts to manufacture guncotton, serious accidental explosions occurred, which delayed its general use as an explosive. Eventually, however, guncotton became universally accepted for use in blasting.

Nitroglycerin, an ester of glycerin and nitric acid, was invented by Asconio Sobrero, an Italian chemist, in 1846. Nitroglycerin was found to be extremely sensitive to even slight shocks, so its commercial use was delayed. This promising explosive was eventually used on a large scale with the invention of dynamite, blasting gelatin, and smokeless powder. Nitroglycerin production facilities were designed for commercial application by Alfred Nobel, a Swedish chemist (Figure 6.1). In 1862, the first plant was constructed at Heleneborg, Sweden.

In 1863, trinitrotoluene (TNT) was prepared by J. Willibrand, a German scientist. TNT had been used for many years in the dye industry; however, it was not used as an explosive until 1904. Thereafter, TNT became one of the most commonly used high explosives. Two years later, nitrocellulose was purified by Sir Frederick Abel, an English chemist. Abel pulped, washed, and compressed nitrocellulose into blocks, sheets, disks, and cylinders. These forms were found to be useful for rock blasting.

In 1866, dynamite was invented by Alfred Nobel by absorbing nitroglycerin (75%) in kieselguhr (diatomaceous earth) (25%). Kieselguhr, an inactive ingredient, stabilized the nitroglycerin and made dynamite a much safer explosive to handle. Dynamites with an *active base* were soon patented by Nobel. In these new formulations, nitroglycerin was mixed with combustibles (sawdust, charcoal, starch, etc.), and oxidizers (sodium nitrate or

Figure 6.1 Alfred B. Nobel, Swedish chemist and inventor of dynamite. (Courtesy of Wikimedia Commons, https://commons.wikimedia.org/wiki/File:AlfredNobel_adjusted.jpg.)

potassium nitrate). By 1884, ammonium nitrate became widely used in dynamite formulations. These additives resulted in a more efficient explosive than earlier dynamite recipes. In 1868, Nobel went on to invent the blasting cap, a device used to initiate larger explosives. Nobel's cap consisted of mercury fulminate in a copper tube. The cap was crimped to one end of a safety fuse and then inserted into the dynamite casing.

In 1875, The Explosives Act was enacted by the British Government after a catastrophic explosion in Birmingham killed 53. The Act called for trained inspectors who were given the power to inspect all factories and storage magazines to ensure that manufacturing, storage, and handling operations were carried out safely. As a result, the number of deaths in explosives factories was substantially reduced.

Smokeless powder was invented in 1884 by Paul Vieille of France. This powder proved valuable on the battlefield, as the enemy was no longer capable of locating a hidden shooter by the smoke of his gun. The shaped charge was discovered accidently in 1888 by Charles Munroe, a scientist at the U.S. Naval Academy. Munroe discovered that a concave-shaped explosive charge was capable of piercing a steel plate. Munroe's discovery went on to have important benefits to both military and industrial applications.

In 1889, cordite was prepared by Dr. W. Kellner. Cordite was patented for the British Government and was adopted as a military propellant named CSP (cordite smokeless powder). The high-explosive cyclonite (RDX) was first prepared in 1899 by Georg Henning of Germany. Starting in 1925, RDX was manufactured at an industrial scale at Picatinny Arsenal, New Jersey. It was not until World War II, however, that the value of RDX as an explosive truly came to be appreciated. Extensive research into RDX manufacturing processes and applications were carried out at that time. Pentaerythritol tetranitrate (later to be termed PETN) was first synthesized in 1894 by nitration of pentaerythritol (Zoltan, 2007).

At the end of the nineteenth century, aluminized explosives, that is, those enriched with powdered aluminum to increase performance, were first proposed in Germany. Ammonal, the first such explosive, contained ammonium nitrate, charcoal, and aluminum. It was not until World War II, however, that the United States and Allied forces realized the benefits of aluminized explosives.

In the early twentieth century, antifreeze for dynamite was researched extensively in many countries, in part as a result of a disastrous explosion during defrosting dynamite in Germany. Sigurd Nauckhoff of Sweden published his work on dynamite antifreeze in 1905, listing requirements for a satisfactory formulation (Fordham, 1980). In the same year, nitrostarch was produced in a stable form. Nitrostarch is similar to nitrocellulose but is lower in strength. Nitrostarch does not cause negative health effects from skin contact as do TNT, nitroglycerin, and dynamite.

Early in the new century, substantial strides were made in development of detonating cord and blasting caps. In 1908, a detonating cord containing TNT instead of black powder was patented in France. This cord had a detonation velocity of 4880 m/s (or 16,000 ft/s). In 1914, lead styphnate (trinitroresorcinol), an initiating explosive, was first prepared by E. von Herz of Germany. Russian Col. A. Solonina was the first to propose using lead styphnate in detonators. Ammonium picrate (Dunnite or Explosive D) was standardized in the United States as a bursting charge for armor-piercing shells. These projectiles could be fired through 12 in of armor plate, and could be detonated by an insensitive primer.

By 1912 TNT was adopted as the standard bursting charge in high-explosive shells for the field artillery of the U.S. Army.

World War I

At the outbreak of war in the summer of 1914, the German General Staff had planned to fight a conflict fueled predominantly by high explosives. The Germans rapidly converted their chemical industrial facilities to production of synthetic ammonia, nitric acid, and sulfuric acid, all required for the manufacture of explosives and chemical warfare agents. The key to German explosives production was the Haber process for producing ammonia from atmospheric nitrogen. Using the Haber process, Germany became independent of foreign nations for its supply of ammonia and nitric acid.

Smoke munitions were used on land and sea by the belligerent powers in World War I. In July 1915, the British used *smoke pots*, vessels filled with pitch, tallow, black powder, and potassium nitrate. The first large-scale smoke operation occurred on September 20, 1915, when the Canadians fired several thousand smoke shells from trench mortars during the attack against Messines Ridge (Belgium) in mid-1917.

About 2,500,000 tons of high explosives were used by the warring powers during the war, resulting in an estimated 10 million casualties.

Interwar Years

During the period between the two world wars, the U.S. Army invested significant funding and resources toward the development of ammunition and weaponry. During these two decades RDX, PETN, ethylenedinitramine (EDNA), lead styphnate, and lead azide were formulated as military explosives. The development of processes for producing toluene from petroleum greatly enhanced the availability of TNT, and permitted the manufacture of powerful and castable explosives such as composition B and pentolite (U.S. Department of the Army, 1990). During World War I, the supply of toluene was quite limited—it was derived primarily from coal as a by-product of coke ovens, and some was extracted from natural gas.

From the 1920s onward, scientists at Picatinny Arsenal (New Jersey) had been searching for a compound having the high brisance (shattering power) of RDX without the sensitivity to friction and impact. Research by chemist George C. Hale and others led to the discovery of EDNA, the first entirely American high explosive. More powerful than TNT, EDNA was slightly less powerful then RDX but was also less sensitive. EDNA's stability gave it an important advantage in terms of manufacturing, loading, storage, transportation, and field use. Named haleite (in honor of Dr. Hale), this new explosive could be loaded into small shells without a desensitizing agent.

World War II

When World War II began in September 1939, the standard United States charge for high-explosive bombs was TNT. Early in the war, however, other fillings were used, such as RDX, an explosive known too its great power and brisance but generally considered too sensitive. The British developed a method of using beeswax to desensitize the RDX, and used this explosive with success in the 2-ton *blockbuster* bombs dropped on Berlin in April 1941. The most sensitive of all high explosives was PETN, which was even more readily detonated than RDX. PETN was therefore, diluted with TNT to desensitize it. The new composition, named pentolite, has been extensively used in detonators, bazooka rockets, rifle grenades, boosting devices, and in the shaped charges of antitank shells (U.S. Department of the Army, 1990).

Owing to the extensive use of armor in World War II, considerable research was devoted to development of antitank weapons, armor-piercing shells, and shaped charge munitions. New special-purpose binary explosives such as tetrytol and picratol were developed for use in demolitions, chemical bombs, and armor-piercing weapons. A number of plastic explosives used for demolition work were developed in Great Britain and the United States, the most important being the C-3 composition based on RDX.

Primacord, a highly accurate detonating cord, was created in 1936 by the Ensign-Bickford Company (Simsbury, CT). Primacord consisted of PETN covered with textiles and waterproofing material. This detonating cord had a velocity of 21,000 ft/s (6405 m/s), and has been used extensively by the armed forces for demolition work.

The development of napalm (*nap* for naphthenic acids; *palm* for the coconut fatty acids that comprised the thickener) by the United States in 1941 made use of gasoline in flame weapons. This gelled mixture made it possible for aircraft to deliver firebombs over difficult areas. Napalm proved to be one of the most effective aerial incendiary agents in the war. On the evening of March 9, 1945, more than 300 B-29 bombers flew over Tokyo, dropping about 2000 tons of incendiaries, mostly clusters of M69 6-lb bomblets. The M69 was a tube that contained a black powder propellant charge that ignited and ejected the napalm filling from the tube (U.S. Department of the Army, 1990). Aerial photos indicated 16 mi^2 had been destroyed by fire. Records examined after the war showed that more than 250,000 buildings in Tokyo were destroyed in this raid. More than 100,000 tons of incendiaries were dropped on the cities of Japan during World War II. Most were M69 bomb clusters.

Post–World War II

As a result of the involvement of the United States in the Korean War (1950–1953) and the Vietnam Conflict (1964–1973), there was an incentive for development of even more effective munitions and more powerful explosives (Figure 6.2). In 1950, metal oxidizer explosives (MOXs) were developed by the National Fireworks Ordnance Corporation (West Hanover, MA), for use in mostly small-caliber antiaircraft shells.

In 1952, plastic-bonded RDX was developed by the Los Alamos Scientific Laboratory of the University of California for use as a mechanical strength explosive—this new material was useful in hardening manganese alloys, among other applications. PB-RDX consisted of 90% RDX, 8.5% polystyrene, and 1.5% dioctylphthalate. By 1960, detacord, detaflex flexible cord explosive, and detasheet flexible sheet explosives were developed by DuPont Company.

Slurry explosives were created by M.A. Cook and H.E. Farnham by adding water to ammonium nitrate to form slurries of the oxidizer salt, ammonium nitrate and sodium

Figure 6.2 An artillery officer directs troops as they fire white phosphorous shells on a Communist-held post in February 1951. (Courtesy of National Archives, http://www.archives.gov/publica tions/prologue/images/korean-war-artillery.jpg.)

nitrate, and a solid fuel sensitizer. Slurry explosives were found to provide many times the detonation force of ammonium nitrate–fuel oil (ANFO) explosives.

In 1992, in the aftermath of the Gulf War, explosives were used to extinguish most of the 700 Kuwaiti oil well fires that had been set by Saddam Hussein's retreating troops. One method involved the placement of high explosives in augered shafts at inclined angles to the well pipe. The explosives removed soil and rock to create a ramp for access to the well pipe and also to crimp the well pipe. Two bombs may be physically placed such that they straddle the well (Freepatentsonline, 2009).

CHARACTERISTICS OF EXPLOSIVES

For a chemical to be considered an explosive, the material must exhibit the following (NATO, 1996):

- *Initiation of reaction*: A reaction must be capable of being initiated by the application of shock, heat, or similar insult to a small portion of the material.
- *Rapidity of reaction*: An explosive reaction is distinguished from a typical combustion reaction by the great speed with which it occurs. Unless the reaction occurs

rapidly, the thermally expanded gases will be dissipated in the medium and there will be no explosion.

- *Formation of gases*: Gases are evolved from the decomposition of solid, liquid, or gaseous fuels. When a carbonaceous substance is burned, the carbon and hydrogen in the fuel combine with oxygen in the atmosphere to form carbon dioxide and H_2O (steam), together with flames, heat, and light.
- *Evolution of heat*: The generation of large quantities of heat accompanies every explosive chemical reaction. This rapid liberation of heat causes the gaseous products of the reaction to expand and generate high pressures. Liberation of heat at slow rates will not cause an explosion.

CLASSIFICATION OF EXPLOSIVES

DOT regulates the transportation of chemical explosives and articles containing explosives. DOT recognizes five divisions of Class 1 (explosives): 1.1 through 1.5 (Figure 6.3). These divisions are explained in Chapter 3.

Figure 6.3 Selected DOT placards for an explosive article.

A number of other systems are possible for classification of energetic materials; for example,

- Pure explosive chemicals versus mixtures
- Chemicals versus use forms (slurries, emulsions and sheet explosives)
- Chemical class (nitroamines versus nitroaromatics versus nitrate esters)
- Rate of decomposition (low explosives versus high explosives)
- Commercial versus military types

In this section, we will discuss the types of explosives based on rate of decomposition, military versus commercial materials, and use forms. This will be followed by a discussion of improvised explosive devices (IEDs).

Rate of Decomposition

Explosives are classified as low or high explosives based upon rate of decomposition. Low explosives burn rapidly (or deflagrate), whereas high explosives detonate (Box 6.1). This classification depends, in part, on how the materials are packaged and used. One of the most important properties involved in rating an explosive is detonation velocity, a value designated for both confined and unconfined conditions. Detonation velocity is the speed at which the detonation wave travels through the explosive. This property is usually measured in an unconfined column of explosive 1¼ inch (3.2 cm) in diameter. Detonation velocity is a function of chemical composition of the explosive, density, particle size, charge diameter, and degree of confinement. Factors that increase detonation velocity include decreased particle size, increased charge (i.e., fuel) diameter, and increased confinement. The confined detonation velocity of commercial explosives varies from about 4000 to 25,000 ft/s (Table 6.1) (Global Security, 2008).

Low Explosives

Low explosives function by deflagration (i.e., rapid combustion). Shock waves of low explosives travel at speeds less than 1130 ft/s (the speed of sound). Low explosives are normally

---

BOX 6.1   BASIC TERMINOLOGY ASSOCIATED WITH EXPLOSIVES

- *Deflagration*—Rapid burning with the generation of intense heat and light. This reaction occurs at subsonic speeds (i.e., less than 1130 ft/s or 343 m/s). Deflagration typically occurs with pyrotechnic materials as well as propellants such as smokeless powder and black powder.
- *Detonation*—An explosive event of almost instantaneous decomposition of fuel. Detonation reactions occur at supersonic speeds (greater than approximately 1130 ft/s). Detonation is a form of energy release that supports a lethal shock wave.
- *Deflagration to detonation transition (DDT)*—The transition from deflagration to a detonation, resulting in an explosion.

Table 6.1 Chemical and Physical Properties of Selected Explosives

Classification	Explosive	Rate of Detonation (ft/s)	Chemical Formula	Density	Sensitivity
Low explosives	Black powder	1312	KNO_3, S, C	Varies	Low
	Smokeless powder	Rapid burning		Varies	Low
Primary explosives	Lead azide	13,400 to 17,000	$Pb(N_3)_2$	4.71 g/cm³, solid	High
	Lead styphnate	17,100	$C_6HN_3O_8Pb$	3.02 g/cm³, solid	High
	Mercury fulminate	11,500 to 21,100	$Hg(CNO)_2$	4.43 g/cm³	High
Secondary explosives	Ammonium picrate	22,500	$C_6H_2(NO_2)_3ONH_4$		
	C-4	26,400			
	Flex-x	22,300			
	HMX	29,900	$C_6H_2(NO_2)_3ONH_4$	1.91 g/cm³, solid	Low
	Nitrocellulose	21,900			
	Nitroglycerin	4900 to 25,400	$C_3H_5N_3O_9$	1.6 g/cm³ at 15°C	High
	PETN	27,200	$C_5H_8N_4O_{12}$	1.77 g/cm³ at 20°C	Medium
	Picric acid	19,000	$C_6H_3N_3O_7$	1.76 g/cm³, solid	
	RDX	26,800	$C_3H_6N_6O_6$	1.82 g/cm³	Low
	Tetryl	25,800	$C_7H_5N_5O_8$	1.73 g/cm³	Insensitive
	Trinitrotoluene (TNT)	21,800 to 22,400	$C_7H_5N_3O_6$	1.65 g/cm³	Insensitive
Tertiary explosives	Ammonium nitrate	3300 to 8200	NH_4NO_3	1.72 g/cm³, solid	

Source: Beveridge, A. (Ed.), *Forensic Investigation of Explosions*, CRC Press, Boca Raton, FL, 1998; U.S. Department of the Army, Military Explosives, Technical Manual, TM 9-1300-214, Washington, DC, 1990; U.S. Department of the Army, Explosives Series. Properties of Explosives of Military Interest, *Engineering Design Handbook*, Washington, DC, 1971.

used as propellants and pyrotechnics, and include black powder and most smokeless powders. Both black powder and smokeless powder are used in military and civilian applications.

Propellants

Propellants are designed to release a gas under controlled conditions to perform useful work functions. Examples include the deflagration of gunpowder for firing a projectile (e.g., bullet) out of the barrel of a gun. The key to safe and effective use of propellants is to maintain a controlled release of gas. When propellants are confined or when control is lost, explosions may occur.

Pyrotechnics

Pyrotechnics are designed to produce light, smoke, heat, and sound. The pyrotechnics we are most familiar with include fireworks, which are designed for entertainment. However, pyrotechnics are also important in the workplace, for example, as ingredients of road flares and other illumination devices.

High Explosives

Whereas propellants or low explosives are designed to produce a controlled release of energy, high explosives are engineered to detonate with a near-instantaneous release of energy. High explosives function by detonation; shock and heat waves travel at speeds greater than 1130 ft/s. Some energetic materials have been measured to attain speeds of more than 29,000 ft/s. By virtue of their destructive force, high explosives are used in military ordnance. High explosives are usually initiated by a blasting cap but high temperatures, shock, or friction may also cause initiation.

High explosives are divided into three classes—primary, secondary, and tertiary—based on their sensitivities to various stimuli. Primary explosives are the most sensitive and tertiary the least sensitive. For first responders attempting to identify the safest course of action in a hazardous situation, understanding sensitivity of an explosive material is critical.

Primary Explosives

Primary explosives are all extremely sensitive and therefore extremely dangerous to handle and transport some common primary explosives include:

- Copper acetylide
- Hexamethylene triperoxide diamine
- Lead azide
- Lead picrate
- Lead styphnate
- Mercury fulminate

BOX 6.2   PRIMARY EXPLOSIVE: LEAD AZIDE

Lead azide is the most popular primary explosive in use today (Figure 6.4). It is rated as highly sensitive to both friction and shock. The velocity of detonation is approximately 17,500 ft/s. Its color varies from white to buff. Lead azide is widely used as an initiating explosive in high-explosive detonator devices. Since lead azide does not react with aluminum, detonator capsules for lead azide are composed of this metal. The hygroscopicity of lead azide is very low, that is, it does not attract water. In addition, water does not reduce its impact sensitivity, as is the case with other primaries such as mercury fulminate. Lead azide is completely stable in storage.

Lead azide is poisonous to biota (Global Security, 2008).

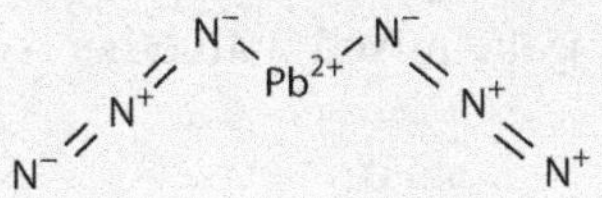

Figure 6.4   Structure of lead azide.

- Nitrogen trichloride
- Nitrogen triiodide
- Silver acetylide
- Silver fulminate
- Silver azide
- Tetramine copper complexes
- Tetryl(2,4,6-trinitrophenyl-*N*-methylnitramine)
- Triacetone triperoxide

The U.S. military had attempted to use a number of primary explosives for conventional munitions; however, because of their extreme sensitivity, such use was abandoned. As a result of their sensitivity, primary explosives are typically used in only small quantities, for example, in blasting caps (Box 6.2). Primary explosives are therefore useful in initiating less sensitive, but more powerful secondary explosives in a so-called firing train.

Secondary Explosives

Secondary explosives are markedly less sensitive than primary explosives and require a significant stimulus (e.g., the energy levels created by another explosion) to detonate; therefore, secondary explosives are initiated by a primary explosive. Secondary explosives are most commonly used in bulk quantities. Some popular examples include the following:

- TNT
- PETN
- Cyclotrimethylene trinitramine (RDX)
- Cyclotetramethylene-tetranitramine (HMX) (Box 6.3)

BOX 6.3   SECONDARY EXPLOSIVE: HMX

HMX, also known as octogen and cyclotetramethylene-tetranitramine, is a powerful and relatively insensitive nitramine high explosive that is chemically related to RDX (see the following discussion). The *HMX* acronym has been assigned a variety of names, for example, *high melting explosive* and *Her Majesty's explosive*; however, the accepted name is *high-molecular-weight RDX* (Figure 6.5).

HMX is the highest-energy solid explosive produced on a large scale in the United States. It explodes violently at high temperatures (534°F and above). Given this property, HMX is used exclusively for military purposes as a component of plastic-bonded explosives, of rocket propellant, and high-explosive burster charges, and to implode fissionable material in nuclear devices (Global Security, 2008). HMX is seldom used alone in military applications but is typically mixed with other compounds such as TNT.

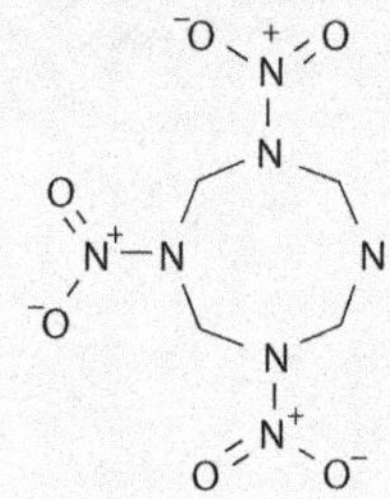

Figure 6.5   Structure of HMX.

Secondary explosives are manufactured to tolerate rough handling. Regardless, however, they must still be handled with extreme caution.

Tertiary Explosives

Tertiary explosives are the most insensitive of high explosives. Most formulations contain the common salt, ammonium nitrate. Ammonium nitrate fuel oil (ANFO) is a common tertiary explosive and a very insensitive substance. ANFO is discussed later in this section. Tertiary explosives require a significant stimulus to cause detonation. A blasting cap, shock, or small flame will not initiate them. Usually, a quantity of secondary explosive (a booster), for example, dynamite, is needed for initiation.

The Firing Train

In military and commercial explosives as well as in terrorist weapons, a sequence of primary, secondary, and often tertiary explosives is used for maximum effectiveness. The firing train (also known as the explosive train) is a specific sequence of steps resulting in progressively larger explosions. The firing train explosions increase in size until the main charge is detonated (Figure 6.6).

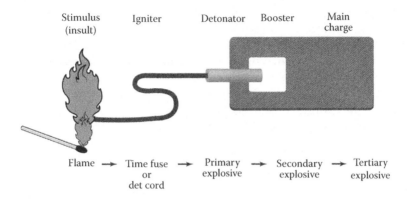

Figure 6.6 Schematic of an explosive firing train.

A minor stimulus begins the train. The stimulus can be fire, an electric pulse, or other insult. If the stimulus is a flame, this will ignite a propellant (e.g., black powder contained within a time fuse). The burning propellant delivers flame to a primary explosive or *detonator* contained in a blasting cap. The primary explosive subsequently detonates, delivering a shock and flame to the secondary explosive. The secondary explosive or *booster* subsequently detonates, delivering a significant shock to the tertiary explosive. The tertiary explosive or *main charge* then detonates, completing the firing train.

Other possible firing trains, which vary in complexity, can be devised. For example, for black powder confined within a steel pipe in an IED, only three steps are needed: (1) a flame ignites a fuse, (2) the fuse ignites the black powder inside the pipe, (3) a DDT, and an explosion occurs (see Box 6.1).

COMMERCIAL AND MILITARY EXPLOSIVES

Military explosives are designed to deliver an enormous quantity of energy very quickly. This ability also allows them to effectively shatter or cut targets. Many commercial explosives have the same characteristics as military explosives; however, numerous commercial explosives are designed to push or heave a target, rather than shatter.

COMMERCIAL EXPLOSIVES

Black Powder

Black powder is composed of 75% potassium nitrate (saltpeter) or sodium nitrate, 10% sulfur, and 15% charcoal, a recipe essentially unchanged since its discovery by Chinese alchemists in the ninth century. Black powder mixtures range in color from black to dark brown, and grains range in size from fine powder to large granules (*prills*). The burning speed of black powder is controlled by granule size (i.e., surface area)—the smaller the granules, the more rapid the burn rate.

Black powder is used as a propellant in weapons such as muzzle-loading rifles and cannons. It is also used as the burning component in safety fuses as well as in some pyrotechnic fireworks and hobby fuses.

Black powder is readily ignited by a spark or squib (a small explosive device), powder fuse, or primer in shotgun cartridges. When initiated, black powder deflagrates; it does not detonate. The rapid burning is an oxidation reaction (Meyer, 2004):

$$32KNO_3(s) + 3S_8(s) + 16C(s) \rightarrow 16K_2CO_3(s) + 16N_2(g) + 24SO_2(g) \tag{6.1}$$

The burning phenomenon occurs so vigorously that it may resemble an explosion. Black powder is such a reactive formulation that it should be stored, transported, and handled as if it were a high explosive. Black powder is indeed classified as a high explosive under DOT regulations. Packages of granular and compressed black powder are labeled EXPLOSIVE 1.1D; transport vehicles are placarded EXPLOSIVES 1.1D.

Black powder does not deteriorate with age. Water may temporarily desensitize it; however, once dry, it regains its original reactive composition. Black powder is extremely sensitive to friction, flame, impact, shock, and static electricity. This characteristic makes black powder one of the most dangerous explosives to handle.

Smokeless powder (Figure 6.7) has replaced black powder in many applications. The term *smokeless* has been used because its combustion products are mainly gaseous, compared to more than 50% solid products for black powder.

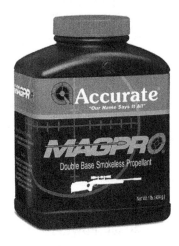

Figure 6.7 Smokeless powder sold as commercial product. (Reproduced with kind permission of Western Powders, Inc.)

Nitroglycerin

Nitroglycerin (1,2,3-trinitroxypropane or glycerin trinitrate) is an oily, pale yellow liquid high explosive (Figure 6.8).

For well over a century, nitroglycerin has been a key ingredient in the manufacture of explosives, specifically dynamite. As early as the 1880s, nitroglycerin was adapted as a military propellant for use in rifles. Nitroglycerin continues to be used in military weapons, as a gellatinizer for nitrocellulose, and as an ingredient in some solid propellants. Nitroglycerin is a popular component of explosives used in the construction and demolition industries. Nitroglycerin also has medicinal uses; it has been used for treatment of heart and certain blood-circulation diseases.

Nitroglycerin is obtained by the nitration of glycerol. Glycerol is added to a mixture of nitric acid and sulfuric acid:

$$
\begin{array}{l}
CH_2OH \qquad\qquad CH_2O-NO_2 \\
| \qquad\qquad\qquad\quad | \\
CHOH + 3HNO_3 \rightarrow CHO-NO_2 + 3H_2O \\
| \qquad\qquad\qquad\quad | \\
CH_2OH \qquad\qquad CHO-NO_2
\end{array}
\tag{6.2}
$$

Sulfuric acid serves as a catalyst in the above reaction.

Nitroglycerin is one of the most powerful explosives, with blast effects comparable with those of RDX and PETN (discussed in "PETN" section). Nitroglycerin is extremely sensitive to shock; even slight physical jarring can cause it to initiate. In addition, nitroglycerin decomposes over time to even more unstable forms. Nitroglycerin is, therefore, extremely dangerous to use or even transport. Due to its high degree of sensitivity (Table 6.1), nitroglycerin is rarely used alone as an explosive. As a result of numerous catastrophic accidents (Central Pacific, 2005), liquid nitroglycerin has been widely banned. More stable explosives such as dynamite and related mixtures have been prepared by mixing nitroglycerin with inert absorbents (diatomaceous earth, sawdust, etc.).

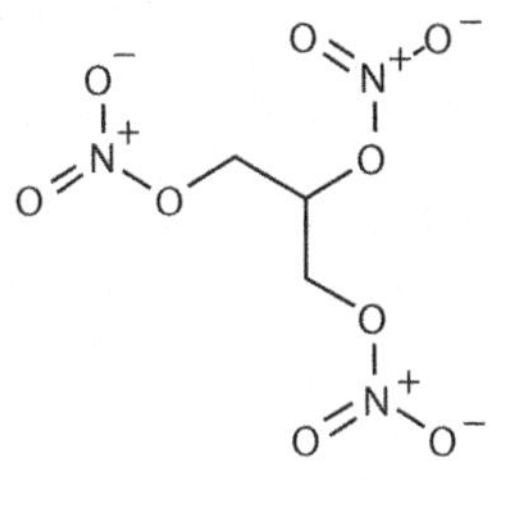

Figure 6.8 Structure of nitroglycerin.

According to U.S. DOT regulations, nitroglycerin is a forbidden explosive. However, when desensitized, DOT regulates the transportation of liquid nitroglycerin as a division 1.1D explosive (49 CFR, 2007).

Nitroglycerin is toxic by ingestion, inhalation, and skin absorption. It causes dilation of small veins, capillaries, and coronary blood vessels, thus leading to severe headaches and decreased blood pressure. After repeated nitroglycerin exposure, tolerance to this vasodilatory activity will eventually occur. Chronic repeated exposures to nitroglycerin, however, have been associated with more serious cardiovascular effects including angina pectoris and sudden death (Global Security, 2008).

Dynamite

Dynamite consists of three parts nitroglycerin, one part diatomaceous earth (i.e., a naturally occurring, chalklike sedimentary rock) and a small amount of sodium carbonate. This mixture was formulated in 1867 by Alfred Nobel, who was concerned with the sensitivity and occupational hazards of nitroglycerin. He discovered that nitroglycerin could be absorbed into a porous material and become much safer to handle than liquid nitroglycerin alone. As noted above, nitroglycerin is highly shock-sensitive; however, when adsorbed onto sawdust or diatomaceous earth, it becomes significantly less sensitive.

Today, dynamite is manufactured by absorbing nitroglycerin in a mixture of sawdust, wood pulp, starch, and similar carbon-rich materials. Calcium carbonate is added to neutralize the nitric acid that forms by spontaneous decomposition. Ethylene glycol dinitrate is added as an antifreeze and oxidizers are also typically added. The mixture is commonly formed into short sticks and wrapped in waxed paper; another popular configuration is as cast boosters (Figure 6.9).

Dynamite is primarily used in mining, quarrying, and construction activities. It is not used for military purposes because of its unstable nature, especially when subjected to

Figure 6.9 Dynamite cast boosters.

freezing. Dynamite has been replaced for combat use by military dynamite, a mixture of TNT, RDX, binders, and antifreeze agents. Military dynamite has approximately 60% of the strength of nitroglycerin-based commercial dynamite (U.S. Department of the Army, 1990).

Dynamites vary widely in composition and are identified by manufacturer and trade name (Apache, Trojan, etc.), strengths (20%, 40%, 60%), application (ditching, quarrying), content of additives (gelatin, nitroglycerin, ammonium nitrate), and form (bulk, slurries, water gels). Three forms of dynamite are in common use: straight dynamite, ammonia dynamite, and gelatin dynamite (Table 6.2). All are composed of the ingredients listed earlier; however, ammonia dynamite and straight dynamite contain ammonium nitrate and sodium nitrate, respectively, as oxidizers; gelatin dynamite contains 1% nitrocellulose that serves to thicken the nitroglycerin and give the dynamite additional shattering power (Meyer, 2004).

By virtue of its enhanced stability over nitroglycerin, dynamite may be transported and used with less hazard of spontaneous detonation. Dynamite is so insensitive that a detonating cap is required to initiate it. Regardless, however, dynamite is considered to be sensitive to heat, shock, and friction and must be handled with extreme care. Aged dynamite can be quite hazardous. Old dynamite sticks that appear to be *sweating*, with salt crystals forming on the outside of the package, dark stains appearing on the package cover, or liquid collecting at the base of a cartridge, indicate the presence of nitroglycerin that has leached from the dynamite. Such a scenario is extremely dangerous and highly susceptible to initiation.

Workers engaged in the production or use of dynamite, or those touching or inhaling fumes from dynamite may become exposed to vapors of nitroglycerin and/or ethylene glycol dinitrate. Initial exposure often results in an intense headache and in some cases dizziness, nausea, palpitations, and decrease in blood pressure. These initial symptoms indicate a shift in blood volume from the central to the peripheral circulatory system initiated by dilation of blood vessels (Global Security, 2008).

DOT regulates the transportation of dynamite as a division 1.1D explosive. The proper shipping name is *Explosive, blasting, type A.*

Table 6.2 Chemical and Physical Properties of Some Forms of Dynamite

	Straight Dynamite	**Ammonia Dynamite**	**Gelatin Dynamite**
Density, g/mL	1.3	0.8–1.2	1.3–1.6
Chemical composition	20–60% nitroglycerin	12–22% nitroglycerin	20–91% nitroglycerin
	23–60% sodium nitrate	15–57% sodium nitrate	40–60% sodium nitrate
	12–50% ammonium nitrate		Gelatinized in nitrocellulose
Detonation velocity, m/s	3600–6000	2700–4600	4000–7400
Ft/s	11,800–19,700	8900–15,000	13,000–24,000
Sensitivity	High	High	High

Source: Meyer, E., *Chemistry of Hazardous Materials*, 4th Edition, Prentice-Hall, Englewood Cliffs, NJ, 2004; U.S. Department of the Army, *Military Explosives*, *Technical Manual*, TM 9-1300-214, Washington, DC, 1990.

ANFO

In 1956, a new blasting agent was developed using a mixture of ammonium nitrate, aluminum powder, and water. The safety and efficiency of this new agent was soon apparent, and subsequent research resulted in the development of slurry explosives and eventually to dry explosive agents.

Ammonium nitrate (chemical formula NH_4NO_3), is a simple salt and a common commercial fertilizer. Mixed with fuel oil and confined, this material can be transformed into a powerful high explosive. ANFO has a broad range of detonation velocities, depending on the reference cited. An approximation for large quantities of blasting agent is roughly half the detonation velocity of C-4, or about 13,000 ft/s (Global Security, 2008). ANFO blasting agents are among the most common industrial explosives used in the United States. ANFO has essentially replaced dynamite for bench blasting during surface mining and quarrying. The most widely used dry blasting agent is a mixture of ammonium nitrate prills and fuel oil.

Explosive-grade ANFO is the least sensitive of all manufactured explosives. For safety reasons, the components are often stored separately and mixed at the point of use. However, the mixed product can also be purchased (Figure 6.10). ANFO is relatively safe and easily handled and can be poured into drill holes in the rock material to be blasted.

Figure 6.10 ANFO mixture. (Courtesy of U.S. Bureau of Alcohol, Tobacco, and Firearms.)

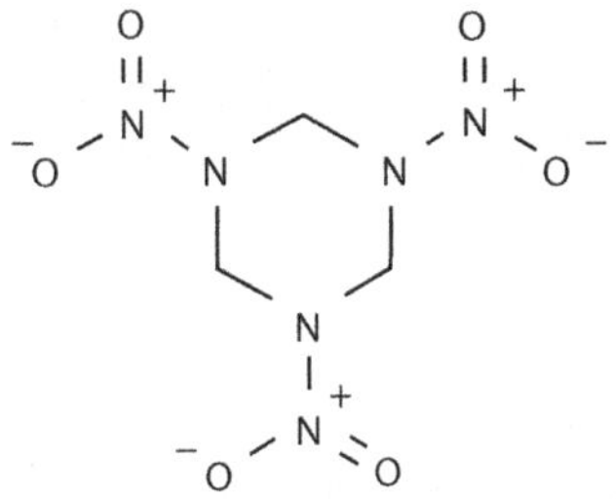

Figure 6.11 Structure of RDX molecule.

MILITARY EXPLOSIVES

Military explosives are not readily available to civilians; however, thefts have occurred, resulting in their incorporation in improvised bombs. For responders, these explosives should be handled with the same safety precautions as those used with commercial explosives.

RDX

RDX is a nitramine compound (chemical formula 1,3,5-trinitro-1,3,5-triazine) whose structure is a heterocycle (Figure 6.11). Several explanations exist for the term RDX, including Royal Demolition Explosive, Research Department Composition X, and Research Department Explosive (Cocroft, 2000). It is more commonly known as cyclonite or hexogen.

RDX was used widely during World War II because petroleum was not required as a raw ingredient. Since World War II, RDX has become the second most widely used high explosive in the military, exceeded only by TNT.

RDX is typically used in mixtures with other explosives, oils, or waxes. It is considered the most powerful and *brisant* of the military high explosives (see Box 6.4). RDX is second in strength to nitroglycerin among common explosive substances. When compressed to a density of 1.70 g/cm³, it has a confined detonation velocity of about 27,000 ft/s (Table 6.1).

BOX 6.4   BRISANCE

Brisance is a measure of the speed with which an explosive produces its maximum blast pressure. This value essentially describes the destructive fragmentation effect of a material on its immediate surroundings. Also known as shattering effect, brisance (from the French briser, meaning *to break*) is of practical importance in determining the effectiveness of an explosion in fragmenting structures.

Factors contributing to brisance include detonation rate and loading density (i.e., degree of compaction of explosives) and the heat of explosion and gas yield. High-brisant explosives are used for blasting hard rock, and low-brisant explosives are used for blasting where a more pushing or heaving than shattering effect is required.

217

RDX has been produced by several methods, but the most common manufacturing process in the United States is the continuous Bachmann process, which involves reacting hexamine with concentrated nitric acid, ammonium nitrate, glacial acetic acid, and acetic anhydride.

$$(CH_2)_6 N_4 + 4HNO_3 \rightarrow (CH_2\text{-}N\text{-}NO_2)_3 + 3HCHO + NH_4^+ + NO_3^- \qquad (6.3)$$

At room temperature, RDX has a high degree of stability in storage; however, it becomes very sensitive when crystallized to temperatures below −4°C. RDX starts to decompose at about 170°C and melts at 204°C (Girard, 2007).

RDX is used alone or with other explosives, including PETN. It is widely used as a component of plastic explosives, detonators, high explosives in artillery rounds, Claymore mines, and demolition kits. RDX can be mixed with plasticizers to make C-4 (a plastic explosive; see "C-4" section). Semtex, another plastic explosive, combines RDX and PETN. RDX forms the base for the following common military explosives (Global Security, 2008):

- Composition-A (RDX melted with wax)
- Composition-B (RDX mixed with TNT)
- Composition-C (RDX mixed with plasticizer)
- HBX
- H-6
- Cyclotol

Civilian applications of RDX include use in fireworks, in demolition, as a heating fuel for food rations, and as a rodenticide. Combinations of RDX and HMX, another explosive, comprise the main ingredients in approximately 75 explosive products.

TNT

TNT (2,4,6-trinitrotoluene) is one of the most common bulk explosives in use today, both in military munitions and in civilian mining and quarrying activities. TNT was first used on a wide scale during World War I. TNT has the chemical formula $C_6H_2(NO_2)_3CH_3$, and its structure, that of a nitroaromatic compound, is shown in Figure 6.12.

The explosive yield of TNT is considered the standard of strength for comparison of explosives (see Box 6.5). TNT is classified as a secondary explosive because it is less susceptible to initiation and requires a primary explosive for ignition. TNT can be used as a

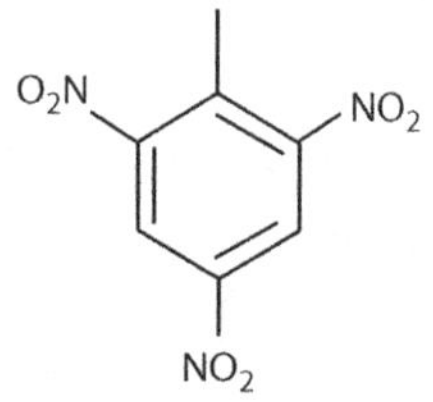

Figure 6.12 Structure of TNT, trinitrotoluene.

BOX 6.5   RELATIVE EFFECTIVENESS FACTOR FOR EXPLOSIVES

The *relative effectiveness (RE) factor* is a measure of the power of an explosive for military demolitions (Table 6.3). The RE factor compares an explosive's effectiveness relative to TNT. This is so engineers can substitute one explosive for another when they are calculating blasting equations that are designed for TNT. For example, if a steel cutting charge requires 1 kg of TNT to work, it would take 0.6 kg of PETN or 1.25 kg of ANFO to create the same effect (Cooper, 1996).

Table 6.3   Examples of RE Factors or Explosives

Explosive	Density (g/cm^3)	Detonation Velocity		RE Factor
		(m/s)	(ft/s)	
TNT	1.65	6900	22,640	1.00
Amatol, 80% TNT + 20% AN	1.55	6570	21,560	1.17
Ammonium nitrate	1.12	5270	17,290	0.42
ANFO, 94.3% AN + 5.7% fuel oil	0.84	5270	17,290	0.8
C-4, 91% RDX	1.74	8040	26,380	1.34
Composition B, 63% RDX + 36% TNT	1.75	8000	26,250	1.35
Gunpowder, 75% KN + 15% C+10%S	1.7	Varies	Varies	0.55
HMX	1.91	9100	29,860	1.70
Nitroglycerin	1.6	7700	25,260	1.50
Octanitrocubane	2.0	10,100	33,140	2.7
PETN	1.77	8400	27,560	1.66
RDX	1.82	8750	28,710	1.60
Semtex, 94.3% PETN + 5.7% RDX	1.78	8420	27,630	1.66
Tetryl	1.73	7570	24,840	1.25
Tetrytol, 70% tetryl + 30% TNT	1.71	7370	24,180	1.20

Source: Cooper, P., *Explosives Engineering*, Wiley-VCH Publishing, New York, 1996; U.S. Department of the Army, *Field Manual 5–25 Explosives and Demolitions*, Washington, DC, 1967.

booster for high-explosive shells and bombs; it can also be mixed with other explosives such RDX and HMX, and it is a constituent of amatol, pentolite, tetrytol, torpex, tritonal, picratol, and others. TNT has been used under trade names such as Triton, Trotyl, Trilite, Trinol, and Tritolo (Global Security, 2008).

TNT is popular in industry and the military because of its insensitivity to shock and friction, which reduces risk of accidental detonation.

TNT is synthesized in a three-step process (U.S. Department of the Army, 1990). Toluene is nitrated with a mixture of sulfuric and nitric acid to produce mononitrotoluene (MNT). The MNT is then nitrated to dinitrotoluene (DNT). Lastly, DNT is nitrated to TNT. The acids used in the manufacturing process are reused.

Upon detonation, TNT decomposes as follows:

$$2C_7H_5N_3O_6 \rightarrow 3N_2 + 5H_2O + 7CO + 7C \tag{6.4}$$

TNT is poisonous to biota. Skin contact causes local irritation, causing the skin to turn a bright yellow-orange. Persons exposed to TNT over prolonged periods (e.g., workers who manufactured TNT during the 1950s) experience increased risk of ailments including aplastic anemia and liver damage (e.g., toxic hepatitis) (ATSDR, 1996). Improved industrial safety practices have resulted in a significant decline in serious health problems related to TNT exposure.

As mentioned earlier, TNT is classified as a nitroaromatic compound (Figure 6.12). The majority of nitroaromatics occurring in the biosphere are industrial chemicals, including explosives, dyes, pesticides, and solvents. Nitroaromatics are *recalcitrant xenobiotic* compounds, that is, they are resistant to natural decomposition processes and tend to persist in the biosphere. In addition, nitroaromatics pose toxic and mutagenic hazards to humans, fish, and other biota.

PETN

PETN is one of the most powerful high explosives known, with a confined detonation velocity of more than 25,000 ft/s and an RE factor of 1.66. PETN is primarily used in booster and bursting charges of small caliber ammunition, in charges of detonators in some land mines and shells, and as the charge within detonating cord (Global Security, 2008). The formula of PETN is $C_5H_8N_4O_{12}$ and its structure is shown in Figure 6.13.

Manufacture of PETN involves nitration of pentaerythritol with a mixture of concentrated nitric and sulfuric acid. An alternative method of nitration uses concentrated nitric acid alone:

$$C(CH_2OH)_4 + 4HNO_3 \rightarrow C(CH_2ONO_2)_4 + 4H_2O \tag{6.5}$$

PETN was first synthesized in 1894 using this method. This formulation was subsequently used by the German army in World War I. PETN is also one of the ingredients in Semtex plastic explosive. Richard Reid (Abdel Rahim) attempted to use PETN to blow up a 767 jetliner traveling from Paris to Miami in 2001.

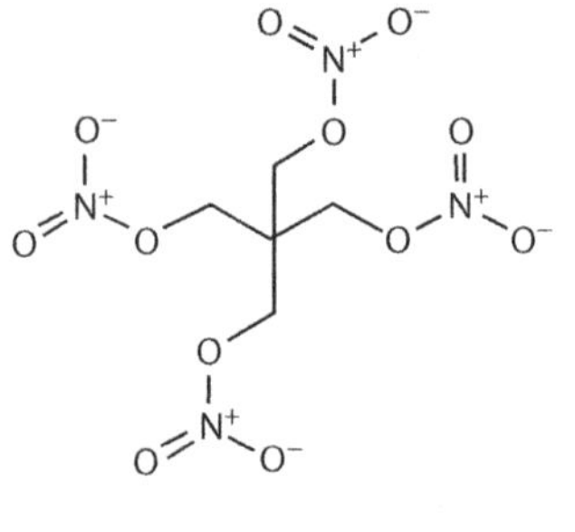

Figure 6.13 Structure of PETN.

PETN also has medical applications; it is used as a vasodilator, similar to nitroglycerin. A treatment for heart disease, Lentonitrat, is nearly pure PETN (Russek, 1966).

Use Forms of Explosives

Pure explosive compounds may be used alone as liquids, powders, or solid casts; however, the majority of explosives require modification to their physical properties. To alter mechanical as well as other properties, pure explosives are blended with other explosives and with inert materials. The mixtures can then be manipulated to form specific explosive products. The chief product forms include:

- Plastic
- Cast
- Sheet
- Emulsion
- Slurries
- Detonating cords
- Blasting caps
- Binary mixtures

Plastic Explosives

In the context of explosives, the term *plastic* indicates a malleable or moldable material, similar to properties of modeling clay (Figure 6.14). Explosives are mixed with a plastic binder and a plasticizer to keep the material from hardening. Several plastic explosives have been popular among military engineers and for commercial (particularly industrial) uses. The most common commercial use of plastic explosives is for hardening high manganese percentage steel (PA&E, 2006). For the emergency responder, it should be noted that the ability of plastic explosives to conform to numerous shapes, while maintaining their destructive capabilities, make them ideal weapons for IEDs for terrorists.

Common plastic explosives include C-4, which is popular with the U.S. military, and Semtex. Other popular plastic explosives and their country of origin are shown in Table 6.4.

C-4

C-4 (*Composition 4*) is a plastic explosive primarily used as a demolition charge, and to cut through steel (Figure 6.14). C-4 is a simple mixture composed of explosives, plasticizer, and binder. As is common with many plastic explosives, the energetic ingredient in C-4 is RDX, comprising about 90% of the C-4 by weight. This formulation also contains about 5% 2-ethylhexyl sebacate (the plasticizer), 2% polyisobutylene (the binder), and 2% motor oil (Liberty, 2008).

C-4 is manufactured by combining RDX slurry with binder dissolved in a solvent. The solvent is evaporated and the mixture is dried and filtered. The final product is an off-white solid that feels similar to modeling clay. It is manufactured in block form.

Figure 6.14 Sample of C-4, a plastic explosive.

C-4 detonates with a blast wave of approximately 8040 m/s (26,400 ft/s). For successful detonation, C-4 requires the heat generated by the shock of a special military blasting cap. Commercial blasting caps are typically not powerful enough to detonate C-4.

When molding C-4, cracks may form in the solid mass. These cracks will prevent the complete detonation of the charge and may result in scattering of a portion of unused explosive. Such a phenomenon is termed a *low-order explosion*, that is, an incomplete detonation. Under such a situation, hazardous material will persist on site, which may be susceptible to accidental detonation.

Military troops have become ill from exposure to C-4, which contains 90% RDX. Field exposures were the result of soldiers either chewing C-4 as an intoxicant or using it as a fuel for cooking. Scores of U.S. soldiers have experienced convulsions owing to RDX ingestion during the Vietnam Conflict.

Table 6.4 Various Plastic Explosives and Country of Origin

Common Name	Country
C3, C4	Greece
CHEMEX (C4), TVAREX 4A	Slovakia
C-4 (Composition C-4), Detasheet, Primasheet, Plastic Bonded Explosives	United States
KNAUERIT	Austria
PENO	Finland
PE4, PLASTRITE (FORMEX P 1)	France
PLASTITE	Switzerland
PE4, DEMEX	United Kingdom
PWM, NITROLIT	Poland
PW-5A Plastic Explosive	Russia
PP–01 (C4)	Yugoslavia
Semtex	Czech Republic
Sprängdeg m/46	Sweden
Sprengkörper DM12, (formbar)	Germany
T-4 Plastico	Italy

Source: Thurman, J.T., *Practical Bomb Scene Investigation*, CRC Press, Boca Raton, FL, 2006; Explosia.cz. http://www.explosia.cz/en/?show=semtex.

Semtex

Semtex is another popular malleable explosive, with characteristics and uses similar to those of C-4. Semtex was first manufactured by the Semtin East Bohemian Chemical Works in the Czech Republic. It is used in commercial blasting, demolition, and in certain military applications. As with C-4, Semtex can be used to cut through thick steel.

Semtex uses high explosive (PETN mixed with RDX), combined with a binder of a synthetic styrene–butadiene rubber binder, resulting in a malleable product. Semtex is brick-orange in color, whereas C-4 is off-white. Semtex has the benefit of being usable over a greater temperature range than other plastic explosives. The two common varieties of Semtex are *A* (for blasting) and *H* (for hardening). Details regarding composition are presented in Table 6.5.

Cast Explosives

Cast explosives typically are shaped within cardboard, plastic, or metal packaging. An example of a cast explosive is dynamite (see Figure 6.9). Cast explosives are relatively insensitive and normally consist of multiple components. A responder should never assume that cast explosives only exist with their exterior packaging intact—such explosives do not require packaging. Unexploded artillery and mortar projectiles have been stolen from ranges at military bases, cut open, and the cast explosives removed and used in IEDs.

Table 6.5 Properties of Semtex A and H Forms

Ingredient	Semtex A	Semtex H
PETN	94.3%	49.8%
RDX	5.7%	50.2%
Dye	Sudan IV (reddish brown)	Sudan I (red-orange)
Antioxidant	*N*-Phenyl-2-naphthylamine	*N*-Phenyl-2-naphthylamine
Plasticizer	Di-*n*-octyl phthalate, tri-*n*-butyl citrate	Di-*n*-octyl phthalate, tri-*n*-butyl citrate
Binder	Styrene–butadiene rubber	Styrene–butadiene rubber

Source: Liberty, 2008. http://www.libertylib.com/semtex.shtml#semtex-ingredients; Hobbs, J.R., Analysis of Semtex explosives, in: *Advances in Analysis and Detection of Explosives*, Kluwer Academic Publishers, The Netherlands, 1993; Yinon, J., Zitrin, S., *Modern Methods and Applications in Analysis of Explosives*, Wiley and Sons, New York, 1993; Answers.com. http://www.answers.com/topic/semtex.

Sheet Explosives

Also known as plastic-bonded explosives (PBX), Detasheet or Flex-x, sheet explosives consist of a mixture of PETN or RDX, and a plastic polymer such as polystyrene. By virtue of its flexibility, its major use is as a cutting charge for irregular surfaces.

In sheet explosive, the fine explosive particles are embedded in a rubbery binder. The combination of explosive and polymer is extruded into rolls, sheets, ribbons, and cord. The sheets measure between 1 and 8 mm thick and are available in rolls with inner layers of waxed paper preventing adhesion of the explosives (Figure 6.15). Sheet explosives for military use are manufactured in olive drab color; however, commercial sheet explosives may be found in any color.

Sheet explosives are extremely insensitive to shock—they require a blasting cap for initiation. Sheet explosives rate among the most powerful and versatile of explosives. They are appealing to terrorists because they can be hidden in envelopes, briefcases, or even sewn into the clothing of a suicide bomber.

Emulsion Explosives

An emulsion is composed of a mixture of two immiscible liquids, that is, those that do not normally mix with one another. One liquid is typically oil-based, whereas the other is water-based. When the appropriate emulsifier is included in the mixture, the two phases blend well together.

Emulsion explosives are prepared as water-in-oil emulsions. One phase is composed of an oxidizer salt solution (e.g., ammonium nitrate) suspended as microscopic-sized droplets surrounded by a continuous fuel phase. An emulsifying agent stabilizes the mixture. As each microcell of the oxidizer is coated with an oily exterior, the emulsion has excellent water resistance. A bulking agent such as ultrafine air bubbles may be dispersed throughout the emulsion matrix, which modifies the sensitivity of the explosive (Zukovich, 2008). Many fuels are incorporated in emulsion explosives, including water-soluble organics such as glycol and alcohols. Some emulsion explosives have a high content of aluminum powder that increases the overall explosive force and imparts a shiny metallic color when the contents are exposed.

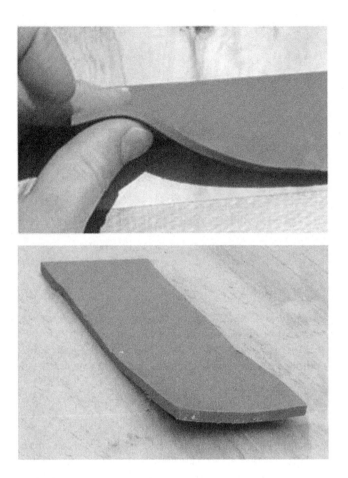

Figure 6.15 Sheet explosive.

Emulsion explosives were originally manufactured for commercial use but now have military applications as well. They can be identified by their packaging in flexible plastic tubes (Figure 6.16). The exterior wrapping can be any color.

Slurries

Slurries, sometimes called water gels, contain a mixture of oily and water-based components in proportions opposite those of emulsions. Whereas an emulsion contains aqueous materials (ammonium nitrate in water) dispersed in a fuel matrix, slurries consist of tiny droplets of fuel dispersed within aqueous oxidizers. Slurries typically contain ammonium nitrate in solution. Depending on the remainder of the ingredients, slurries are classified as either *blasting agents* or explosives. Slurry blasting agents contain nonexplosive sensitizers or fuels such as carbon, sulfur, or aluminum, and are extremely insensitive to initiation. Slurry explosives, on the other hand, contain blasting cap-sensitive ingredients such as PETN or TNT.

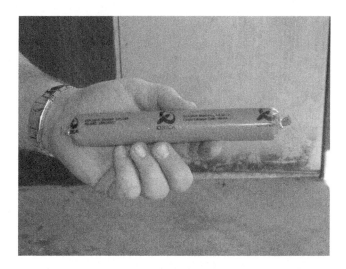

Figure 6.16 Emulsion explosive.

The sensitivity and the detonation properties of the explosive mixture are adjusted by the addition of ultrafine air bubbles. Such air spaces are required for the stable propagation of the detonation wave through the mixture. Slurries are thickened with gelatins, guar gums, and water-soluble polymerizable plastics to impart water resistance (Cooper and Kurowski, 1996).

Blasting Agents

Blasting agents are insensitive explosive mixtures usually made with ammonium nitrate (Figure 6.17) as the oxidizer, plus a petroleum-based fuel. Such agents may contain additional substances such as powdered aluminum to enhance blast effect, or ferrosilicon to

Figure 6.17 Ammonium nitrate prills as a blasting agent.

increase density. Blasting agents may be dry or in slurry forms. As a consequence of their insensitivity, blasting agents are often detonated by a primer of high explosive.

The advantages of using insensitive dry blasting agents are their safety, ease of loading, and low cost. In the free-flowing form, they have a strong advantage over cast explosives because they completely fill a mining borehole. Such close bonding with the walls ensures efficient use of explosive energy.

Binary Explosives

In binary explosives, two nonexplosive components are mixed immediately before use to create a blasting cap-sensitive high explosive. Astrolite is formed when ammonium nitrate is mixed with anhydrous hydrazine. This produces a clear liquid explosive called Astrolite G. Astrolite G generates a very high detonation velocity, almost twice as powerful as TNT (Global Security, 2008). When fine aluminum powder is added to the slurry, another explosive, Astrolite A-1.5, is created.

Blasting Caps

A blasting cap is a small explosive device used to detonate a larger, more powerful explosive (Figure 6.18). A blasting cap contains a highly sensitive primary explosive that provides the activation energy required to initiate a detonation in a more stable explosive. Explosives commonly used in caps include lead azide, lead styphnate, mercury fulminate, sodium azide, and tetryl (Cooper, 1996).

There are two major classifications of detonators—electric and nonelectric. Both contain very sensitive explosives and are highly susceptible to accidental insult. Electric blasting caps consist of a small metal tube closed at one end that contains the primary high

Figure 6.18   Blasting cap. (Courtesy of Timo Halén, https://commons.wikimedia.org/wiki/File:Nalleja.jpg.)

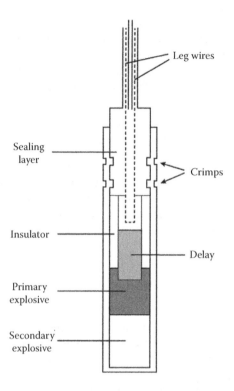

Figure 6.19 Schematic diagram of an electric blasting cap.

explosive. The cap typically contains an ignition charge, an intermediate charge, and a base charge. The firing element consists of two plastic insulated leg wires, an insulated plug holding the leg wires in place, and a small bridge wire connecting the leg wires inside the ignition charge (Figure 6.19).

The cap is triggered using a source of electricity such as a battery. Upon application of electric current, the bridge wire heats to incandescence and initiates the ignition charge. The resulting heat and flame sets off the intermediate charge, which sets off the base charge, which in turn detonates the main charge.

Nonelectric blasting caps are attached to one end of a safety fuse. The other end of the fuse can be ignited with a flame. The ignition charge is designed to amplify the flame from the fuse. This flame front ignites the intermediate charge, which in turn detonates the main charge.

Detonating Cord

A detonating cord (*Det cord*) is a thin, flexible cord packed with high explosive in its core. It is used in a firing train to initiate commercial high explosives. A detonating cord is commonly used in mining, drilling, and demolition work. The core typically occurs as a white pressed form. The cord varies in thickness and the exterior may be a variety of colors (Figure 6.20).

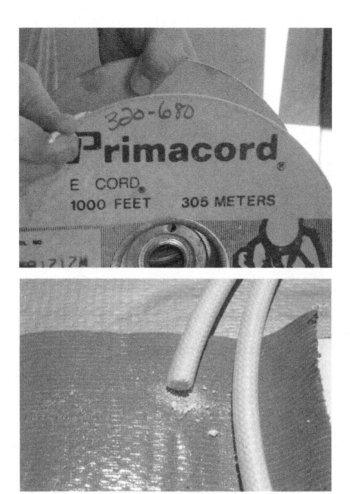

Figure 6.20   Detonating cord.

A detonating cord is actually a high-speed fuse, usually composed of PETN, which explodes rather than deflagrates. It is a relatively insensitive secondary explosive and requires a blasting cap to initiate. The PETN within a detonating cord explodes at 6300 m/s (21,000 ft/s). As a result of this high speed of detonation, a det cord can set off multiple charges simultaneously. A detonating cord will initiate most commercial high explosives (e.g., dynamite) but will not initiate less sensitive blasting agents such as ANFO.

Nonel Shock Tube

Nonel is a shock tube designed to initiate explosions, typically for demolition of buildings and in rock blasting in mines and quarries. As with a det cord, shock tube firing systems use a small plastic tube to deliver the firing impulse to the detonator. The hollow core is coated with a dusting of high explosive, typically PETN and fine aluminum. The

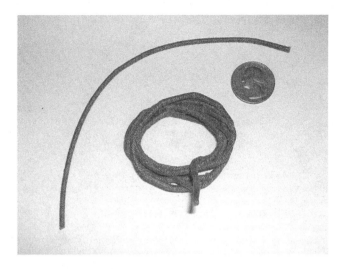

Figure 6.21 Hobby fuse.

shock tube operates by striking a plungerlike device such as a percussion-type fuse lighter that causes the coated plastic tube to transmit a detonating wave. The reaction travels at approximately 2000 m/s (6500 ft/s) along the length of the tubing. At the end of the shock tube is a nonelectric blasting cap.

It is estimated that 1 lb of high explosive can be used for approximately 70,000 ft of tubing.

Safety Fuses

Safety fuses provide a time delay to detonate the main explosive charge from a desired distance. A hobby fuse is composed of a low explosive, typically pressed black powder and potassium nitrate (Figure 6.21).

The fuse is ignited at one end and burns at a controlled rate (allowing the user to reach a safe area) to the other end where a nonelectric blasting cap has been attached. The fuse imparts a flame to the blasting cap and initiates the explosive within. A safety fuse can also be used without a blasting cap to initiate a low explosive device containing black or smokeless powder as the main charge.

Safety fuses are available in many sizes and exterior colors, similar to a detonating cord. Safety fuses can be identified, however, by their central core of black powder. The exterior is coated to protect against abrasion and water penetration.

EFFECTS OF AN EXPLOSION

An explosion undergoes three chief phases:

1. Blast
2. Fragmentation
3. Thermal

The severity of an explosion is a function of the type of explosive (e.g., detonation velocity, degree of brisance), the amount of explosive material involved, and conditions of the explosion (i.e., whether material was confined, proximity to structures).

Blast Phase

The first phase of an explosion involves the instantaneous formation of the characteristic blast (shock) wave. Shock waves can result in widespread damage to the surroundings, including structures and populations.

In the blast phase, the detonation generates gases under high pressure (up to several thousand psi) and high temperatures (approximately 3000–4000°C). The hot gas expands, forcing out the volume it occupies. A layer of compressed air (the blast wave), containing most of the energy released by the explosion, consequently forms in front of this gas volume. The pressure of the blast wave instantaneously increases to a value well above the ambient atmospheric pressure. This overpressure can reach as high as hundreds of pounds per square inch. The overpressure is sufficient to destroy structures and cause severe injuries and death.

The blast wave travels outward like the ripple created by a stone dropped into a pond. The initial blast of outward pressure is called the *positive phase* of the blast. The side-on overpressure rapidly decays as the shock wave expands outward from the explosion source. When pressure from the positive phase extends outward a partial vacuum is created at the seat of the blast. This negative pressure is short-lived and is quickly filled by outside pressure after the blast subsides. Air is rapidly sucked back into the blast seat. This effect is the so-called *negative phase* of the explosion, and the *refilling* effect is termed *implosion*. Implosion is the rapid equalizing of the surrounding air pressure. The negative phase is accompanied by high winds that carry the debris from long distances back into the original blast area. Implosion may last three times longer than the initial explosion (Figure 6.22).

Fragmentation Phase

The second phase of an explosion is the *fragmentation phase*. In this phase, the container of the exploding material is destroyed. Nearby objects are broken to pieces and thrown outward in all directions. Many injuries received from an explosion are fragmentation wounds.

Thermal Effect Phase

The final phase of an explosion is the *thermal effect phase*. This phase involves the release of heat generated from the blast. The rate of heat release and the temperature depend on the explosive material involved, the distance from the blast, and the detonation velocity. Thermal effects can result in severe skin burns, death, and damage to materials such as metals, glass, and polymers.

Figure 6.22 Time-series showing effects of a blast. (1) Predetonation; (2) positive pressure from the blast; (3) stabilization (very brief); (4) negative pressure (suction); and (5) final stabilization.

EXPLOSIVES AND TERRORISM: IEDs

IED is a term used to describe a home-made bomb. Many are made from simple, readily available materials such as steel or polyvinyl chloride (PVC) pipes, standard electrical wiring, home-made switches, and consumer batteries (Figure 6.23). The explosive charge may contain smokeless powder or ANFO, or a more sensitive ingredient. Some IEDs are derived from military explosives attached to a detonating mechanism (Figure 6.24). IEDs are triggered by various methods, including remote control, infrared or magnetic triggers, pressure-sensitive bars, or trip wires.

IEDs are extremely diverse in design and may contain many types of initiators, detonators, penetrators, and explosive loads. Improvised devices generally consist of four

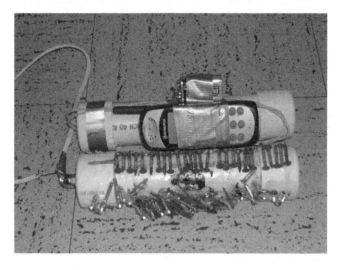

Figure 6.23 Improvised explosive device (IED).

Figure 6.24 Various IEDs recovered from an Iraqi bomb-making factory. These IEDs included U.S. munitions as the primary charge. (Courtesy of the U.S. Department of Defense, http://www .defenselink.mil/news/Nov2.)

components: a power source, an initiator, the explosive charge, and a switch. Shrapnel may be added to the bomb housing.

Power Sources

Most IEDs contain an electric initiator and, therefore, require an electric power source such as a battery. Most commercially available batteries can power an initiator. Batteries can be cut and shaped to make detection more difficult.

Initiators

These consist of blasting caps or flame-producing components such as fuse igniters. Improvised initiators can be easily constructed. Examples include a modified flash bulb or a hobby fuse. Initiator constituents can also be improvised; an example is triacetone triperoxide.

Charge

Explosives take many forms in IEDs. Some are manufactured using old munitions, whereas others contain commercial ingredients (e.g., dynamite). Still others contain simple ingredients purchased from a local gun store (smokeless powder).

Switches

Switches are used as either an arming switch or a fuse and can be simple or complex in design. More than one switch can be included to create redundancy in the system. The

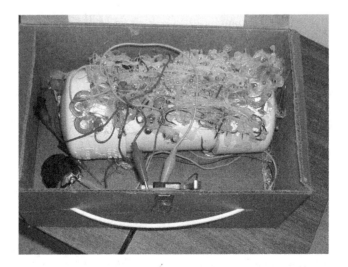

Figure 6.25 Improvised explosive device to which assorted shrapnel have been attached.

arming switch is a safety for the IED and works by disarming (i.e., electrically disengaging) the fusing switch. When the arming switch is engaged, the fusing switch becomes functional. Designs for switches are essentially unlimited so any action by its intended target or a first responder could result in detonation. Switches designed specifically for IEDs can appear quite innocent-looking, completely fitting into the local surroundings.

Fragmentation and Shrapnel

Upon detonation of an IED, the bomb housing and other components can cause injury and death. Fragmentation is a portion of the original casing or the electronics within the IED. In contrast, shrapnel is intentionally added to the device to inflict maximum casualties. Examples of shrapnel include nails, BBs, ball bearings, steel washers, and children's marbles (Figure 6.25).

Delivery of IEDs is discussed in detail in Chapter 7.

QUESTIONS

1. Draw the firing train of an explosion. Include and label all components.
2. The size of an explosion and consequent blast damage will vary as a function of what factors?
3. Define the following terms: deflagration, detonation, xenobiotic, low-order explosion, immiscible.
4. List three examples of primary explosives. Why are these highly energetic materials not commonly used as the main charge of military ordinance?
5. For what other purposes (besides explosives) is ammonium nitrate commonly used?
6. What is the purpose of the *relative effectiveness factor*? Discuss.
7. Nitroaromatic compounds pose what kinds of hazards to humans and other biota? Be specific.

REFERENCES

49 Code of Federal Regulations. 2007. Transportation. Subpart C. Definitions, classification and packaging for class. http://edocket.access.gpo.gov/cfr_2007/octqtr/pdf/49cfr173.50.pdf (accessed November 2, 2010).

Agency for Toxic Substances and Disease Registry (ATSDR). 1996. 2,4,6-Trinitrotoluene. September 1996. See: http://permanent.access.gpo.gov/lps21/tfacts81.html (accessed November 2, 2010).

Beveridge, A. (Ed.). 1998. *Forensic Investigation of Explosions*. Boca Raton, FL: CRC Press.

Central Pacific. 2005. Nitroglycerine! Terrible explosion and loss of lives in San Francisco. Central Pacific Railroad Photographic History Museum, 1866.

Cocroft, W.D. 2000. *Dangerous Energy: The Archaeology of Gunpowder and Military Explosives Manufacture*. Swindon: English Heritage. ISBN 1.85074-718.0.

Code of Federal Regulations. 2014. Vol. 49. New explosives—Definition and procedures for classification and approval. Part 173.56. https://www.gpo.gov/fdsys/granule/CFR-2011-title49-vol2/CFR-2011-title49-vol2-sec173-56.

Cooper, P. 1996. *Explosives Engineering*. New York: Wiley-VCH Publishing.

Cooper, P., and S.R. Kurowski. 1996. *Introduction to the Technology of Explosives*. New York: Wiley-VCH Publishing.

Defense Update. 2004. Sheet explosives. Revisited. http://www.defense-update.com/2004/04/sheet-explosives-revisited.html (accessed November 2, 2010).

Explosia. 2003. Brief history of plastic explosive Semtex®. http://www.explosia.cz/en/?show=semtex.

Fordham, S. 1980. *High Explosives and Propellants*. New York: Pergamon.

Freepatentsonline. 2009. Process for controlling oil well fires. United States Patent 5259454. http://www.freepatentsonline.com/5259454.html (accessed November 2, 2010).

Girard, J. 2007. *Criminalistics: Forensic Science and Crime*. Sudbury, MA: Jones and Bartlett Publishing.

Global Security. 2008 Military: Explosives. http://www.globalsecurity.org/military/systems/munitions/explosives.htm (accessed November 2, 2010).

Hobbs, J.R. 1993. Analysis of Semtex explosives. In: *Advances in Analysis and Detection of Explosives*, ed. J. Yinon and S. Zitrin. The Netherlands: Kluwer Academic Publishers.

Labrude, P., and C. Becq. 2003. Pharmacist and chemist Henri Braconnot. *Revue d'Histoire de la Pharmacie* 51(337): 61–78.

Langford, R.E. 2004. *Introduction to Weapons of Mass Destruction: Radiological, Chemical, and Biological*. Hoboken, NJ: John Wiley and Sons.

Letterman, D. 2003. *The Late Show*. CBS Television.

Liberty, 2008. Semtex. http://www.libertylib.com/semtex.shtml#semtex-ingredients.

Meng, L.K. 2005. Chinese siege warfare. The Pao. August 30, 2005. http://www.grandhistorian.com/chinesesiegewarfare/siegeweapons-earlygrenades.html (accessed November 2, 2010).

Meyer, E. 2004. *Chemistry of Hazardous Materials*. 4th Edition. Cliffs, NJ: Prentice-Hall, Englewood.

NATO. 1996. *NATO Handbook on the Medical Aspects of NBC Defensive Operations*. AMedP-6(B). FM 8.9. Army Field Manual 8.9. Navy Medical Publication 5059. Air Force Joint Manual 44.151. Washington, DC: Departments of the Army, the Navy, and the Air Force, February 1, 1996.

PA&E. 2016. *Explosive Hardening*. Wenatchee, WA: PA&E, Inc. http://pacaero.com/bonded-metals/explosive-hardening/ (accessed February 23, 2016).

Russek, H.I. 1966. The therapeutic role of coronary vasodilators: Glyceryl trinitrate, isosorbide dinitrate, and pentaerythritol tetranitrate. *American Journal of Medical Science* 252 (1): 9–20.

Thurman, J.T., *Practical Bomb Scene Investigation*, CRC Press, Boca Raton, FL, 2006.

U.S. Department of the Army. 1967. Field Manual 5.25 Explosives and Demolitions. Washington, DC.

U.S. Department of the Army. 1971. Explosives Series. Properties of Explosives of Military Interest. *Engineering Design Handbook*. Washington, DC. January 1971.

U.S. Department of the Army. 1990. Military Explosives. Technical Manual. TM 9.1300-214. Washington, DC.

Yinon, J., and S. Zitrin. 1993. *Modern Methods and Applications in Analysis of Explosives*. New York: John Wiley and Sons.

Zoltan, K. 2007. Military use of explosives. In: *New Challenges in the Field of Military Science International Scientific Conference*, November 7–8, 2006.

Zukovich, M., and L.L.C. Wade. 2008. Emulsion explosives technology. http://www.exploenergy.com/services/emulsion-explosives.html (accessed November 2, 2010).

7

Delivery Systems for Weapons of Mass Destruction

Ninety-nine percent is in the delivery.

Buddy Hackett

INTRODUCTION

In military terminology, *delivery systems* refers to missiles, rockets, and other unmanned systems that are specially designed for delivering biological, chemical, or nuclear weapons (Oosthuizen and Wilmshurst, 2004). In terms of use by a terrorist group or individual, however, delivery systems for WMDs embrace a vastly wider range of devices, from the most basic to quite sophisticated. Ultimately, the mode of delivery of a WMD is limited only by the imagination of the perpetrator.

DELIVERY OF BIOLOGICAL AND CHEMICAL AGENTS

In order to plan for and respond to future attacks, governments and response agencies have attempted to visualize biological and chemical terrorist attack scenarios that involve the use of aerosol-delivery technologies to target large populations by air, inside buildings, or in mass transit systems. However, there is relatively little unclassified information on which defense planners can base their understanding of the potential consequences of a large-scale biological or chemical terrorist attack. A 1970 World Health Organization (WHO) study estimated that 50 kg of *Bacillus anthracis* released over an urban population of 5 million would sicken 250,000 and kill 100,000 people. A 1993 Office of Technology Assessment study estimated that between 130,000 and 3 million deaths would follow the release of 100 kg of *B. anthracis*. However, neither of these analyses used field experimental data (Levin and Valadares de Amorim, 2003).

Since World War I, several nations have experimented with innovative technologies to disseminate biological and chemical weapons to produce maximum effect. As discussed in Chapter 4, Japan developed and tested several different biological devices during World War II; more than 1600 bombs were constructed and filled with anthrax spores. Later bombs used cholera, dysentery, typhoid, plague, anthrax, and paratyphoid on Chinese troops (Smart, 1997). Some bombs were designed with ceramic shells for ready release of pathogenic microbes upon impact with the earth.

Many types of equipment can be purchased commercially and used to disseminate liquid or dry biological agents. Such devices tend to be inefficient, as only a small percentage of the agent tends to become airborne in the particle size required for infection (e.g., 1–10 μm for anthrax spores). Regardless, however, their use may still result in extensive casualties.

The biological bomblet munition comes in a variety of sizes and is designed to disseminate an agent using either explosive energy or gaseous energy (Figure 7.1). During the Cold War, the Soviet weapons program focused primarily on explosive energy, whereas the U.S. program concentrated on gaseous energy. Gaseous energy was found to be more efficient in generating more airborne agent, and in the desired particle size.

Point source delivery of biological and chemical agents involves the use of a simple device (a handheld sprayer, for example). The resulting path of the aerosol is dependent on wind speed and direction. As the volume of potentially infective aerosol produced is relatively small, the target area affected by this method is likewise small. In the so-called line source dissemination, a vehicle sprays a plume of biological agent perpendicular to the wind (Figure 7.2). The target can be up to several kilometers downwind from the line of release. Wind transports the biological aerosol toward the target. Line source dissemination is an efficient means of delivering a biological agent provided that meteorological conditions are favorable. Very large targets can be affected, and the aerosol is almost impossible to detect.

Figure 7.1 The E120 was one of several biological bomblets developed by the U.S. military. On impact, the outer shell would shatter. The E120 was developed in the early 1960s and carried 0.1 kg of liquid biological agent. Tularemia bacteria was standardized for use in the bomblet. (Courtesy of Wikipedia, https://en.wikipedia.org/wiki/E120_bomblet#/media/File:E120_biological_bomblet _cutaway.jpg.)

Figure 7.2   Line source delivery of a weapon.

An example of line source delivery (in this example, of a surrogate biological weapon) took place during *Operation Sea Spray* carried out from September 20–27, 1950 by the U.S. Navy, where a ship sprayed spores of *Serratia marcescens* from San Francisco Bay. Based on results from monitoring equipment at 43 locations around the city, it was determined that spores had traveled more than 30 mi, and San Francisco received enough of a dose for nearly all of the city's 800,000 residents to inhale at least 5000 particles (Carlton, 2001; Cole, 1988; Pricenomics, 2014).

After a disseminator releases the agent, a short time span is needed before an aerosol is fully formed. Large particles (>10 µm) do not remain in the air but immediately settle to the ground. After a few minutes, the aerosol comes to equilibrium and is composed primarily of particles measuring 1 to 5 µm in diameter. The aerosol now behaves as a gas and is defined as a primary aerosol. It is this aerosol that is critical in a biological attack; this aerosol requires protective measures.

Terrorist organizations have used a variety of methods to release biological agents. In the 1990s, Aum Shinrikyo attempted to disperse anthrax, botulinum toxin, Q fever, and Ebola against civilian populations and government officials in Japan. Some of their actions included:

- Modifying a car to disperse botulinum toxin through an exhaust system and driving the car around a parliament building
- Attempting to disrupt the wedding of Prince Naruhito by spreading botulinum in downtown Tokyo via an automobile
- Spreading anthrax in Tokyo via a sprayer system from the roof of a building (this was carried out over 4 days)
- Planting three briefcases designed to release botulinum in a Tokyo subway

(No infections or illnesses were reported from these attempts.)

Substantial expertise is required to process biological agents to maximize the effect of aerosol dissemination, but even relatively crude devices could have an impact. Some analysts, however, have questioned whether spores of *B. anthracis* or other microbes could be produced and deployed effectively by terrorist groups without state support. Some experts have asserted that to be used effectively as a biological weapon, *B. anthracis* must be present in dry powdered form, highly concentrated, of uniform particle size, low electrostatic charge, and treated to reduce clumping in order for the bacteria to penetrate spaces deep in the lungs. Some have argued that foggers and crop dusters would not be effective methods to disseminate B. anthracis, because the use of liquid formulations would require a high level of purity to prevent plugging of nozzles and would create agglomerations that would simply fall to the ground rather than remain suspended in the air. Finally, it has been argued that the use of an aircraft to attack a large city with B. anthracis would be ineffective because most of an urban population is inside buildings at any given time, offering some level of protection against breathing air contaminated by spores (Levin and Valadares de Amorim, 2003).

Other methods by which biological or chemical agents may be introduced include (U.S. DHS, 2004):

- Food or water, especially ready-to-eat food (vegetables, salad bars), could be intentionally contaminated with pathogens or toxins. The water supply is less vulnerable because dilution, filtration, and addition of chlorine kill most pathogenic organisms.
- Human carriers could spread transmissible agents by coughing, through body fluids, or by contaminating surfaces.
- Infected animals can cause people to become ill through contact with the animals or contaminated animal products.
- Insects naturally spread some agents such as plague bacteria and potentially could be used in an attack.
- Physically distributed through the U.S. mail.

DELIVERY OF IMPROVISED EXPLOSIVE DEVICES AND RADIOLOGICAL DISPERSAL DEVICES

In many cases, improvised explosive devices are contained or concealed in packaging to remain effective and facilitate delivery to the intended target. Packaging can be of any type of material. Packaging can enhance the destructive effect and disguise the actual contents. Examples of IED packaging include (Figure 7.3):

- Pipes and tubes (steel and polyvinyl chloride)
- Suitcases, briefcases, purses
- Computers
- Postal mail (boxes, letters, cards)
- Toys
- Cellular phones
- Cigarette boxes
- Bottles and jars
- CO_2 gas cartridges
- Fire extinguishers
- Automobiles, trucks, vans
- Electronic appliances
- Fruit baskets, gifts, wrapped packages
- Plaster figures
- Shell casings and cartridges
- Butane, gasoline, propane tanks

Figure 7.3 Vehicle-borne improvised explosive device (VBIED). (From Financial and Banking Information Infrastructure Committee, Vehicle Borne IED Identification Guide: Parked Vehicles, TRIPwire, https://www.fbiic.gov/public/2008/oct/DHSVehicleBorneIEDIdentificationGuideParked Vehicles.pdf. With permission.)

IEDs have been delivered to targets using numerous methods. Vehicles are often used; IEDs may also be placed by hand, thrown, or projected to the target by a mortar or rocket device. A terrorist or an unsuspecting individual such as the postman can deliver an IED to the target.

Package and letter bombs are generally victim-activated. A device that is transported via the mail system is subject to rough handling, so it cannot be designed to be vibration- or movement sensitive. The victim or intended target must activate the device by subjecting it to action other than what it would normally receive during mailing. This action, in most cases, involves opening the package.

Letter bombs do not normally contain timing devices. The mail is not sufficiently predictable for timing devices to be used, as letter bombs are usually aimed at specific targets. Electronic, chemical, or mechanical action long-delay mechanisms may be used, which have an extended time-delay factor of up to a few months.

A number of readily recognizable indicators have been identified among letter and package bombs that have been detected. These include origin in a foreign country, excessive postage, no return address, addressed to a title (e.g., *CEO, Director*) only, restrictive notes (*Do not shake or drop package*), rigid or bulky, uneven distribution of weight in the package, badly typed or written words, and misspelled words (Figure 7.4).

Cars, trucks, motorcycles, bicycles, and boats have been equipped with explosives and have been set to explode by the driver or by remote control. A car bomb can carry thousands of pounds of explosives and may be loaded with shrapnel to increase its deadly effects. Characteristic features of car bombs or vehicle-based IEDs are that they appear weighed down, and in some cases their interiors have been stripped down and rebuilt.

Analysts are expressing alarm that autonomous vehicles (*driverless cars*) can be equipped and programmed to carry an explosive payload to a site and be remotely detonated. Google, along with several major automobile manufacturers, has invested heavily in

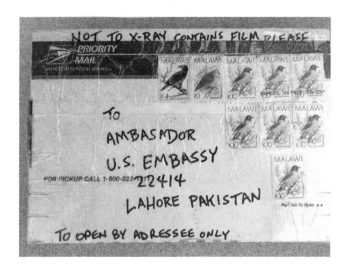

Figure 7.4 Package bomb.

autonomous vehicle technology in recent years. In Syria, an improvised armored vehicle was constructed of armor plate welded to an automobile chassis. The Sham II—so named after ancient Syria—had cameras added and was equipped with a machine gun attached to a PlayStation controller and a TV monitor (Beckhusen, 2012; Lewis, 2015). Although not autonomously operated, the Sham II illustrates the relative ease of converting simple electronic systems for delivery of WMDs.

Boats laden with explosives can be used against ship targets and positions along a coast (e.g., piers, buildings, pipelines). Suicide bombers used a boat-borne IED to attack the USS *Cole*, which was making a refueling stop in the Yemeni port of Aden in October 2000. Seventeen American sailors were killed and 39 were injured. U.S. and U.K. troops have also been killed by boat-borne IEDs in Iraq (BBC, 2006). In 2004, members of a boarding team from the USS *Firebolt* stopped a local fishing boat near the Al Amaya Oil Terminal off the coast of Iraq during a routine inspection. The individuals on the fishing boat detonated hidden explosives in an apparent suicide attack, killing several members of the boarding team and seriously injuring the others (JIEDDO, 2009a; Pelkofski, 2005).

Animals have been used to deliver explosives. In a 1920 attack, a horse-drawn cart was used to deliver 45 kg (100 lb) of dynamite to the target site at the New York Stock Exchange. The blast killed 30 people immediately, and hundreds were seriously injured. During World War II, Mexican free-tailed bats were equipped with a small timed incendiary device and dropped from bombers over Japan. The bats returned to earth by parachute and would roost during the day in attics and barns. Later on, the timers would ignite the bombs. In 2003, eight people were killed when explosives strapped to a horse detonated in a market in Chita, Colombia (BBC, 2003). Colombian authorities blamed the country's largest rebel group, the Revolutionary Armed Forces of Colombia, for the attack. Donkey bombs were a common tactic of the Sendero Luminoso (Shining Path) in Peru. Donkeys have also been used for suicide attacks in Israel (*The Sunday Times*, 1985) and in Afghanistan (*The Sunday Times*, 2009).

Suicide Bombings

Suicide bombing refers to the placement of explosives on an individual who detonates them to kill others and themselves. The bomber conceals explosives on their person, in some cases in a specially made vest (Figure 7.5) along with a trigger to detonate the charge. Some terrorists consider themselves to be *smart bombs* in that they can deliver their weapon to the exact desired point, thus giving the greatest chance of achieving success than any other method of attack. So-called *bra bombs* worn by female suicide bombers have been documented. Concealing the explosives in a bra instead of a vest allows for the women to reveal their midriffs when searched (Rediff, 2004). In 2007, a Tamil Tiger suicide bomber had explosives hidden in her bra, and blew herself up outside the office of a Tamil minister (Agence France-Presse, 2007). The most notorious high-profile suicide attack was by Thenmuli Rajaratnam, who wore either a belt with explosives or a bra bomb for the assassination of Indian Prime Minister Rajiv Gandhi.

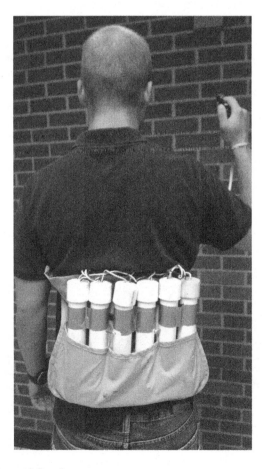

Figure 7.5 (See color insert.) Bomb vest.

In recent years, explosives have been hidden within body cavities. In a 2009 attack in Jeddah, Saudi Arabia, Abdullah Hassan Tali Al-Asiri hid explosives in a body cavity in an attempt to kill Prince Mohammed Bin Nayef, the head of the Saudi security service. Al-Asiri blew himself up in the attack but his target escaped with only minor injuries. By hiding the explosives in a body cavity, he managed to pass security checks before entering the prince's office (Telegraph, 2009).

With the advent of full-body airport scanners, concern is growing over the possibility of suicide bombers having explosives surgically implanted in various parts of the body before boarding airliners. The British secret service agency MI5 has uncovered evidence that al-Qaeda is planning a new stage in its terror campaign by inserting *surgical bombs* inside the body. There is speculation that male bombers would have the explosive secreted near their appendix or in their buttocks, whereas females would have the explosive material placed inside their breasts in the same way as figure-enhancing implants (Leake, 2010).

Recent Use of IEDs

Afghanistan and Iraq

Since the U.S. invasion of Afghanistan in 2001, IEDs have been responsible for more than 60% of all American combat casualties in Iraq and 50% of combat casualties in Afghanistan, including both killed and wounded (U.S. DOD, 2007). Vehicle-borne IEDs are used to strike police stations, markets, and mosques, killing local citizens as well as U.S. troops. Roadside IEDs have targeted U.S. military vehicles and caused immense damage and casualties (Figure 7.6). Afghan insurgents planted 14,661 IEDs in 2010 (Vanden Brook, 2012). The U.S. military recorded 8159 IED incidents in Afghanistan in 2009, compared with 3867 in 2008 and 2677 the year before. The number of IED attacks in Iraq has plummeted, corresponding to the overall decrease in violence in that country. At their peak in 2007, Iraqi insurgents deployed 23,000 IEDs (JIEDDO, 2009b; Whitlock, 2010).

A large proportion of the munitions for constructing IEDs in Iraq may have originated from large Iraqi military ordinance depots looted by insurgents (Glanz and Dwyer, 2004). Department of Defense officials have charged that Iran may have supplied IED technology

Figure 7.6 A Stryker lies on its side following an IED blast in Iraq, 2007. (Courtesy of the U.S. Army.)

to insurgents in Iraq. In Afghanistan, the IED munitions supply is supported by funds from an expanding opium trade (Bergen, 2006). There is concern that IEDs might eventually be used by other insurgents and terrorists worldwide (Sadler, 2005).

In Iraq, small, highly skilled IED cells often hire themselves out to other insurgent groups such as al-Qaeda in Iraq or the Sunni group Ansaar al Sunna. They advertise their expertise on the Internet, and may be contracted on a per-job basis but otherwise remain autonomous (Wilson, 2007). A typical IED terrorist cell may consist of six to eight people including a financier, bomb maker, emplacer, triggerman, spotter, and often a cameraman. Videos of exploding U.S. vehicles and dead Americans are distributed via the Internet to attract new supporters (Wilson, 2007).

U.S. forces are continually developing countermeasures for these devices, for example, by relying on intelligence sources and by disrupting portions of the radio spectrum that insurgents use to trigger IEDs. New technologies being evaluated include electronic jammers and predetonators, radars, X-ray equipment, robotic explosive ordnance disposal equipment, and armor for vehicles and personnel (Lieberman, 2005). However, insurgents quickly adapt to countermeasures, and new, more sophisticated IEDs are subsequently created (Wilson, 2007).

Over the Atlantic, 2009

Umar Farouk Abdulmutallab (Figure 7.7), a Muslim Nigerian citizen, attempted to detonate an improvised device hidden in his underwear while onboard Northwest Airlines Flight 253 en route from Amsterdam to Detroit, Michigan, on December 25, 2009. After spending about 20 min in the airplane restroom Abdulmutallab returned to his seat and covered himself with a blanket. Soon afterward passengers nearby heard popping noises

Figure 7.7 Umar Farouk Abdulmutallab, arrested for attempting to bomb a Northwest Airlines flight using an IED worn in his clothing. (Courtesy of Wikipedia, https://en.wikipedia.org/wiki/Umar_Farouk_Abdulmutallab#/media/File:UmarFarouk.jpg.)

and smelled a foul odor. Some saw fire on Abdulmutallab's clothing and the wall of the plane. Fellow passengers jumped on Abdulmutallab and restrained him as flames were doused with fire extinguishers.

The device consisted of a 6-in (15-cm) packet sewn into his underwear containing both pentaerythritol tetranitrate (PETN) along with triacetone triperoxide (TATP) (Krolicki and Pelofsky, 2009). After being taken into custody, Abdulmutallab informed authorities he had been directed in the attack by al-Qaeda, and that he had received training and obtained the materials for the device while in Yemen. Al-Qaeda in the Arabian Peninsula, the organization's affiliate in Yemen, claimed responsibility for the attack, describing it as revenge for the U.S. role in a Yemeni military offensive against al-Qaeda in that country (Spiegel and Solomon, 2009).

Abdulmutallab was subsequently charged on six criminal counts, including attempted use of a WMD and attempted murder of 289 people. In 2012, he was sentenced to life in prison as a result of his guilty plea to all counts of the federal indictment charging him for his role in the attempted bombing.

Al-Qaeda has made numerous failed attempts to bomb planes over the past decade. On November 1, 2015, a Russian Metrojet flight that was bound for St. Petersburg, was downed by a bomb allegedly planted by Islamic State in Iraq and Syria (ISIS). Table 7.1 lists the events in which bombs destroyed passenger jets in recent decades.

London

On July 7, 2005, a series of coordinated suicide attacks occurred on London's public transport system during the morning rush hour. The bombings were carried out by four British Muslim men—three of Pakistani and one of Jamaican descent.

At 8:50 A.M., three bombs exploded within 50 s of each other on three London Underground trains just outside Liverpool Street and Edgware Road stations, and on another traveling between King's Cross and Russell Square. A fourth bomb exploded at 9:47 A.M. on a double-decker bus in Tavistock Square. The explosions were apparently caused by home-made devices, packed into backpacks and detonated by the bombers themselves, all four of whom died. A total of 56 people, including the four bombers, were killed and about 770 were injured.

The bombers were named as Mohammad Sidique Khan, age 30; Shehzad Tanweer (22); Germaine Lindsay (19); and Hasib Hussain (18). Two of the bombers made videotapes describing their reasons for becoming *soldiers* for their cause. In a videotape aired by Al Jazeera on September 1, 2005 (Figure 7.8), Mohammad Sidique Khan described his motivation.

> I and thousands like me are forsaking everything for what we believe. Our drive and motivation doesn't come from tangible commodities that this world has to offer. Our religion is Islam, obedience to the one true God and following the footsteps of the final prophet messenger. Your democratically elected governments continuously perpetuate atrocities against my people all over the world. And your support of them makes you directly responsible, just as I am directly responsible for protecting and avenging my Muslim brothers and sisters. Until we feel security you will be our targets and until you stop the bombing, gassing, imprisonment and torture of my people we will not stop this fight. We are at war and I am a soldier. Now you too will taste the reality of this situation.

> BBC News, 2005

Table 7.1 Bombs That Destroyed Passenger Jets in Recent Decades

Date	Event
February 21, 1970	*Swissair Flight 330:* A bomb exploded in the cargo compartment of a flight from Zurich to Hong Kong, which had a scheduled layover in Tel Aviv. All 38 passengers and 9 crew members died. A Palestinian militant group claimed responsibility.
October 6, 1976	*Cubana de Aviacion Flight 455:* A passenger jet from Barbados destined for Jamaica blew up soon after takeoff, killing all 73 people aboard. A group of anti-Castro regime Cuban exiles were eventually convicted of carrying out the bombing.
September 23, 1983	*Gulf Air Flight 771:* A flight from Karachi, Pakistan to Abu Dhabi crashed after a bomb exploded in the luggage compartment. All 112 people on board, mostly Pakistani nationals, died. Investigators ultimately linked the attack to a Palestinian militant organization that wanted to punish the Emiratis for not paying it protection money.
June 23, 1985	*Air India Flight 182:* The flight from Toronto was destroyed by a bomb above Irish air space and crashed in the Atlantic Ocean. All 307 passengers and 22 crew members died. The attack was carried out by Sikh separatist militants as retribution for the 1984 anti-Sikh riots in New Delhi.
April 2, 1986	*TWA Flight 840:* A flight from Los Angeles to Cairo was destroyed over Greece by a bomb planted beneath a seat. It blasted a hole in the plane's side, resulting in four deaths. The remaining passengers survived as the pilot made an emergency landing. A Palestinian group dubbed Arab Revolutionary Cells claimed responsibility, citing a struggle against *American imperialism*.
November 29, 1987	*Korean Air Flight 858:* A flight between Baghdad and Seoul was brought down by North Korean operatives, who detonated a device using liquid explosives disguised in liquor bottles. All 115 people on board died.
December 21, 1988	*Pan Am Flight 103:* This flight, scheduled to travel from London to Detroit, blew up over Scotland. Debris landed in the town of Lockerbie and killed 11 residents. All 259 people on board died. The attack was linked to agents from the regime of Libyan dictator Muammar Gaddafi.
November 27, 1989	*Avianca Flight 203:* A flight from Bogota, Colombia to Cali blew up, killing all on board. The incident underscored the depth of violence brought on by drug lord Pablo Escobar; he was possibly hoping to kill a Colombian presidential candidate who decided not to take the flight.

(Continued)

Table 7.1 (Continued)   Bombs That Destroyed Passenger Jets in Recent Decades

Date	Event
August 24, 2004	*Volga-Avia Express Flight 1353* and *Siberia Airlines Flight 1047:* Two planes that flew out of Moscow were destroyed on the same day by a pair of female Chechen suicide bombers. A militant group dubbed the Islamist Brigades claimed responsibility for the attack, which killed a total of 90 people.
November 1, 2015	*Russian airliner:* The Airbus A321 crashed 23 min after takeoff from the Sharm al-Sheikh tourist resort in Egypt's Sinai Peninsula, killing all 224 on board. The plane was brought down by a bomb allegedly planted by ISIS in Egypt. The bombing may be retribution to Russia, which entered the Syrian conflict on behalf of the regime of President Bashar al-Assad.

Source: Tharoor, I. 2015. 10 times bombs brought down passenger jets. *Washington Post.* https://www .washingtonpost.com/news/worldviews/wp/2015/11/06/10-times-bombs-brought-down -passenger-jets/?hpid=hp_hp-cards_hp-card-world%3Ahomepage%2Fcard; Mohamed, A., and M. Georg, Exclusive: Investigators '90 percent sure' bomb downed Russian plane, Reuters, 2015, http://www.reuters.com/article/2015/11/09/us-egypt-crash-russia-flights-tourists -idUSKCN0SX07D20151109#F631oUkdb4mtgmMz.97.

Figure 7.8   Mohammad Sidique Khan, one of the four men who bombed the London transit system in July 7, 2005, in a video aired by Al Jazeera. (Courtesy of Wikipedia, https://en.wikipedia.org/w /index.php?curid=14862374.)

Forensic examiners had initially thought that military-grade plastic explosives were used in the attacks, and, as the blasts were thought to have occurred simultaneously, that synchronized timed detonators were used. However, it was eventually determined that home-made organic peroxide-based devices were used. Each device was believed to contain 10 lb or less of TATP and was small enough to fit inside a backpack.

Oklahoma City, USA

On April 19, 1995, a large vehicle bomb detonated on the north side of the Alfred P. Murrah Federal Building in Oklahoma City, OK (see Figure 1.1). A total of 168 perished in the blast; estimates of injuries varied from 460 to more than 800. The true number may never be known, as many treated themselves and did not seek medical help as they realized that medical facilities in the area were overwhelmed.

The Murrah Federal Building was constructed in 1977 of rebar-reinforced concrete. The structure had nine floors with a basement and parking garages and included more than 300,000 ft^2, providing office space for various federal agencies, a credit union, and child day care center.

The detonation rocked every building in Oklahoma City. The explosion destroyed the Murrah Building, the Water Resources Board, a restaurant, and other structures in the surrounding area as well as breaking windows and doors for 14 blocks. A total of 342 businesses were damaged and 10 structures collapsed. The north face of the Murrah Building was sheared away and numerous vehicles in the parking lot across 5th Street ignited into flames, sending smoke and a massive concrete dust cloud over the area.

The blast was felt 50 mi away, causing security alarms throughout the city to activate. The Oklahoma Geological Survey Station, located 16 mi south of Oklahoma City, recorded a large surface wave at 9:02:13 A.M., followed by a second wave at 9:02:23 A.M.

Oklahoma City Bomb Squad Officers quickly assessed the damage as consistent with a large vehicle bomb and not that of an accidental explosion. As the bombing was of a federal building and federal employees were killed, the Federal Bureau of Investigation (FBI) was designated the lead criminal investigative agency.

Approximately 460 tons of debris was sifted and examined for evidence. All vehicles in the lot across the street were processed and the owners identified. As investigators completed assignments in the outer areas, they were moved to other teams working the inner perimeter.

The first key piece of evidence discovered was a large piece of the vehicle used in the bombing, located 150 ft from the blast site. A rear axle and gear housing from a large vehicle was located in front of the Regency Towers Apartment Building and the axle contained a vehicle identification number (VIN). Investigators initiated a trace of the VIN and found it to be from a 1993 Ford F700 cargo van registered to Ryder Truck Rental and bearing a Florida license.

On the basis of evidence collected at the scene, interviews with witnesses and evidence obtained through the arrest of Timothy McVeigh and execution of several search warrants, the device was determined to be a large vehicle bomb contained in a 1993 Ford F700 20-ft cargo van. The main explosive charge contained approximately 4800 lb of an ammonium nitrate and nitromethane mixture packed in plastic barrels. The firing train of the device included a fuse igniter of approximately 4 ft of safety fuse with a nonelectric detonator.

The explosives boosters could not be identified and may have been a combination of explosives. The main charge was located in the cargo box. It is probable that McVeigh parked the vehicle in the freight zone of the Murrah Building on 5th Street, ignited the safety fuse from the cab, exited, locked the vehicle, and walked away. The fuse was attached to the explosive train through a hole penetrating the cab to the cargo box. The fuse would have burned at approximately 42 s per foot or 2½ min total time.

The vehicle-borne IED detonated at a velocity of 8000 ft/s and generated significant heat that ignited vehicles nearby. A blast pressure wave shattered the glass face of the Murrah Building. Massive injuries resulted from the pressure wave and shock front, as well as from shards of broken glass and flying debris. The blast wave entered the Murrah Building causing failure of the main transfer beam that provided support to the third through ninth floors. As this beam collapsed, all floors along the north wall collapsed in a pancake configuration to the street below. The crater was approximately 30 ft wide and 8 ft deep.

The blast wave penetrated but was also reflected off the nearby Journal Record Building across 5th Street. Vehicles in the area received extensive damage from blast pressures that were traveling at more than 7000 mi/h.

Nine buildings in a four-block area were destroyed by the blast. A tenth structure approximately a quarter mile north of the Murrah site collapsed as a result of reflective pressure. Structural damage was noted as far away as five blocks from the blast seat. Fragments of the vehicle containing the explosives were recovered up to eight blocks from the bomb crater.

Timothy McVeigh was arrested by an officer of the Oklahoma Highway Patrol at 10:22 A.M. on the day of the bombing about 75 mi North of Oklahoma City. Evidence recovered from McVeigh's clothing and vehicle assisted in the device reconstruction. Residue samples of PETN, commonly used in detonating cord, were found on McVeigh's knife and in his pockets. Residues of the explosive chemical ethylene glycol dinitrate were recovered from earplugs removed from McVeigh's vehicle.

On June 2, 1997, McVeigh was found guilty on 11 counts of murder and conspiracy and was sentenced to death. He was executed by lethal injection at a U.S. penitentiary in Terre Haute, Indiana. An accomplice in the bombing, Terry Nichols, was convicted in Federal Court for conspiracy to commit murder of federal law enforcement officers and manslaughter of the federal officers. He was given a life sentence. The State of Oklahoma tried Nichols for the murder of 162 victims. He was convicted at the state level and received a life sentence. A third accomplice, Michael Fortier, was convicted in Federal Court for lying to investigators and transporting stolen property over state lines. He was given a lenient sentence in return for his testimony against Terry Nichols and Timothy McVeigh. He is currently in Federal prison serving a 23-year sentence.

Boston, USA

Monday April 15, 2013, was the 117th running of the Boston Marathon. The 26.2-mi run, held to commemorate the 1775 battles of Lexington and Concord, is celebrated as part of a legal holiday in the state of Massachusetts.

At about 2:50 P.M., with 5600 runners still in the race, two explosions occurred at a short distance from the finish line. The explosions occurred seconds apart and sent shrapnel and fragments flying among the crowds of spectators and runners. The velocity of the shrapnel was sufficiently high to impale victims, and many suffered severe burns. The blasts took three lives and injured hundreds more (Leinwand et al., 2013). Of those 260 injuries, 16 people required amputations because of their injuries.

Two days after the bombing, a lid to a pressure cooker was found atop a structure near the seat of the explosions. This crucial piece of evidence helped investigators to reconfigure the crime scene and the device used.

Three days after the explosions, a police officer at the Massachusetts Institute of Technology was shot and killed by the alleged bombing suspects (CNN, 2014). The shooting prompted a large-scale manhunt. Less than 24 h after the MIT officer was killed, a carjacking occurred in a nearby town. Shots were fired at police after explosives were thrown from the stolen vehicle. Defensive fire was returned, hitting one of the suspects. As the injured suspect was being placed in handcuffs, the driver ran him over; he died shortly afterward. The perpetrators were identified as 19-year-old Dzhokhar Tsarnaev and his 26-year-old brother Tamerlan Tsarnaev. In the evening hours of April 19, 2013, Dzhokhar was captured by police and placed under arrest. On April 8, 2015, Tsarnaev was found guilty on all 30 counts of the indictment. On May 15, 2015, the jury recommended that Tsarnaev be sentenced to death by lethal injection on six of 17 capital counts.

After the incident, forensic scientists were able to recreate the pressure cooker devices and identify the explosive charge and shrapnel (Figure 7.9). In 2004, the Department of Homeland Security was sufficiently concerned about pressure-cooker bombs to issue an alert to federal and state security officials, stating, "The use of pressure cookers as an improvised explosive device is a technique commonly taught in Afghan terrorist training camps" (Crowley, 2013).

MANPADS

Man-Portable Air Defense Systems (MANPADS)—also known as shoulder-fired anti-aircraft missiles—when in the hands of terrorists, criminals, or other nonstate actors, pose a serious threat to passenger air travel, the commercial aviation industry, and military aircraft around the world (Figure 7.10).

MANPADS are surface-to-air missiles that can be carried and fired by a single individual or by a team. Most MANPADS consist of the following: (1) a missile packaged in a tube; (2) a launching mechanism (commonly known as a *gripstock*); and (3) a battery (Figure 7.11). The tubes, which protect the missile until it has been fired, are disposable. Simple sights are mounted on the tube. A single-use battery powers the missile prior to launch (U.S. Department of State, 2011).

MANPADS launch tubes typically range from about 1.2 to 2 m (4 to 6.5 ft) in length and about 70 mm (3 in) in diameter. Their weight, with launcher, varies from about 13 to 25 kg (28 to 55 lb). They are easy to transport and conceal. Some of the most commonly proliferated MANPADS can easily fit into the trunk of an automobile. By virtue of these characteristics, and because a single successful attack against an airliner would have significant consequences for the international civilian aviation industry, MANPADS are highly appealing weapons to terrorists and criminals (U.S. Department of State, 2011).

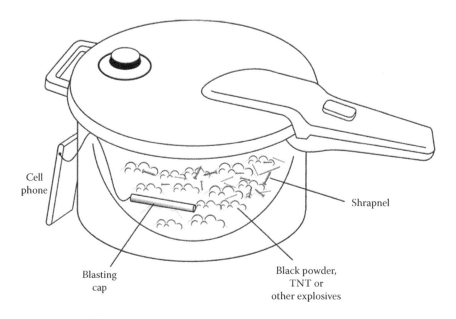

Cell
phone

Shrapnel

Blasting
cap

Black powder,
TNT or
other explosives

Figure 7.9 Schematic of a pressure cooker IED.

Figure 7.10 Iraqi insurgents with SA-7b and SA-14 MANPADS. (Courtesy of the U.S. Department of Homeland Security.)

Types of MANPADS

Since the development of the American Redeye in the late 1950s, it is estimated that more than 1 million MANPADS have been manufactured worldwide. Among the most widespread are the Russian Strela (SA-7 and SA-14), Igla (SA-16 and SA-18), and the U.S.-manufactured FIM-92 Stinger (FAS, 2004).

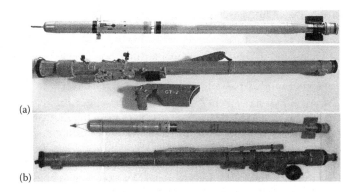

Figure 7.11 An SA-18 (Igla) missile with launch tube and grip stick (a) and an SA-16 (Igla-1) missile and launch tube (b). (Courtesy of Naval Sea Systems Command, https://naveodtechdiv.navsea .navy.mil.)

MANPADS were designed for use by national military forces to protect troops and facilities. They can attain speeds of about twice the speed of sound and strike aircraft flying at altitudes up to approximately 4.5 km (15,000 ft) at a range of up to 5 km (3.2 mi). Most of the older systems are ineffective against modern military aircraft, although civilian aircraft remain vulnerable because of the lack of countermeasures.

Three main types of MANPADS are in use (U.S. Department of State, 2011):

1. Infrared (IR) systems that lock in on an aircraft's heat source, usually the engine or the engine's exhaust plume
2. Command Line-of-Sight systems whereby the MANPADS operator visually locates the target aircraft using a magnified optical sight, and then uses radio controls to guide the missile to the aircraft
3. Laser Beam Riders in which the missile flies along the laser beam and strikes the aircraft where the operator has aimed the laser

Use of MANPADS by Terrorists and Insurgents

There are an estimated 500,000 MANPADS in the world today, many thousands of which are thought to be on the black market and therefore accessible to terrorists and other non-state actors (Kuhn, 2003).

Since 1975, 40 civilian aircraft have been hit by MANPADS, causing more than 800 deaths worldwide (Table 7.2; Figure 7.12) (U.S. Department of State, 2011). All of the incidents, except a November 2002 incident in Mombasa, Kenya, took place in zones of conflict.

About 20 countries have produced or have licenses to produce MANPADS or their components. The United States believes that most MANPADS systems are either stockpiled in national inventories or have been destroyed (U.S. Department of State, 2011). Thousands, however, have not been accounted for and are believed to be outside of the control of national governments.

Table 7.2 Airliners Shot Down by MANPADS Since 1975

Date	Event
March 12, 1975	A Douglas C-54D-5-DC passenger airliner, operated by Air Vietnam, crashed into Vietnamese territory after being hit by a MANPADS. All six crew members and 20 passengers were killed in the crash.
September 3, 1978	An Air Rhodesia Vickers 782D Viscount passenger airliner crash-landed after being hit by a MANPADS fired by forces from the Zimbabwe Peoples Revolution Army. Four crew members and 34 of the 56 passengers were killed in the crash.
December 19, 1988	Two Douglas DC-7 spray aircraft en route from Senegal to Morocco, chartered by the U.S. Agency for International Development to eradicate locusts, were struck by MANPADS fired by POLISARIO militants in the Western Sahara. One DC-7 crashed killing all five crew members. The other DC-7 landed safely in Morocco.
September 22, 1993	A Tupolev 154B aircraft operated by Transair Georgia was shot down by Abkhazian separatist forces, crashed onto the runway and caught fire, killing 108.
April 6, 1994	A Dassault Mystère-Falcon 50 executive jet carrying the Presidents of Rwanda and Burundi and its French flight crew was shot down over Kigali, killing all aboard and sparking massive ethnic violence and regional conflict.
October 10, 1998	A Boeing 727-30 Lignes Aeriennes Congolaises airliner was downed over the Democratic Republic of the Congo jungle by Tutsi militia, killing 41.
December 26, 1998	A United Nations-chartered Lockheed C-130 Hercules transport was shot down over Angola by UNITA forces, killing 14.
January 2, 1999	A United Nations Lockheed L-100-30 Hercules transport was shot down by UNITA forces in Angola, killing nine.
November 28, 2002	Terrorists fired two MANPADS at an Arkia Airlines Boeing 757-3E7 with 271 passengers and crew as it took off from Mombasa, Kenya. Both missiles missed.
November 22, 2003	A DHL Airbus A300B4-203F cargo jet transporting mail in Iraq was struck and damaged by a MANPADS. Although hit in the left fuel tank, the plane was able to return to the Baghdad airport and land safely.
March 23, 2007	A TransAVIAexport Ilyushin 76TD cargo plane was shot down over Mogadishu, Somalia, killing the entire crew of 11.

Source: U.S. Department of State, 2011.

Nonstate combatants acquire MANPADS in a variety of ways, including from black markets, arms dealers, front companies, intermediaries, end-use certificate falsification, and corrupt government officials (U.S. Department of State, 2011). The black market cost of MANPADS varies widely, ranging from a few hundred dollars to more than $100,000, depending on the model and its condition. Given the relatively low cost of some systems, there is the possibility of acquisition by terrorists or other nonstate actors. The United States believes that a number of terrorist organizations, including ISIS and al-Qaeda, already have MANPADS in their possession (Gibbons-Neff, 2014).

Figure 7.12 A DHL Airbus air cargo jet with left wing on fire returns to the airport in Baghdad to make a controlled landing shortly after being hit by a MANPADS fired by an Iraqi insurgent. (Courtesy of U.S. Department of Homeland Security.)

The most frequently used and proliferated MANPADS is the first-generation, infrared-homing system designed by the former Soviet Union known as the SA-7b. This is the most common MANPADS possessed by terrorist groups.

Since 2003, cooperation among several countries has led to the destruction of more than 32,500 excess, loosely secured, illicitly held, or otherwise at-risk MANPADS in more than 30 countries. Some successes include (U.S. Department of State, 2011):

- Bosnia and Herzegovina destroys its government-held stockpile of almost 6000 MANPADS between 2003 and 2004
- Hungary's destruction of more than 1500 MANPADS
- Macedonia's destruction of 156 MANPADS
- Montenegro's destruction of 1500 MANPADS
- Liberia's destruction of 45 MANPADS in 2003
- Burundi's destruction of 312 MANPADS
- Cyprus's destruction of 324 MANPADS in 2009
- Elimination of more than 100 MANPADS in Afghanistan

UNMANNED AERIAL VEHICLES

The acronym *UAV* refers to an aerial vehicle that does not carry a human operator; uses aerodynamic forces to provide vehicle lift; can fly autonomously based on pre-programmed automation systems or be piloted remotely (e.g., directed by a pilot at a ground station); and can carry a lethal or nonlethal payload (Theuav.com, 2015). Other terms include unpiloted aerial vehicle and remotely piloted aircraft (ICAO, 2011). In the mainstream, an unmanned aerial vehicle (UAV) is commonly known as a drone. The definitions just mentioned cover a wide array of aerial vehicles, including even cruise

Figure 7.13 A German crew rolls out a V-1 bomb during World War II. (Courtesy of Homeland Surveillance Electronics Unmanned Aerial Vehicle.)

missiles. UAVs are designed to be expendable or recoverable. This chapter focuses on a narrow category: small devices, often propeller-driven, which can be readily assembled and operated by individuals (Miasnikov, 2005).

UAVs offer practical capabilities: covertness, speed, and accuracy. Until recently, UAVs were deployed for military and special operations; today, however, they are being used in a wide range of civil applications such as search and rescue, reconnaissance, border patrol missions, surveillance, crowd monitoring, and detection of illegal hunting. Other uses include forest fire detection, aerial surveying of crops, fire investigation, and inspection of power lines and pipelines. UAVs are often relied on for duties that are considered too *dull, dirty, or dangerous* for manned aircraft (Atherton, 2013).

In the military, UAVs originally were dedicated to performing intelligence, surveillance, and reconnaissance missions; this remains their predominant function. The roles have expanded to include strike missions, electronic attack, suppression and/or destruction of enemy air defense, communications relay, and combat search and rescue. Such UAVs range in cost from a few thousand dollars to tens of millions of dollars, and the aircraft used in these systems range in size from a Micro Air Vehicle weighing less than 1 lb to large aircraft weighing more than 40,000 lb (Theuav.com, 2015).

Historically, UAVs were simple remotely piloted aircraft; however, autonomous control is increasingly being used. The V-1 flying bomb used by Nazi Germany during World War II flew autonomously (Figure 7.13).

Terrorist Use of UAVs

The operation of commercial UAVs by civilians has spawned significant concerns regarding misuse by terrorists and criminals; UAVs have already been used for the transport of drugs, guns, and other illicit items. Criminals are using small *hobby* UAVs to smuggle drugs and other contraband across the border and even into prisons. Such UAVs are termed *blind mules* (MacKenzie, 2015).

UAVs have an obvious appeal to terrorists: it is difficult to detect them; they are controlled from hidden locations (e.g., a parked minivan) or far away; and they are capable of flying into crowded or remote places, whether a sports stadium or a power plant (please see below the list of attributes of UAVs that are appealing to terrorists). They can be equipped to carry chemical or biological agents, radioactive materials, and explosives (Figure 7.14). Unlike the suicide bomber, no one has to die to complete the mission. Drones, therefore, combine the stealth of a suicide bomber with the power and range of an armed aircraft (Alexander, 2014).

Attributes of UAVs that are appealing to terrorists (Bartsch, 2005):

- Satellite data links can allow UAVs to be controlled and operated from a remote location, including internationally
- Possible to attack targets that are difficult to reach by land
- Possible to carry out a wide-scale attack aimed at inflicting a maximum death rate on a population (e.g., via the use of WMDs in crowded urban environs)
- Covertness of attack preparation
- Flexibility in choice of launch site
- Possible to achieve a long range and good accuracy with relatively inexpensive and increasingly available technology
- There are currently weak air defenses against low-flying UAVs
- Relative cost-effectiveness of UAVs compared with manned airplanes
- Possible to achieve a strong psychological effect by frightening populations and public officials

Defense and terrorism experts have discussed the potential use of UAVs for terrorism. The New York Police Department considers a UAV carrying explosives as a major threat (CBS News, 2009). Authorities in the United States, Germany, Spain, and Egypt have foiled numerous potential terrorist drone attacks since 2015 (Nicas, 2015).

Figure 7.14 It is possible that a terrorist group could equip a UAV to deliver biological or chemical weapons. (Reproduced from Homeland Surveillance and Electronics LLC. With permission.)

The payload of UAV does not have to be large to cause significant damage. This is especially true with regard to WMDs. For example, a computer simulation predicts that if 900 g of weapons-grade anthrax was dropped from a height of 100 m upwind of a large U.S. city, 1.5 million people would become infected (Wein et al., 2003). Even with the most diligent medical measures that can be taken during an epidemic, the model estimates that 123,000 people would die.

Significant damage could be caused by the most popular of terrorist weapons, a mixture of explosives and metal shrapnel. An explosive device delivered by a UAV to a crowded venue could inflict much more damage than the same device carried by a suicide terrorist (armscontrol.ru, 2011).

Drones could be used by terrorists as flying bombs to take down a passenger jetliner. Concerns have been raised that terrorists could fly multiple remote-controlled unmanned aircraft into the engines of a jumbo jet, causing it to crash. These concerns came after it emerged that a drone flew within 6 m (20 ft) of an Airbus A320 as it landed at Heathrow Airport in London in 2014. An official report found that the small UAV narrowly avoided colliding with the passenger jet 210 m (700 ft) above the runway (Brooks-Pollock, 2014). The UAV was not picked up on radar, and the operator of the device could not be traced. One expert stated, "It would be the equivalent of an aerial truck bomb, like a suicide bomb only the terrorist could fly it remotely, with impunity. These drones can be bought anonymously online, piloted anonymously and the attacker would be untraceable because they are completely unlicensed" (Brooks-Pollock, 2014).

In some cases, unmanned aircraft systems or drones are either intentionally or unintentionally being flown into the airspace of commercial aircraft. In summer 2014, a New York City Police helicopter nearly collided with a drone that was about 240 m (800 feet) above ground. In 2015, in San Jose, Costa Rica, a Cessna C-172 collided with a drone 400 m (1300 feet) in the air. No one was hurt (*TicoTimes*, 2015).

Concerns about terrorists using UAVs are well founded. Hezbollah, a Shiite militia based in Lebanon, has been flying UAVs into Israeli airspace for over a decade. In 2014, Israel used a Patriot missile to shoot down a UAV operated by Hezbollah flying off its coast. Hezbollah said it did not own the device, but that it has flown a UAV—one that it assembled from an Iranian design—35 mi into Israel. Hamas claims to have three varieties of UAV. In 2014, Israel shot down a Hamas-operated drone in southern Israel. Hamas has shown video footage of drones armed with rockets, and says it has a design for others that operate more or less like a cruise missile (Cardinal, 2014).

Hezbollah is using drones in its fight against al-Qaeda-led rebels in the border region between Syria and Lebanon. A video released by pro-Hezbollah media showed aerial footage shot by a drone flying over the battlefield near the town of Qalamoun (Masi, 2015). Hezbollah is also believed to be constructing its own drones. Reports from earlier Hezbollah drone strikes and photo evidence of Hezbollah fighters building the aircraft show that they primarily use Misrad (*migrant*) drones, considered the Iranian drone of choice (Masi, 2015). Iran, the key sponsor for Hezbollah, has claimed for several years to have succeeded in manufacturing armed drones (Bergen and Schneider, 2014).

Al-Qaeda has planned to use remote-controlled planes for a range of destructive attacks (see Table 7.3), and ISIS is known to have used them. In August 2014, ISIS released

Table 7.3   Early Reports of Terrorist Attempts to Use UAVs

Year	Attempted Activity
1995	Aum Shinrikyo, the Japanese terrorist group that attacked the Tokyo subway with sarin gas (see Chapter 2), planned to use remote-control helicopters to spray toxic chemicals from the air. The helicopters crashed during testing.
2001	Osama bin Laden considered using remote-control airplanes packed with explosives to kill President G.W. Bush and other heads of state at the G-8 summit in Genoa, Italy.
2002	Quoting a German intelligence official, the Reuters news agency reported that al-Qaeda might be planning to attack passenger aircraft using model airplanes.
2002	Palestinian toy importers in Jerusalem and Ramallah were told to order hundreds of model airplanes for distribution to Palestinian children in hospitals. The model planes were sent to Palestinian workshops for conversion into miniature air bombers with explosive payloads. Militiamen from the Fatah movement were sent to open areas near Jericho to test the new weapons, and discovered they could fly to a distance of 1 km and an altitude of 300 m. The Fatah leadership chose Jerusalem as its target, predicting that it would be some time before Israeli security and intelligence authorities learned how to intercept the new weapons.
2003	The Vremya Novostei newspaper reported in November 2003 the theft of a copy of the newest developmental reconnaissance UAV model from a facility in Israel. The UAV weighs 14 kg and has a wingspan of 1.5 m. The thief was not caught, and there were fears about the possible use of the model by terrorists (Vremya Novostei, 2003).
2003	According to the *London Independent* newspaper, a British national held at Guantanamo Bay, Cuba, confessed to being part of an al-Qaeda plot to acquire a UAV to attack the House of Commons with anthrax (Miasnikov, 2005).
2004	According to Reuters, in early March, Israeli intelligence prevented a terrorist act with a UAV loaded with explosives. Representatives of the administration of Prime Minister Ariel Sharon claimed that a Palestinian extremist group planned to attack a Jewish settlement in Gaza sector.

Source: Miasnikov, E., Threat of Terrorism Using Unmanned Aerial Vehicles: Technical Aspects, Moscow Institute of Physics and Technology, Moscow, Russia, 2005; Polit.Ru, 2004. http://www.polit.ru/news/2004/03/10/izrail/; Vremya Novostei, Moscow, November 11, 2003; DEBKA, DEBKAfile Special Counter-Terror Report, January 14, 2003; Gips, M., A remote threat, Security Management Online, October 2002.

video footage captured by an off-the-shelf drone of a Syrian military base it later attacked. The caption on the video read, "From the drone of the army of the Islamic State." Some have warned that it is only a matter of time that well-funded terrorist organizations such as ISIS will stockpile these inexpensive items (Cardinal, 2014).

In two separate cases in the summer of 2013, German law enforcement personnel raided Islamic militants and right-wing extremists believed to be plotting drone attacks. Police recovered bomb-making materials and a drone from the extremists, who were allegedly planning to use the device to bomb a German summer camp (Nicas, 2015).

Model aircraft built by amateurs demonstrate highly sophisticated capabilities. For example, a 5-kg TAM-5 aircraft was remotely piloted across the Atlantic. The TAM-5 started from Canada, conducted the flight in automatic mode, and landed 39 h later 3000 km away in Ireland (Miasnikov, 2005). In 2012, a Massachusetts graduate student was imprisoned for plotting to attach plastic explosives to small UAVs and fly them into the Pentagon and the U.S. Capitol (Box 7.1) (Alexander, 2014). In 2015, an 18-year-old equipped a UAV with a gun and posted a video on the Internet. The footage appears to show a gun affixed to a drone hovering several feet off of the ground. The gun discharges several times while the drone is in flight. The designer described the device as a "homemade multirotor with a semi-automatic handgun mounted on it" (Corcoran and Connors, 2015). (The designer was arrested shortly after the internet posting.)

Production-run accessories and separate parts such as engines, radio controls, servos, flight stabilization systems, and global positioning system receivers are available commercially; in addition, a wide array of ready-to-fly aircraft kit models are on the market. Some models require experience in piloting, but others that are simple and stable in flight are manufactured specifically for beginners. UAV control and delivery to a target is a more complex operation but is still achievable by nonprofessionals. The most critical component—preparation of the aircraft for a terrorist attack, including assembly and testing—can be conducted legally, because such activity is currently not regulated or controlled (armscontrol.ru, 2014).

Given that UAVs are not burdened by the physiological limitations of human pilots, they can be designed for maximal in-flight times. The maximum flight duration of UAVs varies widely. Internal combustion engine aircraft endurance depends strongly on the percentage of fuel burned as a fraction of total weight (Theuav.com, 2015). Solar electric UAVs hold the potential for unlimited flight, and scores of models are currently available.

Defenses against Terrorist Use of Drones

A key problem facing security officials is that many UAVs are too small to be picked up by radar (MacKenzie, 2015). Larger drones can be detected by radar and shot down. The United States and Israel are improving defenses against smaller ones, however. It is possible to jam the frequencies drones use for navigation or to hack them (Alexander, 2014).

In 2015, a 2.8-lb drone accidentally crashed on the White House grounds. The Secret Service stated that this incident was a recreational flight by a hobbyist; however, the accident highlighted fears of a possible drone terror attack on the president and others. The manufacturer, SZ DJI Technology of China, has pledged to update the software on its drones to prevent them from flying over Washington, DC (MacKenzie, 2015).

U.S. security officials are seeking ways to efficiently track drones to protect potential targets such as critical infrastructure, government buildings, prisons and crowded stadiums (Nicas, 2015). A growing industry is emerging to address the issue, offering systems to detect incoming drones and alert authorities. DroneShield LLC (Washington, DC) has installed about 200 of its audio-based detection systems worldwide, including around prisons, government buildings, and power plants (Nicas, 2015). Resilient Solutions Ltd. (Alexandria, VA) is working with a European defense contractor to develop a sophisticated system that can detect and track a drone and identify whether it is a threat. Sentien Robotics LLC (Fredericksburg, VA) aims to use drones with radiofrequency sensors to help detect potentially unwelcome ones. Many companies, however, acknowledge that such developments are difficult and existing methods are not perfect. They lament that

BOX 7.1   THE FERDAUS PLOT

In April 2011, Rezwan Ferdaus, a graduate of Northeastern University with a degree in physics, provided details of his attack plans to undercover FBI agents posing as members of al-Qaeda. His attack was to be carried out against the Pentagon and Capitol building using three remotely controlled UAVs and six people.

According to court papers, Ferdaus told undercover agents he wanted to create as big a *psychological* impact as possible by killing as many Americans as possible, including women and children he allegedly considered *enemies of Allah.*

In May 2011, Ferdaus traveled from Boston to Washington, DC, to conduct surveillance and take photographs of the Pentagon and Capitol buildings. He identified and photographed sites at East Potomac Park from which he planned to launch the UAVs containing a C-4 explosive (Kimery, 2015).

Ferdaus intended to incorporate an armed ground assault using automatic weapons with the aerial assault. Ferdaus stated, "We can effectively eliminate key locations of the P-building then we can add to it in order to take out everything else and leave one area only as a squeeze where the individuals will be isolated, they'll be vulnerable and we can dominate." Once isolated, Ferdaus planned to *open up on them* and *keep firing* to create *chaos* and *take out* everyone.

Between May and September 2011, Ferdaus researched, ordered, and acquired many of the materials and components for his attack, including an RC F-86 Sabre (Figure 7.15). He also allegedly planned to use an RC F-4 Phantom model plane. Several RC planes can reach top speeds of more than 60 mi/h.

Ferdaus stated he was working to find out how much weight the remote controlled airplane can hold. Nevertheless, he told an FBI undercover operative that the

Figure 7.15   Scale model of a U.S. Navy F-86 Sabre fighter plane, similar to the device constructed by Rezwan Ferdaus. (Courtesy of U.S. Department of Justice, http://ideas.time.com /2013/01/31/criminals-and-terrorists-can-fly-drones-too/.)

"model airplane…can carry a good enough payload and it will detonate on impact" Kimery (2015). Ferdaus received from the FBI undercover operatives 25 lbs. of what he believed was C-4, as well as six fully automatic AK-47 assault rifles and grenades.

In 2012, Ferdaus was sentenced to 17 years in prison.

Prior to the Ferdaus attempt, Christopher Paul, a Columbus, Ohio, resident pleaded guilty in 2008 to planning terrorist attacks in the United States and Europe. According to the indictment in that case, Paul conducted research in 2006 on a variety of remote-controlled UAVs, including a boat and a 5-ft-long helicopter. Paul was accused of joining al-Qaeda in the early 1990s (Cruickshank and Lister, 2012).

many small drones do not show up on radar. Acoustic sensors can miss the buzz of a drone amid city sounds or mistake a weed whacker for one of the devices. Visual sensors do not work well at night and can be inaccurate (Nicas, 2015).

Concerns about drones are causing many government agencies to reconsider security. Authorities in France are investigating a series of illegal drone flights over 14 of its nuclear power plants (*Daily Mail*, 2014). At the University of Texas at Austin, officials were alarmed when a drone flew over the school's packed football stadium during a 2014 game. In 2015, the Secret Service arrested a man who was "trying to launch a drone outside the White House fence" (AP, 2015).

According to some experts, publicizing the dangers of illicit use of UAVs would be a first step toward mitigating the threat. Ensuring that drone manufacturers and training instructors know their customers and are aware of suspicious behavior should be high priority. International protocols regulating export of drone technology must be strengthened with attention to terrorism, with special focus on UAVs that can evade radar. There has been discussion of installing tracking software or *kill switches* into unmanned aircraft; however, practical problems exist (Bloomberg, 2014). Unfortunately, accurately detecting such small and agile devices will pose difficulties for years.

The capabilities of UAVs will continue to improve and their costs will decrease, so that unmanned aircraft will be applied ever more widely in the civilian sector. By 2030, it is expected that 30,000 UAVs may be hovering in U.S. skies alone, most of them devoted to beneficial operations such as emergency response and crop reconnaissance (Bloomberg, 2014). It must be restated that even a small UAV payload (i.e., just a few kilograms) is capable of causing significant death and injury and massive damage to structures. This demonstrates the need for careful assessment of UAVs by regulators. Prospects for terrorist use of larger UAVs seem less likely, although this possibility cannot be dismissed (Miasnikov, 2005).

QUESTIONS

1. List five methods by which biological or chemical agents may be released by a terrorist.
2. What are the technical requirements for a terrorist to successfully release spores of *Bacillus anthracis*?

3. What kinds of countermeasures against IEDs are being developed by U.S. forces?
4. Discuss the IEDs used in the following situations: (a) Northwest Airlines Flight 253, December 25, 2009; (b) London, U.K., July 7, 2005; (c) Oklahoma City, 1995; and (d) Boston, Massachusetts, 2013. What explosive materials were used, and how was the IED designed and constructed?
5. What are the main components of MANPADS?
6. How can MANPADS be acquired by a terrorist organization?
7. List some of the attributes of UAVs that are appealing to terrorists.
8. Check the national and international news from the past 6 months. List the following events: (a) situations where UAVs operated by hobbyists came too close to an airport and/or airplane in flight; (b) terrorist use of a UAV to deliver a weapon; (c) controversial use of a UAV near high-ranking elected leaders.
9. Check the Internet and identify new technologies that have been developed to counter potentially hostile actions by UAVs. For example, what new detection systems have been developed? Have UAV manufacturers installed improved software so that UAVs will avoid sensitive locations such as airports and government buildings?

REFERENCES

Agence France-Presse. 2007. Tamil bra bomber targets Sri Lanka minister. November 27, 2007. http://afp.google.com/article/ALeqM5hypJWWD9ww4hQudZ5VyS1FeKWmhA (accessed November 2, 2010).

Alexander, C. 2014. Hamas bragging rights grow with drones use against Israel. Bloomberg Business. http://www.bloomberg.com/news/articles/2014-07-16/hamas-bragging-rights-grow-with-drones-use-against-israel.

Armscontrol.ru. 2011. The Threat of the Use of Small UAVs by Terrorists: Technical Aspects. Eugene Miasnikov's presentation at the International Seminar on the Law of Armed Conflicts, French Air Force Academy, Salon-de-Provence, France, April 7, 2011. http://www.armscontrol.ru/uav/em040711.htm.

Atherton, K.D. 2013. No one wants to be a drone pilot, U.S. Air Force discovers. Popular Science. http://www.popsci.com/technology/article/2013-08/air-force-drone-program-too-unmanned-its-own-good.

Bartsch, R., Parliamentary Library Lecture, UAS International, Beecroft, NSW, Australia, 2014; Miasnikov, E., Threat of Terrorism Using Unmanned Aerial Vehicles: Technical Aspects, Moscow Institute of Physics and Technology, Moscow, Russia, 2005.

Bartsch, R. 2014. To catch a drone: Security and privacy challenges in a high-tech age. Parliamentary Library Lecture. UAS International, Beecroft, NSW, Australia.

BBC.com. 2003. 'Horse bomb' hits Colombia town. http://news.bbc.co.uk/2/hi/americas/3098746.stm (accessed November 2, 2010).

BBC.com. 2006. Iraq boat attack personnel named. BBC News. February 14, 2006. http://news.bbc.co.uk/2/hi/uk_news/6146844.stm (accessed November 2, 2010).

BBC News. 2005. London bomber: Text in full. http://news.bbc.co.uk/2/hi/uk/4206800.stm.

Beckhusen, R. 2012. PlayStation Controlled DIY Tank May Be the Wildest Weapon Yet in the Syria War. http://www.wired.com/2012/12/rebel-armor/.

Bergen, P. 2006. The Taliban, regrouped and rearmed. *Washington Post*, September 10, 2006. http://www.washingtonpost.com/wp-dyn/content/article/2006/09/08/AR2006090801614.html.

Bergen, P., and E. Schneider. 2014. Hezbollah armed drone? Militants' new weapon. CNN.com. http://www.cnn.com/2014/09/22/opinion/bergen-schneider-armed-drone-hezbollah/.

Bloomberg, 2014. When terrorists have drones. http://www.bloombergview.com/articles/2014-07 -22/when-terrorists-have-drones.

Brooks-Pollock. 2014. Drones 'could be used as flying bombs for terror attack on passenger jet'. *The Telegraph.* http://www.telegraph.co.uk/news/uknews/terrorism-in-the-uk/11290086/Drones -could-be-used-as-flying-bombs-for-terror-attack-on-passenger-jet.html.

Caldwell, A., *U.S. News.* 2015. Man arrested near White House over drone. http://www.usnews.com /news/articles/2015/05/14/man-arrested-near-white-house-over-drone.

Cardinal, D. 2014. Drones provide terrorists with a DIY air force. http://www.extremetech.com /extreme/188941-drones-provide-terrorists-with-a-diy-air-force.

Carlton, J. 2001. Of microbes and mock attacks: Years ago, the military sprayed germs on U.S. cities. *The Wall Street Journal.* http://www.wsj.com/articles/SB1003703226697496080.

CBS News. 2009. NYPD scanning the sky for new terrorism threat. October 29, 2014, 6:57 AM. http:// www.cbsnews.com/news/drone-terrorism-threat-is-serious-concern-for-nypd/.

CNN.com. 2014. Boston Marathon terror attack fast facts. Retrieved November 19, 2014. http:// www.cnn.com/2013/06/03/us/boston-marathon-terror-attack-fast-facts/.

Cole, L.A. 1988. *Clouds of Secrecy: The Army's Germ Warfare Tests Over Populated Areas.* Oxford, UK: Rowman and Littlefield.

Corcoran, F., and B. Connors. 2015. Father says 'flying gun' drone video broke no laws. NBC Connecticut. http://www.nbcconnecticut.com/news/local/FAA-Police-Investigate-Drone-Gun -Clinton-Connecticut-Video-316368531.htmlonnors.

Crowley, M. 2013. A short recent history of pressure cooker bombs. *Time.* April 16, 2013. http:// swampland.time.com/2013/04/16/a-short-history-of-pressure-cooker-bombs/.

Cruickshank, P., and T. Lister. 2012. Terror and toy planes—Not so remote. CNN.com. http://security .blogs.cnn.com/2012/08/07/terror-and-toy-planes-not-so-remote/.

Daily Mail. 2014. Mystery drones fly over French nuclear sites. Associated Press. http://www.daily mail.co.uk/wires/ap/article-2818642/Mystery-drone-flights-French-nuclear-sites.html.

DEBKAfile. 2003. Arafat's New Terror Weapon: Exploding Toy Planes. DEBKAfile Special Counter-Terror Report, January 14, 2003. http://www.debka.com/article/2785/Arafat-s-New-Terror -Weapon-Exploding-Toy-Planes.

Federation of American Scientists (FAS). 2004. MANPADS Proliferation. Issue Brief #1. http://fas .org/asmp/campaigns/MANPADS/MANPADS.html.

Financial and Banking Information Infrastructure Committee. Vehicle Borne IED Identification Guide: Parked Vehicles. TRIPwire. https://www.fbiic.gov/public/2008/oct/DHSVehicleBorneIED IdentificationGuideParkedVehicles.pdf.

Gibbons-Neff, T. 2014. Islamic State might have taken advanced MANPADS from Syrian airfield. https://www.washingtonpost.com/news/checkpoint/wp/2014/08/25/islamic-state-might -have-taken-advanced-manpads-from-syrian-airfield/.

Gips, M. 2002. A remote threat. Security Management Online, October 2002. https://www.questia .com/magazine/1G1-92850644/a-remote-threat-news-and-trends.

Glanz, J., and J. Dwyer. 2004. Looting spree gutted ammo dump. *San Francisco Chronicle.* October 28, 2004.

International Civil Aviation Organization (ICAO). 2011. Unmanned Aircraft Systems (UAS). Montréal, Quebec, Canada. http://www.icao.int/Meetings/UAS/Documents/Circular%20328_en.pdf.

Joint Improvised Explosive Device Defeat Organization (JIEDDO). 2009a. Water-borne IED Threats and the Strait of Hormuz. 09292009-028. https://info.publicintelligence.net/JIEDDO-Hormuz .pdf.

Joint Improvised Explosive Device Defeat Organization (JIEDDO). 2009b. Annual report FY 2009. https://www.jieddo.dod.mil/content/docs/20100804_FULL_2009%20Annual%20Report _Unclassifi ed_v1.pdf (accessed November 2, 2010).

Kimery, A. 2015. The Threat of Small, Manned, Unmanned Aircraft in Washington Airspace has Long Been Known. Homeland Security Today. April 30, 2015. http://www.hstoday.us/columns/the -kimery-report/blog/the-threat-of-small-manned-unmanned-aircraft-in-washington-airspace -has-long-been-known/9c6177043dadfc7a5f064f89a435fc93.html.

Krolicki, K., and J. Pelofsky. 2009. Nigerian charged for trying to blow up U.S. airliner. Reuters, December 26, 2009.

Kuhn, D.A. 2003. Mombasa attack highlights increasing MANPADS threat. *Jane's Intelligence Review.* February 2003.

Leake, C. 2010. Terrorists "plan attack on Britain with bombs INSIDE their bodies" to foil new airport scanners. UK Daily Mail. January 30, 2010. http://www.dailymail.co.uk/news/article -1247338/Terrorists-plan-attack-Britain-bombs-INSIDEbodies-foil-new-airport-scanners.html (accessed November 2, 2010).

Leinwand, D., K. Johnson, and D. Stanglin. 2013. Boston bombs were pressure cookers filled with metal. *USA Today.* April 1, 2013. http://www.usatoday.com/story/news/nation/2013/04/16 /boston-marathon-explosions/2086853/.

Levin, D., and G. Valadares de Amorim. 2003. Potential for Aerosol Dissemination of Biological Weapons: Lessons from Biological Control of Insects. MedScape. http://www.medscape.com /viewarticle/452339.

Lewis, J. 2015. A Smart Bomb in Every Garage? Driverless Cars and the Future of Terrorist Attacks. Start. umd. http://www.start.umd.edu/news/smart-bomb-every-garage-driverless-cars-and-future -terrorist-attacks?utm_source=START%20Announce&utm_campaign=c31100c138-START _Newsletter_Sept2015&utm_medium=email&utm_term=0_a60ca8c769-c31100c138-50041757.

Lieberman, B. 2005. SDSU professor focuses laser research on finding killer explosives in Iraq. SignOnSanDiego.com, December 27, 2005. http://www.signonsandiego.com/articlelink/sdsu foundation4/sdsufoundation4.html (accessed November 2, 2010).

MacKenzie, D. 2015. WSJ: Terror attacks using drones pose huge threat for US. http://www.news max.com/Newsfront/US-terrorists-drones-Secret-Service/2015/01/29/id/621447/.

Masi, A. 2015. Hezbollah allegedly using drones against Al-Qaeda in battle for Qalamoun. *International Business Times.* http://www.ibtimes.com/hezbollah-allegedly-using-drones-against -al-qaeda-battle-qalamoun-1918696.

Miasnikov, E. 2005. Threat of Terrorism Using Unmanned Aerial Vehicles: Technical Aspects. Center for Arms Control, Energy and Environmental Studies, Moscow Institute of Physics and Technology, Moscow, Russia. http://www.armscontrol.ru/uav/em040711.htm.

Mohamed, A., and M. Georg. 2015. Exclusive: Investigators '90 percent sure' bomb downed Russian plane. Reuters. http://www.reuters.com/article/2015/11/09/us-egypt-crash-russia -flights-tourists-idUSKCN0SX07D20151109#F631oUkdb4mtgmMz.97.

Nicas, J. 2015. Criminals, terrorists find uses for drones, raising concerns. *The Wall Street Journal.* http://www.wsj.com/articles/criminals-terrorists-find-uses-for-drones-raising-concerns -1422494268.

Office of Technology Assessment, U.S. Congress. *Proliferation of Weapons of Mass Destruction.* Washington, DC: U.S. Government Printing Office; Publication OTA-ISC-559, 1993.

Oosthuizen, G.H., and E. Wilmshurst. 2004. Terrorism and Weapons of Mass Destruction: United Nations Security Council Resolution 1540. BP 04/01. Chatham House, London.

Pelkofski, J. 2005. Al-Qaeda's Maritime Campaign. Military.com, December 27, 2005. http://www .military.com/forums/0,15240,83909,00.html.

Pike, J.E. 2008. Weapons of Mass Destruction. Tularemia. Global Security. http://www.globalsecurity .org/wmd/intro/bio-tularemia.htm.

Polit.ru. 2004. V Izraile predotvraschyon terakt s ispol'zovaniyem BLA [Terrorist act with UAV employment has been prevented in Israel]. March 10, 2004. http://www.polit.ru/news/2004/03/10 /izrail/.

Pricenomics. 2014. How the U.S. Government Tested Biological Warfare on America. http://price onomics.com/how-the-us-government-tested-biological-warfare-on/.

Rediff. 2004. Sri Lanka probing bra bomb. July 14, 2004. http://www.rediff.com/news/2004/jul /14lanka.htm. (accessed November 2, 2010).

Sadler, B. 2005. Jordan confirms al-Qaeda behind hotel blasts. CNN, November 12, 2005.

Smart, J.K. 1997. History of chemical and biological warfare: An American perspective. In: *Medical Aspects of Chemical and Biological Warfare*, ed. Sidell, F.R., Takafuji, E.T., and Franz, D.R. Borden. Washington, DC: Institute Walter Reed Army Medical Center.

Spiegel, P., and J. Solomon. 2009. Al Qaeda takes credit for plot. *The Wall Street Journal*. December 29, 2009. http://online.wsj.com/article/SB126203574947307987.html (accessed November 2, 2010).

The Sunday Times. 1985. Militia shoot 'donkey bomb' rider. November 4, 1985. http://archive.times online.co.uk/tol/viewArticle.arc?articleId=ARCHIVE-The_Times-1985.11-04.05-003&pageId =ARCHIVE-The_Times-1985.11-04.05 (accessed November 2, 2010).

The Sunday Times. 2009. Donkey 'suicide' bombing is latest tactic against patrols. *Sunday Times.* http:// www.timesonline.co.uk/tol/news/uk/article6194874.ece (accessed November 2, 2010).

Telegraph. 2009. Terrorist hid explosives in his bottom. Telegraph.co.uk. September 21, 2009. http:// www.telegraph.co.uk/news/newstopics/howaboutthat/6212908/Terrorist-hid-explosives -in-his-bottom.html (accessed November 2, 2010).

Tharoor, I. 2015. 10 times bombs brought down passenger jets. *Washington Post.* https://www .washingtonpost.com/news/worldviews/wp/2015/11/06/10-times-bombs-brought-down -passenger-jets/?hpid = hp_hp-cards_hp-card-world%3Ahomepage%2Fcard.

Theuav.com. 2015. The UAV. http://www.theuav.com/.

TicoTimes. 2015. Drone hits small plane over Costa Rica park. http://www.ticotimes.net/2015/11/05 /drone-hits-plane-costa-rica-park.

Union of Concerned Scientists. N.d. An Overview of Emerging Missile State Countermeasures. http://www.ucsusa.org/sites/default/files/legacy/assets/documents/nwgs/cm_ch6-9.pdf.

U.S. Department of Defense. 2007. Personnel and Military Casualty Statistics. Defense Manpower Data Center. Casualty Summary by Reason, October 7, 2001 through August 18, 2007. http:// siadapp.dmdc.osd.mil/personnel/CASUALTY/gwot_reason.pdf (accessed November 2, 2010).

U.S. Department of Homeland Security. 2004 Biological Attack Human Pathogens, Biotoxins, and Agricultural Threats. News and Terrorism: Communicating in a Crisis. http://www.dhs.gov /xlibrary/assets/prep_biological_fact_sheet.pdf.

U.S. Department of State. 2011. MANPADS: Combating the Threat to Global Aviation from Man-Portable Air Defense Systems. Bureau of Political-Military Affairs. July 27, 2011. http://www .state.gov/t/pm/rls/fs/169139.htm.

Vanden Brook, T. 2012. IED casualties dropped 50% in Afghanistan in 2012. http://www.usatoday .com/story/news/world/2013/01/18/ied-casualties-down-afghanistan-2012/1839609/.

Vremya Novostei. 2003. Ukraden izrail'skii samolyot-razvedchik. [An Israeli reconnaissance airplane has been stolen]. November 11, 2003. Moscow.

Wein, L.M., D.L. Craft, and E.H. Kaplan. 2003. Emergency response to an anthrax attack. *Proceedings of the National Academy of Sciences* 100(7): 4346–4351.

Whitlock, C. 2010. Soaring IED attacks in Afghanistan stymie U.S. counteroffensive.

Wilson, C. 2007. Improvised Explosive Devices (IEDs) in Iraq and Afghanistan: Effects and Countermeasures. CRS Report for Congress, Washington, DC.

World Health Organization (WHO). 1970. *Health Aspects of Chemical and Biological Weapons.* Geneva, Switzerland: World Health Organization.

8

Directed-Energy Weapons

We manipulate nature as if we were stuffing an Alsatian goose.
We create new forms of energy; we make new elements; we kill crops;
we wash brains. I can hear them in the dark sharpening their lasers.

Erwin Chargaff

INTRODUCTION

The term *directed energy* had, in the past, been placed solely within the domain of science fiction, but today is a fact of modern life. Laser pointers, CD players, supermarket checkout scanners, and many other commonplace devices are equipped with directed-energy components. Directed-energy technologies have also been under extensive development by police and military programs in many countries. In addition, criminals and terrorist organizations are known to have used weapons equipped with these innovative technologies.

Conventional projectile weapons such as guns and missiles destroy targets by kinetic effects, including direct damage by projectile or shrapnel, overpressure, *spalling* damage, and incendiary effects. The result is structural damage and combustion that destroys the target. A kinetic weapon thus uses stored chemical energy in propellants and warhead explosives (Kopp, 2008). Directed-energy weapons (DEWs) also deliver a large amount of stored energy from weapon to target to produce structural and incendiary damage effects; however, a fundamental difference is that a DEW acts on its target without the use of a projectile. In addition, it delivers its effect at the speed of light rather than supersonic or subsonic speeds typical of projectile weapons (Kopp, 2008). DEWs destroy their target by bombarding it with either subatomic particles or electromagnetic waves. Such weapons include lasers/masers, microwave radiation emitters, sonic weaponry, and particle-beam generators.

At present, DEWs are capable of damaging so-called soft targets, including personnel, or the soft components of hard targets, such as optical components or communications equipment (Globalsecurity.org, 2010a). Efforts at destroying military and other hardened targets are becoming increasingly successful; such devices may soon be used in military combat.

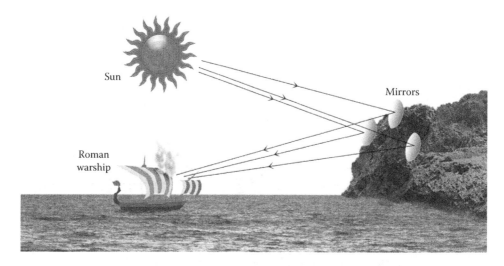

Figure 8.1 Idealized drawing of Archimedes' death ray being used against Roman ships.

HISTORY OF USE OF DEWs

According to legend, the concept of the *death ray* began with Archimedes (ca. 287 B.C.E.–ca. 212 B.C.E.), who is credited with creating a mirror with an adjustable focal length. More likely, the weapon may have been composed of a series of mirrors focused on a common point. The device focused sunlight on ships of the Roman fleet as they invaded Syracuse, setting them aflame (Figure 8.1).

Before and during World War II, both the Allies and Axis powers conducted basic research into the development of primitive DEWs. British scientists calculated that the electronic systems of that period could not generate the power necessary to generate a *death ray*, and research was redirected to radar detection systems (Fisher, 1988).

During the Cold War, the United States and Soviet Union studied the feasibility of particle-beam weapons that could fire streams of subatomic particles or neutral hydrogen atoms at a target. The concept behind such weapons was that the kinetic energy imparted by a particle stream would destroy the target by heating its atoms to the point that it explodes. These weapons were considered for both land- and space-based systems. However, because beam strength was found to degrade rapidly as the particles reacted with atoms in the atmosphere, it was calculated that an enormous power plant would be required to generate a weapons-grade beam. Both countries eventually abandoned particle-beam weapon research as impractical (Roberds, 2006).

MODERN DEWs

Lasers

LASER is the acronym for *l*ight *a*mplification by *s*timulated *e*mission of *r*adiation. In 1917, Albert Einstein described the theoretical basis of lasers; however, it was not until decades later that the first working laser was constructed. Dr. Charles Townes codiscovered the Maser (microwave amplification by stimulated emission of radiation) in 1953 at Columbia University, and later went on to collaborate with Dr. Arthur Schawlow at Bell Labs to create the first Laser in 1958.

Lasers produce narrow, single-frequency (i.e., single-color), coherent beams of light that are much more powerful than ordinary light sources. As a result, laser weapons can concentrate intense light and heat on a target. Depending on the power of the laser, this light can heat the target to the point of melting or combustion, burn out optical devices, or permanently blind those who operate them.

Laser light is generated by a number of systems ranging from rods of chemically doped crystals to energetic chemical reactions to semiconducting diodes. The earliest lasers involved the use of crystal rods such as ruby, or discharges in argon or carbon dioxide gas. The generic crystal-type laser consists of a flash tube, a crystal rod, and two mirrors, one that is *half-silvered*. The flash tube *pumps* the laser, and the crystal rod is the lasing medium (Figure 8.2).

Energy is applied to excite the crystal (e.g., via the flash tube), and many atoms in the crystal consequently shift to an excited state. When the atoms (specifically, their electrons) return to the ground state, a stream of photons of a wavelength specific to the excited atoms is released. The process of the flash tube exciting the atoms is termed *pumping*. Pumping can be achieved using light (flash-lamps or other so-called *pump* lasers), electrical discharges (in gas lasers), electrical current (semiconductor lasers), or shockwaves in gas flows (gas dynamic lasers, chemical lasers) (Kopp, 2008). Some photons are emitted in a direction parallel to the rod's axis, so they bounce back and forth between the mirrors. As these photons pass through the crystal, they stimulate photon emissions in other atoms. When sufficient photons are emitted, the light will pass through the half-silvered mirror (Figure 8.2).

Laser light is very different from normal light and possesses a number of unique properties: (1) the light released is monochromatic—it contains one specific wavelength

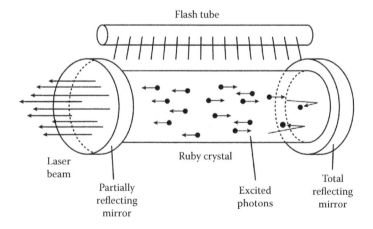

Figure 8.2 Generation of laser light using a crystal tube device.

(i.e., one specific color); (2) the light released is collimated or coherent. In physical terms, it is *organized*—each photon moves in step with the others. This means that all of the photons have wave fronts that launch at the same time (Figure 8.3); and (3) the light is highly directional. A laser light has a tight beam and is very concentrated. In contrast, a flashlight releases light in many directions, and the light is weak and diffuse. Since lasers produce light that is coherent and almost spectrally pure, that light can easily be focused. Such light characteristics are highly valuable for applications in both industry and the military (Table 8.1).

Lasers are designed to generate either continuous beams or short, intense pulses of light in every spectrum from infrared to ultraviolet (UV) (Table 8.2). The power output necessary for a weapons-grade laser ranges from 10 kW to 1 MW.

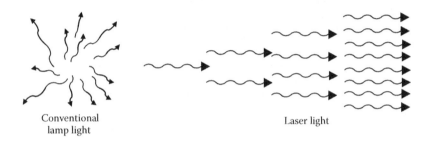

Conventional
lamp light

Laser light

Figure 8.3 Normal versus collimated light produced by a laser.

Table 8.1 Common Uses of Lasers in Industry

Industry	Application
Optoelectronics	CD players and CD-ROM drives
	Data transfer via fiber optic cables
Medicine	Ophthalmology
	Dermatology
Measurement and instrumentation	Mining and tunnel surveying
	Measurement of workpiece surfaces
	Analysis (e.g., in mobile environmental analysis equipment)
Manufacturing technology	Cutting
	Welding
	Surface treatment, etc.
Research	Laser chemistry
	Laser fusion
	Spectroscopy
	Diagnostics
	Measurement of earth–moon distance

Source: Occupational Safety and Health Administration, *OSHA Technical Manual*, TED 01–00-015 [TED 1–0.15A], 2010b. http://www.osha.gov/dts/osta/otm/otm_toc.html.

Table 8.2 Laser Types Based on Selected Operating Factors

	Wavelength	Power	Operating Mode	Applications
Semiconductor Diode Lasers				
Single diodes	Infrared to visible	1–100 mW	Continuous and pulsed modes	Optoelectronics
Diode laser bars	Infrared to visible	Up to 100 W	Continuous and pulsed modes	Pumping light source for solid state lasers
Solid State Lasers				
Nd:YAG laser	1.06 μm	1 W–3 kW	Continuous and pulsed modes	Materials processing, measurementation, medicine
Rubin-Laser	Red	Several MW	Pulsed mode	Measurementation, pulse holography
Gas Lasers				
CO_2 laser	10.6 μm	1 W–40 kW (100 MW in pulsed mode)	Continuous and pulsed modes	Materials processing, medicine, isotope separation
Excimer laser	1963 nm, 248 nm, 308 nm (and others)	1 kW–100 MW	Gepulster Batrieb, Pulslänge 10 ns–100 ns	Micromachining, laser chemistry, medicine
HeNe Laser	632.8 nm (most prominent)	1 mW–150 W	Kontinuierlicher Betrieb	Measurementation, holography
Argon ion laser	515 nm, 458 nm (several)	1 mW–150 W	Continuous and pulsed	Printing technology, pumping laser for dye laser stimulation, medicine
Dye laser	Continuous between infrared and ultraviolet (different dyes)	1 mW–1 W	Continuous and pulsed	Measurementation, spectroscopy, medicine

Source: Fraunhofer, I.L.T., Laser tutorial, 2006. http://www.ilt.fraunhofer.de/eng/100048.html.

Effects of Lasers on Humans

Laser weapons concentrate intense light and heat on a target and will damage exposed parts of the body. The most common cause of tissue damage is, where tissue proteins are denatured because of the temperature increase following absorption of laser energy (OSHA, 2010a). The eye is the most vulnerable part of the body to laser hazards, followed by the skin. Eye damage occurs at much lower power levels than those that affect the skin. Eye damage may be either temporary or permanent, depending on the wavelength and the power of the laser. Some lasers are so powerful that even reflection from a surface can be hazardous to the eye.

Light enters the human eye through the cornea (Figure 8.4). The light is focused on the retina, a small region in the back of the eye. In the retina, an image is formed on photoreceptor cells (also known as rods and cones) that are capable of detecting light. Rods, which detect light and transmit that reception to the brain, are the most sensitive to light. Cones separate light, informing the brain regarding the color of an object.

A person exposed to laser light can become temporarily blinded (*dazzling*), they can be blinded for a prolonged period (photolysis), or they can suffer permanent changes in visual function from retinal lesions or hemorrhages. This includes permanent blindness. If a person is using a see-through optical device such as a telescope or binoculars, the beam strength is magnified and will result in greater injury. Even moderately powered lasers can temporarily blind a person looking through binoculars.

The severity of laser-induced eye injuries depends on the following:

- Nature of the beam
- Exposure location
- Dose
- The atmosphere through which it passes

The attributes of a laser beam include pulse energy, pulse duration, and wavelength of the light. Some infrared radiation from IR-A wavelengths, which range from 700 to 1400 nm, and IR-B wavelengths, which range from 1400 to 3000 nm, is absorbed by the lens (Stewart, 2006) (Figure 8.5). Far-infrared radiation, which ranges from 3000 nm to 1 mm, is absorbed primarily by the cornea (Figure 8.4). A high-energy laser pulse may severely burn or perforate the cornea. Minor laser burns to the cornea may be treated with an eye patch and appropriate eye antibiotics (Stewart, 2006). Laser light in the UV (290–400 nm) or far-infrared (1400–10,600 nm) spectrum can cause damage to the cornea and/or the lens. Laser light from visible and IR-A wavelengths (400–1400 nm) is known as the retinal *hazard region* (Bader and Lui, 1996)—this is the most hazardous range, and is transmitted by the optical components of the eye (e.g., cornea). When this light reaches the retina, most

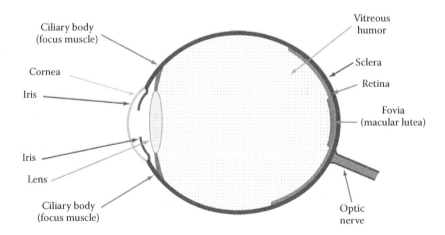

Figure 8.4 Cross section of the human eye.

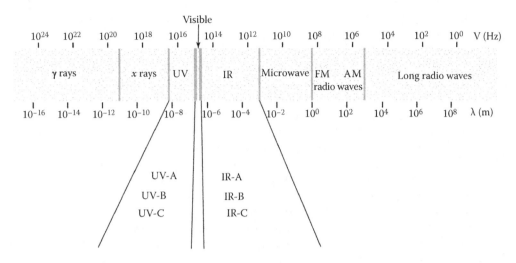

Figure 8.5 Electromagnetic spectrum with emphasis on IR and UV wavelength ranges.

of the radiation is absorbed in the retinal pigment epithelium and in the choroid, a layer with large blood vessels and a high blood flow rate. Laser light in this region can result in scotoma (a blind spot in the fovea). Damage to the retina or hemorrhaging from retinal damage can cause a complete loss of vision (Stewart, 2006). Table 8.3 summarizes several medical conditions caused by lasers as a function of wavelength.

The atmosphere that laser light traverses also affects the energy delivered by the beam; factors include the range, the water content of the atmosphere, atmospheric turbulence,

Table 8.3 Medical Conditions Caused by Lasers as a Function of Wavelength

Photobiological Spectral Range	Eye Effects	Skin Effects
Ultraviolet C (0.200–0.280 μm)	Photokeratitis	Erythema (sunburn)
		Skin cancer
Ultraviolet B (0.280–315 μm)	Photokeratitis	Accelerated skin aging
		Increased pigmentation
Ultraviolet A (0.315–0.400 μm)	Photochemical UV cataract	Pigment darkening
		Skin burn
Visible (0.400–0.780 μm)	Photochemical and thermal retinal injury	Photosensitive reactions
		Skin burn
Infrared A (0.780–1.400 μm)	Cataract, retinal burns	Skin burn
Infrared B (1.400–3.00 μm)	Corneal burn	Skin burn
	Aqueous flare	
	IR cataract	
Infrared C (3.00–1000 μm)	Corneal burn only	Skin burn

Source: Occupational Safety and Health Administration, *OSHA Technical Manual*, TED 01–00-015 [TED 1–0.15A], 2010b. http://www.osha.gov/dts/osta/otm/otm_toc.html.

and pollution (Buck, 1967; Horak, 1966). The potential for eye injuries is increased when lasers are used in open, uncontrolled environments. Laser exposures have temporarily blinded commercial pilots.

Other factors influencing the severity of eye injuries from exposure to laser light include the intensity of the laser and the duration of exposure to the laser.

A number of high-power visible lasers and infrared lasers are now used in industry. These are capable of producing significant skin burns in less than 1 s. Damage at the skin surface may include acoustical effects (analogous to a shockwave), laser ablation (i.e., skin removal), and other effects, depending on the wavelength and pulse duration (Cain et al., 2007). Damage effects may be short-lived and disappear within a few days or may last for much longer periods, including permanent discoloration (Cain et al., 2007) and possibly skin cancer (Stewart, 2006).

Skin injuries from lasers fall into two general categories: thermal injury (i.e., burns) from acute exposure to high-power laser beams, and photochemical injury from chronic exposure to scattered UV laser radiation. Thermal injury is the most common cause of laser-induced tissue damage, and can result from direct contact with a beam or its reflection. Skin tissue proteins are denatured because of the temperature increase following absorption of laser energy. Such injuries may be painful but are usually not serious. The thermal damage process is typically associated with lasers operating at exposure times longer than 10 µs in the near-UV to the far-infrared (0.315–03 µm) region. Tissue damage may also be caused by thermally induced acoustic waves following exposures to submicrosecond laser exposures (UCSD, 2009). The principal thermal effects of laser exposure depend on the following factors (OSHA, 2010b):

- Absorption and scattering coefficients of the tissues at the laser wavelength
- Radiant exposure of the laser beam
- Duration of exposure
- Pulse repetition characteristics
- Extent of local vascular flow
- Size of area irradiated

Photochemical injury may occur over time from UV exposure to the direct beam, *specular* reflections, or diffuse reflections of a laser. The effect on a victim may approximate minor or severe sunburn. Prolonged exposure may promote the development of skin cancer.

Skin injuries usually affect the epidermis only (Figure 8.6). Even if laser injury penetrates the skin, the damage heals readily. Laser-induced skin damage is most pronounced from far-infrared wavelengths such as those produced by the carbon dioxide laser. Skin damage can also be caused by visible or near-infrared wavelengths, but this requires higher laser intensity than for far-infrared wavelengths. This is because the skin reflects most visible and near-infrared wavelengths and absorbs UV-B and UV-C wavelengths. With enough power and duration, a laser beam of any wavelength in the optical spectrum can penetrate the skin and cause deep internal injury (Seeber, n.d.). Proper protective eyewear and clothing may be necessary to control exposure to the skin and eyes (Stewart, 2006).

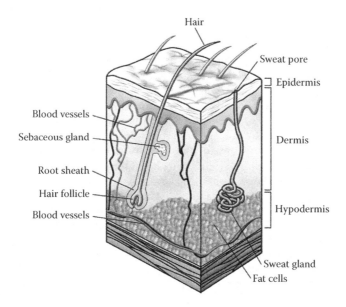

Figure 8.6   Major layers of the skin.

The pain from thermal injury to the skin by most targeting lasers is usually sufficient to alert a victim to move out of the beam path.

Classification of Lasers

In the early 1970s, the International Electrotechnical Commission (IEC) established five classes of laser: 1, 2, 3A, 3B, and 4. This classification was formulated to give the laser user an indication of the degree of hazard to exposed persons (WHO, 1993). Table 8.4 presents the key characteristics and requirements for the classification system as specified by the IEC 60825-1 standard (IEC, 2007), along with typical required warning labels. In addition, classes 2 and higher must use the triangular warning label (Figure 8.7) and other labels are required in specific cases indicating laser emission, laser apertures, skin hazards, and invisible wavelengths.

Use of Lasers as a Weapon

Since laser energy travels at the speed of light, lasers are particularly well suited for use against moving targets such as rockets, missiles, and artillery projectiles. High-power lasers can be used to destroy objects in flight or on the ground. This light can burn out optical devices, temporarily blind or distract, or permanently blind those who operate them. The most likely targets for such systems include optical and electro-optical systems such as gun sights and vision viewers, and the personnel operating them. Any laser beam entering a direct view optical system (e.g., a gun sight) has its power increased by the magnification of the system. Soldiers, civilians, or terrorists using the sight could suffer damage to the eyes.

Table 8.4 International Electrotechnical Commission Classification of Lasers

Class	Requirements/Conditions
1	Safe under all conditions of normal use. The maximum permissible exposure (MPE) cannot be exceeded. This class includes high-power lasers within an enclosure that prevents exposure to the radiation and that cannot be opened without shutting down the laser. For example, a continuous laser at 600 nm can emit up to 0.39 mW, but for shorter wavelengths, the maximum emission is lower because of the potential of those wavelengths to generate photochemical damage. The maximum emission is also related to the pulse duration in the case of pulsed lasers and the degree of spatial coherence.
1M	Safe for all conditions of use except when passed through magnifying optics such as microscopes and telescopes. Class 1M lasers produce large-diameter beams, or beams that are divergent. The MPE for a Class 1M laser cannot normally be exceeded unless focusing or imaging optics are used to narrow the beam. If the beam is refocused, the hazard of Class 1M lasers may be increased and the product class may be changed. A laser can be classified as Class 1M if the total output power is below class 3B but the power that can pass through the pupil of the eye is within Class 1.
2	Safe because the blink reflex will limit the exposure to no more than 0.25 s. It only applies to visible-light lasers (400–700 nm). Class-2 lasers are limited to 1 mW continuous wave, or more if the emission time is less than 0.25 s or if the light is not spatially coherent. Intentional suppression of the blink reflex could lead to eye injury. Many laser pointers are class 2.
2M	Safe because of the blink reflex if not viewed through optical instruments. As with class 1M, this applies to laser beams with a large diameter or large divergence, for which the amount of light passing through the pupil cannot exceed the limits for class 2.
3R	Safe if handled carefully, with restricted beam viewing. With a class 3R laser, the MPE can be exceeded, but with a low risk of injury. Visible continuous lasers in Class 3R are limited to 5 mW. For other wavelengths and for pulsed lasers, other limits apply.
3B	Hazardous if the eye is exposed directly, but diffuse reflections such as from paper or other matte surfaces are not harmful. Continuous lasers in the wavelength range from 315 nm to far-infrared are limited to 0.5 W. For pulsed lasers between 400 and 700 nm, the limit is 30 mJ. Other limits apply to other wavelengths and to ultrashort pulsed lasers. Protective eyewear is typically required where direct viewing of a class 3B laser beam may occur. Class-3B lasers must be equipped with a key switch and a safety interlock.
4	All lasers with beam power greater than class 3B. In addition to posing significant eye hazards, with potentially devastating and permanent eye damage as a result of direct beam viewing, diffuse reflections are also harmful to the eyes within the distance called the Nominal Hazard Zone. Class 4 lasers are also able to cut or burn skin. In addition, these lasers may ignite combustible materials, and thus represent a fire risk, in some cases. Class 4 lasers must be equipped with a key switch and a safety interlock.

Source: International Electrotechnical Commission, Safety of laser products: Part 1. Equipment classification and requirements, IED 60825-1 ed2.0, Geneva, Switzerland, 2007.

Figure 8.7 Laser warning label.

Recent advances in laser technology show promise in use against vehicles, machinery, and other large targets. The U.S. Navy's 30-kW Laser Weapon System aboard the USS *Ponce* is now being fired in operational scenarios by sailors in the Persian Gulf, marking the first-ever deployment of a sea-based DEW (Osborn, 2014). Navy officials are also working on a much more powerful, next-generation 100- to 150-kW laser weapon. Lockheed Martin recently developed the Area Defense Anti-Munitions (ADAM) system, which uses an off-the-shelf 10-kW laser. ADAM can disable targets such as boats, drones and simulated small-caliber rockets from 1.5 km away (Extance, 2015). The primary mechanism of action of the laser on such targets is mechanical shear, caused by reaction when the surface of the target is explosively evaporated.

The U.S. Navy has reported that Iran and other countries were already using lasers to target ships and commercial airliners (Shalal, 2015).

Other examples of laser weapons include:

- The JD-3 laser dazzler is mounted on the Chinese Type 98 main battle tank. It is coupled with a laser radiation detector and automatically aims for the enemy's illuminating laser designator, attempting to overwhelm its optical systems or blind the operator.
- The ZM-87 Portable Laser Disturber is an electro-optic countermeasure neodymium laser device developed by China. It can blind enemy troops at up to 2–3 km range and temporarily *dazzle* them at up to 10 km. It is also reported to damage the photoelectric elements in laser rangefinders and video cameras and missile seekers (Small, n.d.). The ZM-87 was banned by the 1995 United Nations Protocol on Blinding Laser Weapons and is no longer in production. Roughly 22 were made up to year 2000.

Figure 8.8   A PhaSR, a dazzler-type weapon. (Courtesy of U.S. Air Force, http://www.af.mil/shared /media/photodb/photos/051101-F-0000S-012.jpg.)

- Personnel Halting and Stimulation Response (or PHaSR) is a nonlethal handheld weapon developed by the U.S. Department of Defense (Figure 8.8). Its purpose is to *dazzle* or stun a target. It uses a two-wavelength laser.
- The Mid-Infrared Advanced Chemical Laser (MIRACL) is an experimental U.S. Navy laser and was tested against an Air Force satellite in 1997.
- The U.S. Air Force's Airborne Laser, or Advanced Tactical Laser, is a program to mount a CO_2 gas laser or chemical laser on a modified Boeing 747 and use it to shoot down missiles.

Advantages of Lasers as a Weapon

Laser weapons have several advantages over conventional weapons (Possel, 1998):

- Laser beams travel at the speed of light, so there is no need for the user to compensate for target movement when firing over long distances. As a result, it is impossible to evade a laser after it has been fired.
- The extreme velocity of light essentially eliminates the influence of gravity. Therefore, long-range projection does not require compensation for gravity. Wind speed and other variables can also be ignored.
- Depending on power source technology, laser weapons could have limitless *magazine* or *ammunition*.
- Lasers weapons produce little or no recoil.
- Laser beams do not generate sound or light that would be detected by the enemy when emitted, so the weapon cannot betray the user's position when fired.
- The operational range of a laser weapon can be much larger than that of a ballistic weapon, depending on atmospheric conditions and power level.

Technical Problems with Lasers

Several technical problems associated with lasers (Dunn, 2005) include:

- Blooming. Laser beams tend to scatter and disperse energy into the atmosphere. Blooming is more severe in the presence of fog, smoke, or dust in the air.
- Evaporated target material *shades*, and thus protects, the target.
- Beam absorption by air. A laser beam traveling through air can be absorbed or scattered by rain, snow, fog, dust, or smoke.
- High power consumption. Lasers waste significant energy as heat, and thus require substantial power and bulky cooling equipment to avoid damage by overheating.
- Lack of indirect fire capabilities. Indirect fire, that is, attacking a target hidden behind a hill, is not feasible with line-of-sight laser weapons. An alternative would be to mount lasers (or reflectors) on airborne or space-based platforms or unmanned aerial vehicles.

Other practical hazards (OSHA, 2010b) include:

- Explosion hazards. High-pressure arc lamps and filament lamps may shatter during laser operation.
- Nonbeam optical radiation hazards. UV radiation emitted from laser discharge tubes and pumping lamps can damage the eyes and are a hazard to skin.
- Collateral radiation. Radiation, other than laser radiation, may be associated with the operation of a laser, for example, radio frequency energy associated with some plasma tubes and x-ray emission associated with the high voltage power supplies used with excimer lasers.
- Flammability of laser beam enclosures. Enclosure of Class 4 laser beams can result in potential fire hazards if the enclosure materials are exposed to irradiances exceeding $10 \, \text{W/cm}^2$. Enclosure material may be constructed of plastics, so their use and potential for flammability and release of toxic fumes following direct exposure should be assessed. Flame-resistant materials and commercially available products specifically designed for laser enclosures should be considered.
- Electrical hazards. Laser systems have high-energy requirements and complicated circuitry. Precautions against stray electrical current are essential when using laser devices.

Microwave Weapons

In recent years, the modern battlefield has become a *target-rich* environment for high-power microwave (HPM) weapons. Except for the standard rifle, gun, knife, or grenade, virtually all military equipment contains some electronics, all of which may be vulnerable to microwaves. For example, during recent conflicts in Iraq and Afghanistan, the average squad of soldiers was equipped with devices ranging from radios to global positioning system receivers, which they used to provide communication and information about the battlefield. HPM weapons, also known as high energy radio frequency weapons, have

279

been under investigation for years as potential weapons for combat. Criminals have allegedly used microwave weapons, and terrorist groups are also known to be experimenting with them.

Microwaves consist of electromagnetic radiation with wavelengths ranging from as long as 1 m to as short as 1 mm, or equivalently, with frequencies between 300 MHz (0.3 GHz) and 300 GHz (Table 8.5) (Pozar, 1997). The most common microwave applications are within the 1–40 GHz range.

An example of a relatively simple HPM device is a magnetron (Figure 8.9), a cylindrical device commonly used in microwave ovens. A cathode is positioned at the center of the

Table 8.5   Microwave Frequency Bands

Letter Designation	Frequency Range (GHz)
L band	1–2
S band	2–4
C band	4–8
X band	8–12
K_u band	12–18
K band	18–26.5
K_a band	26.5–40
Q band	30–50
U band	40–60
V band	50–75
E band	60–90
W band	75–110
F band	90–140
D band	110–170

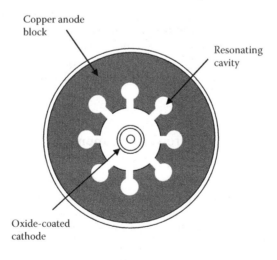

Figure 8.9   Cross section of a magnetron.

unit and is surrounded by an anode. An electrical current is sent to the cathode, causing it to become heated. The heating increases molecular activity, thereby causing electrons to boil off into the zone between cathode and anode. The negatively charged electrons attempt to fly toward the positively charged anode. As the temperature rises and causes more molecular activity, the electrons move at higher speeds.

Two modifications are included in the magnetron's design to modify the motion of the electrons. The anode has slots, termed *resonating cavities*, cut into it. Second, a powerful magnet is placed beneath the anode to generate a magnetic field along the length of the tube. When the electrons try to move from cathode to anode, they travel simultaneously through the electric field (between anode and cathode) and also a magnetic field. The forces of the electric charge, together with the magnetic field, cause the electrons to travel in an expanding circular orbit until they reach the anode. This circular motion of electrons is what produces the microwaves of energy—as the electrons fly past the cavities, the cavities resonate and emit microwave radiation. The microwaves that are generated are collected and channeled in a funnel-like device called a *waveguide* and beamed into the air by an antenna or satellite dish.

Effects of Microwaves

On Humans

Microwave weapons can be used against humans or instrumentation and machinery. The Pentagon's Active Denial System (ADS), revealed in 2001, produces waves at a frequency of 95 GHz and uses an antenna to direct the invisible beam toward its target. Traveling at the speed of light, the energy strikes the victim and reaches a skin depth of about 1/64th of an inch. The microwave energy creates a painful sensation on the surface of the skin (Walters et al., 2000) by heating water molecules on the skin.

The effect is not lethal; however, it strongly motivates the target to flee (JNLWP, 2010). The sensation abruptly stops when the victim moves out of the beam or when the beam is shut off. The ADS weapon was originally developed by the U.S. Air Force Research Laboratory for riot control in Iraq. The device comes in various sizes; smaller units can be attached to a Humvee.

There has been only limited testing for long-term side effects of human exposure to microwave beams. A recent study by the Effects Advisory Panel, an independent panel of nongovernment science and medical experts (Kenny et al., 2008), claims there is minimal risk of both short- and long-term injury because of the shallow penetration depth of energy into the skin at this short wavelength and normal human instinctive reactions to flee.

Although HPM weapons are intended to cause severe pain while leaving no lasting damage, the ADS has been fraught with controversy. Studies at Dortmund University in Germany showed that microwave beams can cause serious burns at levels not far above those required to repel people. This was verified when a U.S. airman was hospitalized with second-degree burns during testing in April 2007. There is also concern as to whether the system could cause irreversible damage to the eyes. The ADS has not been deployed owing to legal issues and safety fears (Hambling, 2009). The Pentagon has subsequently developed a microwave pain-infliction system that can be fired from an aircraft.

On Equipment

Microwave weapons have significant applications against both materials and equipment; they are capable of disabling or destroying *unhardened* (i.e., ushielded) electronics that are susceptible to damage by power surges. A short burst of HPM energy can be lethal to electronics, while having no effect on humans operating the equipment. The low collateral damage aspect of the technology makes HPM weapons useful in many missions where avoiding civilian casualties is a major concern (U.S. Air Force, 2002).

The effects of HPMs on electronics may result in disturbance or permanent physical damage depending on the level of irradiation. Electronics interference may be temporary, that is, the equipment returns spontaneously to full function after the irradiation, or it may cause failure of function—the equipment will require a manual restart or reset. Permanent damage is caused by thermal effects or electrical breakdown in the circuits. In this case, the damaged component or equipment must be repaired or replaced (Bäckström et al., 2002).

Computers used in a wide array of applications—for example, data processing, communications systems, displays, and industrial control applications (including road and rail signaling and those within vehicles), cardiac monitors, digital engine controls, electronic flight controls, and signal processors (found in many types of modern radio equipment)—are all vulnerable to the effects of HPM via *backdoor coupling* (Figure 8.10). Computer networks are especially susceptible because the cabling connecting workstations can act as an efficient radio wave receiving *antenna*. Commercial computer equipment circuits, including those contained in automotive ignition systems and those that operate traffic lights, often include high-density metal oxide semiconductor (MOS) devices, which are very sensitive to pulses of high voltage. Very little energy is required to permanently destroy a MOS device (Stewart, 2006).

Most military-grade radios and electronic equipment are designed to resist some levels of HPMs, but civilian equipment is not adequately shielded against this type of energy. The HPM weapon is therefore a weapon of mass destruction that is well suited to the vulnerabilities of modern cities with significant reliance on computers and other high-end electronics.

Use as a Weapon

The U.S. Navy reportedly used a new class of highly secret, nonnuclear electromagnetic pulse warheads during the opening hours of the Persian Gulf War to disrupt and destroy Iraqi electronics systems (Globalsecurity.org, 2010b).

The Silent Guardian™ Protection System developed by Raytheon Company (2006) uses millimeter wave technology to repel people without causing injury. The mode of operation and effects are very similar to those of the Pentagon's ADS. This capability enables users to stop, deter, and turn away adversaries without the use of lethal force. The system also disrupts an aggressor's ability to effectively use a weapon. Silent Guardian provides the tactical ability to control outbreaks of violence and minimize collateral damage.

Vigilant Eagle is an airport defense system that works by directing electromagnetic radiation at a target—specifically, high-frequency microwaves are directed toward any projectile that is fired toward an aircraft (e.g., a surface-to-air missile). Vigilant Eagle consists of three major components: a missile detect-and-track system, a command-and-control

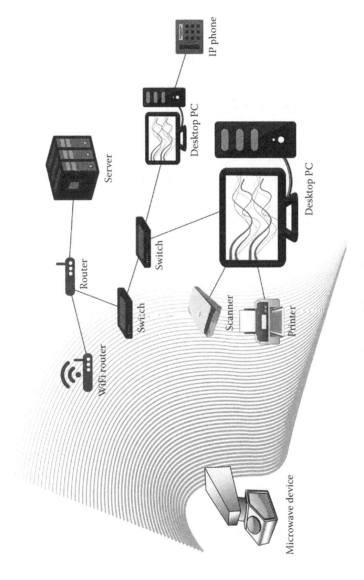

Figure 8.10 Backdoor coupling of a computer network caused by a microwave weapon.

system, and an Active Electronically Scanned Array, which includes a billboard-sized system of highly efficient antennas linked to solid-state amplifiers (Raytheon Company, 2007). This weapon interferes with a surface-to-air missile's guidance system and deflects it away from the aircraft.

A new weapon in the Russian arsenal is a microwave cannon. The gun can reportedly disable drones and warheads at a distance of up to 6 mi. The system is equipped with a high-power generator and reflector antenna, control system, and a transmission system that is fixed to the chassis of BUK surface-to-air missile systems. The *microwave gun* is capable of ensuring perimeter defense at 360° (Limer, 2015).

Advantages of HPMs as a Weapon

Insensitivity to Weather

Microwave frequencies are insensitive to weather, which means that, unlike lasers, microwave emissions can penetrate clouds, water vapor, rain, and dust. As an example, radar (as well as radio and television stations) transmit effectively through rain or dense fog. This is a particular advantage in military operations, because relatively few weapons in military arsenals can function accurately regardless of weather.

Long Reach

With current technologies, the range for a tactical microwave weapon could be in the tens of kilometers, and future advances in microwave technology should permit the development of even longer ranges.

Deep Magazine

Microwave weapons have a *deep magazine*; in other words, they can emit energy as long as there is sufficient power.

Flexibility of Size

Microwave weapons are extremely flexible in terms of size. HPM weapon size depends on the target, delivery application, and desired effects; therefore, HPM weapons are well suited for covert military operations. Human-portable devices may weigh in the tens of pounds; vehicle-mounted devices would weigh in the hundreds of pounds; and airborne systems would weigh in the thousands of pounds (U.S. Air Force Research Laboratory, 1998).

Defenses against HPW Weapons

Some defensive measures that users of electronics equipment can take are as follows (Stewart, 2006):

1. Completely encase susceptible equipment in a heavy-gauge metal shielding or surround it with a special metal screening such as a Faraday cage (Figure 8.11). A Faraday cage can be made from fine metal mesh. The cage is connected to a

Figure 8.11   Faraday cage.

ground and completely encloses the items it protects. Keep all equipment in the cage disconnected from other power supplies.

2. Maintain a supply of spare radio, monitor, and engine ignition spare parts. Keep the spare parts in the Faraday cage. Smaller pieces of equipment can be placed in empty, metal military ammunition containers or similar tightly sealed metal boxes.

Equipment that has been shielded or hardened against electromagnetic discharges may withstand higher electromagnetic fields. Radios and other equipment that use vacuum tube technology will be protected against the effects of microwaves.

Sonic Weapons

Sonic and ultrasonic weapons use sound to injure, incapacitate, or kill its victim. Some sonic weapons are currently in limited use or in research and development by military and police forces. The use of sonic weapons to incapacitate people has occurred both in counterterrorist and crowd-control settings. During the 2009 G-20 Summit in Pittsburgh, police used sound cannons against protestors (Guardian, 2010). In 2005, the crew of the cruise ship *Seabourn Spirit* used a long-range acoustic device (LRAD) to deter pirates who pursued and attacked the ship (Ravilious, 2005). The BBC reported on a sonic device designed to drive *young troublemakers* away from a problem area of the U.K. town of Swindon

285

(BBC.com, 2006). The device works by emitting an ultrahigh frequency pulse (approximately 19–20 kHz) that people under about age 20 are susceptible to and find uncomfortable. Age-related hearing loss apparently prevents the ultrahigh pitch sound from causing a nuisance to those in their late twenties and above. The LRAD sonic device was on hand at protests of the 2004 Republican National Convention in New York City; however, it was not used (ABCnews.com, 2004). Sonic devices had been used at Camp Bucca Iraq and were tested in Baghdad, Fallujah, and other parts of Iraq.

Some sonic weapons produce a focused beam of sound or ultrasound; some create an area field of sound. Others, like the LRAD (see following discussion) use an array of conventional acoustic tweeters, the same as those used in many professional audio applications, all driven together in parallel.

Effects

Sound waves can cause humans to experience nausea or discomfort. This may be sufficient to incapacitate a victim. Some sonic devices produce sufficient output to temporarily disrupt vision by causing vibration of eyeballs (Tandy, 1998). At higher energy levels, a subsonic shock wave may be powerful enough to cause significant damage—extremely high-power sound waves can break a victim's eardrums and cause severe pain or disorientation. Although many sonic and ultrasonic weapons are described as nonlethal, they may possibly kill under certain conditions.

From recent research involving high-intensity audible sound experiments on human subjects, the extra-aural (i.e., unrelated to hearing) effects include the following:

- Tactile sensitivity change
- Muscle contraction
- Cardiovascular function change
- Central nervous system effects
- Vestibular (inner ear) effects
- Chest wall/lung tissue effects

Low-frequency sonic exposure could result in

- Cavitations
- Hypothermia
- Tissue shearing

Cavitation is defined as the formation of vapor bubbles in a flowing liquid. Cavitation affects gas nuclei in human tissue; exposure to ultrasound and can ultimately damage tissue and organs. Exposure to high-intensity ultrasound at frequencies from 700 kHz to 3.6 MHz was found to cause lung and intestinal damage in mice. The threshold for lung and liver damage occurred at 184 dB. Damage increased rapidly as intensity increased.

Heart rate patterns following vibroacoustic stimulation has resulted in serious health effects in humans including arterial flutter and *bradycardia* (Jot Your Life, 2009; Nutley, 2003; Skaggs, 2007). Noise-induced neurologic disturbances have been noted in humans exposed to continuous low-frequency tones for durations longer than 15 min, including

Figure 8.12   (See color insert.) Long-range acoustic device in use by the U.S. Navy. (Courtesy of the National Oceanic and Atmospheric Administration, http://www.vos.noaa.gov/MWL/aug_09 /Images/antipiracytech.jpg.)

development of immediate and long-term damage to brain tissue. The symptoms resembled those of individuals who suffered minor head injuries. Prolonged sound exposure may result in enough mechanical strain to brain tissue to induce a wide range of brain disorders, including degeneration (University of Texas, 2002).

Sonic Weapons Used by the Military

Some sonic weapons are intended for use by American warships to warn incoming vessels that are approaching without permission. Its output, up to 155 db, focused at a distance, is sufficient to produce permanent ear damage and temporarily disrupt vision.

The LRAD has been designed as a crowd-control device (Figure 8.12). It weighs 45 lb and can emit sound in a 30° beam at high frequency (2.5 kHz). At maximum level, it can emit a warning tone that is 146 dB at 1 m, a level that is capable of permanently damaging hearing, and higher than the normal human threshold of pain (120–140 dB). The maximum usable design range extends to 300 m. At 300 m, the warning tone measures less than 90 dB. The warning tone is a high-pitched shrill tone similar to that of a smoke detector. The LRAD possesses excellent directionality; in other words, the device reduces the risk of exposing nearby personnel or peripheral bystanders to harmful audio levels (LRAD Corporation, n.d.).

CRIMINAL AND TERRORIST USE OF DEWs

At present, only military units, some law enforcement agencies, and corporate R&D facilities have the capability to develop and use high-output DEWs.

The FBI and Department of Homeland Security have claimed that al-Qaeda had explored the use of lasers as a weapon, including a possibility of lasing aircraft cockpits to interfere with pilots' ability to operate their aircraft safely (*Los Angeles Times*, 2004). The most vulnerable portion of a flight to such an attack is in landing (Nakagawara et al., 2003).

The Aum Shinrikyo cult in Japan was known to be developing a fluoride laser for terrorism purposes (Bertolli and Pannone, 2009; Olson, 1999).

Aircraft pilots have been targeted by lasers numerous times over the past two decades. Some incidents have occurred in military situations; for example, a Russian ship is suspected of lasing a U.S. military aircraft, resulting in pilot eye injuries; two U.S. helicopter pilots suffered eye injuries in Bosnia after lasers were aimed at them from the ground; and ZM-87 neodymium military lasers are suspected of being used by North Korea on U.S. helicopters in the Korean demilitarized zone (ABC News, 1998; Associated Press, 1999; Bertolli and Pannone, 2009; Federation of American Scientists, 2003; NewsMax.com, 2003). Nonmilitary incidents involving use of lasers at landing aircraft have been documented in Salt Lake City, Utah; Teterboro, New Jersey; Colorado Springs, Colorado; and Sydney, Australia, as well as lasings of police helicopters (Bertolli and Pannone, 2009).

Small-scale microwave weapons can be manufactured by terrorists and other criminals. The primary components of a microwave weapon, that is, power source, microwave generator, and antenna, are all readily available for off-the-shelf purchase and assembly. Civilians have successfully built and tested a range of simple microwave devices. Two inventors from New Mexico suggested gathering magnetrons removed from consumer microwave ovens and lock their output together so that they combine into one coherent beam, that is, making all the magnetrons resonate in synchronization (*New Scientist*, 2006).

News reports have speculated that criminals have used microwave devices to destroy security electronics in banks or warehouses before building entry. With the desperate need for cash by some developing nations, devices such as magnetrons, which are capable of producing multimegawatts, have been offered for sale to other nations and individuals. Hence, HPM weapon capabilities are available not only for military use but also by terrorists and other criminal organizations (Van Keuren and Knighten, 1995). Pevler (1997, p. 107) states: The development of HPM weaponry, and its proliferation into subversive organizations, offers the means to commit the "perfect crime." HPM attacks typically leave no residual evidence and their effects can range from nuisance to catastrophic.

QUESTIONS

1. How does laser light differ from normal light? Provide three specific attributes.
2. Within what range of wavelengths does laser light occur? Microwave radiation?
3. In which range of wavelengths is laser light most destructive to the eyes?
4. List the benefits of lasers as a weapon. List the disadvantages.
5. How do laser light and microwaves differ in terms of transmission through clouds or fog?

REFERENCES

ABC News. 1998. Lasers burn U.S. pilots' eyes. November 4, 1998.

ABCnews.com. 2004. RNC to feature unusual forms of sound. August 25, 2004. http://abcnews.go.com/Technology/story?id=99472&page=1 (accessed October 31, 2010).

Associated Press. 1999. Russian ship's laser caused eye injury, Navy officer says. February 12, 1999. http://www.highbeam.com/doc/1P1-23409696.html.

Bäckström, M., B. Nordström, and K.G. Lövstrand. 2002. Is HPM a threat against the civil society? International Union of Radio Science. *Proceedings of URSI General Assembly and Scientific Symposium.* http://www.ursi.org/Proceedings/ProcGA02/papers/p0453.pdf (accessed October 31, 2010).

Bader, O., and H. Lui. 1996. Laser safety and the eye: Hidden hazards and practical pearls. Lions Laser Skin Centre, Division of Dermatology, Vancouver Hospital & Health Sciences Centre, and University of British Columbia, Vancouver, BC. Presented at the American Academy of Dermatology, Washington, DC, February 10–15, 1996.

BBC.com. 2006. The sound that repels troublemakers. http://www.bbc.co.uk/wiltshire/content/articles/2006/04/04/mosquito_sound_wave_feature.shtml (accessed October 31, 2010).

Bertolli, E.R., and D.R. Pannone. 2009. Lasers: Unconventional weapons of criminals and terrorists. *Police Chief Magazine.* http://policechiefmagazine.org/magazine/index.cfm?fuseaction=display_arch&article_id=1731&issue_id=22009 (accessed October 31, 2010).

Buck, A.L. 1967. Effects of the atmosphere on laser beam propagation. *Applied Optics* 6: 703–708.

Cain, C.P., W.P. Roach, D.J. Stolarski, G.D. Noojin, S.S. Kumru, K.L. Stockton, J.J. Zohner, and B.A. Rockwell. 2007. Infrared laser damage thresholds for skin at wavelengths from 0.810 to 1.54 microns for femtosecond to microsecond pulse durations. *Proceedings of the Society of Photographic Instrumentation Engineers*, Vol. 6435, pp. 64350W1–12.

Dunn, R.J. 2005. *Operational Implications of Laser Weapons.* Los Angeles: Northrop Grumman.

Federation of American Scientists. 2003. Convention on conventional weapons (CCW) news. http://www.fas.org/nuke/control/ccw/news/bosnia981104_laser.html (accessed October 31, 2010).

Extance, A. 2015. Military technology: Laser weapons get real. *Nature.* http://www.nature.com/news/military-technology-laser-weapons-get-real-1.17613.

Fisher, D.E. 1988. *A Race on the Edge of Time: Radar—The Decisive Weapon of WW II.* New York: McGraw-Hill.

Fraunhofer, I.L.T. 2006. Laser tutorial. http://www.ilt.fraunhofer.de/eng/100048.html (accessed October 31, 2010).

Globalsecurity.org. 2010a. Directed-energy weapons. http://www.globalsecurity.org/military/library/policy/army/fm/71–1/711apxlf.htm#sec1 (accessed October 31, 2010).

Globalsecurity.org. 2010b. High-power microwave (HPM)/E-bomb. http://www.globalsecurity.org/military/systems/munitions/hpm.htm (accessed October 31, 2010).

Guardian. 2010. G-20 protesters blasted by sonic cannon. http://www.guardian.co.uk/world/blog/2009/sep/25/sonic-cannon-g20-pittsburgh (accessed October 31, 2010).

Hambling, D. 2009. Microwave weapon will rain pain from the sky. *New Scientist.* http://www.newscientist.com/article/mg20327185.600-microwave-weapon-will-rain-pain-from-the-sky.html (accessed October 31, 2010).

Horak, H.G. 1966. The effect of the atmosphere on laser range determination. SAO/NASA Astrophysics Data System. http://articles.adsabs.harvard.edu/(accessed October 31, 2010).

International Electrotechnical Commission. 2007. Safety of laser products—Part 1: Equipment classification and requirements. Geneva, Switzerland.

Joint Non-Lethal Weapons Program. 2010. Active denial system. https://www.jnlwp.com/ads.asp (accessed October 31, 2010).

Jot Your Life. 2009. Health effects of sonic weapons. September 29, 2009. http://www.jotyourlife.com/2009/09/health-effects-of-sonic-weapons.html (accessed October 31, 2010).

Kenny, J.M., M. Ziskin, B. Adair, B. Murray, D. Farrer, L. Marks, and V. Bovbjerg. 2008. *A Narrative Summary and Independent Assessment of the Active Denial System.* College Station, PA: Pennsylvania State University.

Kopp, C. 2008. High energy directed energy weapons. Technical Report APATR-2008-0501. http://www.ausairpower.net/APA-DEW-HEL-Analysis.html#Background (accessed October 31, 2010).

Limer, A. 2015. Russia says its new microwave cannon can kill drones and warheads with ease. *Popular Mechanics.* June 16, 2015. http://www.popularmechanics.com/military/weapons/a16044/russian-anti-drone-microwave-gun/.

Los Angeles Times. 2004. Terrorists may use lasers to blind pilots, FBI warns. December 10, 2004. http://articles.latimes.com/2004/dec/10/nation/nalasers10 (accessed October 31, 2010).

LRAD Corporation. n.d. LRAD/Product Overview. San Diego, CA. http://www.lradx.com/site/content/view/15/110/.

Nakagawara, V.B., R.W. Montgomery, and K.J. Wood. 2003. *The Effects of Laser Illumination on Operational and Visual Performance of Pilots Conducting Terminal Operations.* DOT/FAA/AM-03/12. Washington, DC: Office of Aerospace Medicine.

New Scientist. 2006. Microwave-over gun. http://www.newscientist.com/blog/invention/2006/10/microwave-oven-gun.html (accessed October 31, 2010).

NewsMax.com. 2003. Report: N. Korea fired laser at U.S. warplanes. May 13, 2003, NewsMax.com. http://archive.newsmax.com/archives/articles/2003/5/13/74427.shtml (accessed October 31, 2010).

Nutley, E.L. 2003. Non-lethal weapons: Setting our phasers on stun? Potential strategic blessings and curses of non-lethal weapons on the battlefield. Occasional Paper No. 34. Center for Strategy and Technology. August 2003. Air University. Maxwell Air Force Base, Alabama.

Occupational Safety and Health Administration. 2010a. Laser safety. http://www.osha.gov/SLTC/laserhazards/.

Occupational Safety and Health Administration. 2010b. *OSHA Technical Manual.* TED 01–00-015 [TED 1–0.15A]. http://www.osha.gov/dts/osta/otm/otm_toc.html (accessed October 31, 2010).

Olson, K.B. 1999. Aum Shinrikyo: Once and future threat? *Emerging Infectious Diseases* 5(4): 513–516. http://www.cdc.gov/ncidod/EID/vol5no4/olson.htm (accessed January 7, 2009).

Osborn, K. 2014. Navy declares laser weapons ready to protect ships in Persian Gulf. http://www.military.com/daily-news/2014/12/10/navy-declares-laser-weapons-ready-to-protect-ships-in-persian.html.

Pevler, A.E. 1997. Security implications of high-power microwave technology. Technology and Society. International Symposium on Technology and Society at a Time of Sweeping Change. Glasgow, UK, p. 107.

Possel, W.H. 1998. *Laser Weapons in Space: A Critical Assessment.* Maxwell Air Force Base, AL.

Pozar, D.M. 1997. Microwave frequencies. In: *Microwave Engineering.* New York: John Wiley & Sons.

Ravilious, K. 2005. The secrets of sonic weapons. *The Guardian.* http://www.guardian.co.uk/science/2005/nov/08/g2.weaponstechnology (accessed October 31, 2010).

Raytheon Company. 2006. *Silent Guardian™ Protection System. Less-than-Lethal Directed Energy Protection.* Tucson, AZ.

Raytheon Company. 2007. Vigilant Eagle: Protection from surface-to-air-missiles. Technology Today. Raytheon Company, Tucson, AZ. http://www.raytheon.com/news/rtnwcm/groups/public/documents/content/rtn08_tech_homesecurity_pdf1.pdf.

Roberds, R.M. 2006. Introducing the particle-beam weapon. *Air University Review,* July–August 1984. http://www.airpower.maxwell.af.mil/airchronicles/aureview/1984/jul-aug/roberds.html (accessed March 15, 2006).

Seeber, F. n.d. *Light Sources and Laser Safety.* Blackwood, NJ: Camden County College. http://spie.org/Documents/Publications/00%20STEP%20Module%2002.pdf (accessed October 31, 2010).

Shalal, A. 2015. U.S. military sees more use of laser, microwave weapons. Reuters. July 28, 2015. http://www.reuters.com/article/2015/07/28/us-usa-military-arms-idUSKCN0Q22HH20150728.

Skaggs, R. 2007. Exploiting technical opportunities to capture advanced capabilities for our soldiers. *Army: AL&T* Oct–Dec: 16–19.

Small, L.A. n.d. *Blinding Laser Weapons: It is Time for the International Community to Take Off its Blinders.* Ryebrook, NY: International Center for Law, Trade and Diplomacy, Inc.

Stewart, C.S. 2006. *Weapons of Mass Casualties and Terrorism Response Handbook.* Boston, MA: Jones and Bartlett.

Tandy, V. 1998. The ghost in the machine. *Journal of the Society for Psychical Research* 62(851): 360–364.

UCSD. 2009. Laser safety program: Biological effects of laser radiation. http://blink.ucsd.edu /safety/research-lab/lasers/effects.html (accessed October 31, 2010).

University of Texas. 2002. *Non-Lethal Swimmer Neutralization Study.* Applied Research Laboratories, University of Texas at Austin. G2 Software Systems, Inc., San Diego; Technical Document 3138; May 2002. http://webcache.googleusercontent.com/unclesam?q=cache:s2NL05udytgJ:www .spawar.navy.mil/sti/publications/pubs/td/3138/td3138cond.pdf+electromagnetic+weapons +affect+heart+rhythm&hl=en&ct=clnk&cd=5&gl=us (accessed October 31, 2010).

U.S. Air Force. 2002. High power microwaves. *Fact Sheet.* Kirtland AFB, NM: Air Force Research Laboratory, Office of Public Affairs.

U.S. Air Force Research Laboratory. 1998. *HPM Overview Briefing.* Kirtland AFB, NM: High Power Microwave Division, Directed Energy Directorate, February 1998.

Van Keuren, E., and J. Knighten. 1995. Use of high power microwave weapons. Security Technology, 1995. *Proceedings, Institute of Electrical and Electronics Engineers 29th Annual 1995 International Carnahan Conference,* October 18–20, 1995. pp. 482–491.

Walters, T.J., D.W. Blick, L.R. Johnson, E.R. Adair, and K.R. Foster. 2000. Heating and pain sensation produced in human skin by millimeter waves: Comparison to a simple thermal model. *Health Physics* 78(3): 259–267.

World Health Organization. 1993. *Safety of Laser Products Part 1. Equipment Classification, Requirements and User's Guide.* IEC publication number 60825–1. Geneva: International Electrotechnical Commission.

9

National Incident Management System and the Incident Command System

The secret of all victory lies in the organization of the non-obvious.

Marcus Aurelius
Roman Emperor, C.E. 121–180

NATIONAL INCIDENT MANAGEMENT SYSTEM

An incident, whether a terrorist attack, a chemical release from a fixed industrial facility, or a highway accident involving hazardous chemicals, typically begins and ends locally. Such incidents are managed on a daily basis at the lowest possible geographical, organizational, and jurisdictional levels. Many incidents occur, however, where successful management and response operations depend on the involvement of many jurisdictions, levels of government, agencies, and/or emergency responder types. Incident response in these situations requires efficient coordination across a broad spectrum of organizations and responsibilities.

The September 11, 2001 terrorist attacks and the 2004 and 2005 hurricane seasons focused attention on the need to improve emergency management, incident response capabilities, and coordination protocols across the country. A comprehensive national approach, applicable at all jurisdictional levels and across functional disciplines, improves the effectiveness of emergency management/response personnel spanning the full spectrum of potential incidents and hazard scenarios. This includes natural hazards, terrorist activities, industrial accidents, and other man-made disasters. Such an approach enhances coordination and cooperation between public and private agencies/organizations in a variety of emergency management and incident response activities.

Under Homeland Security Presidential Directive 5 (February 2003), the Federal government created the National Incident Management System (NIMS). This system directs the creation of a comprehensive national approach to incident management by federal, state, territorial, tribal, and local responders. Presidential Directive 5 also makes NIMS compliance a requirement for any of these entities wishing to receive Federal funds.

Federal and state response agencies and any agencies receiving Federal funds have been given compliance guidance and are working toward educating and training their organizations in becoming NIMS compliant. The Federal government has expanded the definitions of *first responder* agencies beyond the traditional Fire, Hazardous Materials (HAZMAT), Police, and Emergency Medical Services (EMS) to include public works, public health, emergency communications, emergency management, and other agencies involved in disaster preparedness, prevention, response, and recovery activities.

NIMS establishes a uniform set of processes, protocols, and procedures that all emergency responders, at every level of government, will use to conduct response actions.

The six components included in NIMS are

1. Command and management
2. Preparedness
3. Resource management
4. Communications and information management
5. Ongoing management and maintenance
6. Supporting technologies

In addition, NIMS identifies a variety of Federal Preparedness programs that are available to responders.

NIMS Components

The components of NIMS were not designed to stand alone, but to work together in a flexible, systematic manner to provide the framework for incident management.

Command and Management

The Command and Management component of NIMS is designed to enable effective and efficient incident management and coordination by providing a flexible, standardized incident management structure. The structure is based on three key organizational components: the Incident Command System (ICS), Multiagency Coordination Systems, and Public Information. The ICS is described later in this chapter.

Preparedness

Effective emergency management and incident response begins with a range of preparedness activities that must be conducted on an ongoing basis, in advance of any potential incident. Preparedness involves a combination of assessment; planning; procedures and protocols; training and exercises; personnel qualifications, licensure, and certification; equipment certification; and evaluation and revision. It is essential for a response agency that plans and procedures be tested regularly—what does not work must be modified, eliminated, and replaced.

Resource Management

Resources such as personnel, equipment, and supplies are needed to support critical incident objectives. The flow of resources must be fluid and adaptable to the needs of the incident. NIMS defines standardized mechanisms and establishes the resource management process to identify requirements, order and acquire, mobilize, track and report, recover and demobilize, reimburse, and inventory resources.

Communications and Information Management

Emergency management and incident response activities rely on communications and information systems that provide a common framework for all command sites. NIMS specifies the requirements necessary for a standardized system for communications. This is based on the concepts of interoperability, reliability, and portability of communications and information systems.

Ongoing Management and Maintenance

In the 2008 version of NIMS, the former Supporting Technologies component was restructured into Ongoing Management and Maintenance. Within this new component are two sections: the National Integration Center (NIC) and Supporting Technologies.

National Integration Center (NIC)

Homeland Security Presidential Directive 5 required the Secretary of Homeland Security to establish a mechanism for ensuring the ongoing management and maintenance of NIMS, including regular consultation with other federal departments and agencies; state, tribal, and local stakeholders; and nongovernmental organizations (NGOs) and the private sector. The NIC provides strategic direction, oversight, and coordination of NIMS and supports both routine maintenance and continuous refinement of NIMS and its components. It provides guidance to jurisdictions and emergency management personnel as they adopt the system.

Supporting Technologies

As NIMS and its related emergency management systems evolve, emergency management/response personnel will increasingly rely on technology to implement and refine NIMS. The NIC oversees and coordinates the ongoing development of incident management-related technologies.

Mutual Aid Agreements

A large-scale incident (such as release of a weapon of mass destruction) will involve multiple jurisdictions in the response. Coordination of resources and response personnel across several counties and states will be more effective if agreements are already in place, stating what types of resources may be provided.

Mutual aid agreements are the means for one jurisdiction to provide resources, facilities, services, and other required support to another jurisdiction during an incident. Each jurisdiction should be party to a mutual aid agreement with those jurisdictions from which they expect to receive or to provide assistance during an incident. This normally includes all neighboring or nearby jurisdictions, as well as relevant private sector entities and NGOs. States should participate in interstate compacts and intrastate agreements that embrace all local jurisdictions. Mutual aid agreements are also needed with private organizations, for example, the American Red Cross, to facilitate the timely delivery of private assistance during incidents.

An example of a long-standing mutual aid agreement is the Emergency Management Assistance Compact (EMAC), which is a partnership between states and territories of the United States (U.S. FEMA, n.d. [a]). Formulated initially by former Florida Governor Lawton Chiles after the catastrophic 1992 Hurricane Andrew, EMAC is a national interstate mutual aid agreement that enables states to share resources during times of disaster. EMAC has since grown to become the nation's system for providing mutual aid through operational procedures and protocols. Today, all 50 states, the District of Columbia, U.S. Virgin Islands, Puerto Rico, and Guam are members of EMAC.

At a minimum, mutual aid agreements should include the following elements or provisions:

- Definitions of key terms used in the agreement
- Roles and responsibilities of individual parties
- Procedures for requesting and providing assistance
- Procedures, authorities, and rules for payment, reimbursement, and allocation of costs
- Notification procedures
- Protocols for interoperable communications
- Relationships with other agreements among jurisdictions
- Worker compensation
- Treatment of liability and immunity
- Recognition of qualifications and certifications
- Sharing agreements, as required

Authorized officials from each participating jurisdiction must collectively approve all mutual aid agreements.

Summary of NIMS

The components of NIMS are adaptable to any situation, from routine, local incidents to those requiring the activation of interstate mutual aid to those requiring a coordinated federal response, whether planned (e.g., major sporting or community events), notice provided (e.g., hurricane), or no notice (e.g., earthquake). This flexibility is essential for NIMS to be applicable across the full spectrum of potential incidents, including those that require multiagency, multijurisdictional, and/or multidisciplinary coordination. Flexibility in the NIMS framework facilitates scalability of emergency management and incident response activities.

ICS

The ICS is a management strategy designed to address all critical issues that may arise during response to a hazardous incident. ICS may be defined as a program of procedures, communications, facilities, equipment, personnel, and procedures that operate within a common organizational structure to manage resources to respond optimally to an emergency (Figure 9.1).

ICS is especially critical when responding to a terrorist incident. When one considers a catastrophic release of a CBRNE agent, involving many casualties and damage to buildings and infrastructure, the significance of ICS is truly appreciated. Responders initially arriving at the scene may include local police, firefighters, and emergency medical services. Shortly afterward, state and federal investigators, environmental management specialists, utility workers, engineers, the highway department, Red Cross personnel, and many other services (and from many jurisdictions) will arrive. These individuals and agencies are to follow this standardized system to ensure an organized and effective response with optimal distribution of resources and personnel.

History of ICS

The concept of ICS was created in the aftermath of devastating wildfires in California in the early 1970s, in which scores of lives were lost, many hundreds of structures were destroyed, and hundreds of thousands of acres burned. Responding agencies cooperated to the best of their ability during the wildfire event; however, problems with communication and coordination hindered their effectiveness. Subsequent investigations revealed the recurrence of several problems and complications for response agencies (OSHA, n.d.):

- Too many people reporting to one supervisor
- Unclear lines of authority

Figure 9.1 ICS is critical for allocation of personnel and resources in an emergency. (Courtesy of FEMA, https://commons.wikimedia.org/wiki/File:FEMA_-_33205_-_Top_Off-4_Exercise_workers _in_Seattle,_Washington.jpg.)

- Different emergency response organizational structures
- Lack of reliable incident information
- Inadequate and incompatible communications
- Lack of structure for coordinated planning among agencies
- Terminology differences among agencies
- Unclear or unspecified incident objectives

The U.S. Congress subsequently mandated that the U.S. Forest Service design a system that would "make a quantum jump in the capabilities of Southern California wildland fire protection agencies to effectively coordinate interagency action and to allocate suppression resources in dynamic, multiple-fire situations."

The ICS concept was thus developed to manage rapidly moving wildfires, and also to address other emergencies. Municipal, county, state, and federal fire authorities joined to develop the new system, which became known as FIRESCOPE (FIrefighting RESources of California Organized for Potential Emergencies) (U.S. FEMA, n.d. [b]). By the mid-1970s, the FIRESCOPE agencies had formally agreed upon ICS common terminology and procedures and conducted limited field testing of ICS. By 1980, parts of ICS had been used successfully on several major wildland and urban fire incidents. By 1981, ICS was widely used throughout Southern California by the major fire agencies.

In 1980, federal officials transitioned ICS into a national program called the National Interagency Incident Management System, which became the basis of a response management system for all federal agencies with wildfire management responsibilities. Since then, many federal agencies have endorsed the use of ICS, and several have mandated its use.

ICS Organization

Many incidents—whether major accidents (e.g., hazardous material spills), smaller incidents (house fires and utility outages), or emergencies and major disasters (terrorist attack, tornadoes, hurricanes, earthquakes)—require a response from a number of different agencies. To maximize efficiency and productivity of the ICS organization the following sections were created:

- Command
- Command support: safety, liaison, and public information
- Operations
- Planning
- Logistics
- Finance

The relationship among the various ICS components is shown in Figure 9.2.

These components apply during a small-scale emergency, when preparing for a major event, or when managing a response to a major disaster. In small-scale incidents, all of the components may be managed by one person, the Incident Commander (IC). Large-scale incidents usually require that each component, or section, is set up separately. Each of the primary ICS sections may be divided into smaller functions as needed.

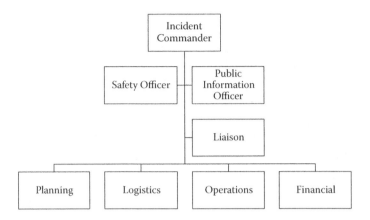

Figure 9.2 The basic Incident Command Structure.

Command

The command function is directed by the IC, who is the person in charge at the incident, and who must be fully qualified to manage the response (Figure 9.3). All incidents, regardless of size or complexity, will be assigned an IC. Major responsibilities for the IC include (U.S. FEMA, n.d. [b]):

- Establish immediate priorities
- Establish an Incident Command Post (ICP)
- Establish an appropriate organization
- Assess the situation and/or obtain a briefing from the prior IC
- Determine Incident Objectives and strategy
- Ensure planning meetings are scheduled as required

Figure 9.3 The Incident Commander is the individual in charge at the incident, and must be fully qualified to manage the response. (From U.S. Army Dugway Proving Ground. With permission.)

- Approve and authorize the implementation of an Incident Action Plan (IAP)
- Ensure that adequate safety measures are in place
- Coordinate activity for all Command and General Staff
- Approve requests for additional resources or for the release of resources
- Keep agency administrator informed of incident status
- Approve the use of trainees, volunteers, and auxiliary personnel
- Authorize release of information to the news media
- Order the demobilization of the incident when appropriate

The IC is responsible for overall management of all incident activities, and also oversees the following staff functions:

- Safety Officer
- Government Liaison Officer
- Public Information Officer (PIO)

The IC has the authority to expand or contract the ICS organization. For example, as incidents become more involved, the IC can activate additional General Staff sections (i.e., Planning, Operations, Logistics, and/or Finance/Administration), as necessary. The decision is based on three major incident priorities:

1. *Life safety.* The IC's first priority is always the life safety of the emergency responders and the public.
2. *Incident stability.* The IC is responsible for determining the strategy that will
   - Minimize the effect that the incident may have on the surrounding area.
   - Maximize the response effort while using resources efficiently. The size and complexity of the command system that the IC develops should be consistent with the complexity (i.e., level of difficulty in the response) of the incident, not the size (which is based on geographic area or number of resources).
3. *Property conservation.* The IC is responsible for minimizing damage to property while achieving the incident objectives.

Initially, the IC will be the senior first responder to arrive at the scene. As more senior officials arrive, command may be transferred to other, more senior personnel. At transfer of command, the outgoing IC provides the incoming IC a full briefing and notifies all staff of the change in command.

Command Staff

The Command position is composed of the IC and Command Staff. Command staff positions are established to assign responsibility for key activities not specifically identified in the General Staff functions (see below). These positions may include the PIO, Safety Officer, and the Liaison Officer, in addition to others as required.

The PIO handles all news media inquiries; this individual is to develop and release information about the incident to the media, to incident personnel, and to other agencies and organizations. The PIO also coordinates the release of information to the media with the Public Affairs Officer at the Emergency Operations Center (EOC).

The Safety Officer monitors safety conditions and develops measures for ensuring the safety of all assigned personnel. This officer must assess and anticipate hazardous and unsafe situations and must develop and recommend measures to the IC for assuring personnel health and safety. The Safety Officer also develops the Site Safety Plan, reviews the IAP for safety implications, and provides timely, complete, specific, and accurate assessment of hazards and required controls (NRT, n.d.).

The Liaison Officer is the on-scene contact for other agencies assigned to the incident. The Liaison Officer's role is to serve as the point of contact for assisting and coordinating activities between the IC and various agencies and groups. This may include local government officials, criminal investigating organizations, and investigators arriving on the scene.

General Staff

The General Staff (Figure 9.2) consists of the following positions:

- Planning/Intelligence Section Chief
- Operations Section Chief
- Logistics Section Chief
- Finance/Administration Section Chief

Each section chief is responsible for the resources and personnel within their respective section; likewise, each section chief reports directly to the IC in a standardized chain of command.

Planning Section

When responding to small events, the IC is the individual responsible for all required planning; however, when the incident occurs on a large scale, the IC establishes the Planning Section. Functions of this section include the collection, evaluation, and dissemination of information about the development of the incident and status of resources (Figure 9.4). Other responsibilities can also include drafting the IAP, which defines the response activities and resource utilization for a specified period.

Operations Section

The Operations Section is responsible for carrying out the response activities described in the IAP (Figure 9.5). These are the tactical experts, the *people on the ground* who extinguish the fire, extricate victims, identify hazardous materials, stabilize the scene, and so on. The Operations Section Chief coordinates Operations Section activities and has primary responsibility for receiving and implementing the IAP. The Operations Section Chief determines the required resources and organizational structure within the section.

Logistics Section

The Logistics Section is responsible for providing facilities, services, materials, and personnel to adequately respond to the incident. This section takes on particular significance

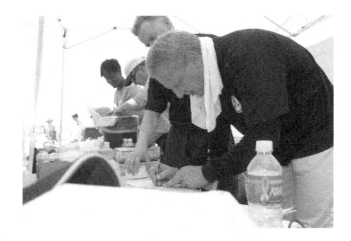

Figure 9.4 Planning for a response must be proactive and must adjust to meet the changing situation. (From U.S. Army Dugway Proving Ground. With permission.)

Figure 9.5 The Operations Section is the *on the ground* tactical team that carries out the requirements set forth in the Incident Action Plan. (From U.S. Army Dugway Proving Ground. With permission.)

in long-term or complex operations. It is important to note that the Logistics Section functions are geared to support the incident responders (i.e., Operations Section). For example, a Medical Unit created within the Logistics Section provides care for the incident responders, not civilian victims.

Finance/Administration

The Finance/Administration Section is critical for tracking incident costs and reimbursement accounting. This section becomes especially important when the incident is of a magnitude that may result in a Presidential Declaration. Costs and financial operations must be meticulously recorded and justified; otherwise, reimbursement becomes difficult or impossible.

SETUP OF THE ICS

The modular organization of the ICS allows responders to scale up or scale down their efforts and apply the parts of the ICS structure that best meet the demands of the incident. In other words, there are no rigid rules for how to expand the ICS organization. Many incidents will never require the activation of Planning, Logistics, or Finance/Administration Sections, whereas others will require their immediate establishment.

A major advantage of the ICS organization is the ability to fill only those parts of the organization that are necessary for response to a particular incident. For some incidents, only a few of the organization's functional elements may be required. However, if there is a need to expand the organization, additional positions exist within the ICS framework to meet virtually any need. For example, in incidents involving responders from a single jurisdiction, the ICS establishes the correct organization for the response. However, when an incident involves multiple agencies and more than one jurisdiction, responders can expand the ICS framework to address the incident (NRT, n.d.).

ICS PRINCIPLES

The effectiveness of the ICS structure has been demonstrated for decades—ICS has been used since the 1970s by response agencies at all governmental levels as well as in industry.

The ICS as required under NIMS can become a complex undertaking for large-scale responses. Therefore, ICS training is required to ensure that all who may become involved in an incident are familiar with its principles.

To be effective, the ICS should include the following components:

- Common terminology
- Modular organization
- Integrated communications
- Unity of command
- Unified command structure
- Consolidated IAPs
- Manageable span of control
- Designated incident facilities

Common Terminology

Over time, a number of response agencies have developed their own vernacular to describe equipment, facilities, duties, and so on, which may not be readily understood by other agencies. Common terminology is essential in any emergency management system, especially when diverse agencies are involved in the response. When agencies have different meanings for terms, confusion and inefficiency are inevitable. For example, not all responders may know *10-codes*, which are common in law enforcement and Citizens Band radio transmissions but not in other agencies. In ICS, terminology is standard and consistent among all agencies involved. Major organizational functions, facilities, and units are predesignated and are assigned titles. Common terminology exists for each of the following elements:

- *Position titles.* A standard set of position titles and major functions exists.
- *Resource titles.* Common names and specifications have been established for all resources used within the ICS.
- *Facilities.* Common terms are used for those facilities in the incident area that will be used during the incident, such as the command post, decontamination line, EOC, and staging areas.

Modular Organization

At any incident, a modular organization is developed from the top down (see Figure 9.2). The term *top–down* means that the Command function is established by the first-arriving responder who becomes the IC. As the incident warrants, the IC activates other functional areas (i.e., ICS sections).

Integrated Communication Procedures

Communications at the incident are managed through use of a common plan and are coordinated through the IC. Integrated communications uses standard operating procedures, common frequencies, and common terminology (Figure 9.6). No special codes are to be used, and all communications should be confined to essential messages. Face-to-face communications are the most effective method of information exchange during an emergency and should be used whenever practical. In-person communications not only minimize the potential for incorrect communication of essential information, but also reduce radio congestion.

Several communication networks may be established, depending on the size and complexity of the incident. If an emergency escalates, multiple radio frequencies can be used simultaneously, for example:

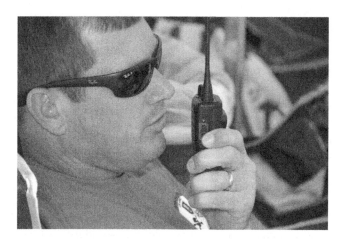

Figure 9.6 Communications at the incident are managed through the use of a common plan. (From U.S. Army Dugway Proving Ground. With permission.)

- *Dispatch.* To issue standby and assistance alerts, all clear, and to request resource response
- *Command.* To link Command with key Command Staff members, tactical division officers, and the dispatch center
- *Tactical.* Tactical frequencies are established when several divisions or groups of resources have a need for radio coordination
- *Support.* Support frequencies may be established to handle requests for support, logistics coordination, and other nontactical needs

Unity of Command

Unity of command is the concept by which each person within an organization reports to only one designated person. In this way, staff will receive work assignments only from their supervisors.

Unified Command

A unified command allows all agencies with responsibility for the incident to manage it by establishing a common set of incident objectives and strategies. This framework does not mean losing agency authority, responsibility, or accountability. Unified command may be applied during incidents that affect more than one political jurisdiction (e.g., adjacent counties). Unified command is also effective in handling incidents involving multiple agencies within a jurisdiction (police, fire, EMS, utilities, highway, etc.).

The concept of unified command means that all involved agencies contribute to the command process by

- Determining overall objectives
- Planning jointly for operations and conducting integrated operations
- Maximizing use of all assigned resources

Under unified command, functions are assigned under a single, coordinated IAP. Also, one Operations Section Chief has responsibility for implementing the IAP. Finally, only one ICP is established. These requirements allow for a streamlined response to an emergency.

The IAP

Every incident response requires an IAP, with the exception of minor incidents of short duration. The IC is charged with the development of the IAP, often with cooperation from the Planning Section.

An IAP formally documents incident goals, objectives for each operational period, and the response strategy. The IAP includes tactics to achieve goals and objectives. Given that incidents will evolve during the course of the response, action plans must be revised on a regular basis (at least once per operational period) to maintain consistent, up-to-date guidance.

The following should be considered for inclusion in an IAP:

- Incident goals (i.e., where we want to be at the end of the response)
- Objectives for the current operational period
- Response strategies (priorities and the approach to accomplish the objectives)
- Response tactics (specific methods developed by Operations to achieve the objectives)
- ICS chart showing primary roles and relationships
- Assignment list with specific tasks
- Updates on resource status
- Health and safety plan (to prevent responder injury or illness)
- Communications plan (how functional units will exchange information)
- Logistics plan (e.g., procedures to support Operations with equipment, supplies)
- Responder medical plan (provides direction for care to responders)
- Incident map (map of incident scene)
- Additional plans specific to the incident

Span of Control

The span of control refers to the number of individuals that a particular leader (e.g., Section Chief) can adequately handle. Safety factors and ability to manage specific response duties will dictate the span of control. Within the ICS, the span of control for any emergency management leader should range from three to seven persons.

Incident Facilities

Several types of facilities may be established in proximity to the incident site. The needs for specific facilities and their locations are based on the requirements of the incident. The following facilities may be established within the ICS:

- *ICP.* This is the single location from which all incident operations are directed. The IC is based at the command post. To ensure consistent and safe operations, the ICP should be located upwind, uphill, and upstream from the site of the incident.
- *Incident Base.* This is where primary support activities are performed. The base is the location of all equipment and personnel support until these resources are sent to a staging area.
- *EOC.* The EOC is a facility located away from the emergency situation and having access to senior facility management (Figure 9.7). The EOC is often a permanent facility, readily available for any type of incident.
- *Staging Areas.* The staging area is established for temporary placement of available resources on very short notice (Figure 9.8).

APPLICATION OF THE ICS: OKLAHOMA CITY, OKLAHOMA

At 9:02 A.M., on Wednesday April 19, 1995, a vehicle-borne improvised explosive device (VBIED) exploded in front of the Alfred P. Murrah Federal Building in Oklahoma City,

Figure 9.7 San Diego Emergency Operations Center's Situation Room. (Courtesy of NASA, http://www.nasa.gov/centers/dryden/news/Features/2007/wildfire_socal_10_07_prt.htm.)

Figure 9.8 Staging area for 16 agencies at an emergency response exercise. (Courtesy of Rockland County, http://www.co.rockland.ny.us/Fire/press/06-24-05pics.htm.)

Oklahoma. The bomb was situated on the north side of the building, near the intersection of NW 5th Street and Robinson Avenue (Figure 9.9). The force of the explosion destroyed approximately one-third of the Murrah Building. Structural damage also extended to the Regency Tower, a 273-unit apartment complex; the two-story Oklahoma Water Resources Board office building; the six-story, historic Journal Record Building; and the three-story Athenian Building.

Figure 9.9 Map of downtown Oklahoma City, showing some of the locations of key emergency management efforts.

The explosion disabled primary and backup telephone lines for the Emergency Medical Services Authority (EMSA), the local ambulance service. As a result, 9-1-1 was the only emergency communication available. The first call for medical assistance was received by EMSA at 9:03 A.M. On hearing the explosion, seven EMS units responded from EMSA headquarters. The emergency response units nearest the scene were at Oklahoma City Fire Department Station One, five blocks away. Emergency personnel from the station responded immediately.

First-in fire companies were faced with an overwhelming rescue operation. As personnel and apparatus approached the scene, firefighters encountered massive debris in the streets, covering several blocks surrounding the Murrah Building. Passages had to be cleared to allow entry of responders and equipment.

Firefighters encountered injured victims leaving the blast site. Two medical triage areas were quickly established. Fire, emergency medical, law enforcement personnel, voluntary organization workers, and many civilians entered the severely damaged structure in a massive search-and-rescue effort. In some areas, human chains were formed to accommodate the safe and rapid removal of victims as they were located. The evacuation of the structure allowed responders to create a controlled perimeter around the unstable site.

Immediately after the blast, an ICS was established by the Oklahoma City Fire Department to manage the intensive search-and-rescue mission. The ICS handled the massive influx of resources that included federal, state, local, and voluntary agency response personnel and equipment, which was placed under the sole command of the Oklahoma City Fire Department. The Oklahoma City Police Department handled traffic and security in coordination with the Oklahoma County Sheriff, state, and federal agencies.

By 9:25 A.M., the State Emergency Operations Center (SEOC), located 3 mi away, was fully operational. State agencies initially represented in the SEOC included the Oklahoma Department of Public Safety, the Oklahoma Department of Human Services, the Oklahoma Military Department, the Oklahoma Department of Health, and the Oklahoma Department of Education. These agencies were soon augmented by the National Weather Service, the Civil Air Patrol, and the American Red Cross.

The incident was reported to the Federal Emergency Management Agency (FEMA), Region VI headquarters, in Denton, Texas, at 9:30 A.M. Regional Director Buddy Young ordered the immediate activation of the Regional Operations Center, the regional federal counterpart to the SEOC.

At 9:45 A.M. Governor Frank Keating ordered a State of Emergency. By 10:35 A.M. Regional Director Young had briefed FEMA headquarters in Washington, DC, and organized staff to accompany him to Oklahoma City. FEMA immediately put Urban Search and Rescue (US&R) Task Forces from Phoenix, Arizona, and Sacramento, California, on alert and at 10:55 A.M. activated each team for deployment to Oklahoma City.

After arriving at the Murrah Building, the Disaster Recovery Manager located the ICP at the intersection of NW 6th Street and Harvey Avenue. He made initial contact with the IC and offered all state assets necessary to supplement the response efforts.

At the time, the most pressing need was to cordon and maintain a secure perimeter around the structure. The option of bringing in National Guard troops and additional public safety officers was agreed upon. The Recovery Manager attempted to make this request to the SEOC via cellular telephone, but was unable to because of a system overload. The transmission was completed via handheld radio.

The first of at least two bomb scares occurred at about this time. People began running north from the Murrah Building, stating that another bomb had been located. Unable to either confirm or deny the threat, the IC made the decision to relocate the command post two blocks north to a vacant parking lot on the southwest corner of NW 8th Street and Harvey Avenue.

After the relocation, other units began arriving, including the Federal Bureau of Investigation (FBI); the Bureau of Alcohol, Tobacco, and Firearms (BATF); and the Drug Enforcement Administration (DEA).

Southwestern Bell Telephone Company brought in a truck for the purpose of issuing free-use cellular phones to all response personnel. They also reported that a temporary *cellular-on-wheels* site was being erected to accommodate the high-traffic cellular use in the downtown area.

Rain was predicted for the afternoon, so a request was made through the SEOC to have the National Guard erect a tent near the ICP.

Owing to the lack of shelter and the increasing number of emergency personnel and equipment arriving at the confined parking lot, the IC made the decision to once again relocate the ICP. The new location was directly across the street in the Southwestern Bell Telephone Company's Corporate Headquarters parking lot (SE corner of NW 8th Street and Harvey Avenue). The new location was more suitable to emergency personnel as it provided a larger parking area and a sheltered garage where voluntary agencies and private organizations could distribute food and store donations. The building itself met the sanitary needs of the emergency and relief personnel and later housed the first two US&R Task Forces.

Additional mobile command units arriving at the ICP represented the U.S. Marshals Service and the Oklahoma Department of Public Safety.

The Oklahoma National Guard erected their tent in the parking lot. Chain-link fencing was placed around the parking lot and access was restricted.

Through the aid of Oklahoma City officials, the FBI secured a vacant building located at 11 NE 6th Street to use as a command post for the investigative element of the crime. The BATF and the DEA joined forces with the FBI in this effort and their respective staff spent the afternoon establishing the operations center, while field operations continued.

Ongoing liaison relationships were maintained with the Oklahoma Department of Public Safety, the National Guard, and the American Red Cross, to attempt to better coordinate a unified effort.

By early afternoon, it became apparent that donated goods would be a problem for the duration of the response. Commercial tractor-trailers, pickups, and other private vehicles began lining up at the corner of NW 8th Street and Harvey Avenue loaded with everything from wheelbarrows to football helmets.

The ICP was not the only location where donated goods were being delivered. Voluntary organizations began storing items as best they could, but new drop-off locations had to be established rapidly, and inventory control became a difficult task. The overall lack of donations coordination was considered a key deficiency in the state and local planning effort (Oklahoma Department of Civil Emergency Management, 1995).

Another escalating problem facing the IC was the increasing influx of media representatives at the scene. The decision was made to locate all media personnel within a vacant parking area, covering approximately one-half a city block, on Harvey Avenue between NW 6th and 7th Streets. The area was roped off, with access allowed to credentialed personnel. Although it was not as close to the Murrah Building as the media had preferred, it did offer an unobstructed view of the structure. Oklahoma City Police and Fire public information specialists provided periodic updates to the media and a joint federal, state, and local press conference was scheduled for the following morning.

The Oklahoma City Fire Department established a Forward Command Post inside the interior loading dock of the Murrah Building. The FEMA Incident Support Team (IST) was activated and colocated in the Forward Command Post. The IST is a trained and equipped unit of operational personnel from around the nation, designed to manage and coordinate the site-specific FEMA response mission during catastrophic disasters. Equipment including electrical power, telephones, copiers, tables, chairs, and other necessary items, was immediately brought in to support their efforts.

At 3:30 P.M. the First Christian Church, NW 36th Street and N. Walker Avenue, was established by the State Medical Examiner's Office as the site of the Family Assistance Center. Immediate family members received briefings directly from the State Medical

Examiner's Office at this location twice daily. The Assistance Center provided information, mental health counseling, and comfort to those who were victims of the incident or who either lost or had missing family members in the building. Center support was provided by many organizations, including the American Red Cross, the Salvation Army, the Oklahoma Funeral Directors Association, and many pastors, chaplains, and mental health professionals throughout the area, state, and nation.

The American Red Cross opened a shelter for those displaced by the explosion. They also activated the National Disaster Services Human Resources Team to administer large-scale disaster assistance to the victims. With donated goods and appropriate distribution becoming an increasing concern, Red Cross logistics support was provided from warehouses at the ICP and at NW 5th Street and Harvey Avenue, inside the damaged U.S. Post Office. Other logistics sites were provided by the Salvation Army.

The Oklahoma City Fire Department established their Technical Logistics Center at 225 NW 6th Street in a covered parking garage. The Oklahoma Restaurant Association had just finished their annual conference when the explosion occurred. They quickly established a 24-h food service operation at the Myriad Convention Center to feed all emergency response workers.

The Convention Center was eventually established as a center for meeting the needs of all personnel responding to the incident. Donated clothing, food, equipment, and supplies were available on a 24-h basis. Other volunteer and donated services included over-the-counter pharmaceutical and personal hygiene items, hair care, optometric, chiropractic, and podiatric care, and massage therapy.

Critical incident stress debriefings and mental health services were offered by professionals from the Oklahoma City Fire and Police Departments, the Oklahoma Department of Mental Health and Substance Abuse Services, the FBI, the American Red Cross, and volunteer private specialists. In addition, crisis hotlines were established throughout the city to meet the needs of the general public.

At 4:00 P.M. CST, President Clinton announced that he had signed Emergency Declaration FEMA-3115-EM-OK. This declaration, under provisions of the Robert T. Stafford Disaster Relief and Emergency Assistance Act, permits the federal government to provide emergency assistance to save lives; protect property, public health, and safety; and to lessen or avert the threat of further damage. The signing of this declaration gave the federal government primary responsibility for responding to the disaster. It also authorized 100% federal financial reimbursement for all eligible response missions performed by local and state governments.

Even though the Presidential Emergency Declaration provided authority and responsibility to the federal government, the chain of command did not change—the Oklahoma City Fire Department still controlled the search-and-rescue mission and the FBI was still in charge of the investigation of the federal crime that was committed. Strategy meetings at the SEOC were held early every morning. Situation reports were developed and distributed daily to both the Governor and the President. The FBI held investigative meetings twice daily, and all key players briefed the public at press conferences, on a minimum schedule of once per day.

The search-and-rescue mission continued at the site for 17 days. Shortly after midnight on May 5, search-and-rescue operations were determined to be officially complete. It was anticipated at that time that three bodies remained in the rubble. Due to the perceived location and potential safety hazards, the decision was made to leave the remaining bodies in the rubble until after the implosion of the structure (Oklahoma Department of Civil Emergency Management, 1995).

The ICS diagram for the Oklahoma City response appears in Figure 9.10.

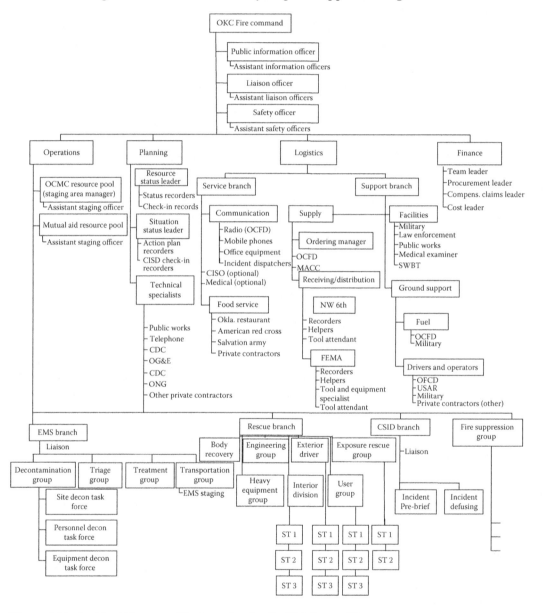

Figure 9.10 Incident Command System plan for the Oklahoma City response.

QUESTIONS

1. When an incident *initially* occurs, who serves as the IC?
2. In the ICS, which section is responsible for drafting the IAP? Which section is responsible for arranging for out-of-state responders and heavy equipment to be ordered for the affected site? Which individual/section is responsible for ensuring optimum communication between external agencies and the IC?
3. The ICP should be located ____ from the incident site.
4. The ICS is part of the NIMS and is the national standard for incident response. True or false?
5. A semitrailer has fallen over on an interstate highway. The driver has been seriously injured and the driver of a car has also been injured. Hazardous liquid (hydrochloric acid) is leaking from the trailer. Can the ICS be used to respond to this event? Why or why not?

REFERENCES

National Response Team. n.d. Incident Command System/Unified Command (ICS/UC) Technical assistance document. http://www.nrt.org/Production/NRT/NRTWeb.nsf/AllAttachments ByTitle/SA-52ICSUCTA/$File/ICSUCTA.pdf? OpenElement (accessed October 26, 2010).

Occupational Safety and Health Administration. n.d. Incident command system. http://www.osha .gov/SLTC/etools/ics/what_is_ics.html (accessed October 26, 2010).

Oklahoma Department of Civil Emergency Management. 1995. *After Action Report: Alfred P. Murrah Federal Building Bombing.* April 19, 1995 in Oklahoma City, OK.

U.S. Federal Emergency Management Agency. n.d. [a] Emergency Management Assistance Compact (EMAC). http://www.fema.gov/pdf/emergency/nrf/EMACoverviewForNRF.pdf (accessed October 26, 2010).

U.S. Federal Emergency Management Agency. n.d. [b]. *Introduction to the Incident Command System.* Emergency Management Institute, Emmetsburg, MD.

10

Personal Protective Equipment for Emergency Response, Decontamination, and Remediation

Know, first, who you are; and then adorn yourself accordingly.

Epictetus

Carelessness in dressing is moral suicide.

Honoré de Balzac

I base most of my fashion sense on what doesn't itch.

Gilda Radner

PERSONAL PROTECTIVE EQUIPMENT FOR EMERGENCY RESPONSE

The purpose of personal protective equipment (PPE) is to shield responders from the chemical, biological, and physical hazards that may be encountered during operations involving hazardous materials. For any given situation, equipment and clothing can be selected that provide an adequate level of protection (Figure 10.1). It is important that users of PPE appreciate that no single combination of ensemble and protective equipment is capable of protection against all hazards; therefore, PPE should be used in combination with other protective methods. For example, engineering controls (ventilation, barrier emplacement, etc.) may be needed as an additional measure to prevent responder exposure to hazards.

Figure 10.1 Proper protective equipment (PPE) is essential when working in hazardous conditions. (Courtesy of U.S. Department of Transportation, http://www.phmsa.dot.gov/staticfiles/PHMSA /SideContentSets/Images/risk-management.jpg.)

Protective clothing must be worn whenever the user may face hazards arising from chemical exposure. In the context of terrorism and WMDs, examples include the following:

- Terrorist incident (release of chemical, biological, radiological/nuclear, explosive materials)
- Chemical manufacturing and process industries
- Hazardous waste site cleanup and disposal

During an emergency response, the following activities require use of PPE:

- *Site reconnaissance.* The initial investigation of a hazardous materials incident is often characterized by a high degree of uncertainty, and will require the highest levels of protection.

- *Search and rescue.* PPE may be required when entering a hazardous materials area to remove a victim. Special consideration must be given to how the selected PPE may affect the ability of the wearer to conduct the rescue.
- *Spill mitigation.* Entering a hazardous materials area to prevent a potential spill or to reduce the hazards from an existing spill (i.e., applying a chlorine kit on a railroad tank car) will require PPE. Protective clothing must accommodate the required tasks without sacrificing protection.
- *Monitoring.* PPE is needed for personnel who are observing a hazardous materials incident without entry to the affected site.
- *Decontamination.* PPE must be worn by personnel who conduct decontamination on responders or equipment leaving the site. In general, a lower level of protective clothing is used by personnel involved in decon compared with those entering the hot zone.

The use of PPE can itself create significant wearer hazards such as heat stress and psychological stress, in addition to impaired vision, mobility, and communication. In general, the greater the level of chemical protective clothing, the greater are the associated risks.

RESPIRATORY PROTECTION

Respiratory protection systems (i.e., respirators) protect the user by preventing inhalation of toxic airborne contaminants and/or by providing oxygen in an oxygen-deficient atmosphere. Many forms of respirators are available; however, the two primary classes are air purifying and supplied atmosphere respirators. We can further divide these classes, for example, into type of fit and mode of operation.

Type of Fit

So-called tight-fitting respirators include face masks composed of flexible molded rubber, neoprene, or other materials. Designs include rubber or woven elastic head straps. Tight-fitting respirators are available in three basic configurations: (1) A quarter-mask covers the mouth and nose, and the lower sealing surface rests between chin and mouth; (2) The half-mask fits over the nose and under the chin. Half-masks are designed to seal more reliably than quarter-masks, so they are preferred for use against more serious hazards (Figure 10.2); and (3) The full-facepiece covers from the hairline to below the chin. Full-facepiece masks provide the greatest protection, usually seal most reliably, and provide eye protection as well (Figure 10.3) (U.S. DOJ, 2002).

Loose-fitting respirators enclose the head at a minimum. A typical configuration includes a hood, that is, a light flexible device covering only the head and neck (Figure 10.4). As these respirators are loose fitting, it is essential that sufficient air be provided to maintain a slight positive pressure inside the hood relative to the environment immediately outside. In this way, contaminants are prevented from entering the wearer's breathing zone.

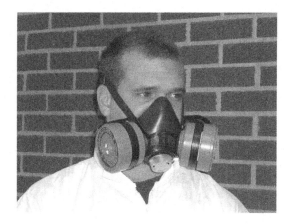

Figure 10.2   Half mask air-purifying respirator.

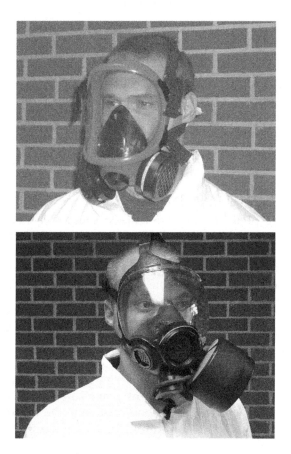

Figure 10.3   Full-facepiece air-purifying respirator.

318

Figure 10.4 Hood respirator. (From U.S. Army Dugway Proving Ground. With permission.)

Air-Purifying Respirators

Air-purifying respirators (APRs) are of the tight-fitting category and contain a replaceable filter, cartridge, or canister that removes a specific contaminant by passing ambient air through purifying media before it is inhaled by the wearer (Figure 10.5). Cartridges that remove particulates are termed *filters*; those that remove vapor or gas are termed *chemical cartridges* or *canisters*. Two critical aspects regarding air-purifying cartridges must be made clear to the user:

1. These respirators do not supply oxygen. They can only be used when the atmosphere of the work zone contains sufficient oxygen to sustain life.
2. The concentration of the atmospheric contaminant must be below the concentration limits of the air-purifying cartridge. Otherwise, the cartridge will quickly become saturated and allow toxic vapors to break through to the user.

Filters and canisters are the key functional components of APRs, and they can be removed and replaced once their effective life has expired.

APRs are grouped into three functional categories: particulate removing, vapor and gas removing, and combination. These respirators may be nonpowered or powered.

1. Particulate-removing respirators are designed to reduce inhaled concentrations of harmful dusts and aerosols by filtering contaminants from inhaled air before they enter the breathing zone of the wearer. Different types of filtration technologies include (1) mechanical filters [high-efficiency particulate air (HEPA) and ultralow penetration air]; (2) electrostatic filters (which incorporate electrostatic charges into the filter medium); and (3) membrane technologies (which physically separate air particles based on their size and geometry). The simplest and least expensive (and least reliable) of the APRs are filtering facepiece respirators, commonly referred to as dust masks, disposable respirators, or single-use respirators (Figure 10.6).

Figure 10.5 Cartridges used in APR. Cartridges can be selected for removal of a particular contaminant (e.g., hydrocarbon vapors, HCl, asbestos, etc).

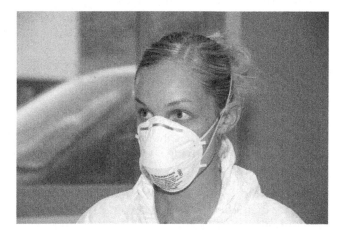

Figure 10.6 A dust mask is the simplest and least costly, but the least effective of all respirator types. (From U.S. Army Dugway Proving Ground. With permission.)

2. Vapor- and gas-removing respirators use sorbent chemicals such as activated charcoal or catalysts to remove (*adsorb* or *absorb*) specific gases and vapors from ambient air before they can enter the breathing zone of the wearer.
3. Combination cartridges and canisters are available to protect against particulates as well as vapors and gases. An example of a combined particulate and vapor removal technology is the C2A1 canister, a component of the M40 protective mask. The C2A1 canister contains a HEPA filter layered with a tetraethylene diamine activated carbon vapor filter.

Filtration Mechanisms

Some particulate filters use simple screening (sieving) to remove particles from the air—that is, they exclude the particles that are larger than the pores. These are termed *absolute filters*. Most respirator filters, however, are nonabsolute, which means they contain pores that are larger than the particles to be removed. Nonabsolute filters rely on a variety of mechanisms to remove particulates, including interception capture, sedimentation capture, inertial impaction capture, diffusion capture, and electrostatic capture. The filtration mechanisms that occur within the media depend on the flow rate through the filter and particle size.

1. *Interception capture.* As a stream of air approaches a fiber situated perpendicular to its path, it splits and compresses to flow around the fiber. If a particle in the airstream comes sufficiently close to the fiber surface, it is captured. As particle size increases, the probability of interception capture increases.
2. *Sedimentation capture.* Only large particles (2 μm and larger) are captured by sedimentation. This type of capture relies on gravity to pull particles from the airstream. Flow rate through the filter must therefore be low.
3. *Inertial impaction capture.* As the airstreams split and change direction to pass around the fiber, particles with sufficient inertia cannot change direction to avoid the fiber. Thus, they impact on the surface of the fiber. The size, density, speed, and shape of the particle determine its inertia.
4. *Diffusion capture.* The motion of small particles is affected by air molecules colliding with them. The particles randomly cross the airstream and encounter the fiber as they pass. This random motion is dependent on particle size and air temperature. As particle size decreases and air temperature increases, the diffusive activity of the particle increases, which increases the probability of capture. Lower flow rate through the filter also increases probability of capture because the particle spends more time in the area of the fiber.
5. *Electrostatic capture.* Target particles have a natural charge, and filter fibers can be designed with the opposite charge. Therefore, the particles are attracted to the fiber surfaces. The electrostatic capture mechanism aids the other capture mechanisms, especially interception and diffusion (U.S. DOJ, 2002).

Mechanisms for Removal of Vapors and Gases

Vapors and gases are removed from cartridge respirators by a physicochemical process termed *sorption*. In the cartridge, contaminant molecules come into contact with a granular, porous sorbent material. In addition to sorption, some respirators use chemical catalysts, which react with the contaminant to produce a less toxic vapor or gas (U.S. DOJ, 2002).

Three mechanisms are responsible for vapor and gas removal.

1. *Adsorption* retains the contaminant molecule on the surface of the sorbent granule by physical attraction. The intensity of the attraction varies with the type of sorbent and the characteristics of the contaminant. Sorbent molecules tend to have extremely large surface areas for reaction with the contaminant of interest.

Adsorption by physical attraction holds the adsorbed molecules weakly. If chemical forces are involved, the bonds between contaminant and sorbent granules are much stronger and can be broken only with difficulty.

Granular activated charcoal (GAC) is by far the most common adsorbent used in cartridge respirators. It is used primarily to remove organic vapors. Activated charcoal also can be treated with various substances to make it act selectively against specific gases and vapors. Examples are GAC impregnated with iodine to remove mercury vapor, with metallic oxides to remove acid gases, and with salts of metals to remove ammonia gas. Other sorbents used in vapor- and gas-removing respirators include activated alumina and silica gel (U.S. DOJ, 2002).

2. *Absorption* involves the incorporation of a molecule deep within the pores of the sorbing material. This mechanism can remove certain vapors and gases in addition to particulates. Vapor and gas molecules usually penetrate deeply into the molecular spaces throughout the sorbent and are held there chemically. Absorbents do not have as large a specific surface area as do adsorbing media. Furthermore, absorption tends to be slower than adsorption, which occurs instantaneously. Most absorbents are used for protection against acid gases. They include mixtures of sodium or potassium hydroxide with lime and/or caustic silicates.

3. *Catalysts* increase the rate of chemical reaction between substances without themselves changing. One catalyst used in respirator cartridges is hopcalite, a mixture of porous granules of manganese and copper oxides. A common ratio is approximately 3:1 manganese dioxide/copper oxide. In cartridges that remove carbon monoxide, hopcalite speeds the reaction between carbon monoxide and oxygen to form carbon dioxide.

Within the respirator cartridge, vapor and gas removal is essentially 100% efficient until the sorbent's capacity to adsorb vapor and gas (or catalyze specific reactions) is exhausted. Then the contaminant will pass completely through the sorbent and into the facepiece. This dangerous phenomenon is termed *breakthrough*.

Powered APRs

Breathing in ambient air through an APR takes effort on the part of the user such that it may eventually result in user fatigue. A powered air-purifying respirator (PAPR) uses a blower to force ambient air through the cartridge to the wearer (Figure 10.7). PAPRs reduce the burden caused by drawing air through the filter element, thereby allowing the wearer to breathe with less difficulty.

PAPRs have been designed in several different configurations. One consists of the air-purifying element(s) attached to a small blower that is worn on the belt and connected to the respiratory inlet by a flexible tube. The device is usually powered by a small battery, either mounted separately on the belt or as part of the blower. Some units are powered by an external DC or AC source. Another type of PAPR consists of a helmet or facepiece to which the air-purifying element and blower are attached. The battery is carried on the belt.

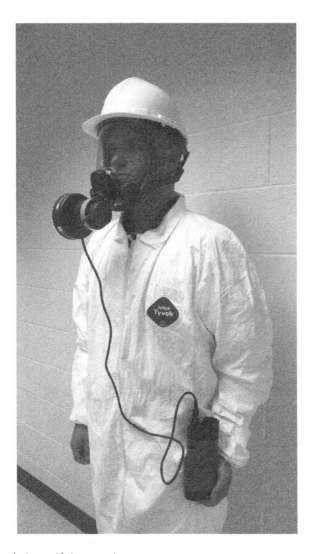

Figure 10.7   Powered air purifying respirator.

Supplied Atmosphere Respirators

Supplied atmosphere respirators provide clean breathing air separate from the local atmosphere, rather than removing contaminants from ambient air. Such respirators are tight-fitting, and are classified by the method used to supply air and the way in which the air supply is regulated. The principal classes of atmosphere-supplying respirators are self-contained breathing apparatus (SCBA) and supplied-air respirators (SARs).

   1. The SCBA (Figure 10.8) is similar to a scuba tank. Air is supplied from a compressed air cylinder that is worn on the back, into a full-face mask. This generally allows greater movement than an SAR; however, the air supply is limited,

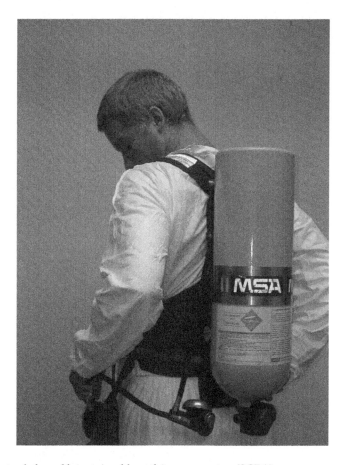

Figure 10.8 Air tank for self-contained breathing apparatus (SCBA).

typically to 30–60 min. These times may be cut in half with moderate to heavy workloads.

2. SARs (also called *airline respirators*) usually involve a face mask or hood connected by a hose to a stationary source of compressed air. The air is delivered continuously in a sufficient volume to meet the wearer's breathing requirements. There are limitations as to the length of the hose connection—most airline hoses extend no farther than 300 ft. There are also dangers of damage to or crimping of the hose.

Airflow Regulators

Regulators within atmosphere-supplying respirators provide three types of airflow: demand (negative pressure regulator), pressure demand (positive pressure regulator), and continuous flow.

In a demand regulator, the air supply valve stays closed as long as there is positive pressure in the facepiece (during exhalation). Inhalation creates negative pressure in the facepiece and the supply valve opens, allowing air into the facepiece. In other words, air flows into the facepiece only on *demand* by the wearer.

A pressure-demand or positive pressure regulator is similar to a demand type except for a spring that holds the supply valve slightly open, theoretically allowing continual air flow into the facepiece. A combination of modified regulator and special exhalation valve is designed to maintain positive pressure in the facepiece at all times. As a result of the positive pressure, any leakage should be outward; therefore, a pressure demand system provides excellent respiratory protection to the wearer.

Continuous-flow regulators maintain airflow at all times, rather than only on demand. By design, either the control valve cannot be closed completely, or a continually open bypass is provided to allow air to flow around the valve, maintaining a positive flow rate. Continuous-flow regulators are used only with SAR, not SCBAs.

THE PPE ENSEMBLE

There is no single *PPE suit* that is appropriate for all situations. Selection of PPE must include an ensemble of clothing and equipment that are integrated to provide both an appropriate level of protection and still allow the responder to carry out activities involving hazardous materials. The primary components that may comprise the chemical protective ensemble are as follows:

- Protective clothing (suit, coveralls, hoods, gloves, boots)
- Respiratory equipment (SCBA, APR)
- Cooling system (ice vest, air circulation, water circulation)
- Communications device
- Head protection (hard hat)
- Eye protection
- Ear protection
- Inner garment
- Outer protection (overgloves, overboots, flashcover)

Levels of Protection

The U.S. Environmental Protection Agency, in collaboration with the Occupational Health and Safety Administration, has established four levels of protection in an occupational environment that are labeled A, B, C, and D. The levels described below are not strict ensembles and should be used as guidelines only; the levels should be adjusted to meet the needs of the responder and the situation.

Level A
The Level A ensemble provides the highest level of respiratory, skin, and eye protection from solid, liquid, and gaseous chemicals. Level A includes a pressure-demand full-face SCBA, inner and outer chemical-resistant gloves, and chemical-resistant safety boots (Figure 10.9). Two-way radio communication is strongly recommended for this ensemble, as ordinary verbal communication is extremely difficult through the suit.

Figure 10.9 (See color insert.) Two examples of Level A PPE. (From U.S. Army Dugway Proving Ground. With permission.)

Level A is necessary in situations where the composition of the atmosphere is unknown. Level A is also used when the composition of the atmosphere has been identified and is found to pose a significant hazard to the respiratory system, skin, and eyes. The Level A ensemble is also required for operations conducted in oxygen-deficient locations, for example confined spaces or other poorly ventilated areas.

Optional components for the Level A ensemble may include a cooling system (e.g., an ice vest; Figure 10.10), outer gloves, and a hard hat.

It is obvious that the Level A suit must resist permeation by the chemicals present at the response site. In addition, ensemble components must allow integration without loss of performance; for example, a respirator must fit within the hood of the Level A suit.

Level B

The Level B suit is used when the chemical(s) in the response zone have been identified and do not require a high degree of skin protection. The primary hazards associated with

Figure 10.10 Ice vest for PPE ensemble. (From U.S. Army Dugway Proving Ground. With permission.)

Figure 10.11 Level B PPE.

site entry are from liquid and not vapor contact. Level B provides the same level of respiratory protection as Level A, but less skin protection.

The Level B ensemble includes a liquid splash-protective suit, a pressure-demand, full-facepiece SCBA, inner chemical-resistant gloves, and chemical-resistant safety boots (Figure 10.11). As with the Level A suit, a two-way radio communication system is appropriate.

Level C
The Level C ensemble is used when contact with site chemicals will not affect the skin. In addition, airborne contaminants have been identified and their concentrations measured, and concentrations are less than immediately dangerous to life and health levels.

Figure 10.12 Level C PPE. (Courtesy of Nebraska Department of Health & Human Services, http://www.hhs.state.ne.us/images/meth/PPELevel-C.jpg.)

Sufficient oxygen is present (at least 19.5% v/v), and an APR is used to remove the specific atmospheric contaminants. The ensemble includes a protective garment (e.g., a lightweight Tyvek™ suit); a full-facepiece, air-purifying, canister-equipped respirator; chemical-resistant gloves; and safety boots (Figure 10.12).

The degree of skin protection provided by the Level C ensemble is the same as in Level B; however, a lower level of respiratory protection is provided, via the APR. Level C provides minimal liquid splash protection and minimal protection against chemical vapors or gases.

Level D

The Level D suit is considered the standard, day-to-day clothing ensemble for responders. Level D is used when the atmosphere contains no known hazard (i.e., the atmosphere must contain at least 19.5% oxygen and concentrations of hazardous constituents are either negligible or below detectable limits). Work functions preclude splashes, immersion, potential for inhalation, or direct contact with hazardous chemicals (Figure 10.13).

The Level D ensemble may include coveralls, safety boots/shoes, safety glasses, or chemical splash goggles. This level is not appropriate for emergency response and should not be worn in the hot zone.

Figure 10.13   Level D personal protective equipment. (Courtesy of U.S. Department of Labor, http://www.osha.gov/SLTC/etools/evacuation/images/firemen_02.jpg.)

Selection of Ensemble Components

What criteria should be used to select a certain level of protection? As we shall see, factors beyond those of the immediate hazardous situation must be considered.

- *Chemical hazards.* Chemicals present a variety of hazards such as toxicity, corrosiveness, flammability, reactivity, and oxygen deficiency. Depending on the chemicals present, any combination of hazards may exist.
- *Physical environment.* The response site can occur in industrial or commercial settings, along highways or in residential areas. Ambient temperatures may be in the extremes, that is, very hot or very cold. The exposure site may be cluttered, presenting physical hazards; activities may involve entering confined spaces, heavy lifting, climbing a ladder, or crawling along the ground. The choice of ensemble components must account for these conditions.

Duration of exposure. The protective qualities of ensemble components may be limited to certain exposure levels. The decision for ensemble use time must be made assuming the worst-case exposure.

Protective clothing or equipment available. Ideally, an array of different clothing and equipment is available to workers to meet all intended applications. Reliance on one particular clothing or equipment item may severely limit an agency's ability to handle a broad range of exposures. When purchasing PPE, the agency should attempt to provide a high degree of flexibility, while choosing protective clothing and equipment that is easily integrated and provides protection against most potential hazards.

Ease of decontamination. The degree of difficulty in decontaminating protective clothing may dictate whether disposable or reusable clothing is used, or a combination of both.

Chemical protective clothing standards. Buyers may wish to specify clothing that meets specific standards, such as 40 CFR 1910.120 or National Fire Protection Association standards.

Cost. Users of protective clothing should obtain the broadest range of ensemble components and protective equipment with available funds to meet their specific application.

Other factors that affect the selection of ensemble components include how each item accommodates the integration of other components. Certain ensemble components may be incompatible (e.g., some SCBAs may not fit within a particular chemical protective suit or provide for acceptable mobility when worn). Another example is the ease of interfacing ensemble components without sacrificing required performance (e.g., a poorly fitting overglove may greatly reduce wearer dexterity). Selection of ensemble components also affects donning time.

Chemical Resistance of PPE

There is no PPE material that is 100% resistant to all hazardous chemicals. When entering the hot zone, the chosen suit material must resist permeation, degradation, and penetration by the contaminant chemicals.

Permeation is the process by which a chemical dissolves in or migrates through a PPE material at the molecular level (Figure 10.14). Typically, there is little visible evidence of chemicals permeating a material.

Permeation breakthrough time is used to assess material compatibility with chemicals. The rate of permeation is a function of several factors, including chemical concentration, material thickness, humidity, and temperature. Most material testing is carried out using a concentrated form of a chemical over an extended exposure period. The time it takes for the test chemical to permeate through the material is termed the *breakthrough time*. A material is considered acceptable for use in emergency response situations when the breakthrough time exceeds the expected period of PPE use. However, the effects of temperature and pressure may accelerate permeation and reduce the safety factor.

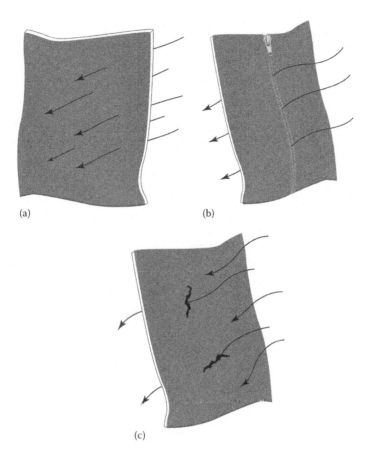

Figure 10.14 Permeation versus penetration in PPE fabric: (a) Permeation at the molecular level; (b) penetration through the zipper; (c) penetration through cracks in PPE material.

Penetration is the movement of chemicals through zippers, seams, or imperfections in PPE material.

Degradation is the result of a chemical reaction between the contaminant and the protective material. Degradation involves physical changes in the material as a result of chemical exposure, routine use, or exposure to natural conditions (e.g., sunlight). The most commonly observed material degradation effects include discoloration, swelling, loss of physical strength, or deterioration. Degradation can cause PPE material to shrink or swell, or become brittle or too soft. Such changes may enhance permeation or allow penetration of the contaminant.

Published data are available that indicate the relative effectiveness of various protective materials against generic classes of chemicals (Table 10.1). Most data tables only reflect the ability to resist degradation, however. Such tables are useful when used with discretion and when the degree of hazard is properly evaluated.

Table 10.1 Selected Commercial Products Used in Manufacturing PPE

Trade Name	Manufacturer	Description
4H™	Safety 4, Inc.	Multilayer laminate of polyethylene and ethylene-vinyl alcohol. Offers protection against exposure to many chemicals and mixtures.
Barricade™	DuPont	A chemical barrier fabric (multilayer laminate) that provides excellent chemical resistance.
Chemrel™	Chemron UK	Multilayered film barrier composites, laminated onto a soft polypropylene substrate; encapsulated suits made from different Chemrel™ fabrics are available providing protection against different chemicals and gases.
Kevlar™	DuPont	Aramid (aromatic polyamide) fiber—tough textile fiber used in protective clothing where resistance to cuts, heat, bullets or flying fragments is needed.
Nomex™	DuPont	High temperature–resistant aramid (aromatic polyamide) fiber; resistant to a wide range of industrial chemicals and solvents.
Responder™	Life-Guard	Multifilm material designed to offer a high degree of permeation resistance to a broad range of chemicals; also used in level A protective suits.
Saranex™	Dow Chemical Company	Multilayer coextruded film made from polyethylene, polyvinylidene chloride, and ethylene-vinyl acetate. Used as a coating for protective clothing.
Silver Shield™	Siebe North Inc.	A laminate material that offers excellent protection against a wide range of chemicals and solvents but does not have good cut-resistance. Can be used as an inner glove to enhance protection where cuts/mechanical damage are likely.
Teflon™	DuPont	Fluorocarbon polymers made from tetrafluoroethylene or from a mixture of tetrafluoroethylene and hexafluoropropylene. Has excellent chemical and thermal resistance but poor physical strength properties; is combined with other materials in protective clothing.
Trellchem™	Trelleborg Protective Products AB	Trade name of a range of chemical protective suits. All are made with a polyamide fabric coated with different materials for the outside and inside layers offering protection against exposure to wide range of chemicals; some suits meet NFPA flammability test criteria. Examples of Trellchem materials: Trellchem HPS (High Performance Suit)™—Viton and butyl rubber outside, and a polymer barrier laminate inside.

(Continued)

332

Table 10.1 (Continued)   Selected Commercial Products Used in Manufacturing PPE

Trade Name	Manufacturer	Description
		Trellchem VPS (Vapor Barrier Suit)™—chloroprene rubber outside and a polymer barrier laminate inside.
		Trellchem Super™—Viton™ and butyl rubber outside and butyl rubber inside.
		Trellchem Butyl™—butyl rubber outside and inside.
		Trellchem Light™—polyvinyl chloride outside and inside.
		Trellchem TLU™—polymer barrier laminate outside and inside.
		Trellchem TLU-A™—ensemble comprising an aluminized fiberglass fabric cover and a Trellchem TLU suit.
Tychem™	DuPont	Offers protection against exposure to wide range of chemicals and is more tear- and puncture-resistant than Barricade™ material.
Viton™	DuPont Dow Elastomers	Series of synthetic fluororubbers, elastomers based on polymers made from hexafluoropropylene and vinylidene fluoride or vinyl fluoride; other fluorocarbons may be used in some Viton™ products.
Zetex™	Newtex	Clothing products are woven from highly texturized silica yarns—an alternative to asbestos for gloves, etc., for protection against heat, flames and sparks.

Source: Canadian Centre for Occupational Health & Safety, Personal protective clothing—Trade names, manufacturers, 2005. http://www.ccohs.ca/oshanswers/prevention/ppe/trade_name.html.

PPE Material Types

Decades of research have been devoted to engineering materials that can withstand chemicals ranging from simple industrial products to complex mixtures to highly destructive chemical weapons.

Table 10.1 lists the names of some commercial products used in the manufacture of certain personal protective clothing (e.g., gloves, suits). The list in Table 10.1 is not intended to be comprehensive.

Limitations with PPE Use

Wearing PPE is not without some inherent drawbacks. A number of practical factors must be considered when choosing PPE for a response activity.

- *Communication.* Talking to team members while wearing PPE is difficult. This problem is especially apparent in the Level A ensemble, when the responder's face is covered with at least two layers—the respirator mask and the encapsulating suit. Communications systems (i.e., push-to-talk radios) are extremely useful in such situations. Otherwise, hand signals are imperative. All signals must be agreed upon (and practiced) before site entry.

- *Recognition of team members.* During a response, problems may arise with recognition of support personnel; for example, when the entry team is suited up, how to recognize who is in charge? Also, entry teams will want to recognize each member. To alleviate this problem, duct tape of a specific color or labeled using a marker can identify team members. The Team Leader may have a separate label on his/her shoulder or hood.

Other Practical Considerations

- *Donning.* Properly donning PPE takes time. It is useful, if not essential, to have a team member (a *buddy*) to assist in donning PPE.
- *Dexterity.* Dexterity is greatly impaired by donning multiple pairs of gloves. It is therefore imperative for responders to prepare as much of their supplies and equipment as possible before entry into the hot zone. For example, fill in spaces on forms; have evidence labels clearly marked; peel back the outer layer of selected packaging.
- *Mobility.* When wearing PPE, movements are slow and sometimes difficult.
- *Impaired vision.* Due to the often narrow facepiece, peripheral vision is impaired.

Beyond the above practical difficulties are several significant risks associated with PPE use. Heat stress can occur even when working in a cold environment. Level A and B ensembles do not allow for loss of perspiration (and hence cooling of the body). It is important to monitor core body temperature and blood pressure of all entry team members, both before and after response work. Team members must be sure to watch their buddies for any sign of heat stress. Psychological stress may also come into play during a response. Heavy, multiple-layer PPE can trigger a claustrophobic reaction in some. In others, there is the simple fear of not being able to get out of their suits without assistance.

SITE CONTROL

Site control involves the establishment of specific work zones during response to a hazardous incident. The goals of site control are to minimize potential contamination of workers, protect the public from site hazards, and prevent unauthorized persons from accessing a site affected by a WMD incident.

A number of site control procedures should be implemented to reduce worker and public exposure to WMD hazards, for example:

- Draft a site map
- Establish work zones
- Establish site security measures
- Establish decontamination procedures for personnel and equipment

The degree of site control depends on the type of hazard, site characteristics, and proximity to surrounding populations. The site control program should be established during the planning stages of a response; it is modified based on new information and site assessments as the response proceeds.

Site Map

A site map indicating the actual hazards (e.g., fires, chemical releases, presence of WMDs), topographic features, prevailing wind direction, drainage, and location of structures is valuable for

- Planning activities
- Assigning personnel to specific duties
- Identifying access routes, evacuation routes, and problem areas
- Identifying areas that require use of PPE

The map must be prepared prior to site entry and updated throughout the response operation to indicate

- Location of immediate hazards (e.g., improvised explosive devices, hazardous chemicals, fires)
- Changes in site activities
- Hazards not previously identified
- New equipment and materials brought to the site
- Current and predicted weather conditions

To reduce the accidental spread of hazardous substances by workers from the contaminated area to the clean area, zones are delineated indicating where specific operations will occur; in addition, the flow of personnel among the zones must be controlled. The establishment of work zones will help ensure that personnel are properly protected against the hazards present where they are working; in addition, work activities and contamination are confined to the appropriate areas. With established work zones, personnel can be located and evacuated in an emergency (OSHA, n.d.).

Work zones at an incident include:

- Exclusion zone (hot zone), that is, the contaminated area
- Contamination reduction zone (warm zone), the area where decontamination takes place
- Support zone (cold zone), the uncontaminated area where workers should not be exposed to hazardous conditions

Delineation of zones is based on factors including visual observation, sampling and monitoring results, wind direction, and evaluation of potential routes of contaminant dispersion in the event of a release. Movement of personnel and equipment among these zones should be minimized and restricted to specific access control points to prevent cross-contamination. A layout of work zones for a hypothetical WMD event is shown in Figure 10.15.

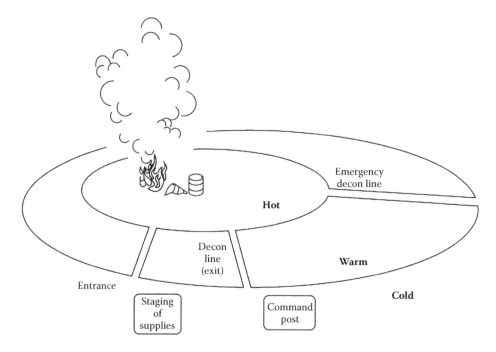

Figure 10.15 Work zones for a hypothetical WMD incident.

Work Zones

Exclusion Zone

The exclusion zone (hot zone) is the area of immediate hazard; this is where contamination occurs (or may occur). Activities performed in the hot zone relevant to WMD/terrorism response include:

- Site characterization, such as mapping, photographing, and collecting samples
- Extrication of victims
- Site cleanup, including removal of hazards
- Detoxification of structures
- Cleanup work, such as moving drums containing hazardous materials

The outer boundary of the exclusion zone, termed the Hotline, should be established according to the criteria listed below. The line should be clearly marked by hazard tape, cones, and/or signs. Access control points are established at the periphery of the exclusion zone to regulate the flow of personnel and equipment into and out of the zone. When feasible, separate entrances and exits should be established to separate personnel and equipment movement into and out of the exclusion zone.

Criteria for establishing the hotline (U.S. DOL, n.d.):

- Visual survey of the immediate site environs
- Determine locations of

- Hazardous materials
- Drainage, leachate, and spilled material
- Visible discoloration of soil, plants, structures, etc.
- Evaluate data from the initial site survey indicating the presence of
  - Combustible gases
  - Organic and inorganic gases, particulates, or vapors
  - Ionizing radiation
- Evaluate the results of soil and water sampling
- Consider the distances needed to prevent an explosion or fire from affecting personnel outside the hot zone
- Consider the physical area necessary for site operations
- Consider meteorological conditions and the potential for contaminants to be dispersed from the area

Personnel working in the exclusion zone may include the Field Team Leader, work teams, and specialized personnel such as heavy equipment operators. All personnel within the exclusion zone must wear the level of protection required by a Site Safety Plan.

Contamination Reduction Zone

The contamination reduction zone, also known as the warm zone, is the transition area between the contaminated area and the clean area (cold zone). The purpose of the warm zone is for decontamination of those responders exiting the hot zone, thus reducing the probability of carrying contamination into the cold zone.

Decontamination procedures take place in a designated area within the warm zone called the contamination reduction corridor, or decon corridor. At least two lines of decontamination stations should be set up within the decon corridor, that is, one for personnel and one for equipment. Access into and out of the warm zone from the hot zone is through access control points. An emergency decon corridor should be established in the event of an accident along the original decon corridor.

The warm zone must be designed to manage:

- Decontamination of equipment, personnel, and samples.
- Emergency response—transport for injured personnel (safety harness, stretcher), first aid equipment, containment equipment (absorbents).
- Worker temporary rest area—toilet facilities, chairs, liquids, and shade. Drinking, washing, and toilet facilities should be located in a safe area.
- Drainage of water and other liquids used during decontamination.

Personnel within the warm zone should be required to maintain internal communications, line-of-sight contact with work parties, work party monitoring (e.g., for air time left, fatigue, heat stress, hypothermia), and site security.

Support Zone

The Support Zone (cold zone) is the location of the administrative and other support functions needed to keep the operations in the hot and warm zones running smoothly. The

Table 10.2   Activities Carried Out in the Cold Zone

Facility	Function
Command Post	Supervision of all field operations and field teams.
	Maintenance of communications, including emergency lines of communication.
	Recordkeeping, including: – Accident reports – Chain-of-custody records – Daily logbooks – Manifest directories and orders – Medical records – Personnel training records – Site inventories – Site safety map – Up-to-date Site Safety Plans
	Providing access to up-to-date safety and health manuals and other reference materials.
	Interfacing with the public: government agencies, local politicians, medical personnel, the media, and other interested parties.
	Monitoring work schedules and weather changes.
	Maintaining site security.
	Sanitary facilities.
Medical Station	First aid administration.
	Medical emergency response.
	Medical monitoring activities.
	Sanitary facilities.
Equipment and Supply Centers	Supply, maintenance, and repair of communications, respiratory, and sampling equipment.
	Maintenance and repair of vehicles.
	Replacement of expendable supplies.
	Storage of monitoring equipment and supplies. Storage may be here or in an onsite field laboratory.
Administration	Sample shipment.
	Interface with home office.
	Maintenance of emergency telephone numbers, evacuation route maps, and vehicle keys.
	Coordination with transporters, disposal sites, and appropriate federal, state, and local regulatory agencies.

(Continued)

Table 10.2 (Continued)   Activities Carried Out in the Cold Zone

Facility	Function
Field Laboratory	Coordination and processing of environmental and hazardous waste samples. Copies of the sampling plans and procedures should be available for quick reference in the laboratory.
	Packaging of materials for analysis after the decontamination of the outsides of the sample containers, which should be done in the CRZ.
	Shipping papers and chain-of-custody files should be kept in the Command Post.
	Maintenance and storage of laboratory notebooks in designated locations in the laboratory while in use, and in the Command Post when not in use.

Source: U.S. Department of Labor, Occupational Safety and Health Administration, Site Control, n.d. https://www.osha.gov/Publications/complinks/OSHG-HazWaste/9-10.pdf.

Command Post Supervisor should be present in the cold zone. Other personnel present will depend on the functions being performed. Activities carried out in the cold zone are listed in Table 10.2.

Personnel may wear normal work clothes within the cold zone. Any potentially contaminated clothing, equipment, and samples must remain in the warm zone until decontaminated.

Site Security
Site security is necessary to

- Prevent the exposure of unauthorized, unprotected people to site hazards.
- Avoid interference with safe working procedures.
- Prevent theft.

To maintain site security during working hours:

- Maintain security in the cold zone and at access control points.
- Establish an identification system to identify authorized persons.
- Erect a fence or other physical barrier around the site.
- If the site is not fenced, post signs around the perimeter and use guards to patrol the perimeter.

Guards must be trained to be fully aware of the hazards involved and trained in emergency procedures. Trained site personnel must accompany visitors at all times; visitors must be provided with appropriate protective equipment.

To maintain site security during off-duty hours:

- Install warning signs and fences to prevent exposure to site hazards of unauthorized and unprotected people.
- If necessary, use security guards to patrol the site boundary.
- Enlist the local police department if the site presents a significant risk to local health and safety.
- Secure all equipment.

DECONTAMINATION

Decontamination may be defined as the reduction or removal of chemical or biological agents so they are no longer hazardous. Agents may be removed by physical means, they may be neutralized chemically, or they may be detoxified. Decontamination processes may be labeled based on who or what is being treated:

- Oneself—personal decon
- Victims—casualty decon
- Responders—personnel decon
- Equipment and structures

In the event of a mass casualty incident (e.g., CBRNE attack or accidental release of an industrial chemical), decontamination should be performed before victims are transported to a hospital. Hospitals should not accept patients who have not been thoroughly decontaminated, as they could possibly introduce hazardous substances to the facility.

Many hospitals and hazmat (hazardous materials) response teams have limited experience in handling large numbers of persons exposed to hazardous chemicals. During a WMD event, where scores or possibly hundreds of victims may require attention, a typical city hazmat team will not possess the necessary numbers of personnel and equipment. At a mass casualty incident, persons of all ages and both sexes will be affected. Victims may show symptoms of exposure to CBRNE materials and have traumatic injuries. In addition, victims may have preexisting medical conditions, be untrained in emergency response, multilingual, or under extreme mental stress, all of which will complicate a decontamination process.

TYPES OF DECONTAMINATION

Several decontamination approaches are available, depending on the incident and the persons or equipment exposed. The types of decontamination to be discussed in this section include mass, emergency, secondary, technical, and equipment.

Mass Decontamination

Mass decontamination refers to the rapid physical removal of agent from the skin of many contaminated victims, typically referring to the general public (i.e., not responders) (Figure 10.16). Other terms associated with mass decontamination are emergency, gross, and immediate. The mass decon procedure must be performed as quickly as possible. A low-pressure, high-volume water system is recommended. High-pressure water systems are discouraged because contaminants may be forced into the victim's skin, or spread further over the victim. High-pressure sprays can also spread contamination to the local environment.

One of the most effective methods for providing mass decontamination for large numbers of contaminated victims is the use of elevated master streams that use fog nozzles

Figure 10.16 Mass decontamination. (From the Santa Clara County Fire Department. With permission.)

operating at low pressure to shower the victims. The ladder-pipe decontamination system has been shown to be highly effective for mass decontamination (Figure 10.17). A decon line using multiple hoses allows for a long corridor for decontamination that can accommodate numerous victims.

Other effective mass decontamination methods make use of facilities such as chlorinated swimming pools, school shower facilities, car washes, or other locally available facilities for rapid decontamination (U.S. DHS, 2007).

Figure 10.17 Mass decontamination of civilians using ladder-pipe system. (Reproduced from Global Security.org, http://www.globalsecurity.org/security/system/mvdecomtam.htm. With permission.)

341

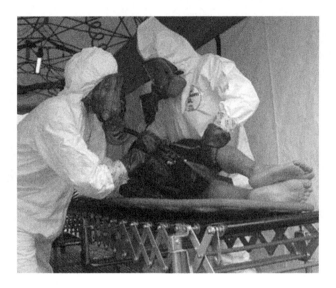

Figure 10.18 (See color insert.) Secondary decon of a victim. (Courtesy of Alaska Department of Environmental Conservation, http://www.dec.state.ak.us/SPAR/perp/gallery/MassDeconJune2007 /images/MassDecon_June2007_p009.jpg.)

Secondary Decontamination

Secondary decontamination is performed following mass decon and is performed on an as-needed basis. If a victim has received proper decontamination treatment and continues to display symptoms of contamination, a secondary decon may be necessary. This procedure may be applied only to limited areas of the body and is more thorough than mass decontamination (Figure 10.18).

Secondary decon may consist of one to several stations, depending on the degree of hazard. A decontamination team must be present to assist in the handling of victims and to supervise the operation. To control the spread of contaminants, low-pressure water should be used and overspraying and splashing should be kept to a minimum. The decontamination corridor should be established in a location where runoff can be contained and controlled.

Emergency Decontamination

Emergency decontamination can occur at any time during an incident response. Should an emergency occur during a response action (e.g., a responder collapses while carrying out assigned duties), immediate steps must be taken to manage the emergency, while practicing contamination avoidance. Speed is crucial in emergency decon.

Technical Decontamination

Technical decontamination refers to the planned cleaning of response personnel and their equipment after they have completed their assigned duties. The goal of technical decon is to completely remove the agent from a responder's PPE. Responders are cleaned using brushes, hoses, water and soap, and so on (Figure 10.19). Technical decontamination should be performed on responders with their arms out and their legs apart (i.e., the *star* configuration; Figure 10.20). The responder should be washed from the top down; hence, elevated wash systems such as overhead showers are useful. Technical decontamination is not time-constrained—there is no need to rush through the process. Technical decontamination should be conducted in a location separated visually from victim decontamination.

Figure 10.19 Technical decontamination of emergency responders. (Courtesy of FEMA, http://www.photolibrary.fema.gov/photolibrary/photo_details.do?id=16934.)

Figure 10.20 **(See color insert.)** *Star* configuration used in emergency decon.

Equipment Decontamination

Decontamination is not limited to victims and responders; all equipment that had entered the hot zone must also be decontaminated. Many such items pose practical problems.

Air monitoring and sampling equipment are often fragile and extremely sensitive to environmental conditions; for example, an atmosphere rich in hydrocarbon or acid vapors may permanently damage sensors and render the equipment inoperable. Such equipment is also difficult to clean without damaging, once it has been contaminated. Therefore, before entering the hot zone, personnel should carefully wrap sensitive instrumentation in plastic such that it will operate correctly (Figure 10.21).

Trucks, bulldozers, backhoes, or other heavy machinery may require decontamination in certain situations. Such equipment is decontaminated using a high-pressure water wash, steam cleaning, and/or hand scrubbing with a decontamination solution (Figure 10.22). Runoff from the area must be captured by the prior installation of plastic tarp in the decon zone. In addition, a sump system may be installed. Wipe tests of equipment are recommended to determine the success of decontamination.

Area Decontamination

Surfaces may be slightly contaminated in a limited number of locations (e.g., pavement and building walls). In the case of surficial contamination, site cleanup may take the form of high-pressure spray-washing using specialized cleaning agents to loosen contaminants for collection and treatment (Figure 10.23).

A series of stringent decontamination procedures were used at the Reston, Virginia Primate Facility where 450 monkeys were destroyed when the Ebola virus was discovered (Peters and Olshaker, 1997; U.S. DHS, 1995). The monkeys were disposed and supplies were incinerated, and all particulate matter was scraped from surfaces. Surfaces and

Figure 10.21 Wrapping sensitive air monitoring equipment in plastic will ensure that the instrument is not damaged in a hazardous atmosphere.

Figure 10.22 Equipment decontamination. (Courtesy of Department of Military Affairs, Wisconsin, http://dma.wi.gov/DMA/news/2015news/15062.)

Figure 10.23 Decontamination of cars of the Tokyo Metro after the 1995 sarin attacks. (Courtesy of Environmental Health Perspectives, http://ehp.niehs.nih.gov/docs/2001/109-11/gas.jpg.)

drains were subsequently drenched with bleach. Thirty-nine electric frying pans were placed on timers and filled with paraformaldehyde mixed with water. Every seam in the building was taped and the paraformaldehyde was boiled off with a target concentration of 10,000 ppm. The building was put up for sale but eventually demolished (Muller Vogt and Sorensen, 2002).

Decontaminating the monkey fecal matter was a difficult process. The U.S. Army Medical Research Institute of Infectious Diseases proposed to soak the fecal matter in Clorox® and dispose of it in the sewer. However, Virginia environmental officials objected to sending large volumes of disinfectant down the sewer. Permission was finally given to proceed with the disposal when the Army stated that they would leave it for the state to dispose of (Muller Vogt and Sorensen, 2002).

DECONTAMINATION MEDIA

An ideal decontaminant will rapidly and completely remove or detoxify all known chemical and biological warfare agents from clothing, PPE, and skin (Baker, 1985; Chang, 1984; Hurst, 1997). Desirable traits of a skin decontaminant are listed below. A range of substances, many of which are commercially available, have been evaluated for possible use in decontamination of both PPE and skin. Household products have been investigated for decontamination of civilians and soldiers; for example, timely use of water alone, soap and water, or baking flour followed by wet tissue wipes have proven effective.

Desirable aspects of a skin decontaminant (Chang, 1984):

- Neutralizes all chemical and biological agents
- Is safe (i.e., nontoxic and noncorrosive)
- Applied easily by hand
- Readily available
- Acts rapidly
- Produces no toxic end-products
- Stable in long-term storage
- Stable in the short-term (i.e., after application)
- Inexpensive
- Does not enhance agent absorption through skin
- Is nonirritating
- Is hypoallergenic
- Easily disposed with no hazardous residues

Decontaminants must be acquired and stocked well in advance of any incident. They must be accessible, clearly labeled, and routinely tested for viability (i.e., strength). Responder training must stress the importance of decontaminants, application methods, and possible risks of use (e.g., skin irritation). Several effective decontamination solutions are discussed next.

Soap and Water

Both freshwater and seawater physically remove chemical agents from the body and from PPE; additionally, they serve to both dilute the contaminant and initiate hydrolysis of toxins. Unfortunately, however, chemical warfare agents tend to be of low solubility; therefore, water alone tends to limit agent hydrolysis rate (Chang and Ciegler, 1986).

When soap, particularly an alkaline formulation, is used with water, the rate of chemical hydrolysis reactions increases. Soap and water serves as an effective and inexpensive decon solution. Whereas some personal decontamination solutions irritate the skin, are toxic and/or costly, soap and water pose no such problems for decontamination. According to the U.S. Army Medical Research Institute of Chemical Defense, timely use of soap and water followed by wet tissue wipes produced results equal to—or, in some instances, better than—those produced by the use of Fuller's Earth, Dutch Powder, and other decontamination compounds (U.S. DHS, 2007).

Sodium Hypochlorite

Sodium hypochlorite, the active ingredient in household bleach, is highly favored for disinfecting tools, equipment, and structures. Dilute hypochlorite solution should be made fresh daily with a pH in the alkaline range (pH 10–11).

Although dilute hypochlorite (0.5%) is an effective skin decontaminant, most responders have discontinued the use of bleach because of skin irritation. This effect is attributed to the oxidizing and corrosive properties of the hypochlorite ion. Concentrated mixtures may cause corneal injuries. Emergency responders must abide by jurisdictional requirements and consult with medical personnel to determine whether to use bleach for patient decontamination.

Absorbents

Commercially available materials may be used to remove gross chemical contamination from surfaces. Several nonaqueous (i.e., without water) materials provide for contaminant removal, and are available in dry, gelled, or powdered forms. Common absorbents include soil, flour, Fuller's earth, baking powder, sawdust, charcoal, ash, activated carbon, silica gels, and clays. The effectiveness of these materials in removing contaminants varies substantially. Contamination transferred to the absorbent material must be treated as contaminated waste and disposed appropriately.

The U.S. Department of Defense uses the M-291 and M-295 Skin Decontamination Kits, which use a charcoal-based resin absorbent. The M-291 kit is considered highly effective as a dry decontaminant for skin (see Box 10.1). Both the M-291 and M-295 kits are effective in removing localized spots of liquid chemical agent; in other words, they may not be suitable for treating mass casualties. The small size of the decontamination pad and the time needed to clean large amounts of contamination from a victim may also limit its utility in the field.

Dry Powder Decontaminant

Some decontaminants incorporate dry powders for the absorption of toxins; for example, FAST-ACT®, a powder developed by NanoScale Materials, is designed to remove and chemically treat toxic chemical hazards. FAST-ACT is proven to remove more than 99.6% of VX, GD (soman), and HD (sulfur mustard) from surfaces in less than 90 s, converting the agents to relatively safe by-products. FAST-ACT has also been demonstrated to neutralize acids and other toxic industrial chemicals such as caustic gases, phosphorus compounds, and some organics (U.S. DHS, 2007).

It should be noted that natural processes may enhance decontamination. For example, high temperatures tend to increase the rate of chemical degradation. Agents may become dispersed by the wind, thus reducing concentrations on skin and PPE. Moisture (e.g., rain) tends to dissolve and sometimes break down chemical agents. In contrast, biological agents dehydrate in low humidity. The ultraviolet light occurring in sunlight may also serve to inactivate microbial pathogens and decompose certain toxins.

BOX 10.1   THE M-291 RESIN KIT

The M-291 Skin Decontamination Kit consists of a wallet-like carrying pouch containing six individual tear-open decontamination packets. This is sufficient to carry out three complete skin decontaminations. Each packet includes an applicator pad filled with a nontoxic/nonirritating decontaminating compound, Ambergard XE-555 resin (Rohm and Haas Co., Philadelphia, PA). The M-291 Kit is designed to completely decontaminate the skin through physical removal, absorption, and neutralization of toxic agents (Figure 10.24).

Each pad has a loop that fits over the hand. Holding the pad in one hand, the user scrubs the pad over contaminated skin. The chemical agent is rapidly transferred into and trapped within the resin particles. The presence of acidic and basic groups in the resin promotes the destruction of trapped chemical agents by acid and base hydrolysis (Braue et al., 1997).

Figure 10.24   The M-291 Resin. (Courtesy of the U.S. Army, http://www.army.mil/-images /2008/07/01/18410/army.mil-2008-07-01-153742.jpg.)

THE DECONTAMINATION CORRIDOR

As mentioned earlier, the warm zone contains the decontamination corridor and any access control points through which personnel and equipment enter and exit the hot zone. Key variables affecting the size and design of the warm zone include:

- Physical conditions of the site (topography, drainage, buildings, obstructions, etc.)
- Physical, chemical, and toxicological characteristics of the chemical(s) present
- Contaminant concentrations measured in the field
- Weather conditions including wind direction
- Possible atmospheric dispersion of toxic chemicals as predicted by air dispersion models
- Potential for fire or explosion
- Adequate roads, power sources, and water

Additional factors regarding the site and the equipment to be considered include the following:

- Availability of decontamination supplies and facilities.
- How will nonambulatory persons (handicapped, elderly) be accommodated?
- Handling of animals—are animals contained until after victims are decontaminated?
- Visibility—can all activity within the warm zone be observed?
- Runoff of decontaminants and management of solid and hazardous wastes.

A sample decon corridor is shown in Figure 10.25.

The decon corridor should be of sufficient size within the warm zone and be placed upwind, uphill, and upstream of the hot zone.

Responders should make use of readily available materials and equipment for the setup of the decon corridor. Examples include mobile trailers designed for mass decontamination, portable showers, and children's wading pools. Hoses can be set up overhead in corridors to provide a fine spray for victims to walk through. If a school or community center shower or pool (or even car wash) are accessible, these may be used for decontamination using low-pressure, high-volume water. Equipment has been specifically designed for mass decontamination in which low-pressure, high-volume water sprays or fog nozzles with low pressure can be sprayed onto victims.

DISPOSAL OF CONTAMINATED MATERIAL

All materials and equipment used for decontamination must be properly disposed of. Nondisposable clothing (e.g., respirators, boots, gloves) must be completely decontaminated before removal from the warm zone.

In many incidents responders use disposable clothing. Such items must be bagged and labeled, and placed in drums or other secure containers. These items are to be disposed with other contaminated substances from the site. Additional items used at the incident such as

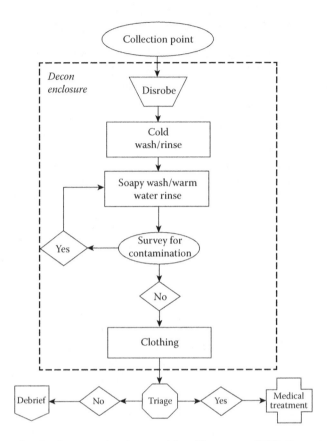

Figure 10.25 Example of a decontamination corridor. (Courtesy of U.S. Department of Homeland Security, Weapons of Mass Destruction, Technical Emergency Response Training, PER-260, Center for Domestic Preparedness, Anniston, AL, 2005.)

brushes, tools, wash, and rinse solutions, which cannot be decontaminated must be secured in drums, labeled and disposed with substances having similar chemical contamination.

Environmental Concerns

Section § 107 (d) (1) of the Comprehensive Environmental Response, Compensation, and Liability Act (CERCLA), is often known as the *Good Samaritan* provision:

> No person shall be liable under this subchapter for costs or damages as a result of actions taken or omitted in the course of rendering care, assistance, or advice in accordance with the National Contingency Plan (NCP) or at the direction of an on-scene coordinator (OSC) appointed under such plan, with respect to an incident creating a danger to public health or welfare or the environment as a result of any releases of a hazardous substance or the threat thereof.

U.S. Environmental Protection Agency, 2000

This provision, however, does not preclude costs for damages caused by "gross negligence or intentional misconduct by the state or local government." Therefore, once all threats to human health or life are managed, responders should immediately make every reasonable effort to contain contamination and to mitigate environmental consequences. During decontamination, the obvious priority is to ensure that all victims are decontaminated. The second priority should be to contain runoff so that it does not contaminate the local environment. The Incident Commander should check with the state environmental agency or the Environmental Protection Agency (EPA) On-Scene Coordinator for guidance regarding disposal options. All areas that had been contaminated should be marked for remediation.

SITE REMEDIATION

Chapters 1 through 8 have addressed the effects of CBRNE attacks and/or industrial releases on human health, and, in the case of nuclear and explosive releases, on structures. At this point, it is necessary to address how to decontaminate a site affected by CBRNE weapons or industrial chemicals. Residual chemicals may pose both short- and long-term effects on human populations and the environment, and must be removed and/or stabilized quickly to prevent harm.

As mentioned earlier, surfaces may only be slightly contaminated in limited locations following a CBRNE release. In more extreme cases, however, contamination may be extensive— chemicals or other toxins may saturate soil and may percolate to significant depths and ultimately contaminate groundwater. Surface water bodies and vegetation may become saturated with toxic chemicals as well. Such sites are contaminated to a point that intensive cleanup (*remediation*) practices are necessary to restore it to a safe and usable condition.

Environmental Site Assessment

The first step involved in effective site remediation is assessment of the degree of hazard. Specifically, this involves identification of site contaminants along with the location of contamination (both aerial and with depth). In the case of actual or suspected long-term industrial releases, the conventional procedure is to conduct a Phase I Environmental Site Assessment (ESA), followed by a Phase II and finally remediation of the site. The Phase I ESA is a study of the historical use of the site and the materials used, generated, and stored on-site. Such information will provide a guideline for eventual sampling and chemical analysis of environmental materials. The Phase II ESA involves detailed sampling of soil, sediments, surface water, groundwater, building materials, and other relevant site attributes to provide an accurate picture of where the chemicals of interest are occurring at the site.

In the case of a single significant release of an agent by a terrorist group or industry, the Phase I ESA can be omitted, as historical information about the site may not be relevant. The Phase II, however, will provide scientists, engineers, and planners with a detailed snapshot of the site regarding soil and geologic attributes, where the contaminants are occurring, and, ultimately, how to remove them. The Phase II will include recommendations as to how to conduct site cleanup (Figure 10.26). On the basis of soil, landscape,

Figure 10.26 Substantial planning among scientists, engineers, planners, and other stakeholders may be required before conducting a remediation activity. (Courtesy of FEMA, http://www.photo library.fema.gov/photolibrary/photo_details.do?id=44793.)

geologic, hydrologic, and numerous other practical considerations, decisions can be made as to how to best address cleanup goals.

Remediation Process

Techniques for removal of a hazardous agent have evolved greatly over the past three decades; gone are the days when soil removal and disposal in a landfill is considered the optimal solution for site restoration. Many innovative technologies use sophisticated engineering systems and may involve use of exotic chemicals and/or extremely high temperatures. Other approaches, however, rely on natural solutions, for example, the use of microorganisms and/or plants to clean a site. This section provides a brief overview of several selected remediation technologies for sites affected by CBRNE agents. The published literature, plus web sites offered by the U.S. EPA, state environmental agencies, and private environmental firms provide many more options.

Selected Technologies

Soil Removal

Among the most straightforward methods to remedy a site affected by hazardous substances is to excavate and relocate the contaminated soil. Backhoes, bulldozers, and other conventional earth-moving equipment remove the soil (Figure 10.27) and transfer it to a secure disposal facility, that is, an engineered landfill equipped with impermeable liners and leak detection systems. Drawbacks to this method are that it is expensive and may actually create new hazards, by causing soil and dust to disperse into the air and be carried significant distances. Ultimately, the contaminant is not truly being destroyed; rather, it is simply being relocated.

Figure 10.27 Soil excavation and removal is often considered a last resort for site remediation. (Courtesy of U.S. Environmental Protection Agency, http://yosemite.epa.gov/R10/CLEANUP .NSF/9f3c21896330b4898825687b007a0f33/c1f04dcab85cd0018825699a00633013/$FILE/Removal +of+Contaminated+Soil.jpg.)

Soil/Sediment Incineration

In cases of contamination with highly toxic yet combustible chemicals (e.g., chemical warfare agents) and biological agents (cultures, spores, etc.), excavated soils can undergo controlled incineration. Incineration units can be permanent facilities, or mobile units can be transported to the affected site. The contaminated media may need to be sieved or otherwise cleared of large debris (logs, tires, etc.) before charging into the unit. The incineration chamber is designed to operate at temperatures sufficiently high to destroy most hydrocarbon compounds (approximately 1600–1800°F, higher for some halogenated substances). It is essential that flue (waste) gases be captured and treated, as necessary, to remove toxins such as halogenated gases, mercury, and other volatile wastes. The residual ash will also need to be tested for potential toxicity and disposed accordingly.

Pump-and-Treat

Should groundwater and/or surface water be contaminated, the water can be extracted by wells and pumps and transported via pipeline to a designated treatment area. Once at the treatment facility, the water can be chemically and/or biologically treated to destroy the contaminants of concern. Treatment may be as simple as applying pulverized limestone (e.g., to neutralize acids) or addition of microbial cultures and oxygen (to destroy certain explosive residues, nerve gases, or other carbon-containing toxins). More complex and/or *recalcitrant* (resistant) compounds can be removed from water by passage through a bed of absorbent material such as activated charcoal or synthetic resin. A key disadvantage of pump-and-treat is that the process may take years for removal of significant contamination from groundwater. Furthermore, only a portion of the contaminant will be removed; much will remain attached (adsorbed) to soil materials such as clay, organic matter, and hydrous iron oxides. These latter contaminant phases require a more rigorous treatment for removal.

Chemical Treatment

Hazardous chemicals can be extracted from the site or they may be fixed in place. The decision depends in part on the toxicity of the contaminants. In the case of VX, a highly toxic nerve agent, which is also highly persistent, it is critical to remove and/or destroy the contaminant. In contrast, if only scattered *hot spots* of a radionuclide occur in soil, the optimal procedure may be to immobilize it in place.

Soil Washing/Flushing

Soils contaminated with toxins can, literally, be washed; in other words, a solution of appropriate chemical formulation is applied to a site to flood it. The goal is for the contaminant to dissolve in the washing solution and percolate downward, where it is collected in strategically placed wells and underdrains (Figure 10.28). This technology is subject to interferences and complications; for example, the contaminant of concern may adsorb tightly to soil and not be readily solubilized by the washing solution; in addition, improper placement of recovery wells may cause the soluble contaminants to migrate off site.

Destruction in Place

Certain contaminants, particularly hydrocarbon-based substances such as explosive residues and nerve gas, may be destroyed by the addition of selected chemicals to soil. Oxidizing or reducing chemicals can be pumped underground directly into the contaminant plume. Ozone (O_3) and concentrated hydrogen peroxide (H_2O_2) are extremely effective for hydrocarbon destruction by the process of oxidation, that is, incorporation of oxygen into the contaminant of concern. Once these additive compounds react with the plume, ideal products would include carbon dioxide and water (plus heat). However, not

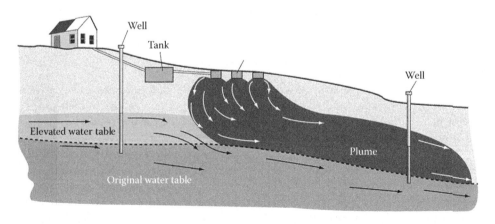

Figure 10.28 Basic soil washing technology. (Courtesy of U.S. Environmental Protection Agency, http://www.epa.gov/nrmrl/pubs/625r00008/html/3-8.gif.)

all contaminants will decompose completely in the presence of oxidizing agents; in some unusual cases, the contaminant will react with an oxidizing agent to generate even more resistant and hazardous chemical forms.

Fixation in Place

For certain compounds that occur in relatively small areas and may be highly toxic (e.g., an accumulation of VX nerve gas or high-level radioactive debris), it may be appropriate to *fix* the material in place. Depending on the chemical composition of the contaminant, solidification/stabilization can take place using fixative materials as simple as Portland cement (for aqueous-based contaminants) or asphalt or polyethylene (for hydrocarbon-based contaminants) (Figure 10.29).

For situations in which the contaminant is extremely toxic and thereby precludes the possibility of removal (e.g., soil affected by plutonium debris), soil can be *vitrified* by heating to extremely high temperatures. A series of electrodes are placed into the ground and a voltage is passed between them. The soil heats to the point that it *fuses* to a bright viscous orange mass (typical temperatures of 2900–3600°F occur) (Pichtel, 2007). Carbon-based contaminants (e.g., chemical weapons, biological agents, explosives) are destroyed in the melt by thermal processes. Potentially hazardous gases that may be released (e.g., fluorine arising from sarin destruction) are captured in a fume hood that is positioned over the work zone. The voltage is subsequently shut off, allowing the mass to cool and harden to a glassy material (Figure 10.30). Those contaminants that are noncombustible (e.g., radio-actives) are securely retained in the glass. Given the very high cost of the technology, its application is limited to situations of contamination by highly toxic substances.

Figure 10.29 Solidification of contaminated soils using Portland cement is highly effective for fixing toxic materials in place. (Courtesy of U.S. Department of Transportation, http://www.fhwa.dot .gov/engineering/geotech/pubs/gec8/images/f120.gif.)

Figure 10.30 Following *in situ* vitrification, the affected soil is converted to a solid block of glass-like material after cooling. (Courtesy of Savannah River National Laboratory, http://srnl.doe.gov /images/vitrification.jpg.)

Biological Treatment

Microbial Remediation

Microorganisms that occur naturally in soils, sediments, and water can be used to decompose hydrocarbon-based contaminants. Soil bacteria and fungi are particularly well suited to degradation of carbonaceous substrates; the microbial cell extracts energy and carbon to support growth. So-called bioremediation processes have been in use for decades to treat sites contaminated with crude oil, fuels, solvent wastes, pesticides, and other toxic and recalcitrant compounds; additionally, bioremediation has shown success in the decomposition of explosives and their residues. It is also feasible to apply bioremediation to soils affected by chemical weapons such as nerve agents and blister agents.

Engineered bioremediation processes may be relatively simple and involve the injection of nutrients and oxygen to indigenous populations of soil microorganisms occurring at the site of contamination. Additives may be applied at a substantial depth below the land surface (Figure 10.31) or directly on the surface. The ultimate goal is for microbial populations to exploit the hydrocarbon contaminant (explosive, VX, sulfur mustard, etc.) as sole carbon source, leaving behind simpler, less toxic compounds such as carbon dioxide and water. A simplified reaction showing the bacterially catalyzed decomposition of trinitrotoluene (TNT) is shown in Figure 10.32.

Current research in biodegradation of toxic chemicals is focusing on identification of organisms or mixed microbial populations with broad degradation capabilities. Much work is being devoted to genetic engineering of bacteria and fungi to accelerate the decomposition of target compounds.

Figure 10.31 Nutrient injection tanks, pumps, and related equipment in a process trailer for an *in situ* bioremediation program. (Courtesy of Pacific Northwest National Laboratory, http://bioprocess .pnnl.gov/projsum/PNNL_SA_32879.Point.Mugu.Demonstration.Project.Summary.htm.)

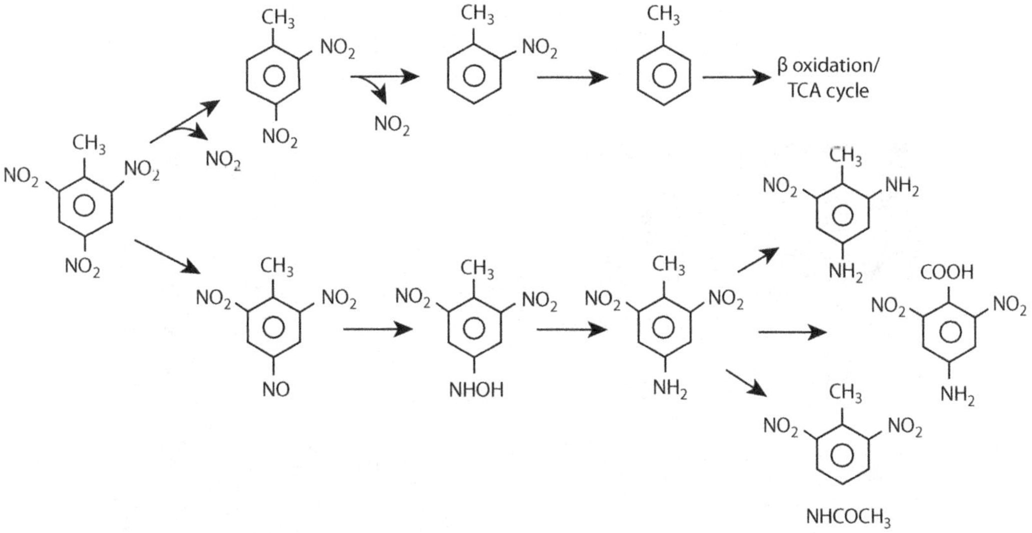

Figure 10.32 Reaction showing the bacterially catalyzed decomposition of TNT.

Phytoremediation

Plant-based remediation (phytoremediation) involves the use of green plants, selected for a specific capability, to remove and/or destroy hazardous compounds in place.

- *Phytoextraction.* Certain plants have been identified with the ability to hyper-accumulate metals such as lead and mercury (both of which occur in primary explosives) (see Chapter 6). Others can hyperaccumulate radioactive metals from soil. Hyperaccumulation is defined as the extraction, uptake, and storage of soil metals in plant tissue in extremely high concentrations (Figure 10.33). The metal- or nuclide-enriched plant tissue must be harvested at the end of the growing season and chemically or physically treated to recover the metals. Treatment may involve ashing followed by acid extraction of the metals, or smelting in a furnace to recover the contaminant of concern. Alternatively, the metal- or nuclide-enriched plant tissue can be compacted and disposed as a hazardous waste.

- *Rhizosphere-enhanced degradation.* Green plants are known to possess highly active microbial populations within the *rhizosphere* (i.e., root zone). In addition, the rhizosphere harbors a much greater microbial diversity (i.e., more microbial types and physiologic processes) compared with nonvegetated soil. In many cases, the microbes present in the root zone carry on the identical reactions discussed above for bioremediation (e.g., breakdown of complex organic compounds); however, rhizosphere microbes proliferate because of the abundance of compounds exuded from the plant root. Microbial reactions may be more rapid and efficient and result in more complete decomposition of the target contaminants as compared to processes in nonvegetated soil. The combined decomposition processes carried out by green plants in concert with soil microbes is termed *rhizosphere-enhanced degradation.*

    Obviously, the success of phytoremediation is limited by depth—the process will work only where roots can effectively reach the contaminant.

Figure 10.33 (See color insert.) Phytoremediation is a very promising, low-cost technology that can be used for the destruction and/or removal of soil contaminants.

Other Innovative Technologies

Extensive research at laboratory, pilot, and field scale continue to offer more effective, efficient, and rapid technologies for the destruction of highly toxic compounds, including various weapons and their debris, in soil, sediments, and groundwater.

Plasma Incineration

Conventional incineration typically works at operational temperatures of 1800–2000°F; however, there are situations in which a highly toxic and/or recalcitrant chemical may require significantly higher temperatures to ensure complete destruction.

A plasma torch produces an arc that contacts a conducting portion of a specialized reactor vessel. The heat generated by the plasma torch brings the feed material to temperatures sufficient to melt soil (typically about 3000°F; however, temperatures as high as 50,000°F have been documented). This intense heat melts contaminated soil, incorporating any inorganic and metal components into a stable material. Organic components are volatilized by the heat of the plasma and oxidized by the air. Oxygen may also be added in a primary chamber to enhance combustion of organics (U.S. EPA, 1992). As with conventional incineration, there is still a need to capture waste gases and ash, which may themselves pose toxicity hazards.

QUESTIONS

1. Explain how permeation of a hazardous chemical into PPE differs from degradation and penetration. Provide examples of each.
2. A wide range of material types are available for PPE, depending in part on the chemicals a responder may encounter. What suit materials are appropriate for exposure to HCl vapors, vinyl chloride vapors, asbestos particles, and CCl_4? Check the web sites of several vendors of PPE to support your response.
3. Complete the table given here. Which level of PPE would be appropriate for the following hazardous situation?

Contaminant in Atmosphere	PPE Level
Unknown	
Nerve agent (sarin)	
Blister agent (sulfur mustard)	
Blood agent (HCN)	
Choking agent (chlorine)	
Biological agent (anthrax spores)	
Radiological particulates	
No contaminant; $[O_2] = 14.5\%$	

4. Compare and contrast the following decontamination modes: mass, technical, and emergency, How do they differ in terms of persons treated? Time constraints?
5. Describe the operation of the M-291 Skin Decontamination Kit. What is the active ingredient, and how does it work?

6. In the mass decon of a large group of males and females, how could you set up a decon system allowing for maximal privacy with minimal availability of supplies? Draw an example of the decon train.

REFERENCES

Baker, J.A. 1985. COR Decontamination/Contamination Control Master Plan Users' Meeting. September 11–13, 1985. Decontamination 353.

Braue, E.H., C.H. Boardman, and C.G. Hurst. 1997. In: *Medical Aspects of Chemical and Biological Warfare*, ed. Sidell, F.R., Takafuji, E.T., and Franz, D.R. Washington, D.C.: Borden Institute Walter Reed Army Medical Center.

Canadian Centre for Occupational Health & Safety. 2005. Personal protective clothing—Trade names, manufacturers. http://www.ccohs.ca/oshanswers/prevention/ppe/trade_name.html (accessed November 1, 2010).

Chang, A.M.H., and A. Ciegler. 1986. Chemical warfare: I. Chemical decontamination. *NBC Defense and Technical International* 1(40): 60.

Hurst, C.G. 1997. Decontamination. In: *Medical Aspects of Chemical and Biological Warfare*, ed. Sidell, F.R., Takafuji, E.T., and Franz, D.R. Washington, DC: Borden Institute Walter Reed Army Medical Center.

Muller Vogt, B., and J.H. Sorensen. 2002. How Clean is Safe? Improving the Effectiveness of Decontamination of Structures and People Following Chemical and Biological Incidents. Oak Ridge National Laboratory. Final Report ORNL/TM-2002/178. Prepared for the U.S. Department of Energy Chemical and Biological National Security Program. Washington, DC.

Peters, C. J., and M. Olshaker. 1997. *Virus Hunters*. New York: Anchor Books (Doubleday).

Pichtel, J. 2007. *Fundamentals of Site Remediation for Metal- and Hydrocarbon-Contaminated Soils*. 2nd Edition. Rockville, MD: Government Institutes, Inc.

U.S. Department of Health and Human Services. 1995. *Proceedings of the Seminar on Responding to the Consequences of Chemical and Biological Terrorism*. Public Health Service, Office of Emergency Preparedness. Uniformed Services University of Health Sciences, Bethesda, MD, July 11–14, 1995.

U.S. Department of Homeland Security. 2007. Weapons of Mass Destruction. Technical Emergency Response Training. Center for Domestic Preparedness. Anniston, AL.

U.S. Department of Justice. 2002. *Guide for the Selection of Personal Protective Equipment for Emergency First Responders. NIJ Guide 102-00*, Volume I. Washington, DC: Office of Justice Programs, National Institute of Justice.

U.S. Department of Labor. Occupational Safety and Health Administration. n.d. Site Control. https://www.osha.gov/Publications/complinks/OSHG-HazWaste/9-10.pdf.

U.S. Environmental Protection Agency. 1992. Retech, Inc., *Plasma Centrifugal Furnace*. EPA/540/A5–91/007. Washington, DC: Office of Research and Development.

U.S. Environmental Protection Agency. 2000. First Responders' Environmental Liability due to Mass Decontamination Runoff. EPA 550-08-009. Office of Solid Waste and Emergency Response, Washington, DC. http://nepis.epa.gov/Exe/ZyNET.exe/P1002ZKP.txt?ZyActionD=ZyDocument&Client=EPA&Index=2000%20Thru%202005&Docs=&Query=&Time=&EndTime=&SearchMethod=1&TocRestrict=n&Toc=&TocEntry=&QField=&QFieldYear=&QFieldMonth=&QFieldDay=&UseQField=&IntQFieldOp=0&ExtQFieldOp=0&XmlQuery=&File=D%3A\ZYFILES\INDEX%20DATA\00THRU05\TXT\00000019\P1002ZKP.txt&User=ANONYMOUS&Password=anonymous&SortMethod=h|-&MaximumDocuments=1&FuzzyDegree=0&ImageQuality=r85g16/r85g16/x150y150g16/i500&Display=p|f&DefSeekPage=x&SearchBack=ZyActionL&Back=ZyActionS&BackDesc=Results%20page&MaximumPages=1&ZyEntry=1.

APPENDIX A: GLOSSARY

Action plan: See **Incident Action Plan**.

Acute exposure: Exposure to a toxic substance that occurs in a short or single period.

Acute toxicity: Any poisonous effect produced by a single short-term exposure. The LD_{50} of a substance is typically used as a measure of the acute toxicity of a substance.

Allotrope: Elements that can exist in two or more different structural forms. In each allotrope, the element's atoms are bonded together in different positions.

Alpha radiation: Form of radiation consisting of two protons plus two neutrons. A relatively heavy, low-energy form of radiation.

al-Qaeda: An international terrorist organization founded in the late 1980s by Osama bin Laden and Muhammad Atef. al-Qaeda calls for the use of violence in bringing about the end of non-Islamic governments, and, in particular, a goal to drive U.S. armed forces out of Muslim lands. Establishing training camps in areas such as Afghanistan, Pakistan, Kenya, and Saudi Arabia, al-Qaeda is responsible for the proliferation of terrorists throughout the world and providing them with military equipment and financing.

Anhydrous: Without water.

Area Command: An organization established to (1) oversee the management of multiple incidents that are each being handled by an Incident Command System or (2) oversee the management of a very large incident that has multiple Incident Management Teams assigned to it. Area Command has the responsibility to set overall strategy and priorities, allocate critical resources based on priorities, ensure that incidents are properly managed, and ensure that objectives are met.

Area denial weapon: Weapon that will, by virtue of its toxicity and persistence, render an area unsafe for entry.

Asymmetric warfare: War between belligerents whose relative military power differs significantly, or whose strategy or tactics differ significantly.

Atom: The simplest structural unit of any element that can exist, while still retaining the unique chemical and physical characteristics of the element.

Atomic mass: The number of protons plus neutrons in an atom's nucleus.

Atomic number: The number of protons in a nucleus.

Base: See Incident base.

Bequerel (Bq): The number of disintegration of a radioactive atom over a period of time. One Bq is equal to one disintegration per second.

Beta radiation: Radioactive particle ejected from an atom's nucleus at high speed. About the size of an electron, a beta particle has no charge.

Biological agent: Organisms which can be used to harm living organisms (e.g., anthrax, smallpox, or any infectious disease).

Biological warfare: Warfare involving the use of living organisms (as disease agents) or their toxic products as weapons.

Biotoxins: Toxins that are extracted from a living source such as plants, animals, or bacteria.

Blasting agent: Explosives that are so insensitive to shock that they must be detonated by a booster of secondary explosive. Blasting agents are commonly used in large-scale mining and construction operations. A common blasting agent consists of ammonium nitrate and fuel oil.

Blepharospasm: Involuntary closure of the eyes and lids.

BLEVE: Boiling liquid expanding vapor explosion. An explosion that results from the rupture of a container of liquid well above its atmospheric boiling point.

Branch: The organizational level in ICS having functional or geographic responsibility for major aspects of incident operations. Branches are identified by functional name (e.g., medical, security).

Breakthrough: When a chemical permeates the protective material of an air-purifying respirator (or other worker protection), thus allowing a contaminant to enter the breathing space or contact skin.

Breakthrough time: Time for a test chemical to permeate through a material (e.g., in respirator cartridges of an APR) or contact skin.

Brisance: Measure of the speed with which an explosive produces its maximum blast pressure. This value describes the destructive fragmentation effect of a material on its immediate surroundings. Also known as shattering effect.

Carcinoma: A malignant tumor.

Cation: An element or molecule that has lost an electron and becomes positively charged.

Catalyst: Substance that accelerates the rate of a chemical reaction without itself being changed.

Chain of Command: A series of management positions in order of authority.

Chain of Custody: A process used to maintain and document the chronological history of collected evidence. Documents should include name of the individual collecting the evidence, each person or entity subsequently having custody of it, dates the items were collected or transferred, agency and case number, victim's or suspect's name, and a brief description of the item.

Charge, explosive: The explosive material itself.

Chemical warfare: Tactical warfare using incendiary mixtures, smokes, or irritant, burning, poisonous, or asphyxiating gases.

Chemical weapon: A chemical compound (e.g., incendiary mixtures; smokes; irritants; burning, poisonous, or asphyxiating gases) used during warfare.

Chief: The ICS title for individuals responsible for command of the functional sections Operations, Planning, Logistics, and Finance/Administration.

Chloropicrin (PS): A heavy colorless insoluble liquid compound that causes tears and vomiting; used as a pesticide and as tear gas.

Chronic: Effects that may occur after long-term exposure to a substance.

Combustible liquid: One that does not meet the definition of any other hazard class and has a flash point >141°F (60.5°C) and ≤200°F (93°C).

Command Post: See Incident Command Post.

Command Staff: In ICS, the Command Staff consists of the Information Officer, Safety Officer, and Liaison Officer. These individuals report directly to the Incident Commander.

Contamination: The unwanted transfer of material from another source to the body, PPE, equipment, or physical evidence.

Contamination reduction zone (CRZ): *Warm Zone.* This area separates the contaminated area from the clean area and acts as a buffer to reduce contamination of the clean area. Decontamination of personnel and equipment occurs in the CRZ.

Control/blank sample: Material from a known source that was presumably uncontaminated during the commission of a crime. May be used in laboratory/forensic analysis.

Critical mass: The quantity of nuclear fuel capable of sustaining a chain reaction.

Cross-contamination: The unwanted transfer of material between two or more sources of physical evidence.

Curie (Ci): The number of disintegrations of radioactive atoms over a period of time. One Ci is equal to 37 billion (37×10^9) disintegrations per second.

Cyanosis: Bluish discoloration of the skin and mucous membranes. Cyanosis is a sign that oxygen levels in the blood are dangerously low.

Cytotoxic: Toxic to cells.

Decay scheme, radioisotope: A timeline of radioactive decay of an isotope that identifies the types of ionizing radiation emitted, the range of energies of the radiation emitted, and the half-life of the decaying radioisotope.

Decontamination: A systematic process to remove contamination (of a hazardous chemical or radioactive material) from victims, responders, equipment, etc.

Deflagrate: Rapid burning with the generation of intense heat and light. This reaction occurs at subsonic speeds (i.e., less than 1130 ft/s) (343 m/s).

Degradation (of PPE): Physical changes that occur in a material as the result of chemical exposure, use, or environmental conditions (e.g., UV radiation).

Delegation of Authority: A statement provided to the Incident Commander by the Agency Executive delegating authority and assigning responsibility. The Delegation of Authority can include objectives, priorities, expectations, constraints, and other considerations or guidelines as needed. Many agencies require a written Delegation of Authority to be given to Incident Commanders before their assuming command.

Deputy: A fully qualified individual who, in the absence of a superior, could be delegated the authority to manage an operation or perform a specific task. In some cases, a Deputy could act as relief for a supervisor and therefore must be fully qualified in the position. Deputies can be assigned to the Incident Commander, General Staff, and Branch Directors.

Detonation: An explosive event of almost instantaneous decomposition of fuel. Detonation reactions occur at supersonic speeds (greater than approx. 1130 ft/s) and generates a lethal shock wave.

Detonation velocity: Speed at which the detonation wave travels through an explosive.

Detonator: The primary explosive in a firing train.

Deuterium: Stable isotope of hydrogen (^{2}H), having one proton and one neutron (atomic mass = 2). Also called *heavy hydrogen*.

Diphosgene (DP): Also known as trichloromethyl chloroformate ($ClCO_2CCl_3$), a compound originally developed for chemical warfare. At room temperature, it is a stable, colorless liquid with a vapor pressure of 10 mm Hg at 20°C. It decomposes to phosgene at approximately 300°C.

Direct action mechanism: Direct attack on a molecule by ionizing radiation followed by destruction of the molecule.

Director: The ICS title for individuals responsible for supervision of a Branch.

Dispatch Center: A facility from which resources are assigned to an incident.

Division: Divisions are used to divide an incident into geographic areas of operation. A Division is located within the ICS organization between the Branch and the Task Force/Strike Team.

Domestic terrorism: The unlawful or threatened use of force or violence by a group or individual based and operating entirely within the United States, without foreign direction, and whose acts are directed at elements of the U.S. Government or its population, in the furtherance of political or social goals.

Dyspnea: Difficulty breathing or labored breathing.

Edema: Swelling from excessive accumulation of watery fluid in cells, tissues, etc.

Edema factor: The component of the anthrax toxin that produces edema when combined with the protective antigen.

Electromagnetic pulse (EMP): Radiation from a nuclear detonation ionizes air molecules, imparting an electric charge to them. These ionized air molecules interact with the earth's magnetic field to create a surge of electromagnetic energy, the EMP.

Electron: A subatomic particle having a negative charge and orbiting the nucleus of an atom.

Emergency decontamination: Procedures taken for the rapid removal of agent from the victim, when an emergency arises during the response process.

Emergency Medical Technician (EMT): A healthcare specialist with particular skills and knowledge in prehospital emergency medicine.

Emergency Operations Center (EOC): A predesignated facility established by an agency or jurisdiction to coordinate the overall agency or jurisdictional response and support to an emergency.

Emulsifier: A substance that promotes the suspension of one liquid in another.

Emulsion: A suspension of droplets of one liquid in another liquid. The two liquids do not chemically combine but are instead suspended within one another (e.g., oil suspended in water).

Eschar: A black, necrotic mass of tissue.

Event: A planned, nonemergency activity. ICS can be used as the management system for a wide range of events (e.g., concerts, parades, sporting events).

Explosion: The rapid expansion of matter into a greater volume. Three categories of explosions exist: chemical, nuclear, mechanical.

Explosive device: Any device designed to explode, with concomitant release of a blast wave, gases, light, heat, and sound.

Explosive range: See Flammable range.

Explosive train: See Firing train.

Extremist: Person who advocates extreme political measures; a radical.

Extrication: To free or remove from an entanglement or difficulty.

Fallout: See Radioactive fallout.

Fatwa: A legal opinion or decree handed down by an Islamic religious leader.

Fedayeen: Highly capable sleeper commandos trained in languages, science, and trade.

Finance/Administration Section: The ICS section responsible for all incident costs and financial considerations. Includes the Time Unit, Procurement Unit, Compensation/Claims Unit, and Cost Unit.

Fire point: Temperature at which the vapors will continue to burn after the vapor flash occurs.

Fireball (nuclear): The extremely hot sphere of air and gaseous weapon residues immediately following a nuclear detonation.

Firing train: The specific sequence of steps resulting in progressively larger explosions. In the firing train, explosions increase in size until the main charge is detonated.

First Responder: The initial responding public safety official arriving at the scene before the arrival of the investigator in charge.

Fissile isotope: A nuclide capable of undergoing neutron-induced fission.

Fission (nuclear): Splitting of an atom.

Fissionable isotope: Isotope capable of fission.

Flammable liquid: A liquid having a flash point of ≤60.5°C (141°F).

Flammable range: The range of vapor concentrations that will support combustion in the presence of an energy source such as a flame.

Fragmentation: A portion of the original casing or the electronics within an IED.

Fragmentation phase (of an explosion): Phase of a detonation where the container of the exploding material is destroyed and thrown outward in all directions.

Free radical: An atom or molecule that has a single unpaired electron in one orbit

Fusion (nuclear): The joining of two atoms to form a new element; e.g., hydrogen + hydrogen = helium.

Gamma radiation: Electromagnetic radiation emitted during radioactive decay and having an extremely short wavelength and high penetrating power.

General Staff: The group of incident management personnel reporting to the Incident Commander. Consists of Operations Section Chief, Planning Section Chief, Logistics Section Chief, and Finance/Administration Section Chief.

Gray (Gy): Unit of radiation exposure equal to 100 rads.

Ground state: The lowest energy state of an atom or electron.

Ground zero: Specific point of an incident (e.g., an explosion).

Group: In ICS, groups are established to divide the incident into functional areas of operations. Groups are composed of resources assembled to perform a special function not necessarily within a single geographic division.

Gun-type nuclear device: Nuclear weapon in which two pieces of fissionable material, each below critical mass, are rapidly brought together to form a single, supercritical unit. The gun-type assembly is achieved in a tube in which a high explosive blasts a subcritical piece of fissionable material from one end into a second subcritical piece held at the opposite end.

Half-life: Time required for half the atoms of a radioactive sample to decay to nonradioactive forms.

Hard x-rays: The highest energy x-rays, typically those with energies greater than 10 keV.

Hazardous material: Any substance that poses a hazard to humans, other biota or the environment. Hazardous materials occur as explosives, flammable and combustible substances, corrosives, poisons, and radioactive materials.

Highly enriched uranium (HEU): Uranium having more than 20% of the ^{235}U isotope, used for making nuclear weapons or fuel for nuclear power reactors.

Hydrogen bomb: See Thermonuclear bomb.

Hygroscopic: Has a high affinity for water; bonds readily with water molecules.

Hypotension: Abnormally low blood pressure.

Hypoxemia: An abnormal deficiency in oxygen concentration in the blood.

Hypoxia: Abnormally low oxygen concentration in organs or tissues of the body.

Immediately dangerous to life and health (IDLH): The atmospheric concentration that poses an immediate threat to life, causes irreversible or delayed adverse health effects, or interferes with a person's ability to escape from a dangerous atmosphere.

Immiscible: Substances that do not normally mix with one another.

Improvised explosive device (IED): Device constructed in an improvised manner incorporating destructive, lethal, noxious, pyrotechnic or incendiary chemicals, designed to destroy, disfigure, or intimidate. IEDs may incorporate military materials, but are normally devised from nonmilitary components.

Incident Action Plan: Plan that contains objectives reflecting the overall incident strategy and specific tactical actions and supporting information for the next operational period. The Plan may be oral or written. When written, the Plan may have a number of forms as attachments (e.g., traffic plan, safety plan, communications plan, map).

Incident Base: The location at which primary logistics functions for an incident are coordinated and administered. There is only one Base per incident. The Incident Command Post may be located with the Base.

Incident Command Post (ICP): The location at which the primary command functions are executed. The ICP may be located with the Incident Base or other incident facilities.

Incident Command System (ICS): A standardized on-scene emergency management concept specifically designed to allow users to adopt an integrated organizational structure equal to the complexity and demands of single or multiple incidents, without being hindered by jurisdictional boundaries.

Incident Commander: The individual responsible for the management of all incident operations.

Incident objectives: Statements of guidance and direction necessary for the selection of appropriate strategies and the direction of resources. Incident objectives are based on realistic expectations of what can be accomplished when all allocated resources have been effectively deployed. Incident objectives must be achievable and measurable, yet flexible enough to allow for strategic and tactical alternatives.

Indirect action mechanism: Damage to cells or tissue when water in the cell is irradiated. The water molecule is split and the resulting free radicals subsequently damage the cell.

Information Officer: A member of the Command Staff responsible for interfacing with the public and media or with other agencies requiring information regarding an incident. There is only one Information Officer per incident.

Initial Responding Officer: The first law enforcement officer to arrive at the scene.

Internal hazard: Substance that must enter the body to cause biological damage (e.g., alpha radiation).

International terrorism: The unlawful use of force or violence committed by a group or individual who has some connection to a foreign power or whose activities transcend national boundaries against persons or property, to intimidate or coerce a government, the civilian population, in furtherance of political or social objectives.

Intubation: The process of placing a tube into a hollow organ or passageway, often into the airway, to keep it open.

ISIS: See Islamic State of Iraq and Syria.

Islamic:
1. The religious faith of Muslims including belief in Allah as the sole deity and in Muhammad as his prophet
2. The civilization erected upon Islamic faith
3. The group of modern nations in which Islam is the dominant religion

Islamic State of Iraq and Syria (ISIS): Also known as the Islamic State of Iraq and the Levant or Islamic State of Iraq and al-Sham, is a jihadist militant group that follows an Islamic fundamentalist doctrine of Sunni Islam. The group is also known as Daesh.

Isotope: Any of two or more species of atoms of a chemical element with the same atomic number and nearly identical chemical behavior, but with differing atomic mass.

Jihad: Translated as *struggle*, a Muslim holy war against infidels.

Jurisdiction:
1. The power, right, or authority to interpret and apply the law
2. The authority of a sovereign power to govern or legislate
3. The power or right to exercise authority
4. The limits or territory within which authority may be exercised

Kind: Resources described by function (e.g., a patrol car or a bulldozer).

Lachrymating: Causing the eyes to tear involuntarily.

Latency period: Period from the time of exposure to an environmental insult to the time of the appearance of symptoms or signs.

Lavage: The washing of a hollow organ (typically the stomach or colon) by flushing with fluids.

LC_{50}: Concentration of an inhaled substance, expressed in mg/cm^3 of air, which is necessary to kill 50% of test animals exposed within a specified time.

LD_{50}: Dosage, administered by any route except inhalation, which is necessary to kill 50% of exposed animals in laboratory tests within a specified time. The LD_{50} is ordinarily expressed in mg/kg body weight.

Left wing:
1. The leftist division of a group (as in a political party)
2. Those professing views usually characterized by desire to reform or overthrow the established order, especially in politics and usually advocating change in the name of the greater freedom or well-being of the common man
3. A radical as distinguished from a conservative position

Lethal factor: A virulence factor of the anthrax toxin that, when combined with a protective antigen, results in death of host cells.

Liaison Officer: A member of the Command Staff responsible for coordinating with representatives from assisting agencies.

Logistics Section: The section responsible for providing facilities, services, and materials for the incident response.

Low-order explosion: An incomplete detonation; not all of the charge is consumed.

Lower explosive limit (LEL): The lowest concentration of a vapor that will produce a fire when an ignition source (flame, spark, etc.) is present. Expressed in percent of vapor or gas in air by volume.

Mach stem: The shock front formed by combining the incident and reflected shock fronts from a detonation.

Macule: A small, flat, distinct colored dermatological lesion that is less than 10–15 mm in diameter.

Management By Objectives: In ICS, this is a top–down management activity that involves a three-step process to achieve the incident goal. The steps are establishing the incident objectives, selection of appropriate strategy(ies) to achieve the objectives, and selecting the tactical direction associated with the chosen strategy. Tactical direction includes selection of tactics, selection of resources, resource assignments, and performance monitoring.

Mass decontamination: The rapid physical removal of agent from the skin of numerous contaminated victims.

Mediastinitis: Inflammation of the tissues in the mid-chest, or mediastinum.

Miosis: Constriction of the pupils of the eyes.

Mobilization: The process and procedures used by all organizations—federal, state, and local—for activating, assembling, and transporting all resources that have been requested to respond to an incident.

Mujahedeen: Islamic guerrilla fighters, especially in South Asia and the Middle East.

Multi-Jurisdiction Incident: An incident requiring action from multiple agencies that have a statutory responsibility for incident mitigation. In ICS, such incidents will be managed under Unified Command.

Muriatic acid: Hydrochloric acid.

Muslim: An adherent of Islam.

Mutual Aid Agreement: Written agreement between agencies and/or jurisdictions in which each agree to assist one another upon request by furnishing personnel and equipment.

Myalgia: Muscle pain.

National Incident Management System (NIMS): Developed by the Secretary of Homeland Security, the National Incident Management System integrates effective practices in emergency preparedness and response into a comprehensive national framework for incident management. NIMS enables responders at all levels to work together more effectively to manage domestic incidents no matter what the cause, size, or complexity.

Necrosis: Death (of tissue, cells).

Negative phase (of an explosion): Phenomenon that occurs immediately after an explosion, when air is rapidly drawn back into ground zero.

Nerve agent antidote kit (NAAK): The nerve agent antidote used by the U.S. Armed Forces in the treatment of nerve agent poisoning. The kit consists of four separate components: the atropine autoinjector, the pralidoxime chloride autoinjector, a plastic clip, and a carrying case.

Neutron: Subatomic particle with no net electrical charge and a mass approximately equal to that of a proton.

Neutron activation: Process in which a nonradioactive atom absorbs a neutron and becomes a radioactive isotope having one additional mass unit.

Nuclear:
1. Being a weapon whose destructive power derives from an uncontrolled nuclear reaction
2. Of, produced by, or involving nuclear weapons
3. Armed with nuclear weapons

Nuclear chain reaction: Series of nuclear fissions in which neutrons released by splitting one atom leads to the splitting of others. The process cascades, resulting in the release of tremendous quantities of energy.

Officer: ICS title for the personnel responsible for the Command Staff positions of Safety, Liaison, and Information.

Oil of vitriol: Sulfuric acid.

Operational period: The period scheduled for execution of a given set of operation actions as specified in the Incident Action Plan. Operational Periods can be of various lengths, although they usually do not exceed 24 hours.

Operations Section: The section responsible for all tactical operations at the incident. Includes Branches, Divisions and/or Groups, Task Forces, Strike Teams, Single Resources, and Staging Areas.

Overpressure: Increase in atmospheric pressure as a result of a detonation.

Papule: Small solid rounded bumps rising from the skin that usually measure less than 1 cm in diameter.

Pathogen: Disease-causing.

Penetration (of PPE): Movement of chemicals through zippers, seams, or imperfections in PPE material.

Permeation: Process by which a chemical dissolves in or moves through a PPE material at the molecular level.

Permissible exposure limit (PEL): A legal limit, established by OSHA, for exposure of an employee to a chemical substance. The established limit is usually expressed in ppm or sometimes in milligrams per cubic meter (mg/m^3). A PEL is usually given as a time-weighted average. Unlike the threshold limit value (see below), the PEL is an enforceable limit.

Persistence (of a chemical weapon): The ability to persist in an environment. A persistent weapon will not readily volatilize or be decomposed by chemical reactions or biological processes.

Personal protective equipment (PPE): Articles such as disposable gloves, masks, and eye protection that are used to provide a barrier to keep biological or chemical hazards from contacting the skin, eyes, and mucous membranes.

Petechiae: Small red or purple spots caused by bleeding into the skin.

Phagocytes: White blood cells that protect the body by ingesting harmful foreign particles, bacteria, and dead or dying cells. Phagocytes are essential for fighting infections and for subsequent immunity.

Photolysis: The breaking apart of a molecule by the action of light.

Planning Section: ICS section responsible for the collection, evaluation, and dissemination of tactical information related to the incident, and for the preparation and documentation of Incident Action Plans. The Planning Section also maintains information on the current and forecasted situation and on the status of resources assigned to the incident. Includes the Situation, Resource, Documentation, and Demobilization Units, as well as Technical Specialists.

Positive phase (of an explosion): The initial blast of outward pressure immediately following an explosion.

Presumptive test: A nonconfirmatory test used to screen for the presence of a substance.

Prodrome: Early nonspecific symptoms that might indicate the start of a disease before specific symptoms occur.

Prompt ionizing radiation: Radiation produced within approximately 1 minute from a nuclear detonation. Prompt radiation is composed mainly of neutrons, gamma rays, x-rays, and alpha and beta particles, and is highly destructive.

Proton: Subatomic particle occurring in the nucleus of an atom and having a single positive charge.

Pustule: A small inflamed elevation of skin containing pus.

Pyrophoric: Substance that spontaneously ignites in air.

Rad: (Radiation absorbed dose), a unit of absorbed radiation. The rad was defined in CGS units in 1953 as the dose causing 100 ergs of energy to be absorbed by 1 g of matter. The rad was restated in SI units in 1970 as the dose causing 0.01 J of energy to be absorbed per kilogram of matter.

Radioactive; radioactivity: Property possessed by some elements (such as uranium) or isotopes (carbon-14) of spontaneously emitting energetic particles (such as alpha particles or gamma rays) by the disintegration of their atomic nuclei.

Radioactive fallout: The fine radioactive dust created when a nuclear weapon detonates. The residual radiation hazard from a nuclear detonation that falls out of the atmosphere following a detonation.

Radioisotope: Radioactive isotope.

Radiological: Relating to nuclear radiation.

Radiological dispersal device (RDD): A radiological weapon that combines radioactive material with conventional explosives.

Radionuclide: Radioactive isotope. Also known as radioisotope.

Recalcitrant: Resistant to decomposition, whether by chemical or biological means.

Relative effectiveness factor (RE Factor): Measure of the power of an explosive for military demolitions. The RE factor compares an explosive's effectiveness relative to that of TNT.

Remediation: To remedy. In the context of environmental contamination by CBRNE agents, remediation is the process of removing, detoxifying and/or stabilizing contamination.

Resources: Personnel and equipment available for a response action.

Resources Unit: Functional unit within the Planning Section responsible for recording the status of resources committed to the incident. The Resources Unit also evaluates anticipated resource needs.

Right wing: Individuals professing opposition to change in the established order and favoring traditional attitudes and practices and sometimes advocating the forced establishment of an authoritarian order (as in government). A conservative, reactionary position.

Roentgen equivalent man (REM): The dosage of ionizing radiation that will cause the same amount of injury to human tissue as 1 Roentgen of x-rays.

Safety Officer: A member of the Command Staff responsible for monitoring and assessing safety hazards or unsafe situations and for developing measures for ensuring personnel safety.

Secondary decontamination: Removal of agent from a victim, already processed through mass decontamination, who shows continued signs of contamination.

Section: The organizational level with responsibility for a major functional area of the incident (e.g., Operations, Planning, Logistics, Finance/Administration).

Septicemia: Contamination of the bloodstream by pathogenic microorganisms from a point of infection.

Service Branch: A branch within the Logistics Section responsible for service activities at the incident. Includes the Communications, Medical, and Food Units.

Shock front: See Shock wave.

Shock wave: A very strong pressure wave in air, water, or other media. A shock wave can carry significant kinetic energy and can be quite destructive.

Shrapnel: Items which are intentionally added to an IED to inflict maximum casualties. Examples include nails, BBs, ball bearings, steel washers, and children's marbles.

Sievert: A measure of radiation dose deposited in body tissue, averaged over the body. One sievert is equivalent to 100 rem.

Single resource: An individual, a piece of equipment plus its personnel complement, or a team of individuals that can be employed at an incident.

Slow neutron: Neutron whose kinetic energy is below 1 keV.

Soft x-rays: Low-energy x-rays, typically those with energies less than 10 keV.

Span of control: The number of responders that a supervisor can effectively manage during an incident. The supervisory ratio of from three to seven individuals, with five-to-one being optimum.

Specific activity (of a radionuclide): The number of radioactive disintegrations per unit mass. For example, a curie (Ci) of activity represents 37 billion atoms decaying every second (37 billion dps).

Staging area: Locations set up at an incident where resources can be placed while awaiting a tactical assignment. The Operations Section manages staging areas.

Supercritical mass: Amount of uranium or plutonium that exceeds the mass necessary to support a chain reaction.

Supervisor: ICS title for individuals responsible for command of Division or Group.

Supply unit: Functional unit within the Support Branch of the Logistics Section responsible for ordering equipment and supplies required for incident operations.

Support resources: Nontactical resources under the supervision of Logistics, Planning, Finance/Administration Sections, or the Command Staff.

Technical decontamination: The removal of contamination from response personnel and their equipment.

Technical specialists: Personnel with special skills that can be used anywhere within the ICS organization.

Thermal effects phase (of an explosion): Final phase of an explosion. This phase involves the release of heat generated from the blast.

Thermonuclear weapon: A nuclear weapon in which fusion of light nuclei, such as deuterium and tritium, contributes the main explosive energy. The high temperatures required for such fusion reactions are obtained by means of an initial fission explosion. Also referred to as a hydrogen bomb.

Threshold limit value (TLV): Level of a substance at which a worker can be exposed daily for a working lifetime without adverse health effects. The TLV is defined as a concentration in air, typically for inhalation or skin exposure. The TLV is an estimate based on the known toxicity to humans or animals of a given chemical substance and the reliability of the latest analytical methods. The TLV is a recommendation by the American Conference of Governmental Industrial Hygienists.

Toxemia: High concentrations of toxins in the blood.

Toxicology: A branch of science that deals with poisons and their effects.

Transuranic: Atoms heavier than uranium (*beyond uranium* in the Periodic Table of the Elements).

Tritium: Radioactive isotope of hydrogen with a nucleus containing one proton and two neutrons (atomic mass = 3). Chemical symbol is ^{3}H.

Type: Refers to resource capability. A Type 1 resource provides a greater overall capability because of power, size, capacity, etc. than would be found in a Type 2 resource. Resource typing provides managers with additional information in selecting the best resource for the task.

Unified Area Command: A Unified Area Command is established when incidents under an Area Command are Multijurisdictional.

Unity of Command: The concept by which each person within an organization reports to only one designated person.

Upper explosive limit: The maximum concentration of a gas above which the substance will not explode when exposed to a source of ignition.

Vesicant: Chemical compound that causes severe pain to skin, eyes and mucous membranes. Vesicants result in large, painful blisters on the tissue of victims.

Viremia: Contamination of the bloodstream with a virus.

Virion: Individual virus particle.

Vitrify/vitrification: Process used to physically and chemically fix a contaminant permanently in soil by heating to extremely high temperatures.

Volatile organic compound (VOC): Any organic compound having a high vapor pressure (i.e., one that evaporates readily to the atmosphere).

Volatility: A measure of how rapidly an agent will evaporate. The more volatile an agent, the more rapidly it will evaporate. Temperature, wind speed, and humidity at the incident site influence how rapidly an agent will evaporate.

Walk-through: Site reconnaissance. Initial assessment of a scene conducted by carefully walking through to evaluate the situation, recognize potential evidence, and determine resources required. Also, a final survey conducted to ensure the scene has been effectively and completely processed.

Weapon of mass destruction: Any device that is designed or intended to cause mass destruction and/or death (Refer to Title 18 USC, Section 2332a for a detailed definition).

Weapons-grade uranium: Nuclear material that is most suitable for the manufacture of nuclear weapons: uranium enriched to 93% ^{235}U.

Whole-body hazard: Radiation that will cause damage to both internal and external tissue. Gamma radiation, x-rays, and neutrons are whole-body hazards.

Xenobiotic: (*Foreign to nature.*) Substances that are man-made and often exotic; xenobiotics tend to be resistant to natural decomposition processes and persist in the biosphere.

X-rays: Electromagnetic radiation of high energy having wavelengths shorter than those in the ultraviolet region, i.e., less than 10^{-6} cm.

Yield: The explosive power of a nuclear weapon. This value is typically expressed in terms of the quantity of TNT that would release an equivalent amount of energy.

APPENDIX B: ACRONYMS

AC	Hydrogen cyanide
ALF	Animal Liberation Front
APR	Air-purifying respirator
ATSDR	Agency for Toxic Substances and Disease Registry
BLEVE	Boiling liquid expanding vapor explosion
BW	Biological weapon
C8 Paper	Chemical Agent Detector Paper
CAM	Chemical agent monitor
CBRNE	Chemical, biological, radiological, nuclear, and explosives
CDC	Centers for Disease Control and Prevention
CERCLA	Comprehensive Environmental Response, Compensation, and Liability Act
CERT	Community emergency response team
CFR	Code of Federal Regulations
CG	Phosgene
CK	Cyanogen chloride
Cl	Chlorine
CW	Chemical weapon
CWC	Chemical Weapons Convention of 1993
CX	Phosgene oxime (blister agent)
DDT	Deflagration to detonation transfer
DHHS	Department of Health and Human Services
DHS	Department of Homeland Security
DOD	Department of Defense
DOE	Department of Energy
DOJ	Department of Justice
DOT	Department of Transportation
DP	Diphosgene (choking agent)
ELF	Earth Liberation Front
EMP	Electromagnetic pulse
EMS	Emergency medical service
EMT	Emergency medical technician
EOD	Explosive ordinance disposal
EOP	Emergency Operations Plan
EPA	Environmental Protection Agency
ERG	Emergency Response Guidebook
FBI	Federal Bureau of Investigations
FEMA	Federal Emergency Management Agency
GA	Tabun (nerve agent)
GB	Sarin (nerve agent)

GD	Soman (nerve agent)
H	Sulfur mustard
Hazmat	Hazardous materials
HCl	Hydrochloric acid
HEPA	High efficiency particulate air
HMRU	Hazardous Materials Response Unit
IAP	Incident Action Plan
IC	Incident Commander
ICAM	Improved chemical agent monitor
ICP	Incident Command Post
ICS	Incident Command System
IDLH	Immediately dangerous to life and health
IED	Improvised explosive device
JOC	Joint Operations Center
JTTF	Joint Terrorism Task Force
L	Lewisite (blister agent)
LC_{50}	Lethal concentration (to kill 50% of test organisms)
LD_{50}	Lethal dose (to kill 50% of test organisms)
LEL	Lower explosive limit
M256A1	Chemical agent detector kit
M8 Paper	Chemical agent detector paper
M9 Paper	Chemical agent detector paper
MCI	Mass casualty incident
NAAK	Nerve agent antidote kit
NAERG	North American Emergency Response Guidebook
NBC	Nuclear, biological and chemical
NCP	National Contingency Plan
NFPA	National Fire Protection Association
NIMS	National Incident Management System
NIOSH	National Institute for Occupational Safety and Health
NRC	Nuclear Regulatory Commission
NRP	National Response Plan
ODP	Office for Domestic Preparedness
OSHA	Occupational Safety and Health Act
PAPR	Powered air-purifying respirator
PEL	Permissible exposure limit
PID	Photoionization detector
PIO	Public Information Officer
PPE	Personal protective equipment
PS	Chloropicrin (choking agent)
RDD	Radiological dispersal device
RPG	Rocket-propelled grenade
SAR	Supplied air respirator
SCBA	Self-contained breathing apparatus
SOP	Standard operating procedures

STEL	Short-term exposure limit
SWAT	Special Weapons and Tactics
TIC	Toxic industrial chemical
TLV	Threshold limit value
TWA	Time-weighted average
UAS	Unmanned aerial system
UAV	Unmanned aerial vehicle
USAMRIID	U.S. Army Military Research Institute for Infectious Disease
USDA	U.S. Department of Agriculture
VBIED	Vehicle-borne improvised explosive device
VEE	Venezuelan equine encephalomyelitis
VHF	Viral hemorrhagic fever
VOC	Volatile organic compound
VX	VX (nerve agent)
WHO	World Health Organization
WMD	Weapon of mass destruction

APPENDIX C: SELECTED CHEMICAL AND PHYSICAL PROPERTIES OF CHEMICAL WEAPONS

Selected Chemical and Physical Properties of Chemical Agents

Agents	Chemical Agent; Formula; Symbol	Molecular Weight	State at 20°C	Odor	Vapor Density (Air = 1)	Liquid Density (g/ml)	Freezing/ Melting Point (°C)	Boiling Point (°C)	Vapor Pressure (mm/Hg)	Volatility (mg/m³)
Choking agents	Phosgene; $COCl_2$; CG	98.92	Colorless gas	Newly-mown hay or grass; green corn	3.4	1.37 at 20°C	−128	7.6	1.173 at 20°C	4,300,000 at 7.6°C
	Diphosgene; $C_2Cl_4O_2$; DP	197.85	Colorless liquid	Newly-mown hay or grass; green corn	6.8	1.65 at 20°C	−57	127–128	4.2 at 20°C	45,000 at 20°C
Nerve agents	Tabun; $C_5H_{11}N_2O_2P$; GA	162.3	Colorless to brown liquid	Faintly fruity: none when pure	5.63	1.073 at 25°C	−50	240	0.037 at 20°C	610 at 25°C
	Sarin; $C_4H_{10}FO_2P$; GB	140.1	Colorless liquid	Almost none when pure	4.86	1.088 at 25°C; 1.102 at 20°C	−56	158	2.9 at 25°C; 2.10 at 20°C	22,000 at 25°C; 16,090 at 20°C
	Soman; $C_7H_{16}FO_2P$; GD	182.178	Colorless liquid	Fruity; camphor when impure	6.33	1.0222 at 25°C	−42	198	0.4 at 25°C	3900 at 25°C
	Cyclosarin; $C_7H_{14}FO_2P$; GF	180.2	Liquid	Sweet; musty; peaches; shellac	6.2	1.1327 at 20°C	−30	239	0.044 at 20°C	438 at 20°C
	$C_{11}H_{26}NO_2PS$; VX	267.38	Colorless to amber liquid	None	9.2	1.0083 at 20°C	Below −51	298	0.0007 at 20°C	10.5 at 25°C
	"V-Sub X"; V_x	211.2	Colorless liquid	None	7.29	1.062 at 20°C	–	256	0.007 at 25°C; 0.004 at 20°C	75 at 25°C; 48 at 20°C
Blood agents	Hydrogen cyanide; HCN; AC[a]	27.03	Colorless gas or liquid	Bitter almonds	0.990 at 20°C	0.687 at 20°C	−13.3	25.7	742 at 25°C; 612 at 20°C	1,080,000 at 25°C
	Cyanogen chloride; CNCl; CK	61.48	Colorless liquid or gas	Pungent, biting; can go unnoticed	2.1	1.18 at 20°C	−6.9	12.8	1000 at 25°C	2,600,000 at 12.8°C; 6,132,000 at 25°C
	Arsine AsH_3 SA	77.93	Colorless gas	Mild garlic	2.69	1.34 at 20°C	−116	−62.5	11,100 at 20°C	30,900,000 at 0°C

(Continued)

Selected Chemical and Physical Properties of Chemical Agents (Continued)

Agents	Chemical Agent; Formula; Symbol	Molecular Weight	State at 20°C	Odor	Vapor Density (Air = 1)	Liquid Density (g/ml)	Freezing/ Melting Point (°C)	Boiling Point (°C)	Vapor Pressure (mm/Hg)	Volatility (mg/m³)
Blister agents	Distilled mustard; $C_4H_8Cl_2S$ HD	159.08	Colorless to pale yellow liquid	Garlic or horseradish	5.4	1.268 at 25°C; 1.127 at 20°C	14.45	217	0.072 at 20°C	610 at 20°C
	Nitrogen mustard; $C_6H_{13}Cl_2N$ HN-1	170.08	Colorless to pale	Fishy or musty	5.9	1.09 at 25°C	−34	194	0.24 at 25°C	1520 at 20°C
	Nitrogen mustard; $C_5H_{11}Cl_2N$ HN-2	156.07	Dark liquid	Soapy in low concentrations; fruity in high concentrations	5.4	1.15 at 20°C	−65 to −60	75 at 15 mmHg	0.29 at 20°C	3580 at 25°C
	Nitrogen mustard; $C_6H_{12}Cl_3N$ HN-3	204.54	Dark liquid	None if pure	7.1	1.24 at 25°C	−3.7	256	0.0109 at 25°C	121 at 25°C
	Lewisite; $C_2H_2AsCl_3$ L	207.35	Colorless to brownish	Variable; may resemble geraniums	7.1	1.89 at 20°C	18	190	0.394 at 20°C	4480 at 20°C
	Mustard–lewisite mixture; 37% HD 63% L by weight HL	186.4	Dark, oily liquid	Garlic	6.5	1.66 at 20°C	−25.4 (pure) −42 (plant purity)	<190	0.248 at 20°C	2730 at 20°C
	Phenyldichloroarsine; $C_6H_5AsCl_2$; PD	222.91	Colorless liquid	None	7.7	1.65 at 20°C	−20	252 to 255	0.033 at 25°C	390 at 25°C
	Ethyldichloroarsine; $C_2H_5AsCl_2$; ED	174.88	Colorless liquid	Fruity, but biting; irritating	6.0	1.66 at 20°C	−65	156	2.09 at 20°C	20,000 at 20°C
	Methyldichloroarsine; CH_3AsCl_2; MD	160.86	Colorless liquid	None	5.5	1.836 at 20°C	−55	133	7.76 at 20°C	74,900 at 20°C
	Phosgene oximedichloroforoxime; $CHCl_2NO$; CX	113.94	Colorless solid or liquid	Sharp, penetrating	3.9	–	35–40	129	11.2 at 25°C (solid) 13 at 40°C (liquid)	1800 at 20°C
Vomiting agents	Diphenylchloroarsine; $(C_6H_5)_2AsCl$; DA	264.5	White to brown solid	None	Forms little vapor	1.387 at 50°C	41–445	333	0.0036 at 45°C	48 at 45°C
	Adamsite; $C_6H_4(AsCl)$–$(NH)C_6H_4$; DM	277.57	Yellow to green solid	None	Forms little vapor	1.65 (solid) at 20°C	195	410	Negligible	Negligible
	Diphenylcyanoarsine; $(C_6H_5)2AsCN$; DC	255.0	White to pink solid	Bitter almond-garlic mixture	Forms little vapor	1.3338 at 35°C	31.5–35	350	0.0002 at 20°C	2.8 at 20°C

a These properties and values subject to change by subsequent effort to be performed by SBCCOM.

Special Characteristics of Chemical Warfare Agents

Agents		Physiological Action	Protection Required	Stability	Decontamination	Use
Choking agents	CG	Damages and floods lungs	Protective mask	Stable in steel if dry	None needed in field; aeration in closed spaces	Delayed-action casualty agent
	DP	Damages and floods lungs	Protective mask	Unstable; tends to convert to CG	None needed in field; steam, ammonia, and aeration in closed spaces	Delayed- or immediate-action casualty agent
	GA	Cessation of breath—death may follow	Protective mask and clothing	Stable in steel at normal temperatures	Bleach slurry, dilute alkali, or DS2; steam and ammonia in confined area; M291, M295	Quick-action casualty agent
	GB	Cessation of breath—death may follow	Protective mask and clothing	Stable when pure	Steam and ammonia in confined area; hot soapy water; M291, M295	Quick-action casualty agent
Nerve agents	GD	Cessation of breath—death may follow	Protective mask and clothing	Less stable than GA or GB	Bleach slurry, dilute alkali; in confined area, hot soapy water; M291, M295	Quick-action casualty agent
	GF	Cessation of breath—death may follow	Protective mask and clothing	Relatively stable in steel	Bleach slurry, dilute alkali, or DS2; steam and ammonia in confined area; M291, M295	Quick-action casualty agent
	VX	Produces casualties when inhaled or absorbed	Protective mask and clothing	Relatively stable at room temperature	STB slurry or DS2 solutions; hot soapy water; M291, M295	Quick-action casualty agent
	V_x	Produces casualties when inhaled or absorbed	Protective mask and clothing	Relatively stable	STB slurry or DS2 solution; hot soapy water; M291	Quick-action casualty agent
Blood agents	AC	Interferes w/ body tissues' oxygen use; accelerates rate of breathing	Protective mask; protective clothing in unusual situations	Stable if pure; can burn on shell explosion	None needed in field	Quick-action casualty agent
	CK	Chokes, irritates, causes slow breathing rate	Protective mask (high concentration; may penetrate filter)	Tends to polymerize; may explode	None needed in field	Quick-action casualty agent
	SA	Damages blood, liver, and kidneys	Protective mask	Not stable in uncoated metal containers	None needed	Delayed-action casualty agent

(Continued)

Special Characteristics of Chemical Warfare Agents (Continued)

Agents		Physiological Action	Protection Required	Stability	Decontamination	Use
Blister agents	HD	Blisters; destroys tissue; injures blood cells	Protective mask and clothing	Stable in steel or aluminum	Bleach, fire, DS2, M291, M295	Delayed-action casualty agent
	HN-1	Blisters; affects respiratory tract; destroys tissue; injures blood cells	Protective mask and clothing	Adequate	Bleach, fire, DS2, M291, M295	Delayed-action casualty agent
	HN-2	Similar to HD Bronchopneumonia possible after 24 hours	Protective mask and clothing	Unstable	Bleach, fire, DS2, M291, M295	Delayed-action casualty agent
	HN-3	Similar to HN-2	Protective mask and clothing	Stable	Bleach, fire, DS2, M291, M295	Delayed-action casualty agent
	L	Similar to HD, plus may cause systemic poisoning	Protective mask and clothing	Stable in steel and glass	Bleach, fire, DS2, caustic soda, M291, M295	Moderately delayed-action casualty agent
	HL	Similar to HD, plus may cause systemic poisoning	Protective mask and clothing	Stable in lacquered steel	Bleach, fire, caustic soda, M291, M295	Delayed-action casualty agent
	PD	Irritates; causes nausea, vomiting, and blisters	Protective mask and clothing	Very stable	Bleach, DS2, caustic soda, M291, M295	Delayed-action casualty agent
	ED	Damages respiratory tract; affects eyes; blisters; can cause systemic poisoning	Protective mask and clothing	Stable in steel	None needed in field; bleach, caustic soda or DS2 in closed spaces, M291, M295	Delayed-action casualty agent
	MD	Irritates respiratory tract; injures lungs and eyes; causes systemic poisoning	Protective mask and clothing	Stable in steel	Bleach, DS2, caustic soda, M291, M295	Delayed-action casualty agent
	CX	Violently irritates mucous membrane of eyes and nose; forms wheals rapidly	Protective mask and clothing	Decomposes slowly	None entirely effective; wash w/ large amounts of water or DS2	Rapid-action casualty agent
Vomiting agents	DA	Like cold symptoms, plus headache, vomiting, nausea	Protective mask	Stable if pure	None needed in field; caustic soda or chlorine in closed spaces	Former training and riot control agent
	DM	Like cold symptoms, plus headache, vomiting, nausea	Protective mask	Stable in glass or steel	None needed in field; bleach or DS2 in closed spaces	Former training and riot control agent
	DC	Like cold symptoms, plus headache, vomiting, nausea	Protective mask	Stable at normal temperatures	None needed in field; alkali solution or DS2 in closed spaces	Former training and riot control agent

Selected Chemical and Toxicological Data for Chemical Warfare Agents

Type	Symbol/Common Name	CAS Number	LCt$_{50}$^{a} (mg min/m³)	ICt$_{50}$ (mg min m³)	LCt$_{50}$^{c} ppm	ICt$_{50}$^{c} ppm	IDLH ppm	PEL ppm
Choking	CG/Phosgene	75-44-5	3200 [1,2,6]	1600 [1,2,6]	791	395	2	0.1 [5,6]
	Cl/Chlorine	7782-50-5	3200	1600	6561	622	30	1.0 [4,5]
	GA/Tabun	77-81-6	135–200 [5,6] 400 [3] 200 [1]	300^a [2]	60 20 [5]	45	0.03 [5,6]	0.000015 [6]
	GB/Sarin	107-44-8	70–100 [1,2] 70 [5,6]	35–75^a [1,2] 35 [5]	12–17	8	0.03 [5]	0.0000017 [6]
Nerve	GD/Soman	94-64-0	70 [1,2,5,6]	50–300^a 35 [5,6]	9	8	0.008 [5]	0.000004 [6]
	VX	50782-69-9	30–100 [1,2] 30 [5,6]	24–50^a [1,2] 25 [6]	3–9	3	0.0018 [5]	0.0000009 [6]
	H/HD	505-60-2	1500 [1,2,6]	150^b [2] 200 [1,5] (eyes)	231	23 30 [5]	0.0005 [5]	0.0005 [6]
Blister	HN-1	538-07-08	1500 [2,6]	200^b [2,6]	(216)	(29)	0.0004	0.0004 [6]
	HN-2	51-75-2	3000 [2,6]	100^b [2,6]	(470)	(16)	NS	NS
	HN-3	555-77-1	1500 [2,6]	200^b [2,6]	(179)	(24)	NS	NS
	HT	505-60-2	1500 (approx. same as H) [1,2]	200^b (approx. same as H) [1,2]	Approx. same as H	Approx. same as H	0.0005 [5]	0.0005 [6]

(Continued)

Selected Chemical and Toxicological Data for Chemical Warfare Agents (Continued)

Type	Symbol/Common Name	CAS Number	LCt$_{50}$[a] (mg min/m³)	ICt$_{50}$ (mg min m³)	LCt$_{50}$[c] ppm	ICt$_{50}$[c] ppm	IDLH ppm	PEL ppm
	CX	35274-08-9	3200 [1,2,6]	>3[b] [2,6]	687	0.6	Unknown	Unknown
	L	541-25-3	1200–1500 [1,5,6] 1400 [2]	<300[b] [2,5,6]	165 [2] 141–177 [1]	Unknown <35 [2,6]	0.0004 0.00035 [5]	0.00035 [6]
Blood	AC	74-99-8	2000–4000 [1,2]	Varies[a] [2]	3600	Varies	45	10 [5]
	CK	506-77-4	11,000 [1,2,6]	7000[a] [1,2,6]	4375	2784	Unknown	0.2 [6]

Note: The calculations for converting mg/m³ to parts per million (ppm) is provided as follows: A lethal dose has been calculated for a 70 mg/man. An individual is in a concentration of agent measured at 20 mg/m³. How long will it take him to become a casualty? An individual breathes at approximately 15 L/min. There are 1000 L in a cubic meter; therefore, 20 mg/m³ = 20 mg/1000 L (20 mg/1000 L) (15 l/min) = 0.3 mg/min. Therefore, it would take 70/0.3 or 233 min. to achieve the legal dose. To convert mg/m³ to ppm: ppm = $\dfrac{(mg/m^3)(24.45)}{MW}$, where 24.45 is a constant representing roughly the molar volume of any gas and MW is the molecular weight of the agent. NS, no standard.

[a] Respiratory.
[b] Ocular.
[c] Assuming 1 min exposure, breathing 10 l/min.

REFERENCES

1. Chemical Agent Data Sheets, Volume I, Edgewood Arsenal Special Report EO-SR-74001, Edgewood Arsenal, Aberdeen Proving Ground, MD, December 1974, Unclassified Report (ADB028222).

2. Department of the Army, Department of the Navy, Department of the Air Force. Potential Military Chemical/Biological Agents and Compounds. Army Field Manual No. 3-9; Navy Publication No. P-467; Air Force Manual No. 355-7. Headquarters, Washington, DC, December 12, 1990, PCN 320 008457 00.

3. Budavari, S., M. O'Neil, A. Smith, P. Heckelman, and J. Obenchain, *Merck Index*, 12th edition. CRC Press, Boca Raton, FL, 1996.

4. *CRC Handbook of Chemistry and Physics*, 69th edition. CRC Press, Boca Raton, FL, 1998.

5. U.S. Army Center for Health Promotion & Preventive Medicine. Detailed Chemical Facts Sheets. Office to the Deputy for Technical Services. Aberdeen Proving Ground, MD, 1998. http://www.911emg.com/Ref%20Library%20ERG/US%20Army%20Chem%20Fact.pdf.

INDEX

Page numbers followed by f, t, and b indicate figures, tables, and boxes, respectively.

391

Made in the USA
Monee, IL
27 August 2022